Cuban Underground

Cuban Underground Hip Hop

Black Thoughts, Black Revolution, Black Modernity

Tanya L. Saunders

University of Texas Press, Austin

This book is a part of the Latin American and
Caribbean Arts and Culture publication initiative,
funded by a grant from the Andrew W. Mellon Foundation.

First edition, 2015

Requests for permission to reproduce material from this work should be sent to:
Permissions
University of Texas Press
P.O. Box 7819
Austin, TX 78713-7819
http://utpress.utexas.edu/index.php/rp-form

♾ The paper used in this book meets the minimum requirements
of ANSI/NISO z39.48-1992 (R1997) (Permanence of Paper).

Library of Congress Cataloging-in-Publication Data
Saunders, Tanya L., author.
    Cuban underground hip hop : black thoughts, black revolution,
black modernity / Tanya L. Saunders.
        pages cm — (Latin American and Caribbean Arts and Culture Mellon)
    Includes bibliographical references.
    ISBN 978-1-4773-0237-8 (cloth : alk. paper)
    ISBN 978-1-4773-0770-0 (pbk. : alk. paper)
    ISBN 978-1-4773-0771-7 (library e-book)
    ISBN 978-1-4773-0772-4 (e-book)
    1. Hip-hop—Cuba. 2. Music—Political aspects—Cuba. 3. Blacks—Cuba—
Ethnic identity. 4. Blacks—Political activity—Cuba. 5. Racism—Cuba.
6. Cuba—Race relations. I. Title.
    F1789.N3S28 2015
    781.64'9097291—dc23   2014048855

To my mom ☺

To the Cuban artists, intellectuals, and artivists working for social change

Contents

Acknowledgments

This book began with an undergraduate research opportunity at St. Mary's College of Maryland (SMCM). I'd like to thank Jorge Rogachevsky and SMCM for supporting my undergraduate research in Cuba. I really appreciated Jorge's mentorship while I was a student at SMCM, which included an introduction to Miguel Barnet. Thank you to Miguel Barnet and the researchers and scholars at the Fernando Ortiz Foundation for their support of my undergraduate and graduate research in Cuba. As an undergraduate and during the first few years of my graduate studies, I also met Cuban scholars who have become my mentors: Víctor Fowler Calzada, Tomás Fernández Robaina, Roberto Zurbano Torres, Graciela Chailloux Laffita, and Norma Guillard Limonta.

I would also like to thank artists, activists, scholars, and friends, including Yesenia Fernández Selier, Sahily Borrero, Odaymara Cuesta, Olivia Prendes, Wanda Cuesta, Yompi of the Junior Clan, David of Grupo OMNI, Etián "Brebaje Man" Arnau Lizaire, DJ Leydis Freire, DJ Yari, Yanelis Valdes, La Yula, Grisel Hernández, NoNo12 (known informally simply as NoNo), Alexey–el tipo este, Magia MC, Alexis "DJ D'Boys," Rodríguez, Mikel El Extremo, Ivonne Chapman Mill, Mariela Castro Espín, Yarima, Yuri, Pablo Herrera, Ariel Fernández, La Fina, La Javá, Las Positivas, La Real, La Reyna, Miki Flow, Randy Acosta, Apolonia Guilarte, Sekou, Vanessa Díaz, Julio Cadenas, Cross, Rodolofo Rensoli, Michael Oremas, La Fina, La Real, Lourdes "La Cinmarrona" Suárez, Ángel Candeaux, Jessel Fernández, Isnay "El Jugue" Rodríguez, Lou Piensa, Telmary Díaz, Nehanda Abiodun, María Teresa Linares, and many, many more who all shared with me their homes, experiences, and friendship. Thank you to Larry La-Fountain-Stokes, Celiany Rivera-Velázquez, Aisha Durham, Yaba Blay, Gladys Mitchell, Ivonne Chapman Mil, Yuri, Yarima, Yinet "La Habichuela" Rodríguez, Esther, Zulma Oliveras Vega, Christina Hanhardt, R. L'Heureux

Lewis-McCoy, Eli Jacobs-Fantauzzi, Gayatri Gopinath, Isabel Cordova, Jafari S. Allen, Teiji Maeda, Agustín Lao-Montes, Marysol Asencio, Enid Logan, Alfred DeFreece, Chavella Pittman, Vera Fennell, Seth Moglen, Monifa Bandele, Abel Sierra Madero, Ariel Meilich, Dalia Acosta, Sujatha Fernandes, Mignon Moore, Kelly Anderson, and Salvador Vidal-Ortiz for their support and feedback over the course of this project. Thanks to Kim Greenwell for sharing my vision for this project and helping me see it to fruition. I'd also like to send a shout out and thank you to Lehigh University, especially to my colleagues in the Africana Studies and Women's Studies Program for their support. And thanks to my family, including my uncle Fred McRae Jr., who thought it was a great idea to start talking to an eight-year-old kid about "the revolution."

Cuban Underground Hip Hop

Introduction

Ariel Fernández, a Cuban hip hop producer, DJ, and foundational member of Cuba's hip hop generation who is now based in New York, posted the following on his Facebook page on January 26, 2014:[1]

> Arsenio Rodríguez, Mongo Santamaría, La Lupe, Celia Cruz, Chano Pozo, Olga Gillot, Miguelito Valdez, Mario Bauza, Cachao, Pérez Prado were born, bred, and raised in Cuba. They were Cubans. Not Latinos. I repeat: not Latinos. Rumba, Son, Mambo, Cha Cha Cha, Guaguanco, Boleros, Pilón, Mozambique, Afro-Cuban are Cuban genres, not Latino. Without all those rhythms invented and created by Cubans in a country named Cuba and later brought to the U.S. would not exist what is called Salsa today and Latin Jazz. Period. One hundred percent fact checking. And I am only doing this because this Cuban identity and contribution is often dismissed, hidden, and manipulated in this country. So why am I a divisive person when I claim what my ancestors did? . . . Who gets offended? And why? Does the truth hurt? Who? We are Cubans and Caribbeans . . . Not Latinos. What is in the end . . . Latin?

Here Fernández challenges the politics of "Latin@ness" in the United States and the way in which it is used to erase the contributions of Cubans to the development of U.S. music culture and Caribbean music cultures. He also mentions the contributions of Cubans to music cultures that are known as Afro-diasporic musical traditions. Fernández points to the way in which these contributions are not bounded by the geopolitical borders of nations: when Cubans leave Cuba, they are still *Cuban*. What he argues here is that people carry those subjectivities with them and reproduce them within sound, no matter where they are. Fernández invokes the term "Afro-Cuban" as "Cuban," referring to the African origins of Cuban culture, and argues that redefining Cubans as "Latino" erases part of what it means to be Cuban: their African cultural legacies. He does, however, self-identify as a Black man.

THIS BOOK is the product of a semilongitudinal study that analyzes the artivism of the members of the first generation of the Cuban Underground Hip Hop Movement (CUHHM), "the old school" of Cuban hip hop (active from about 1995 to 2006).[2] I started participating in the CUHHM as a concertgoer in 1998. That year was important, for by that point hip hop had become conscious of itself as a music genre, the CUHHM had started to conceptualize itself as a social movement, and Cuba's younger generation of socially critical artists had begun to enter into the movement and develop their own discourses aimed at broad-based social change. I use 2006 as the marker for the end date of the early years because this was when the movement saw the last major exodus of many of the founding artists of the Cuban Underground Hip Hop Movement to other countries. During that time, it also became clear that the movement had taken root throughout the Island, with Santiago de Cuba and other cities establishing their own local hip hop movements.[3] Many of the groups in these cities (such as Las Positivas in Santiago de Cuba) have also emerged as influential national acts. Meanwhile a younger generation of artists in Havana came of age and began to fill the void left by the earlier generations. The groups and artists who stayed in Cuba began to change artistically over time, initiating newer types of artistic projects. As discussed in chapter 8, contemporary underground Cuban hip hop is a different artistic and social project from the original Cuban Underground Hip Hop Movement examined here. The CUHHM went into decline in 2006 when artists started to leave the Island. Another major shift in the movement occurred in 2011 when Obsesión, foundational members of the CUHHM leadership, returned from a tour in Canada. They learned that Magia, a member of Obsesión, had been replaced as the head of the Cuban Agency of Rap, an institution founded in 2002 to represent the interests of hip hop artists.

The effects of this recent leadership change have yet to be fully understood. Between 1998 and 2006 I traveled to Cuba two to three times a year; I began regularly returning to Cuba in 2010. The trips ranged from two weeks to three months. My work in Cuba was done primarily in Havana and on several tours with hip hop artists throughout the Island. In 2006 the majority of the first generation of Cuban hip hop artists left Cuba. They went primarily to the United States, Canada, Mexico, Norway, Spain, England, and Finland. I stayed in contact with many of these artists and attended their shows and symposia in the United States and Canada. Additionally, I organized a conference on contemporary Cuban music and scholarship in 2008 at Lehigh University in Bethlehem, Pennsylvania, where global hip hop scholars, activists, and Cuban hip hop scholars presented their work.[4]

I draw from ethnographic data collected in Havana between 1998 and 2006 and 2010 and 2013, including interviews with twenty hip hop artists in Cuba, five artists living outside of Cuba, and ten state officials affiliated with the movement between 2004 and 2013, for a total of thirty-five formal interviews. The interviews lasted an hour and a half to two hours. Participant observation was a central part of this project. I passed as Cuban when moving through public space in Cuba. This was very important in gathering data. For example, Cuban taxi rides offered a wealth of information. I would sit quietly in the taxis while the drivers talked about their lives, new government policies, and current events or just vented about things that happened in their everyday experiences. A few times people noticed that I was quiet and double checked to see if I was Cuban, at which point I would just sigh, roll my eyes, and stare out of the window. They would laugh and keep talking. I learned over time how to move through space and to "pass." While I was with artists, the racism and forms of harassment that we experienced were impressive.

If it became known that I was a foreigner, everyone with me would have had a problem in numerous situations. Until approximately 2005 it was illegal for Cubans, specifically Black people, to interact with "tourists." When we were stopped by the police, it was important to know when to be silent and how to move to a position so that the police would focus on the others present—who knew how to negotiate with the police—so that I would never have to speak. Several friends commented: "You know what, Tanya, we like you because you pay attention to what's happening around you and you know when to be quiet." All this is to say that what I write is informed not only by hip hop lyrics, interviews, and music videos but by my witnessing of some pretty complicated experiences. We always had an interesting conversation afterward. It is important to note that much of what I write is also informed by my experiences during my own everyday life in Cuba.

When I started research in Cuba, beginning in 1998, when I did preliminary fieldwork for my undergraduate senior thesis, I wanted to understand more about social marginalization there. I focused on race, gender, and sexuality. I wanted to learn whether the state had been successful in addressing prerevolutionary social inequality. Back in 1998 much of the academic literature on Cuba was still centered on the antiquated debate of whether or not Cuba was a totalitarian state or a socialist utopia. Dialogue about race let alone a critique was virtually absent. Carlos Moore and John Clytus were among the small number of scholars and writers to engage the question of race in contemporary Cuba. I knew that there had to be more to Cuba than what was represented in U.S. and Western European literature, media, and popular culture. As my experiences in Cuba confirmed this suspicion, I became frustrated with the absence of a nuanced, multilayered analysis of life in Cuba.

As I continued my work in Cuba at the graduate level, I started participating in the Cuban underground hip hop scene, at first simply as a place to socialize and listen to music after a day of research. Several scholars who had been mentors since I began going to Cuba as a twenty-year-old started to introduce me to Cuban peers who shared the same interests. As I moved forward in my work, I became frustrated. At the doctoral level, I was required to pursue formal research affiliations with institutions. Given that my work centered on sexuality, I decided to apply for an affiliation with research institutions such as the National Center for Sexual Education (CENESEX). I kept my informal affiliation with the Fernando Ortiz Foundation, but my research affiliation with it was not renewed in 2005. I became suspicious of the additional roadblocks that I faced in continuing my work. Several colleagues saw my disappointment the day I was told that my research affiliation would not be renewed. The University of Michigan demanded that I have a formal research affiliation in order to do my fieldwork, so in order to finish my doctoral work I complied.

The contradiction, as I understood full well, was that attempting to formalize anything with the Cuban state, especially in the area of sociology, was pretty much a death knell in terms of accomplishing research. As I left the building, one of the younger scholars, Abel Sierra Madero, followed me out the door. "Tanya," he said, "You don't need us. You know enough people here, so don't focus on institutions, focus on people. You can accomplish your doctoral research alone. You have been coming here for years now." Later that day, as I recounted the story to Cuban scholar and poet Víctor Fowler-Calzada, his only response was: "Culture. Focus on culture."

I replied: "Yes, I know, in Cuba if you want to focus on 'contentious issues' you have to frame it as a historical project, before 1959, or as a cultural project. I get it. But how do I interview people about contemporary realities? Also, I don't want to take the time to do an analysis of visual art, etc."

He just repeated: "Culture. Focus on the cultural sphere. Just focus on the cultural sphere."

After I went to sleep that night, frustrated and saddened about having to redesign the project completely, his advice clicked. I woke up in the middle of the night and thought: "Hip hop! The cultural sphere!" I realized that my friends and the circles in which I was roaming all centered around the hip hop movement. Everyone in the movement was talking about the issues that I was interested in, from the artists on the stage to the people who formed the movement's public. I understood that by focusing on the group Las Krudas CUBENSI and female rappers and MCs such as Magia MC, La Yula, DJ Leydis, and others I could learn about feminism, gender, and sexuality in Cuba. All this time I had been attending underground lesbian parties, hip hop after-parties, concerts, conversations, symposia—I had a wealth of ethnographic data about everyday life in Cuba. Most importantly, I became aware that I had been talking to activists working for social change all along.

Nonetheless, after realizing that I already had access to a lively sphere of critique and debate on these issues, another question arose: "Why was this happening in the cultural sphere?" In the literature on the Soviet Union, to which Cuban society, history, politics, and culture are unfairly equated, the answer was that culture was where all the disenfranchised political actors went to vent. Given my experiences in Cuba, however, and the way in which the work of artivists was hotly debated and discussed in state media, it was clear that something else was happening. That is how this project originated.

In August 2005, a week before Hurricane Katrina landed in New Orleans, I sat with cultural worker and artistic director Rodolfo Rensoli at his apartment in the Havana suburb of Alamar. Rensoli, a Rastafarian and key figure in Cuba's alternative culture and arts scenes, talked about art, race, and the history of cultural politics in Cuba. During the interview, Rensoli linked cultural politics, racial equality, and social change in Cuba to a longer historical struggle against the legacies of colonialism. He mentioned a meeting that a friend of his (one of the few Black students to graduate from Cuba's state-run arts institutions) organized with the minister of culture to talk about race and cultural production in Cuba. Rensoli described what happened in our interview in Havana in 2005:

Y convocó con el Ministro de Cultura, donde yo planteé que el único problema que hay en Cuba . . . que el único factor que entorpecía el desarrollo de la raza negra en Cuba es . . . era que todos los parámetros de legitimación son blancos, céntricos, euro-céntricos u occidentales. Que le cabía cualquier. Nosotros nos hemos creado un propio parámetro de medir la capacidad del individuo . . . nos estamos guiando por un discurso humanista de Francia de que sé yo que lugar, que siempre contiene al otro con una diferencia. Aquí no acabamos de asumir la nación mestiza como decimos en la cultura, no es así. Ahí en ese encuentro se dijo de alguna manera, Diego lo dijo, la actitud de la policía con el negro es vergonzosa. Se refiere al movimiento de rastafary. La justificación es que somos consumidores de marihuana . . . Pero ¿quién constata el valor de lo que producen los rasta como cultura? . . . hay un inmenso talento en la comunidad rastafary en Cuba . . . músicos de tremenda capacidad, pero somos tenidos como escoria. Igual pasa con el Rap.

O sea, entonces, la subordinación se ahí se expresa ahí o la intención de la continuidad de la subordinación colonial. Tienes que tener un discurso complaciente, tienes que tener una imagen que esté acorde con las concepciones de otro de lo que es una imagen agradable.

> And he convened a meeting with the minister of Culture, where I proposed that the only problem in Cuba . . . that the only factor that hindered the development of the Black race in Cuba . . . was that all parameters of legitimation are white, centric, Eurocentric, or Western.[5] That come from whichever one [Western European country]. We have created our own parameter to measure the ability of the individual in which we are guided by a French humanist discourse, really I don't know from which place, which always contains the other with a difference. Here we have not stopped assuming that the nation is a mestiz@ nation, as we say in the culture; it's not. There in that meeting, it was said somehow, Diego said it, the attitude of the police toward Blacks is shameful. He referred to the Rastafari movement. The rationale is that we are marijuana users. . . . But who notes the value of what Rastas produce as culture? . . . there is immense talent in the Rastafari community in Cuba . . . musicians of tremendous ability, but we are counted as slackers. The same goes with Rap.
>
> So, then, the subordination there expresses itself or the intention of continuing colonial subordination. You have to have a discourse that is accommodating; you have to have an image that is consistent with the views of the other as to what is an agreeable image.

Rensoli and his cultural production group, Grupo Uno, are the founders of the Cuban Underground Hip Hop Festival; they are considered to be the producers who initiated the movement. In this quotation Rensoli reflects on what he sees as one of the biggest issues facing Black Cubans, particularly Black Cuban artists: the Eurocentrism of Cuban culture. This Eurocentrism is both a historical legacy and a continued manifestation of the colonial subordination of Cuba's Afro-descendant population. It remains a central feature of discourse defining what and who count as *Cuban*. While internationally known dissidents are marginalized because of their direct challenge to the post-1959 state's legitimacy to govern, nearly the entire Black population in Cuba has been historically, economically, and politically marginalized because of its cultural and aesthetic (including corporal) "differences." Although questions surrounding economic and political equality reemerged in public discourse in Cuba during the 1990s, the role of Afro-descendant people in Cuba's public sphere as contributors to the formation of Cuban culture and the nation has been downplayed, if not rendered invisible, throughout Cuban history.

According to Rensoli, continued colonial subordination has been hidden through the national discourse of *mestizaje*. This discourse posits that race does not exist in Cuba because everyone is racially and culturally mixed, yet it simultaneously depends on the cultural marginalization of that which is coded as African or Black. Through his discussion of the "other," Rensoli critiques Western ontology and rejects it: in a country like Cuba, the only way for those who are defined as other to represent themselves in Western Eurocentric culture is to represent themselves as other in terms of the European, that is, as a different kind of being than a European. As Alexander Weheliye (2005), Rensoli, and numerous scholars and artists have argued, the cultural logic underlying hegemonic notions of Western modernity is premised upon the othering of Africans and Afro-descendants who have been and are formative in the emergence of the West or that which is Western.

The othering of Africans and Afro-descendants in the Americas is intertwined with the institutionalization of an African-centered forced labor system as a foundational element of colonial economic structures in the Americas. African peoples and their various cultural logics have been formative in the emergence of the West, yet the only intelligible way in which they are incorporated as part of the West is as the other. This process of othering accounts for the seemingly contradictory ways in which Black and Afro-descendant people who are clearly a part of the West are both included in and also excluded from the narrative of Western modernity (Gilroy 1993a; Nwankwo 2005; Weheliye 2005). Thus, in the case of Cuba, an African-descendant country guided by Eurocentric humanist discourse, there is a process of othering for Black and mulat@ Cubans,[6] despite nationalist discourses arguing that Cuba is mixed and integrated. Rensoli contends that Cuba is culturally African and that it is in fact white Cubans' anxious awareness of this that fuels their attempts to impose racial hierarchies that deny this cultural reality. For many of Cuba's socially critical artists such as Rensoli, improving the political, economic, and social situation of Black Cubans and indeed of the country itself demands a culturally based challenge to the legacies of colonialism in Cuban culture. It requires exposing the ways in which anti-Black racism serves as the fulcrum of white supremacy (Nakagawa 2012). Such a challenge highlights the manner in which Eurocentrism and whiteness (as oppressive ideologies, subject positions, and ways of being in and interpreting the world) structure social inequality in the West (especially in the Americas), while at the same time exposing and acknowledging the contributions of Africans and their descendants in the formation of Cuban society and, as I argue in this book, the West.

This book examines the Cuban Underground Hip Hop Movement (CUHHM) from 1998 to 2006 as part of a transnational Afro-diasporic challenge to the coloniality of American culture (regionally speaking). In this text I focus on the emergence and activism of the CUHHM as a formative element in the emergence of localized Black identity politics in Cuba during the Special Period (1989 to the early 2000s), the years in which contemporary Black Cuban identity politics were in formation. By situating Cuba's contemporary national Black identity debates, which were largely publicly spurred in the 1990s and early 2000s by the Cuban Underground Hip Hop Movement, in conversation with the circulation of hemispheric discourses concerning blackness, I show how localized Black identity politics, like the identity politics of Black U.S. Americans, Brazilians, and Puerto Ricans, have emerged in relation to and in conversation with Black identity politics throughout the Americas. By decentralizing essentialist notions of Black U.S. identity politics and centralizing Cuba as one node in the production of Black praxis within the Americas,[7] I show how Black Cuban politics reverberate throughout the diaspora—even after a fifty-year embargo and the state's institutionalization of cultural discourses of "racelessness" via *mestizaje*.

In debates about what constitutes Black U.S. identity politics, claims regarding their geopolitical boundaries and exceptionality negate the continued influence of the U.S. South on notions of Black identity within the United States, as well as rendering invisible the profound influence of Puerto Ricans, Jamaicans, Cubans, Haitians, and so many more from the Americas on the formation of Black U.S. culture, identities, and identity politics. It also obscures the contradictory space that Black people still hold in contemporary U.S. society. The Black experience in the Americas has always had a global element: our relationships to geopolitical borders were fluid until abolition, and national discourses concerning our ability to access the full benefits of American (regionally speaking) citizenships have always been and continue to be tenuous. These tensions have their origins in the colonial period. As such, I focus on the coloniality of Cuban culture and its effects on the possibilities available for Black and Afro-descendant Cubans in the emerging postembargo Cuba. Artists in the Cuban Underground Hip Hop Movement—the majority of whom were Afro-descendant youths—worked to decolonize their own and their fellow citizens' hearts and minds, as a means of contributing to the progress of revolutionary change in Cuba. In conversation with artists, activists, and intellectuals throughout the Americas and indeed throughout the world, the CUHHM used hip hop as a means to expose and challenge the continued coloniality of the Cuban nation and the region. Hip hop serves as a cultural conduit for exchanging ideas, memories, local histories, and strategies with Afro-descendant populations in various American contexts. It is a continuation of longer legacies of music and orality within the African diaspora in the Americas that have been central in the emergence of what Weheliye (2005) calls "sonic Afro-modernity."

The public presence of socially critical artists in Cuba contradicts its depiction as a totalitarian state (though it is clearly a repressive state at the time of this writing). The tendency of international onlookers to recognize only Cuban dissidents who seek to overthrow the state completely as potential and legitimate agents for change obscures the presence of a history of political activism within Cuba's cultural sphere. The development of the Cuban Underground Hip Hop Movement in the late 1990s and early 2000s sparked significant media attention outside of Cuba because it was seen as one of the few notable manifestations of public activism. What is important to stress here, however, is that the movement became notable only when aspects of its discourse and practice became intelligible as political within hegemonic (U.S. and European) understandings of what constitutes "politics" and "political expression." Had Cuba's cultural sphere, or any cultural sphere, been taken seriously as a site of political activism and organization, the media would have realized that several generations of political activism have existed on the Island. To be sure, the CUHHM complicated and challenged the dominant discourses of race, gender, sexuality, political economy, and culture in Cuba, but it drew on both historical traditions and transnational networks of critique and contestation in order to do so.

An analysis of this movement highlights the sociopolitical significance of arts-based political activism as a propeller of social change. For the artivists of the CUHHM, "revolution" is centered on a profound and long-lasting disruption of social inequality, effected by altering individual and collective consciousness. Artivists expect to bring about a fundamental change in the structure of society by disrupting the social norms, practices, beliefs, and structures of feeling that reproduce economic and political disenfranchisement as well as human alienation. They work to effect social change by revealing existing realities and contradictions and offering an alternative vision of society. This is a form of cultural politics: "a collective and incessant process of producing meaning that shapes social experiences and configures social relations" (Alvarez et al. 1998, 3). The Cuban Underground Hip Hop Movement serves as a valuable case study of a social movement centered on cultural politics as a path to decolonization.

The CUHHM's culturally based activism has focused on "knowledge-practices": spurring social change through creating new discourses and knowledge frameworks for Cuban citizens by drawing from and calling attention to the memory and continued presence of African cultural legacies and other alternatives to hegemonic Eurocentric visions of Western modernity (Casas-Cortés et al. 2008). The movement aimed to help its members and its audience develop a critical consciousness, a key component in envisioning an alternative society and spurring citizens to act for social change. Through hip hop, the CUHHM empowered a generation of youth, now adults, in Cuba to name and understand the various forms of oppression that they face.

The economic crisis of Special Period Cuba challenged the legitimacy of state discourses and social policies centered on material-based social equality and inclusive citizenship. The CUHHM and numerous actors in Cuba's politicized cultural sphere challenged the state's material-based discourse both during the Special Period and now. The CUHHM is largely a sphere of racialized social critique of the limitations of the state's material-based approach to citizenship and equality. It is also a movement whose aim was liberation not only of Black Cubans but also of the Cuban nation, the environment, and the world. In addition to the movement's critiques of continued racism and racialization, it provided critiques of class inequality, sexism, homophobia, and heteronormativity.

The CUHHM's critique of coloniality, in which artists also included a racialized critique of gender and sexuality, challenges the key hegemonic ideology in the region: that racism is an issue of individual prejudice, not a systemic, culturally, and by extension materially based problem. According to that ideology, racism ended with Spanish and Portuguese colonialism, only exists in and is perpetuated by the United States, and disappeared from Cuba with the 1959 Revolution. The CUHHM offers a pro-Black, antiracist critique in a socialist country that has pronounced the elimination of racism within its borders. CUHHM artists link racialized oppression to the legacies and ongoing forms of colonialism, imperialism, and rampant global capitalism. By making a cultural intervention against social oppression, however, artivists highlight that such oppression is rooted in ideology and culture and thus is not something that has been or can *only* be resolved by the state's redistributive policies. Artivists challenge the underlying ideological basis of nearly every aspect of social and economic life as a means of spurring long-lasting, profound social change.

The Racialization of Culture and the
Contradiction of Modernity in Latin America

In his interview Rensoli points out that aesthetics and artistic cultures coded as white in Cuba (for example, abstract painting, rock music, and folk music) are seen as contributing to canonical and contemporary culture, while those classified as Black are seen as problematic and excluded from national culture. The racialization of culture, knowledge, and experience was central to colonial domination in the Americas. While corporal coercion was a standard form of violence aimed at the control of African and indigenous populations during the colonial period, reshaping epistemic, affective, and erotic structures was also central to the project of colonial subjugation.[8] This expansive ideological campaign is captured by the term "coloniality." The coloniality of American culture reproduces a reality in which, despite having the legal designation "citizens," Black, multiracial, indigenous, gender, and sexual minority individuals are not *symbolically* recognized as citizens in the Americas.[9] Historically, these culturally marginalized groups have been classified via medical and criminal discourses as unfit or unable to contribute to society as healthy citizens (Bronfman 2005). This multilayered system of stratification is too easily obscured because citizenship was officially conferred on all, regardless of racial classification, with no regional equivalent to U.S. Jim Crow or South African–type legislation by which people were explicitly classified and legally separated on the basis of race. Yet, within this region, the colonial legacies embedded in culture (racism, sexism, classism, and heteronormativity),[10] which are reflected in laws concerning good taste, appearance, and proper conduct, the neo-colonial policies implemented by twentieth-century regimes (socialist and capitalist) and the neo-liberal turn in global capitalism have served to perpetuate and obscure the existence of massive inequalities.

This book locates Cuba culturally, politically, and ideologically within the Americas and more specifically within the Caribbean. I recognize Cuba as a country that has a significant impact on the cultural and intellectual currents circulating throughout the Americas, a region where power struggles concerning competing visions of Western modernity continue to this day.[11] As part of what is often referred to as the Atlantic or Black Atlantic, much of the region has yet to recognize or resolve its contradictory history of race. The Caribbean, in which some scholars include Brazil, was the first part of the Americas to be colonized and the place where the overwhelming majority of African enslaved and free people lived and worked. Before the United States came into existence, colonial European powers created settlements on the Atlantic coast of

Latin America, on the Gulf Coast, and on the islands and coasts of the Caribbean, where a significant portion (in many cases the overwhelming majority) of the population was African or of African descent. As the colonies of the southeastern United States developed, their political and economic structures were largely modeled after and in conversation with the colonies of the Caribbean (including the Central American and Brazilian plantation economy systems).

When Western European modernity became defined in racialized, European cultural terms (beginning in the late eighteenth century and intensifying in the nineteenth century), many of the countries in the Americas faced a conundrum: how to fit their overwhelmingly Black, African-descendant, and indigenous nations into a vision of Western European modernity based on European cultural, racial (read: white) supremacy, and emergent anti-Black/anti-African racism.[12] More specifically, this part of the hemisphere faced two contradictions. The first was the contradiction of exploiting African labor and creative energies while simultaneously purporting to create new nation-states that secured the rights of all. Over time a transnational discourse concerning race evolved that attempted to resolve this contradiction by allowing African bodies to be defined as commodities, essentially defining those enslaved or classified as Black as being outside of humanity. The second contradiction facing the emerging nations of Latin America and the Caribbean was that in hegemonic Eurocentric Western discourses they were not defined as being *of* the West even though they were located *in* the West, as the majority of their peoples were racially classified as nonwhite, mestiz@, indigenous, Black, and "Latin@." The Eurocentric elite living in the region needed to find a way to write themselves into Western European modernity and to keep secret the reality that racially and most importantly culturally they were not European. But they also had to contend with Afrodescendant and indigenous populations who did not sit idly by and let Europeans and their descendants who were classified as white simply determine the development of the emergent nations.

Nonetheless, assimilating to European culture offered tremendous economic, social, and political benefits. Cultural Europeanization became an aspiration for many in the Americas because it gave access to colonial power (Castro-Gómez 2008). The contemporary hegemony of French, German, and Anglo countries (the United States and Canada classify themselves as European, which is also a highly questionable proposition to say the least) in what is now considered "Western Europe" and North America (sans Mexico in the Eurocentric imaginary) has rendered invisible an important part of Western European history: the Spanish Empire and Portuguese Empire. After the reconquest of the Iberian Peninsula, the struggles for power among Iberian powers played out in the Americas, a source of Iberian wealth after the fall of the Moorish Empire. Within these empires, difference was largely based on ethnic and religious differences. Whiteness during this period was largely linked to ethnicity, religion, and relationship to the royal court (nobility). The colonial significance of whiteness as a status marker, as an ethnic marker, and as the foundation of an entire cultural imaginary still organizes social relations within the Americas today.

Countries that were part of the first wave of colonization in the Americas had to reconcile their realities on the ground with the changes that occurred during the second wave of colonialism. Settler colonialism emerged, and a new discourse of race was exported to build "European societies" within the Americas and later in Asia and Africa (Quijano 2000b). During this second and third wave, cognitive and genetic racial differences were increasingly understood as written on the body and encoded in blood. The light-skinned wealthy elites of Latin America and the Caribbean began to contest this increasingly racialized vision of modernity that left them vulnerable to the new reality of their non-whiteness (read: non-Europeanness).

The primary method used to challenge the emergent discourses coming from the United States, France, Germany, and England was to reclassify culturally African and indigenous populations not as African or indigenous but as something else. By developing a discourse of *mestizaje*, light-skinned elites in the Americas enacted a selective embrace of only certain aspects of African culture, while simultaneously leaving whiteness culturally and phenotypically intact as a Eurocentric ideal (Arroyo 2003; Castro-Gómez 2008). The undesirable elements of culture and phenotype became associated with blackness (and in some parts of the Americas with indigeneity), while desirable elements were associated with whiteness. Blackness and indigeneity came to represent that which could be defined as outside of modern national culture or at best as representing a "primitive" element of national culture, physiology, and evolutionary history. The continued existence of a racialized Black/African culture has become encoded as a remnant of the "past" according to the national discourse of many countries in the Americas and the Caribbean. It is this continued strategy of selective appropriation and disavowal that allows racism to continue in the region today.

What the United States achieved through state laws that explicitly restricted the political and economic rights of certain groups Latin America and the Spanish-speaking Caribbean were able to achieve through laws that defined "custom." What these countries defined as acceptable and unacceptable social practices supported the racist, sexist, classist, and heteronormative discourses of the time. They had legal codes concerning morality and productivity and legal codes that criminalized African culture and racialized non-normative sexuality. All of this further compounded the "Black" or "African" body as the sign of non-normativity (Ferguson 2004; Helg 1995; Moore 1997; Somerville 2000). Some examples of the racialization of culture are the criminalization of Yoruba religious instruments and African religious practices and secret organizations (Bronfman 2005; Helg 1995; Miller 2009; Moore 1997). In countries such as Cuba and Brazil, practicing Ifá, Candomblé, Umbanda, Santería, and other African and indigenous religions was and is still associated with the "lower classes," which include Blacks, indigenous people, mixed-race people (depending on their physical features), and "Africanized" or "nativized" poor whites. Even today in Brazil, for example, Evangelical, Catholic, and other Christian groups are working intensely to have these religious traditions banned because of their "barbarity."[13]

Laws concerning "decency" governed social life, explicitly addressing what was considered acceptable morality. They designated what was "high culture" and what was "low culture" and racialized African and indigenous cultural practices and knowledge as criminal or indicative of criminal intent. In essence, while the work of sociologist Pierre Bourdieu (1984) illustrates how culture is used to legitimate class-based social inequality, the racialization of culture in the Americas, especially the racialization of "discriminating taste," is used to legitimate race-based social inequality, in which culture is used as a supplement for race. Race and culture thus became contested stakes among European whites, "Latin/creole" white elites, and African, Afro-descendant, mixed-race, and indigenous populations that assert competing claims to and interventions into what would constitute Western modernity. Because racialized hierarchies of culture, aesthetics, and taste continue to legitimate and reproduce social inequality today, a significant number of politicized social actors focus on cultural politics when working for social change. In this book I begin from the perspective that the term "West" is an ideological construct imbued with coloniality, meaning that its emergence as a concept has its origins in the colonial history of the Americas. In this way I locate the Americas as central to the evolution of contemporary Western ontology and epistemology (Mignolo 2006; Weheliye 2005).

Cultural Politics and Arts-Based Activism in Cuba and Latin America

Nearly all social movements in Latin America and the Caribbean in particular enact a form of cultural politics, as struggles for cultural hegemony are still very much ongoing throughout the region (Alvarez et al. 1998, 6). Hence the reach of these social movements is much greater than that of movements that focus on a single issue, lifestyle, or form of material inequality. Instead they confront multiple nodes of power within society simultaneously, as activists seek to reconfigure the meanings that are integral to social relations. Social movements in this region also foreground questions of national identity, which in turn have broader institutional and social effects, as they challenge the parameters of who is included in the nation and what is considered legitimately "political." In short, cultural politics and social movements in the Americas are not simply about a competition for recognition or representation; they are struggles over competing visions of modernity. And hip hop is just one of the latest forms of Afro-descendant aesthetic and cultural interventions into hegemonic notions of modernity within the Americas.

The artivists of the CUHHM are part of a generation that came of age during a radically changing economic and political context: the Cuba of the 1990s that was struggling to respond to the economic, and subsequently political, instability unleashed by the fall of the Soviet Union. The 1989 to 1998 economic downturn is referred to as the Special Period. During this time the Cuban state also undertook its "Rectification" campaign (beginning in 1986 but formally understood to be from 1987 to 1990), whereby the state began to apologize for what it referred to as the "errors" of the Revolution. Through a series of unprecedented actions, the state signaled a new acceptance of religion when Pope John Paul II was invited to visit Cuba and Fidel Castro visited the houses of prominent Yoruba priests. In 1994 the film *Fresa y chocolate* was released and interpreted by many as heralding the state's recognition of its mistreatment of Cuba's lesbian, gay, bisexual, and transgender (LGBT) population.[14] The state also liberalized its economy and permitted the ownership of small businesses by Cuban families. As Cuba became increasingly integrated into the world capitalist system, racially based material inequality reemerged, affecting Afro-descendant Cubans in particular and revealing the racialized limits of socialist ideology. Black, mulat@, and antiracist white youth began to mobilize to address the conceptual void in socialist ideology, while also demanding that the Cuban government live up to its promise of creating an egalitarian society. Although the 1990s represented a series of social, economic, and political crises, they were also a moment of hope for a new generation of Cuban youth, who realized that they were in the middle of another period of rapid and profound social change.

It is crucial to recognize that the new wave of cultural activism during the Special Period built upon the work of the CUHHM's predecessors. The critical public space in which CUHHM artivists leveled their social critique was a result of the knowledge-practices undertaken by older generations of utopian artivists, intellectuals, and activists within and outside of the Cuban state. The emergence of Cuba's particular cultural sphere is a result of its critical artists and intellectuals' attempts to "socialize culture" and to develop a cultural politic that directly works to alter cultural regimes and expand political participation among citizens (Moore 2006). During a nearly fifteen-year period of intense and overt political tensions among Cuban artists, many of these actors were formally excluded from Cuba's civil society because of their political investments as well as their aesthetic preferences and their race, class, gender, and sexuality. Despite the state's attempts at censorship and intimidation during the early years of the revolution, the public engagement of critical artists and intellectuals (artivists) did not always play out as the state intended. As noted by Desiderio Navarro (2002), one of the central contradictions of the Cuban state's socialization of culture (providing a socially critical education combined with critical artistic literacy) is that the state was fairly successful in creating the mechanisms to build the foundation for the emergence of educated socially critical citizens (Borges-Triana 2009; Martín-Sevillano 2008; Moore 2006) while at the same time expecting and even coercing the population to be less critical. The result was an intensification of frustration within the Cuban population, as several generations gained access to the tools and resources to understand their larger historical, political, and economic context, were encouraged to "act" and to *be* revolutionary, but then were forbidden actually to do so in any way that was not approved by the Cuban state. Resisting this, Cuba's critical artists and intellectuals institutionalized a revolutionary, anticapitalist, and anticolonial ideological framework as part of Cuba's cultural sphere, which has had a tremendous influence on the worldviews of younger generations of Cuban artists born after 1959. It is this framework that provides the foundation for the CUHHM.

The Cuban Underground Hip Hop Movement highlights the importance and value of examining cultural politics in action. It shows that the separation of "culture" from "politics" in empirical work restricts the tools necessary to explain the profound social changes occurring within Cuba and the Americas. This argument is familiar for those working within cultural studies. The social sciences, however, particularly sociology, still have much to learn from cultural studies in terms of moving beyond recognizing that the cultural is political to asking critical questions about cultural politics and recognizing the ways in which cultural workers often initiate or propel social change. When disciplines such as sociology reduce the diverse forms of political mobilization occurring within the arts to being simply "cultural expressions" that are "prepolitical" or simply not political at all, they also limit the ability to understand how cultural activism has been integral to expanding democratic praxis and developing relevant theories of social change. Within the social sciences, particularly in the United States, this ideological division between art/culture and politics has meant that arts-based activism and social movements are rarely understood as a viable form of political activism or recognized as social movements at all. Arts-based activism is often understood primarily as a tool to attract participants to political rallies or as a movement's catharsis, an affective release linked to the collective frustrations resulting from socioeconomic ("political") oppression.

Engagement with cultural studies theorists can be useful in informing sociological theories of social change. One of art's radical qualities is that it helps those who are engaged in it as producers or consumers to connect with and critically reflect on reality (Marcuse 1978). In other words, art allows the articulation of the contradictory nature of reality, as it is experienced and felt, in a way that cannot be articulated by other means of expressing human experience and need. Contemporary political discourse is often centered on the "economy," frequently utilizing a Eurocentric aesthetic that frames certain discourses as rational (and thus legitimate).

The key difference in approaches to democracy and political enfranchisement in much of Latin America and the Caribbean is that culture, particularly the cultural sphere, is not conceptualized as being separated from other spheres of social life. Culture is understood as another sphere in which political mobilization and organized political action can occur; cultural politics are understood as key to social change. Efforts seeking change in Latin America and the Caribbean tend to center on culture as being constitutive of economic and political praxis (Alvarez et al. 1998; Avritzer 2002; Camnitzer 2003, 2007, 2009; Craven 2006). As such, the ultimate goal of arts-based social movements is to eradicate social inequalities largely shaped by cultural practices. While these movements have had successes in changing policy, they are also a challenge to the very meanings of citizenship, political representation, participation, and redefining the role of the state (Alvarez et al. 1998, 2; Yúdice 2003).

Political processes proceed from the ground up in Latin America and the Spanish-speaking Caribbean: people living in this region tend to address their needs at the local level in town squares and then expect that local needs will be addressed at the state level (Avritzer 2002). In many places, what count as deliberative processes in town squares proceed differently than those political processes that occur in Western European conceptualizations of "civil society" or the "bourgeois public sphere." The southeastern U.S. coast, Latin America, and the Caribbean are primarily inhabited by people of African and indigenous descent, who use dance, music, poetry, and other cultural forms of expression and orality that are often classified as "art" as key aspects of social/political deliberative processes. Although these practices are not considered integral to legitimate politics within the region, they often structure political debate, inform larger communities of social, political, and economic issues, propel political organizing, theorize about things ranging from cosmology to political economy, and help to set political agendas. It is for this reason that Chuck D of the U.S. group Public Enemy once referred to hip hop during its early decades as the "CNN of Black America." Cuban music—and more specifically the Cuban alternative music scene, of which the Cuban Underground Hip Hop Movement is a part—has emerged as a recent example of how Cuba's politicized artivists have been able to create a nascent civil society in a nation that is defined as a totalitarian state, where political activism that challenges state policy is assumed to be nonexistent (Borges-Triana 2009; Martín-Sevillano 2008).

Hemispheric Blackness, Black Identity Politics, and the African Diaspora

CUHHM artivists not only challenge traditional notions of what actions count as political but also redefine the boundaries and scale of political community, political processes, and national identification. Located within its regional context, the CUHHM highlights the way in which blackness in the Americas has a significant regional dynamic, including in its relationship to Africa and African cultural legacies. American blackness has historically challenged the hegemony of Eurocentric national identities within the region and within the hemisphere. It asks what exactly it means to be "American," regionally speaking, and makes an intervention into our understandings of Afro-U.S. American, U.S. American, Afro-Cuban, Cuban, Black Puerto Rican, and Puerto Rican, for example. When we consider the regional geopolitics of race rooted in European colonialism, what does it mean, for example, to be Surinamese, Martinican, Haitian, or Jamaican? CUHHM artists challenge the discreteness of national boundaries associated with identity politics and systemic racialized oppression within the Americas and in the West by participating in and invoking notions of transnational Black solidarity. The CUHHM reflects the ways in which Afro-descendant people continue to challenge the exclusion of African culture and worldviews in the articulation of Western modernity. This is reflected in the multiple centers of ideological production found within the African diaspora in the Americas, which includes religious institutions and the various technologies of knowledge production centered on music and orality (Gaunt 2006; Perry 2004; Richardson 2006; Weheliye 2005). The CUHHM has an important ideological tie to transnational Black liberation cultural movements and what Cedric Robinson refers to as the Black radical tradition (2000). These movements challenge the underlying logics of Western modernity, which fail to recognize the humanity of all Black people, especially Black citizens living in Western democracies, and the foundational contributions that the African diaspora has made to the emergence of the Americas and the "West" (Ferguson 2004; Gilroy 1993a; Jameson 1984; Quijano 2000b; Robinson 2000).

The CUHHM is a manifestation of Black American vision(s) of modernity, involving perspectives that are centered on or include African worldviews, such as West and Central African cosmologies. Hemispheric blackness, the experience of being Black, is profoundly understudied (Dixon and Burdick 2012).[15] It includes those whose phenotype indicates a "nonwhite" social classification vis-à-vis a visible presence of an African heritage that precludes being classified as white (however whiteness is interpellated within that country) and being embedded in a broader political context that draws from the cultures, histories, identities, and experiences of people of African descent living in the Americas and the transnational nature of systemic and institutionalized racisms there.[16] That is, the theoretical work that has been produced on global blackness or blackness in the West has ignored an entire region of people who have been formative in the development of U.S., Western, and global articulations of blackness and Westernness. If U.S. blackness were to be read within its regional context, it would raise questions about and highlight the fact that the United States is also not as European as it would like to claim to be.

The lack of empirical research that takes a regional approach to understanding American blackness(es) has led to a situation within academic scholarship, specifically in the social sciences, where there is difficulty in understanding the very existence of Black identity and Afro-descendant identity politics in the region, their origins, and how these identities are understood among people engaged in them. The United States is implicitly (and often explicitly) assumed to be the origin of contemporary Black American politics and even racism. So when questions surrounding blackness within the hemisphere emerge, it is assumed that the work being produced is simply a mimicry of U.S. racial structures.

For example, Danielle P. Clealand (2013) empirically addresses how systemic institutionalized racism in contemporary Cuba is experienced by Black Cubans. She shows that these experiences have been important in influencing the development of in-group identity during the Special Period and afterward. Clealand decided to undertake an empirical study of racial identity and experiences of racism as a means to challenge the hegemony of the ideology of "racial democracy" that tends to dominate academic scholarship on the region. Clealand (2013) writes:

Race in many Latin American countries, including Cuba, has been narrated through the ideology of racial democracy, which negates the importance of race as social cleavage. The ideology rests on the assumptions that (1) race as social cleavage is not relevant and is replaced with a universal national identity; (2) consequently there is an absence of racial hierarchies such that race is not connected to life chances or to socioeconomic status; and (3) racism and discrimination are foreign problems (primarily within the USA) and while individual prejudice may still exist, it only manifests in isolated incidents that cannot be connected to a larger social structure. (1621)

Mark Q. Sawyer (2005) also empirically addresses the relationship between race and racial identity in Cuba:

despite the use of numerous racial categories by interviewers, there was a strong degree of agreement between self-described racial category and the category ascribed by the interviewer. This indicates that the racial categories are seen to be quite distinct. . . . While many social scientists have taken to putting the term "race" into quotation marks, especially in the context of Latin America . . . it is incorrect to assume that race mixing and the existence of multiple racial categories in Cuba make race a confusing and poorly understood construct in daily life . . . people are able to discern who fits into what category. (137)

Sawyer not only found less "fluidity" in racial categories (but instead an increased number of racial categories where textures of hair, lightness of skin, and physical features are taken into consideration to make the classification) but also found that race affects life chances in both the peso economy and the dollar (and now Cuban Convertible Currency/CUC) economy. This challenges the idea that the economic parity continued for those who, when paid in pesos, were dependent on the centralized state economy. Engaging the work of Cuban social scientists in this area, Sawyer also presents empirical data showing that racial attitudes among Cubans have not changed since the Revolution, with white Cubans being less likely to believe that all racial groups have "equal values, levels of decency, and intelligence" (142). Additionally, the mean levels of explicit racism were higher in Cuba than in Puerto Rico, the Dominican Republic, and the United States.

Cuban psychologists Yesenia F. Selier (who in the 1990s conducted the first studies on racial identity in Cuba since the 1960s) and Penélope Hernández (Selier and Hernández 2009) challenge the commonly held wisdom that national identity is more important for Black Cubans than racial identity. In their study the 68 percent of the people who are classified as Black and see themselves as Black, actively participate in social organizations associated with blackness and Africanness (such as practicing an African-based religious tradition), and "believe that racial identity is as or more important as national identity" (35). The important intervention that these Cuban scholars make in studying race in Cuba is highlighting the link between racial identity and membership in cultural practices and organizations commonly associated with blackness and African cultural practices.

Unfortunately, political actors throughout the Americas, who engage the question of blackness and racial inequality from the perspectives of Afrodescendant populations facing systemic racism, are read as "trafficking race." Race is reduced to being a product of the consumption of U.S. cultural products such as hip hop. Additionally, as Cleland notes, taking this perspective renders the realities of race unimportant in terms of determining opportunity, life chances, affect, identity, and even self-esteem. While blackness is not equitable throughout the region, it certainly exists: race, blackness, and racial identity are all formed in relation to each other throughout the hemisphere. It is important to take the reality of blackness seriously, empirically engaging what that looks like in various American contexts. Hip hop studies in the region have become a lightning rod for debates about whether or not blackness even exists in countries outside of the United States. What is important to note is that blackness, in whatever country, is constantly in formation and ever changing, depending on economic and political contexts. The assumed rigidity of Black identity is another limitation of the way in which assumptions about U.S. blackness have become essentialized in academic literature. That is why it is important to place various Black identity politics in the Americas in relation to and in conversation with each other in academic work, because they already are so in reality.

These debates concerning the other side of authenticity play out in academic scholarship on the experience of blackness in countries in the Americas. Latin America and the Caribbean are removed from the West and placed in the "Global South," "non-Western" category. This erases their continued formative influence on Western modernity, which implicitly allows for Western modernity to be defined as white and European. In order for the United States and Canada to be able to position themselves as white European, Western nations, certain histories and realities are rendered invisible, complete with regional separation.[17] The dismissal of the reality of American blackness(es) allows for the possibility of then placing Brazil, Jamaica, Cuba, and Puerto Rico, for example, as "global," outside of a regional context, via the accepted wisdom of racial fluidity, malleability, and miscegenation in the Americas (sans the United States and Canada). That makes it possible for the existence of blackness in the Americas to be considered a myth, imaginary, which includes rendering invisible the presence (or even hegemony) of African cultural legacies and worldviews. This further allows the classification of many American countries as non-Western: they are global spaces that also suffer the influence of U.S. cultural imperialism, in the same way as Japan and Croatia, for example. Acknowledging the hemispheric nature of Black U.S. identity, including discourses of miscegenation and indigeneity, would certainly destabilize the discursive hegemony of a Eurocentric vision of Western modernity.

Let us be clear: a Black, African, or Afro-centric consciousness did not come to Cuba with hip hop. Nor has Cuba been isolated from the discourses of liberation circulating within the Black Atlantic in general, and the Americas specifically, for much of its history (Brock and Castañeda Fuertes 1998; Guridy 2010; Nwankwo 2005; Thompson 1983).[18] Black identity politics and Afro-centric cultural discourses have been a key part of Cuba's culture, history, and national consciousness for centuries (Fernández Robaina 1998a; Helg 1995; Miller 2009; Moore 1997). There was constant cultural contact between the African continent and the Americas via the transatlantic slave trade well into the nineteenth century, with voluntary immigration also connecting the regions in the present. The African diaspora has also been engaged in extensive regional-based migration and movement since the beginning of the colonial period. Additionally, with the invention of the phonograph, technology helped to continue and in some ways intensify the speed of exchanges that circulated the musicality and orality of African diasporic cultures throughout the Americas and the rest of the world (Weheliye 2005).

By the time of the Cuban Revolution in 1959, formerly enslaved Africans were living on the Island, along with a large number of Cubans whose parents, grandparents, and other relatives had been enslaved and still had memories of enslavement and Africa (Barnet 1968). The constant arrival of Caribbean immigrants in the United States, the frequent travel of Black U.S. Americans to the Caribbean, and the transregional movements of Black people within the United States demonstrate the continued circulation of people, ideas, and worldviews in the African diaspora in the Americas. In countries such as Brazil, large-scale illegal immigration from countries such as Haiti has become a policy concern, even while Brazil continues to be a destination for scores of African immigrants to the Americas. As such, for the diaspora in the Americas, the cultural legacies of African cultures and worldviews are not simply a distant memory, the dream of a "return" to some place with which Blacks share a tenuous connection. Instead, the existence of African cultural legacies in the Americas is very much tied to a longer historical cultural circuit, in which the struggle for freedom was not simply a struggle for physical autonomy but also a struggle to liberate consciousness and to recognize African cultures and worldviews as continuously formative elements of Western modernity.

Agustín Lao-Montes (2007) argues against the reduction of the African diaspora, specifically Blacks in the West, to a group of people who share the legacies of the terror of enslavement and social subordination. Lao-Montes (2007) conceptualizes the African diaspora as

> a *project* of affinity and liberation founded on a translocal ideology of community making and a global politics of decolonization. The African Diaspora can be conceived as a project of decolonization and liberation embedded in the cultural practices, intellectual currents, social movements, and political actions of Afro-Diasporic subjects. The project of Diaspora as a search for liberation and transnational community-making is grounded on the conditions of subalternization of Afro-Diasporic peoples and in their historical agency of resistance and self-affirmation. (310; emphasis in the original)

Lao-Montes (2007) goes on to write that Black feminist and queer perspectives from the African diaspora address the reality that not all people who consider themselves to be part of the African diaspora would like to hear "all subaltern subjects speak" (315). He thus argues that "the African Diaspora should be conceptualized as a contested terrain of gender and sexual politics where the very definitions of project, identity and agency are at stake" (315). Just as importantly, the African diaspora also signifies a cosmopolitan project. In the West, cosmopolitanism is central to the definition of Eurocentric Western modernity, associated with a form of sophistication, a familiarity, and a level of comfort engaging with persons and cultures from all over the world (Diouf and Nwankwo 2010; Mignolo 2000). But this conceptualization of cosmopolitanism has its origins in colonialism. The way that Europeans thought of themselves vis-à-vis the rest of the world was racialized, later racist, and always Eurocentric. Through the colonization of the Americas, the region and its colonies reinforced an imaginary cosmopolitan exchange that ideologically excluded non-Europeans.

Conversely, Africans and Afro-descendant populations had their own ideas about what cosmopolitanism and modernity meant—and they continue to do so today (Lao-Montes 2007; Nwankwo 2005). Ifeoma Nwankwo (2005) describes Black cosmopolitanism as follows:

The Blackness of Black cosmopolitanism inheres not in the race of the individuals who express it . . . but rather in the ways individuals and entities seek to define people of African descent and articulate the relationship among them and between them and the world at large. Faced with dehumanization and the Atlantic power structures' obsession with preventing the blossoming of their cosmopolitanism, people of African descent decided to stake their claim to personhood by defining themselves in relation to the new notions of "Black community" and ubiquitous manifestations of cosmopolitanism that the Revolution produced. (10–11)

The revolution that Nwankwo is talking about is the Haitian Revolution, but it should be noted that this revolution stands not only for Haiti but for all of the insurrections and slave revolts that broke out (often through coordination) during that tumultuous historical period (Dubois 2004). Black and African agency and self-determination scared the elites of the colonies. It was clear that Africans and their nonwhite descendants had their own ideas about what types of societies would emerge upon liberation. This idea that those nonwhite, enslaved, culturally "primitive" people previously racialized as "outside" of Western European Enlightenment ideals and cosmopolitanism would apply these ideals to themselves was a frightening prospect for those classified as white and non-Black (Dubois 2004).

After the Haitian Revolution, "blackness" became a point around which the peoples in the African diaspora in the Americas could define themselves as cosmopolitan subjects both within the diaspora, regardless of national boundaries and ethnic differences, and as a collective with shared historical and cultural affinities (Lao-Montes 2007). Most importantly, this diaspora speaks back and demands acknowledgment of its influence on the evolution of Western modernity. Scholars such as Lao-Montes (2007) argue that more needs to be considered when conceptualizing what constitutes the African diaspora. Specifically, we must seriously consider the impact of African worldviews in the development of American cultures (Marable and Agard-Jones 2008; Walker 2001). An Afro-diasporic perspective can help us to rethink the relationship of memory, culture, and structures of power beyond the limits of the nation-state as both a unit of analysis and the basis for political community—and, as a result, develop a politic of decolonization that is not limited to or reduced to nationalism (Ferguson 2004; Lao-Montes 2007). Many Cuban artists thus use hip hop as a vehicle to represent a Black radical and hemispheric Black consciousness that has long existed on the Island. Most importantly, the artists used hip hop to redefine what blackness would come to mean in Special Period and post–Special

Period Cuba (Robinson 2000).[19] If we contextualize the CUHHM within the ideological circuits of the Black radical tradition and the African diaspora, it becomes clear that the CUHHM is not simply the imitation of hegemonic, globalized music cultures emanating from the United States. A sector of hip hop has emerged and developed as part of a longer Afro-descendant challenge to Eurocentric visions of Western modernity; it is part of a continued struggle over cultural hegemony in the Americas that occurs within the arts.

Toward a Black Feminist Critique and a Queer of Color Critique

Centering Black identity politics within the Americas includes using an intersectional approach that takes into consideration the region's Black feminism(s) and antiheteronormativity politics, which also undertake an important project of placing Black U.S. feminism(s) within regional and historical contexts. It is important to undertake this type of analytical study, where academic scholarship begins to do the work of placing American (regionally speaking) Black feminisms into conversation with each other. This can aid in understanding how regionally based, transnational structures of power—which have their origins in the colonial period and have been formative in the emergence of the modern "West"—operate nationally, transnationally (especially regionally), and locally. Considering these power relationships is crucial for thinking through the politics of transnational feminist solidarities in a region in the midst of cultural decolonization and is central to understanding regional and local Black identity politics and political activism.

The sonic component of Black subjectivity and Black identity formation and competing visions of Western modernity include interventions into bodies and pleasures, genders and heteronormativity. Black women and nonheteronormative subjects are also a part of the Black public sphere even though, as Lao-Montes noted, not everyone in the hegemonic Black public sphere may want to hear what they have to say. Nonetheless, Black women and nonheteronormative subjects are also formative participants in the articulation of Black identity and identity politics.

"A Black Feminist Statement" by the Combahee River Collective (2000) explicitly outlines a Black feminist epistemology. The text frames the oppression of Black women as the simultaneous result of homophobia, the non-normative status of Black women, and materially and ideologically based inequality that has its origins in colonialism and slavery but also continues to structure the lives and experiences of Black women in the present. The Combahee River Collective sees Black feminist politics as a struggle against racism, sexism, homophobia, and classism and argues that all of these forms of discrimination simultaneously affect the lives of Black women. The collective asserts that their Black feminist consciousness emerged organically, because, as Barbara Smith (2000) points out, these intersecting dynamics were "driving them crazy." A Black feminist consciousness emerges when someone learns how to love and value herself and other Black women. The collective rejects the mandate to separate their struggle from the struggles of the larger Black community, because they are interconnected. No socialist revolution, antiracist movement, or feminist revolution will guarantee Black women's liberation. Their goal as Black feminists is to examine the "multilayered texture of Black women's lives," as a means of developing the theories and practices necessary for achieving Black women's liberation (Combahee River Collective 2000, 268). These are also central points articulated by the CUHHM's group Las Krudas CUBENSI, who developed this perspective nearly in isolation from the debates occurring within second-wave feminism.

Black feminists have also theorized about how oppression affected women or any oppressed group at the level of the erotic. Here I am referring to Audre Lorde's definition of the erotic as sexual desire and "an assertion of the life-force of women; of that creative energy empowered, the knowledge and use of which we are now reclaiming in our language, our history, our dancing, our loving, our work and our lives" (Lorde 2007, 55). Lorde's work was groundbreaking because it included a critique of how affect, pleasure, and desire have been taken up and reorganized in a capitalist, patriarchal system—imbued with coloniality, I would add.

The transnational anticolonial and revolutionary nationalist struggles of women in countries like Cuba have also had a profound effect on second-wave, leftist Black feminism within the United States (Higashida 2013). The histories of Black feminism in the United States reveal that Black feminist leftists were significantly influenced by transnational struggles against heteropatriarchy that were also a part of revolutionary nationalist and transnationalist struggles for liberation. Hence the queer of color critique, emerging from Black feminism, is not reflective of ideas that emerged as a result of U.S. exceptionalism but consists of ideas and discourses that emerged in relation to transnational discourses concerning Black liberation, in which Black U.S. leftist feminists took part. These transnational conversations also included critiques of blackness and the relationship between hegemonic notions of blackness and the heteropatriarchy embedded in nationalist struggles.

Blackness is also a lived reality and can be deployed as resistance in the face of white colonization (Johnson 2003). Hegemonic blackness is wrapped up in notions of heterosexuality, which E. Patrick Johnson (2003) refers to as the imperialism of heteronormativity within Black culture. This imperialism functions through hegemonic Black masculinity and "faggotry," in which femininity is sutured to homosexuality within the hegemonic Black cultural politic (Johnson 2003). As Johnson writes: "Because femininity is always already devalued in patriarchal societies, those associated with the feminine are also viewed as inferior. Given the ways in which effeminacy in men is read as a sign of homosexuality, particularly in the United States, it follows that homosexual men [and by extension Black women] are devalued" (69). Thus the queer of color critique has always been a part of radical Black feminist activism, especially in internationalist feminism. Black women have been aware of the ways in which questions of race, heteronormativity, nation, and colonialism/imperialism are mutually reinforcing axes of power that have a profound effect on their lives (Higashida 2013).

The queer of color critique emerged from this multilayered perspective of Black feminism to make a similar intervention in the field of queer studies. Roderick A. Ferguson (2004) notes that women of color feminist scholarship and activism highlights how racialized discrimination is interconnected with gender and sexuality-based violence and social inequality. Black feminism and a queer of color critique highlight why liberal ideologies (which include socialist and Communist ideologies) are limited in their articulation of a liberatory politic for racialized, particularly Black, subjects. Discourses concerning the nation, Black liberation, and notions of freedom based on liberal ideology are rooted in naturalized—and oppressive—categories of race, gender, the family, and sexuality (Ferguson 2004; Muñoz 1999).

Broadly speaking, race continues to be treated as an addendum in gender and queer studies despite the work of feminists of color. This unacknowledged racialization of queerness provides the basis for José Muñoz's theory of "disidentification." Disidentification is both a politicized and psychological survival tactic among queers of color. To disidentify is a strategy "clearly indebted to anti-assimilationist thought" (Muñoz 1999, 18), through which queers of color can construct an identity from multiple subjectivities that at the same time deny the queer subject's existence. Muñoz notes, for example, that Frantz Fanon, a key pro-Black, canonical, revolutionary, antiracist, and anticolonial subject, doubted and then dismissed the existence of homosexuality in Martinique. Nonetheless, a Black queer person may still identify with the antiracist, anticolonial elements of Fanon's writing, while simultaneously identifying with elements of white queer theorizing that fail to consider race. Disidentifying subjects remain critical of the exclusionary aspects of their multiple subjectivities. In this way an openly and visibly queer of color person actively challenges the multiple cultural codes that converge to define that person out of existence. This notion of disidentification is at the core of the views of CUHHM and other Cuban activists, including LGBT activists and queers of color. They identify with the ideals of the Cuban Revolution and disidentify with politics and ideologies that may define Black subjects and queer subjects, for example, out of the national or cultural imaginary.

While Ferguson focuses on the materiality of the organization of bodies along racial, gendered, and sexual boundaries and Muñoz acknowledges the psychic significance of a queer of color subjectivity, Manolo Guzmán (2005) considers the psychic effect of the intersections of race and sexuality on the organization of the erotic. Thus gayness is a racial matter even before it intersects with or reflects the experience of racialized subjects. Queer theory needs to offer more of an account of the way in which the erotic is racialized at the level of the subconscious, which affects conscious sexual choice and feelings of desire and disgust. This is a point that Jafari Sinclaire Allen (2011) engages. This text is discussed further in chapter 4, which engages racial identity in Cuba in 1998–2006.

The result of the racialization of erotic desire has been to foster racialized reproduction through reducing the source of all forms of erotic pleasure to the organs necessary for the reproduction of offspring, opposite gender, and homoracial object choice, all harnessed in order to produce heterosexuality (Guzmán 2005). Roderick Ferguson (2004) comes to a similar conclusion when he contends that a materially based argument is not sufficient for addressing the particular social inequalities facing racialized nonheteronormative subjects, as these arguments generally depend on racialized gender and racialized sexual ontology. Not interrogating a racialized ontology results in the naturalizing of the ontological foundations of racialized Western social inequality, including inequalities concerning sexualities.

As I have argued elsewhere (Saunders 2009a, 2009b), the racialization of homoerotic desire works in multiple ways against Black Cuban lesbians. For non-Black lesbians, Black women are an inappropriate object choice in terms of hegemonic homoracial erotic desire. Within the transgressive erotic space of the Cuban lesbian social scene, gender is racialized in such a way that Black women are coded as masculine and are not an appropriately gendered object of erotic desire for lesbians.

Black Music Cultures, Hip Hop, and the Sound of Revolution

During a visit to Trujillo Alto, Puerto Rico, I once said to a Puerto Rican friend and colleague that as a U.S. American in Latin America and the Spanish-speaking Caribbean I would be really nervous if a massive group of people started yelling all of a sudden. She looked at me, confused. "Actually," I said, reconsidering, "maybe I would actually run to someplace in Latin America or the Spanish-speaking Caribbean where massive groups of people are all yelling, because then I'd know that the revolution was about to start."

"What are you talking about?" she asked, perplexed.

I responded: "¿Tu no sabes? Aquí, cada lucha revolucionaria empezó con 'un grito'" (You don't know? Here, every revolution began with "a yell/shout").

She began to laugh. The joke was a play on the word "grito," which means a shout, a yell, a scream. A "Grito de Guerra" is a call to arms. Whenever there is a "Grito de ———," it is named after the place where it occurred. Further, *grito* usually refers to a call to arms to fight against some form of social oppression. Some examples are Grito de Yara (Yara, Cuba, 1868: War of Independence) and Grito de Lares (Lares, Puerto Rico, 1868: War of Independence).

The idea of insurrections being named after a sound or a yell in the public sphere that calls people to arms illustrates the importance of sound in mass mobilization, in hailing the subject, a subject, or a group of subjects. *Un grito* is also reflected in the graffiti behind Sekou of the CUHHM group Anónimo Consejo (fig. 1.1). Behind Sekou is the image of an Afro-descendant male with dreadlocks, yelling. The dreadlocks are important in the context of a country that encourages people with tightly curled hair to straighten or shave their hair. People who not only refuse to do so but also grow dreadlocks are rejecting the hegemony of European aesthetics in Cuban culture and embracing their blackness. Behind the man in the drawing are the head of a microphone, what appears to be the head of a can of spray paint, and a map of the Americas. The message: *Hip hop es el grito de los negros en las Américas*/Hip hop is the call for the revolutionary struggle of the African diaspora in the Americas.

But given the cultural and linguistic differences within this diaspora, how can hip hop resonate with so many throughout the region? Simply reducing the emergence of hip hop scenes to U.S. global capitalism is not an empirically sound argument to make, as I learned from my interviews with hip hop artists and cultural workers in Cuba and Brazil. As break dancing, rapping, graffiti, and DJing (the four elements of hip hop) emerged in the Bronx, they were also emerging at the same time in Cuba and Brazil, which has also been noted by scholars and filmmakers (Díaz and Díaz 2006; Pardue 2008). The particular U.S. contribution to the emergence of hip hop in the Americas is in the naming of hip hop and the initial framing/theorizing of it as a culture centered on knowledge production and consciousness as well as fun and enjoyment. Artists and intellectuals in Cuba and in Brazil often argue that the elements of hip hop were openly practiced throughout the Americas within several years of its emergence

Figure 1.1.   Sekou, of the underground group Anónimo Consejo, standing in front of graffiti in Havana depicting a screaming Afro-descendant male youth, with a map of the Americas behind him. (Courtesy of Claira M. Guilarte/graffiti by the graffiti artist NoNo12)

in the United States. How? Why? One of the reasons why it is difficult to capture much less understand this dynamic lies in the ways in which we think about race, ethnicity, the discreteness of national boundaries, the Black subject, and the movement of ideas between Black subjects in the Americas.

Fred Moten (2003) argues that Black performance is inherently radical because it produces a profound rupture in Western ontology: the (Black) commodity speaks and expresses emotion. The act of performing, singing, and making noise is a profound rupture in a society that has historically framed people of African descent as inhuman and as objects. Alexander G. Weheliye (2005) engages this history by arguing for the centrality of "sonic Blackness" in the formation of contemporary Western modernity. He contends that one of the ways in which the Black subject was rendered invisible is linked to the delegitimization of musicality and orality as legitimate forms of subject representation, in favor of writing and printing. Because of limitations of access to writing and hegemonic literary cultures, and because music and orality are also central elements of West African cultural and intellectual production, Black people were limited in their ability to represent themselves as subjects. With the invention of the phonograph, however, the sonic nature of Black subjectivity took on a different role, challenging the visual and written bias of Western modernity (Somoroff 2006) and enabling Black subjects to articulate themselves beyond the geographical borders of the United States and the Western Hemisphere. Weheliye (2005) writes: "Examining the sonic is an important zone for theorizing 'the fundamentality of Afro-Diasporic formations to the currents of western modernity, since this field is the principal modality in which Afro-Diasporic cultures has been articulated,' though it is not the only one" (4).

Kyra D. Gaunt explores similar themes through an analysis of the hand-clapping games and rhythms of Black girls across the United States. Gaunt (2006) argues that "Black musical style and behavior are *learned* through oral-kinetic practices that not only teach *an embodied discourse of Black musical expression,* but also inherently teach *discourse about appropriate and transgressive gender and racial roles* (for both girls and boys) in African American communities" (2; emphasis in the original). By including Black girls and women in analyses of Black subjectivity, we can learn more about the ways in which the musicality and orality of Black subjectivity (which is, of course, also gendered and sexualized) are both sonic and corporal. Gaunt defines "kinetic orality" as "the transmission and appropriation of musical ideals and social memories passed on jointly by word of mouth and by embodied musical gestures and formulas" (4). In order to show the regional significance of local Black subject formation in the Americas, with its continuing reverberating effects on how blackness is conceptualized within the United States and outside of the Americas, in this book I center on Cuba as a point of reference. It serves as an example of how these dynamics play out regionally and locally, in a country that without a doubt has had a significant ideological impact globally without the material wealth and militarism associated with the ideological reach of the United States. As hip hop artists have argued in the United States, Cuba, and Brazil, people started doing and hearing hip hop before it became defined as a culture. Musicality, orality, and kinetic orality have been central components of Black American subject identity formation and sonic Black modernity, even within hip hop.

The Emerging Field of Hip Hop Studies

Hip hop studies began to emerge as a new field of scholarship in the mid-1990s. The literature examining hip hop is expansive, with scholars making various kinds of interventions vis-à-vis the genre and representations of it. I began working on this project as an undergraduate in 1998. By the time I finished my doctoral work in 2008, a vast field of scholarship had appeared. To this end, this book is very much in conversation with hip hop studies and highlights several key issues that have emerged in the scholarship, as opposed to making a particular theoretical or analytical intervention within it. Throughout the text, I have included the pieces that have been particularly and personally influential in shaping my thinking in general and my analysis in this book. To the extent that my work makes a unique contribution to this scholarship, it does so by beginning specifically with Cuba and a desire to situate the emergence of an underground hip hop movement there in relation to the complex historical conditions of that post–Special Period space. I consider its implications for questions of identity and social change in the American Black Atlantic. The kinds of questions that I ask here about hip hop are then in conversation with the more thematic interventions made by other scholars who interrogate "gender and sexuality and hip hop" or "Black feminism and hip hop," or "African cultural legacies and hip hop."

Nonetheless, it is important to note the profound intellectual significance of hip hop studies in understanding contemporary social movements, racial, gender, and sexual identity politics, contemporary global (consumer) capitalism, and a whole host of social issues and theory. This is widely recognized in the field of cultural studies and acknowledged in the humanities but still virtually invisible within the social sciences. The asymmetry with which the field has been taken up in various disciplines is unfortunate, for hip hop provides a powerful lens through which to understand many different aspects of contemporary social life, including cultural politics, urban youth, arts-based social movements, and activist mobilization. Hip hop scholarship has engaged the social and political significance of hip hop (Rose 1994) and hip hop's link to Black and African political and cultural legacies (George 1998; Gilroy 1993a; Lipsitz 2007; Neal 1999, 2003; Osumare 2007; Rose 1994). Some scholars engage questions surrounding corporality, commodification, Black cultural production, and feminist, queer, gender, and sexual politics (Gaunt 2006; Morgan 2011; Pough 2007, 2011; Saunders 2009b; Snorton 2013). Others focus on specific components of hip hop such as break-dancing and B-boying and B-girling (Schloss 2009) and explore the relationship of hip hop, *latinidad,* and the Caribbean Latino population (specifically Puerto Ricans and Cubans, who were formative in the emergence of hip hop) (Flores 2000; Rivera 2003; Schloss 2009). My goal here is not to review this vast literature but rather to highlight those themes that speak most directly to my analysis of the CUHHM: (1) hip hop as a component of and contribution to a transnational Black political public sphere; (2) what it means and who is included and excluded when hip hop is designated as Black, African, or

Latin music; and (3) the intersectional analyses of hip hop feminism and queer of color critiques.

Hip Hop as Black Public Sphere

Black music cultures have been a key way in which members of the African diaspora in the Americas have continued to reach beyond colonially imposed national boundaries and continuously re-create alternative public spheres in the face of racial oppression (Black Public Sphere Collective 1995; Neal 1999; Rose 1994). Framing hip hop as a Black public sphere highlights how hip hop has come to function as a space where those of African descent, who have often been excluded from the bourgeois public sphere of previous generations, can organize to challenge social exclusion and racial violence (Black Public Sphere Collective 1995). It is a space where critical practice and visionary politics take place. The tools of deliberation within this sphere, such as music, radio shows, churches, and street corners, include practices (for example, singing, dancing, fashion) commonly and easily accessed by those often excluded from the hegemonic public sphere. These spheres attempt to extend social inclusion, such that those who have historically been excluded from public spheres have the opportunity to address their needs in an easily accessible democratic space (Black Public Sphere Collective 1995). Scholars such as Robin D. Moore (2006) and Mark Anthony Neal (1999) argue that having fun, specifically within poor and marginalized communities, is itself political and socially transgressive.

Tricia Rose (1994) describes hip hop as Black music and an example of Black Diaspora practices. Rose links the emergence of hip hop to changes in urban America's relationship to global capitalism. In a similar vein, scholars argue that hip hop's ideological intervention is a product of the sociopolitical losses for the post-1960s generation, including the unfulfilled promises of social mobility and the lack of social welfare safety, such as the weakening of affirmative action and the continued lack of opportunities for poor Blacks (Kitwana 2002; Clay 2012).

Even when music is "commercialized," this does not necessarily mean that its message is apolitical or supportive of capitalism or market interests. Commercialization serves as a means of mass dissemination. In the case of hip hop, as with all forms of Black music culture, when music becomes commercialized in such a way that artists are limited in their ability to articulate their own ideological stance, they find alternative ways to continue their social critique (Neal 1999). Similarly, Black artists used album covers and inserts as a way to educate, to disseminate ideologies concerning blackness, and to participate in Black identity politics through commercial media institutions (Gilroy 1993b). By means of creative practices such as these, artists participating in Black music cultures can use commercial media tools to expand the reach of the Black public sphere. Black identities, experiences, and ideologies of liberation are exchanged not only through music itself but also through visual images and performances, T-shirts, and graffiti. All of these visual forms have become means to communicate the ideas and experience of blackness through symbolism. These images are tools that help to facilitate Black identity formation for collective mobilization and empowerment (Gilroy 1993b). Using the educational and affective codes of images, artists explicitly and implicitly target their art to specific audiences, such as members of the African diaspora (Pardue 2008; Yúdice 2003).

When we consider hip hop as a diasporic music culture in an American (regionally speaking) context, the term "hip hop nation" has particular resonance among socially conscious or underground hip hop fans (Morgan and Bennett 2011, 177). The global reach of the hip hop nation, as an identity politics and politicized transnational public sphere, can be found in the manifestos of hip hop collectives throughout the world and in the lyrics of global hip hop artists who proclaim that they work for social change. One specific and immediately tangible example of this is the proliferation of Zulu Nation chapters throughout the world and the transnational work of organizations such as CUFA (Central Única das Fevalas/Central Union of the Slums).[20] They work for social change through the promotion of hip hop culture as a tool for mobilizing, consciousness-raising, and educational and self-esteem building in poor communities around the world, particularly in urban Afro-descendant communities.

Halifu Osumare (2007) writes:

> I reason that this aesthetic in hip-hop culture is the current manifestation of a historical continuum of cultural practices that are, in fact, African-based expressivity underpinned by a philosophical approach that extended itself into the African Diaspora as a result of the transatlantic slave trade. . . . The Africanist aesthetic in the Americas continues to reflect similar musical, dance, and oral practices that resemble those in West and Central Africa, the source of the Atlantic slave trade . . . in the United States . . . it still retains enough resonances in the performer's attitude, artistic methodology, and relationship to audience to make apparent its connections to African expressive practices. (13)

These cultural practices were classified as "low-cultural" in the Americas. Osumare (2007) argues that hip hop also reflects structures of feeling: as such, hip hop is linked across national boundaries by "connective marginalities":

"These are hip-hop perceived linkages across agency in the face of lingering social inequalities in the postcolonial era" (15). Examples of connective marginalities are culture, class, and historical oppression.

Picking up on this last point, Adreanna Clay looks at how youth identity is also a central identity in social justice organizing. Clay (2012) notes how "the incongruity of the gains in civil liberties accompanied by continued racism, sexism and heterosexism constitutes a cognitive and communal crisis for youth" (5). Here she echoes Bakari Kitwana's description of the hip hop generation (those born between 1965 and 1984).[21]

Clay goes on to note that the promises of the LGBT and feminist movements also evoked a backlash. Like members of the civil rights movement, younger generations also saw the failure of the promises of gender and sexual equality. One of the things that characterizes members of the hip hop generation is the way in which they approach their activism: it is fragmented and diverse (Clay 2012). Social inequality could no longer be reduced to an explicitly white supremist state or to a racist capitalism system (which now included middle-class and wealthy Blacks). As such, contemporary social movements among post-1960s generations tend to take more diffuse, nontraditional forms and are often unrecognized as social movements (Clay 2012).

Relocating Blackness and Latin@ness in National, Regional, and Global Hip Hop Studies

The relationship between blackness and *latinidad* is a complex one. Raquel Rivera (2003) addresses the tensions among blackness, Africanness, Caribbeanness, and U.S. notions of *latinidad*. Rivera contends that Puerto Ricans are culturally part of the African diaspora. She argues that the tensions of racialization, racial identity, cultural identity, and cultural production are reflected in downplaying or ignoring the role of Puerto Ricans in the creation of hip hop as a means of maintaining the racial distinctions between blackness and *latinidad*. Puerto Ricans themselves, especially second-generation Puerto Ricans, find themselves in a situation where they have to navigate the artificial separation between blackness and *latinidad*, especially since the "Latin@" culture they come from is also an Afro-diasporic culture. Rivera explores the cultural convergences of Black southeastern U.S. culture and Puerto Rican culture which are based in shared African heritages. Through focusing on these points of shared cultural history, Black U.S. Americans and Puerto Ricans were able to live, fight oppression, and build a cultural movement together. Rivera and scholars such as Tricia Rose (1994) and Alan West-Durán (2004) highlight the transnational context in which hip hop emerged, noting, for example, that the founders of hip hop in the United States were from the U.S. South, New York City, and the Caribbean (largely from Jamaica and Puerto Rico). The impact of Cuban immigrants and their descendants on the development of Black U.S. and Caribbean identities and music cultures has been seriously understudied, including their formative influence on hip hop.

As Fernández pointedly asks in his post, "What is in the end . . . Latin?" Questions of immigration, racism, and colonialism are unresolved tensions among Latin@s (Flores 2000). For example, the immense importance of Puerto Rican contributions to American society are often unrecognized. Puerto Rican identity and culture are rendered invisible in hegemonic narratives of Latin@ ness in the United States, which tend to focus on Mexican American and Chicano/Latino identity (Flores 2000). Additionally, as Caribbean Latin@s, Puerto Ricans culturally share as much with their African American counterparts as they do with some of their non-Caribbean Latin@ counterparts. Though it is clear that Puerto Ricans have also had a tremendous impact on Black U.S. culture and identity politics, Puerto Ricans are written out of Black U.S. history by virtue of their classification as Latin@. The absence of Puerto Ricans in the history of hip hop — or, better said, the absence of a narrative of hip hop as being Caribbean or even Latin@ in origin — is a primary example of how Puerto Rican cultural contributions continue to be unrecognized, especially since Bomba is one of the key musics that form the foundation of hip hop culture. As a Caribbean immigrant to the United States, Fernández is highlighting similar tensions that Cubans, particularly Black Cubans, face, much like their Puerto Rican counterparts.

Frances Negrón-Muntaner (2004) also picks up on this tension of Latin@ ness, Puerto Ricanness, and blackness. In her chapter entitled "Jennifer's Butt: Valorizing the Puertorican Racialized Female Body," she theorizes about the intercultural, and implicitly interracial, tensions surrounding the casting of Jennifer Lopez to play Tejana star Selena. Negrón-Muntaner (2004) notes that Selena moved from being a Tejana (which she describes as a territorialized "regional" identity) to being a "Latina" (which she argues refers to a national "ethnic minority") when she expanded her repertoire to include Caribbean, South American, and pan-Latin American genres (231). According to Negrón-Muntaner (2004), at this point "Latin@"

> refers less to a cultural identity than to a specifically American national currency for economic and political deal making, a technology to demand and deliver emotions, votes, markets, and resources on the same level—

and hopefully at an even steeper price—as other racialized minorities. It is also an appeal for ethno-national valorization, a way for diverse groups who are similarly racialized to pool their resources. (231)

The trick here is that while "Latin@ness" until recently has largely been bounded by U.S. political and economic interests (it is a classification that is relevant in a U.S. racial hierarchy), blackness or identifying with the African diaspora as a subject position and identification was not bounded in the same way. Specifically, "Latin@" does not exist as a racial classification in Cuba and many countries throughout Latin America and in the Spanish-speaking Caribbean, but "Black" does. In the case of the tensions surrounding Lopez's casting as Selena, Mexican Americans were frustrated that Lopez, a Puerto Rican, was selected for the part. Implicit in the tensions was the racialization of Puerto Ricans as potentially Black and therefore not Latina in the same way that Selena is Latina. Much of the tension centered on Lopez's butt, which was an implicit marker of her Africanness. Lopez, in response, mobilized Black and Latin@ discourses to challenge the critiques of her body as racist and her racialized (possibly Black) body as beautiful, while mobilizing discourses concerning pan-*latinidad* to argue for her Latin@ness. This again reflects the tensions that Puerto Ricans face, especially New York Ricans such as Lopez: they must navigate the boundaries, by virtue of their Caribbeanness, between blackness and *latinidad*. The longer they are in the United States, the more they are associated with blackness (African Americanness). Negrón-Muntaner (2004) describes how all of these tensions were negotiated:

> Even if "race" was hardly mentioned in this debate over curves and buttocks, for any Caribbean interlocutor, a reference to this part of the human anatomy is often a way of speaking about the African in(side) America. Not coincidentally, the major work on racism by a Puerto Rican author, Isabelo Zenón Cruz, is titled *Narciso descubre su trasero* (Narcissus discovers his rear end). And despite the fact that Selena was Chicana, an ethnicity not associated in the Caribbean popular imagination with big butts, her measurements, which according to her seamstress actually match Jennifer's, characterized her as not specifically Mexican American but "Latina," and hence more easily embraced as one of our own. (233)

Because of the presence of Latin@s who are from Afro-descendant countries and are phenotypically or culturally of African descent, the boundaries of *latinidad* in the United States are blurred and unstable. The ever-present reality of blackness, which is code for "African" in the Americas, lurks underneath a

U.S. classification that claims to be independent of blackness or Africanness. In essence, African diaspora studies implicitly, and explicitly, challenge the stability of "Latin@ness" as a category of "nonblackness." This approach allows for writing the African diaspora in the Americas out of Western history, and implicitly supports a more insidious discourse, one that assumes the only "Blacks" or "Africans" outside of Africa are U.S. American. While I note the importance of Latin@s in terms of a U.S. experience in the development of hip hop, I also note that most of those Latin@s were Caribbean immigrants (and their descendants). It is important to render visible a history of Black Spanish-speaking immigrants who were also formative in Black U.S. identity formation but are written out of this history because they are defined as Latin@—not Black and not Caribbean.

The movement of hip hop across the globe has largely been linked to U.S. global capitalism, in which blackness became a sign of "difference" for various communities, which allowed a hip hop movement to emerge in Japan and Colombia, for example (Condry 2006; Dennis 2012). In returning to the diasporic origins of hip hop, via the inclusion of Caribbean Latin@s, Joseph Schloss writes the following: "As Raquel Rivera explains, 'The long-standing tradition of street drumming among New York Puerto Ricans and Cubans—in which African Americans also have participated—strongly influenced the music that was recorded as soul and funk, which was later played as *break-beats* at hip-hop jams'" (Rivera 2003, 35; emphasis in the original; cited in Schloss 2009, 20). Schloss then goes on to quote Ned Sublette: in the 1970s "conga drums had become one of the signature sounds of African American musical nationalism, ultimately even acquiring a faux-African pronunciation unknown in Cuba: kungaz. Along with the one-chord groove tune that the conga helped define, the instrument was an important part of the sound of another of America's great cultural achievements: funk" (20). Schloss notes several important things in his book. First, all of the different aspects of hip hop culture are diasporic in origin. Second, the music that B-boys and B-girls dance to constitutes a canon: recordings are historical documents: the B-boys and B-girls interact with the emotion and the feeling encoded in the documents. And most importantly, a canon expresses a cultural or national identity. Thus hip hop, specifically breaking, has a canon that is diasporic in origin.

It is still quite common for U.S. and global hip hop studies not to take an intersectional approach to their analyses. That is, these texts do not weave the presence of women and their discourses into the overall analysis of hip hop, if the subject is addressed at all. There are of course some exceptions. For example, Derek Pardue (2008) engages questions about gender and organized Black feminist politics in Brazil (and its relationship to the emergence of hip hop feminism there). Interestingly, in Geoff Baker's book (2011) the voices of women artists are notably absent and reduced to the assumed limited visibility of women in hip hop. This absence is especially notable, because it is widely acknowledged in Cuban media and Cuban scholarship that one of the significant contributions of the CUHHM was the public articulation of feminist discourses, after fifty years when feminist identity politics were not a part of Cuba's public sphere. The word "feminist" is not in the index of Baker's book. In global hip hop movements, particularly those with an articulation of Black identity politics within the hip hop scene, a Black feminist/Black woman centered presence is a key part—even if those women have to struggle for visibility, they are still present and profoundly influence the discourses of their respective movements. These women typically are the most invested in Black identity politics because blackness, Eurocentric standards of beauty, and their effects on self-esteem and everyday treatment are a central aspect of the experience of femininity for Afro-descendant women. Hence the absence of hip hop feminists in texts that posit race as fluid (Dennis 2012) or not relevant to national hip hop scenes (Baker 2011) is not surprising.

Hip Hop Feminism Takes on Race, Gender, and Sexuality

Outside of the view of the larger public sphere, Black women have had equal participation in and at times have even dominated Black music cultures (Davis 1998). Describing hip hop as a Black public sphere, Gwendolyn D. Pough (2011) argues that Black women have always been vocal members of the genre. She views women's participation in hip hop as part of a new generation of Black feminist critique and argues that this generation has used hip hop as a way to critically engage issues such as sexism and homophobia in the larger public sphere. Similarly, Tricia Rose (1994) identifies hip hop as a key site of contemporary Black feminist critique. Many in the larger public sphere are not aware of or do not understand the presence and influence of politicized Black women artists within hip hop, as Black music cultures and their leaders are often gendered (and marketed) as male and misogynistic by the music industry (Davis 1998; Durham 2007). As commercialized hip hop, particularly in the United States, became gendered and racialized as Black and male, it has also been racially sexualized as hyper-heterosexual and hyper-phallocentric.

Numerous critiques describe how the oppositionality of hip hop has been commercialized and marketed to a larger public sphere obsessed with blackness as a form of social deviancy (Pough et al. 2007). As commercialization of the genre has progressed, women's critical voices and participation within hip hop have been narrowed to being objects of male sexual gratification and subjects who crave objectification. Some hip hop feminists have pointed out and protested Black male complicity in the sacrificing of Black women for economic gain (Durham 2007). But despite the ways in which commercialized hip hop has come to represent hip hop in the larger American public sphere, women still actively participate in both commercial and noncommercial hip hop. Tricia Rose, like Evelyn Brooks Higginbotham (1995), points out that the intersections of race and class encourage a form of solidarity across gender lines within the Black community, because race functions as a metalanguage, especially in the way gender and sexuality are understood. Racial solidarity results in cross-gender alliances within the Black community (including blackness within *latinidad*) that are difficult to re-create between Black women and their white feminist and white lesbian peers. This difficulty is largely a result of discourses surrounding femininity and sexuality that marginalize nonwhite women's gender expression and sexuality. Black women involved in any aspect of hip hop are often portrayed by white feminists as women who have been duped or co-opted into being unconscious sexual objects of men (Pough 2011; Rose 1994). This erasure of Black women's agency within hip hop ironically obscures the important role and critiques of women artists within the Cuban Underground Hip Hop Movement.

The emerging body of work concerning hip hop feminism challenges the assumption that women are absent from hip hop, including socially critical hip hop. It also challenges the idea that when women are present they only serve as objects of male sexual desire. I offer a regionally situated definition of hip hop feminism that draws upon the work of Aisha Durham (2007) and Gwendolyn D. Pough et al. (2007). Pough et al. (2007) define hip hop feminism as "a worldview, . . . an epistemology grounded in the experiences of communities of color under advanced capitalism, [and] a cultural site for rearticulating identity and sexual politics" (vii). Durham (2007) argues that hip hop feminism is "a sociocultural, intellectual and political movement grounded in . . . situated knowledge" (306). The situated knowledge is that of African and Afro-descendant women from the Atlantic's post-1960s generation,[22] "who recognize culture as a pivotal site for political intervention to challenge, resist and mobilize collectives to dismantle systems of exploitation," which I add are rooted in the legacies of colonialism (Durham 2007, 306). According to both Durham and Pough, a Black feminist identity is central to hip hop feminism. This identity is a hybrid epistemological standpoint composed of multiple subjectivities that borrow from multiple theoretical frameworks, especially personal experiences, in order to articulate itself (Hill Collins 2000; hooks 2000; Smith 2000). Hip hop becomes a mobilization for people often not recognized as participants in political processes to work for social change (Gupta-Carlson 2010). The presence of gays and lesbians is also erased from hip hop history and representation, though some scholars such as Cheryl L. Keyes (2011) and Adreanna Clay (2008) have acknowledged the presence of lesbian hip hop/neo-soul artists, such as Queen Pen and Me'Shell Ndegeocello during the early years of commercial hip hop. Clay (2008) argues that Me'Shell Ndegeocello marks an important turn in Black feminism and reflects the complexities and contradictions of hip hop feminism (53). For queer women of color raised after the canonization of Black feminist theory who grew up as a part of the hip hop generation, Me'Shell Ndegeocello's presence in national media was groundbreaking: she was visibility.

In considering the relationship between hip hop feminism and sexuality Nikki Lane (2011) argues that a gendered Black body is privileged in hip hop and that male and female interactions are framed via heterosexual metaphors concerning power (776). Hence it is a queer act for a woman to enter into hip hop and make an intervention into non-normative behaviors. Thus (as I argue in chapter 7 on Las Krudas CUBENSI) it is possible, if not probable, to find openly queer women artists within hip hop because the female presence within hip hop is a queer presence in and of itself. As such, a queer female subject is one of many queer female subjectivities within hip hop (the bad girl, the femme fatal, the conscious Black woman, the Afro-centric Black woman, the Black lesbian).

Plan of the Book

In chapter 2 I offer some background information on the process of the socialization of culture in Cuba. This chapter also historicizes race and cultural politics in Cuba, which is important in understanding the intervention that Cuban underground hip hop artivists are making.

Chapter 3 focuses on the emergence and development of the Cuban Underground Hip Hop Movement and racial identity politics in contemporary Cuba. It pays particular attention to Cuba's racial structure, its relationship to persistent social inequality, and CUHHM mobilization to challenge racism.

Chapter 4 provides a discussion of whiteness and mulat@ness in Cuba. I explore how and why the discourse of "racial fluidity" (a hegemonic discourse that argues that "races" do not exist in Cuba or in much of the Americas because of racial intermixture) is both pervasive and highly problematic. As many scholars, artists, and activists have noted, this discourse is interwoven into the racial structures that continue to oppress and disenfranchise people of African descent, while preventing/limiting the possibility of people to mobilize to challenge racialized social inequalities.

Chapter 5 examines the terminology used by CUHHM artivists, noting the various ways in which words and concepts are reworked and redeployed. Through examining the regional lexicon of the movement, I offer insight into the agenda of the artivists who interrogate and employ terminologies as a means of articulating and defining the terms of their own political struggle.

Chapter 6 engages the feminist debates that emerged in the movement and CUHHM hip hop feminists' intervention into racism, sexism, and heteronormativity. Drawing from the work of the artivists and their interviews, this chapter highlights the social and economic difficulties facing women, specifically Black Cuban women after the Special Period, with particular attention to how revolutionary discourse limits the possibilities available to women to address these issues.

Chapter 7 engages the discursive intervention of the group Las Krudas CUBENSI. The CUHHM was successful in stimulating national debates at the state level concerning racism, sexism, and homophobia. This chapter is a case study of how one group, as part of a larger movement, was able to push for gender and sexual equality as a key part of the CUHHM discursive intervention. By extension the group used the CUHHM as a national platform on which to address the needs of Cuba's sexual and gender-nonconforming minorities, bringing specific attention to those classified as female at birth. The concluding chapter addresses the post-CUHHM generation and the lasting impact of the CUHHM on political life, particularly Black political life, in Cuba. I address major changes that have occurred since 2006, when a significant number of the first generation of the CUHHM left Cuba for the diaspora, discussing not only why 2006 is seen by many as the "end" of the CUHHM but also the problems with such a diagnosis.

2

Historicizing Race, Cultural Politics, and Critical Music Cultures in Cuba

My field notes from Havana (August 2005) describe a going-away party and how the police reminded us that we were Black:

> The incident began when we left a farewell party for a colleague. We were a mixed group of artists, academics, and a few tourists. Our colleague, a Black Cuban man who had just recently married a white European foreigner, was leaving the following morning. The police saw our racially mixed group walking, stopped us, and asked all of the Black people in the group, including me, for identification. They did not ask the same of the whites who were present, many of whom were Cuban. [I was the only Black person who was a foreigner.] I waited, purposefully, and watched as they walked to every Black Cuban who had identification out, waiting for the customary harassment. The police took people's personal information and recorded their activities for the night, noticeably skipping over every white person present. Everyone remained silent. I stood apart from the group and waited until it was clear that they were only going to check the identification of the Black people in the group. As I quietly distanced myself from the Black Cubans present, I caught the eye of the newlywed for several seconds. I saw a glimmer in his eye. He understood what I was doing as I moved just far enough away that it was clear that I was a part of the group, but also an outlier within it. Realizing that they had one Black person left — me — the two officers looked at me perplexed. I had not taken out any identification.
>
> I waited a bit longer, until both of the officers became upset. They walked over to me and demanded that I present my Cuban identification card. I handed them my United States passport, and they did a hor-

Figure 2.1. Odaymara Cuesta Rosseau (*second from right*) of the Cuban underground hip hop group Las Krudas CUBENSI intervening in an unethical police stop. She challenged the police's targeting of a group of visibly queer men: if the police are going to stop people for no legitimate reason, then they should stop and check the identification of everyone. Unnerved by the intervention and by the subsequent flashes of my camera, the policeman inquired into his handset whether he should continue with the stop. The response: "No. Leave." December 2013. (Photo by Tanya L. Saunders)

rified double take; it did not take them long to realize what had just happened and how they looked in front of a Black U.S. American foreigner. Shocked and embarrassed, they quickly decided to ask everyone for their identification, including the whites present. By this point, there was a small crowd of people watching from across the street and passersby were stopping to ask what was happening. Once they were told the story, they stayed, angry that the police were harassing Cubans, and apparently felt accountable for their actions only when it became clear there was a foreigner present. After the police checked the white folks' identification, they returned to their police car. Everyone was sad about what had just happened, but suddenly our newly married friend walked over to the police car and said, "What you just did was racist, and not only did you embarrass us, you embarrassed your country." The police quickly jumped out of the car and began to arrest him. Seeing this, people flooded into the streets.

Friends intervened and attempted to get the police to change their minds. A mass of people surrounded the police car, and the large crowd (about thirty people) that had formed across the street ran over to give their testimony of the events. The crowd was also racially mixed, and everyone seemed upset about the blatant racism. Another police car appeared, and the first car drove away with our friend inside. Another police car appeared to manage the crowd, which was growing larger. While people were airing their grievances with the police, we tried to figure out where our friend had been taken. I lingered a bit and listened as some of the police officers admitted that they, too, were frustrated with their job and frustrated at feeling pressured to harass fellow citizens by other police officers. They agreed that it was problematic to target Blacks, and some stated that they thought things were changing, though they also noted that there were still a lot of "assholes" in the department. The "jerks" in the police department were the source of their frustration, because they felt that the "jerks" gave the police a bad public image. I would like to emphasize that these were discussions that took place between Black, white, and mulat@ Cubans and the police officers. They did not include the white tourists who were standing in front of the Capitolio, bewildered. . . .

After the conversations with the police, about twelve of us sat in front of the police station waiting to hear about our friend. At least ten of the twelve present expressed sadness (many of this mixed-gender and race group cried); they felt that "the state of things" in their society was such that the only option available to them was to leave. They supported the ideals of the revolution, though many felt that the revolution did not support them. The Black Cubans were frustrated at the constant racism and the lack of options available to them as young, educated professionals and artists. They felt constantly harassed by the police. One dark-skinned Black woman, an artist with dreadlocks who dressed in hippie fashion like her white friends, commented that she loved her country but she wanted to leave. She leaned over and said, "You know I love my country but sometimes people make me hate it. Do you know that sometimes when I am walking down the street people call me 'nigger'? They call me a 'nigger' in my own country. Sometimes I just really want to leave." She spoke in Spanish, but said the word "nigger" in English. In comparison, white and mulat@ Cubans were frustrated by a lack of options, the harassment they experienced when they were in groups of three or more, and the constant harassment of their Black friends. Two people in the group remained quiet for most of the discussions. They were supporters of the revolution.

When asked about their constant support, they said, while shaking their heads with tears in their eyes, "It is the best option."

After waiting for a few hours, we went back over to the Capitolio. Some people went home, but a few of us decided to wait. About four hours after the incident started, a police car came speeding around the corner. It stopped in front of us, and our friend stepped out. He shook the hands of the police. They said to him, "We understand where you're coming from, but there are better ways to handle a situation like that than just putting us on the spot. But you're right, though." And they drove away. We asked our friend what happened. His response: "We drove to the other side of the building and sat and chatted for a few hours." Who knows what really happened during those moments that he was away with the police. What I witnessed at the Capitolio is reflective of the contentious position of Blacks in contemporary Cuba.

This chapter explores three aspects of the Cuban context that are crucial for understanding the significance of the Cuban Underground Hip Hop Movement: the tangled history of race on the Island and in the region more generally; the varied forms and central importance of cultural politics in the country; and the critical music traditions out of which the CUHHM emerged and with which it remains in dialogue. The chapter analyzes the evolution of Cuba's racialized, post-1959 cultural sphere as a means of framing the social context in which CUHHM artists are working.

Historicizing Race in Cuba

Central to the formation and reproduction of the contemporary racialized social structure in much of Latin America and the Spanish-speaking Caribbean are questions such as: Who is classified as white? Who is light enough to be white? Or, better, who is light enough to not be Black? How do you know when someone is not white in a country where there so much gradation in phenotypes and the cultural imperative is to self-identity as "not Black"? As a Cuban colleague once said: "Everyone knows who's white, but not everyone is sure who's Black." These questions highlight the significance of aesthetic practices in everyday interactions in Cuba: what you do with your body and what cultural traditions you publicly embrace indicates your social racial classification and your racial self-identification. Aesthetics are political in such a way that "form" functions as a political discourse. The racialization of culture and the imposition of Euro-centric aesthetics as the cultural and corporal ideal are central to cultural practices in Latin America and the Caribbean; they are also central to identity formation throughout the hemisphere. While race is largely defined by blood and phenotype in the United States, it is primarily defined by phenotype in Latin America and the Spanish-speaking Caribbean. Additionally, the racial hierarchy of this region is largely centered around the ideologies of *mestizaje* and lightening, both which aim to achieve a national body where the overwhelming majority of the population would appear to be phenotypically "European." The negative misrepresentation of African cultures, bodies, histories, and civilizations has created a level of disidentification among those who are light enough to be considered "not Black." For those who are not light-skinned enough to make this claim, it has created a subject position suffused with low self-esteem and "auto-racism." This term is commonly used in Cuba to refer to a form of internalized racism that is not necessarily directed at others but instead functions as a conscious form of intense self-hate among those who are socially interpellated as Black.

Nonetheless, in Latin America and the Spanish-speaking Caribbean, "racism" is often defined in terms of U.S. Jim Crow laws and South African apartheid, whereby Blacks are targeted for social exclusion. As a result, a significant number of Cuban citizens do not see "race" as being a problem in their country, where no such explicit policies exist. Some people who experience racism on a daily basis often do not recognize it as racism, because it is understood (assumed) that everyone in Cuba is racially mixed on some level. To the extent that racial discrimination does exist, it is considered to be the problem of a few individuals and not a larger systemic issue. Thus, though purportedly nonexistent, "the rigid social hierarchies of class, race, and gender that typify Latin American social relations prevent the vast majority of de jure citizens from even imagining, let alone publicly claiming, the prerogative to have rights" (Alvarez et al. 1998, 12). Yet Cuba clearly had a culturally and materially based "race problem" for much of its colonial and postindependence history. As discussed in the introduction, the racialization of Cuba's cultural sphere is linked to a longer history of racialization with origins in the colonial period, during which race as an ideology emerged as a central justification for the maintenance of chattel slavery. It is this history that we must understand in order to make sense of how race continues to structure life in Cuba today.

The Colonial Period

The large Black and mulat@ and small white populations complicated the relationship between race and class in colonial Cuba, particularly with the ascendance of scientific discourses of race in the nineteenth century. Cuba's population was overwhelmingly African or of African descent, so members of the national elite rejected efforts to define themselves and their nation according to emerging notions of racial purity, because this new racial logic would define them as "non-European," "primitive," or "not modern." At the same time, however, the colonial elite continued to look to Europe and the United States as exemplars of modern culture, economy, and society. They implicitly and explicitly embraced European notions of modernity, which at their core linked whiteness to European cultural and racial superiority (Arroyo 2003; Bronfman 2004; Fernández Robaina 1998a; Helg 1995; Moore 1997). Additionally, given the large number of people of African descent on the Island, the elite had to address the political needs of the Black and mulat@ populations if there was to be any independence from Spain.

The success of the Haitian Revolution had significant repercussions in slaveholding societies throughout the Americas. In Cuba in particular, whites feared that Cuba would "become another Haiti" (Ferrer 1999; Helg 1995; Knight 1970; Scott 1985). White Cubans trusted neither Cuba's mulat@ population nor its Black population and feared that most nonwhites would aid Africans in establishing a "barbaric" African nation in Cuba (Helg 1995).[1] Much of the nineteenth-century discussion of the "intentions" of Cuba's Black population centered on this crucial issue: who would assume power when and if the country became independent from Spain? Cubans of African descent had to avoid being considered insurgents intent on establishing a "Black republic" (Helg 1995). Unable to debate publicly what the future Cuban nation would look like during the colonial revolutionary period, Cuba's elite addressed these issues through the cultural sphere, which existed outside of the official public sphere dominated by the Spanish Crown (Arroyo 2003; Ferrer 1999; Lane 1998; Moore 1997).

The result was the emergence of an ideology of Cuban "exceptionalism," a national ideology based on cultural and corporal intermixture in which Black and white Cubans died together on the battlefield during the Wars of Independence and Cubans fought a common enemy (Lane 1998). Black Cubans began to rely on a largely raceless discourse in order to press for social equality as "Cuban citizens." Writers of the period such as the Cuban national hero José Martí contended that "Our America" was one where whites and Blacks lived together. For Martí, there were no races; he and others of his time, such as mulato general Antonio Maceo, rejected the "textbook races" of U.S. racial discourse (Martí 1999). This ideology of a raceless Cuba was embedded within a universalized, culturally based vision of modernity. For all its recognition of hybridity and mestizaje, this vision still retained whiteness as an unquestioned ideal and put the power to define Cuban national culture firmly in the hands of the white and light-skinned Cuban elite (Arroyo 2003; Ferrer 1999).[2]

After the Cuban Wars of Independence, citizenship in Cuba was predicated on racial intermixture and a silence surrounding persistent racial inequality as a means of solving white Cuban fears of a looming race war.[3] Nonetheless, members of Cuba's elite had to acknowledge that they were not culturally "European." Instead of embracing their Afro-descendant culture, however, they classified Cuban culture as being exceptional, as being something else. As Jossianna Arroyo (2003), Ginetta Candelario (2007), Robin Moore (1997), and others have argued, the elites of Latin America and the Spanish-speaking Caribbean nations were able to define "Africanness" out of existence by nationalizing and redefining blackness/Africanness as "Cuban," for example, and embracing a form of racial and cultural ambiguity that would allow a white supremacist social order to function.

In order to understand this complicated, seemingly contradictory racialization of Latin Americans, the liminal category mulat@ needs further discussion. Cuba has a phenotypically based racial classification system, in which individuals can marry "lighter" until their descendants "look white" and are socially perceived and thus accepted as such. As a result, people who appear racially mixed (and are racially classified as mulat@) have some social fluidity: they are accepted (tolerated) in both white- and Black-dominated social spaces. Mulat@s are also considered more socially acceptable as intimate partners than darker-skinned persons, though they still face anti-Black racial discrimination. It is important to note, however, that class status mediates an individual's socio-racial classification. For example, a darker-skinned wealthy Black Cuban who culturally rejects African aesthetics will be tolerated within white- and mulat@-dominated spaces. What is socially discouraged is being physically *and* culturally Black (such as practicing African religion or looking or acting "African").

Mulat@s and nonwhite "whites" (a classification of whiteness based on a history of *mestizaje*) challenge researchers to engage what it means to be Afro-descendant in Latin America and the Caribbean. The paradox is that the racial ambiguity represented by mulat@ness as an "in-between category" is precisely what allows for whiteness to exist in this region. By having a mulat@ category, it becomes difficult to discern where the boundaries of blackness begin. This in turn allows people to disidentify with blackness and challenge its existence altogether (through the discourse that "everyone" is mixed), all while policing the physical manifestations of blackness via micro-social forms of racial discrimination. In essence, the category mulat@ness allows for the possibility of whiteness in predominantly Afro-descendant (or indigenous) societies in which transnational, hegemonic discourses of whiteness — centered on U.S. and European scientific racism—might otherwise have rendered whiteness an impossibility. This complex racial discourse of the Americas allows for variations from hegemonic transnational discourses concerning whiteness in localized contexts, while the disdain for blackness or Africanness remains nearly universal across geopolitical boundaries. This topic is also taken up in chapter 3.

Postindependence Cuba

After independence and the U.S. American occupation of Cuba from 1898 to 1902, national political discourses were largely influenced by the Platt Amendment (1901) and U.S. Jim Crow ideology, which restricted Cubans of African descent from becoming equal members and participants in the postwar economy, political structure, and larger civil society. The Platt Amendment stated that the United States would reoccupy Cuba if it suspected civil unrest there. This created even more pressure for Black Cubans to be cautious about organizing to demand redress as citizens. Using U.S. racism to their advantage, members of the white Cuban elite argued that protesting the implementation of U.S.-style racism would mean sacrificing the nation for Black leaders' own political interests. From 1902 to 1912 Black Cubans' attempts to address persistent racism through political organization were met with legislative challenges that prohibited political organizing along racial lines.

Unable to mobilize politically as a race, and marginalized within political groups because of race, several prominent Black leaders organized a protest. In 1912 Black people took to the streets in the eastern (predominantly Black) part of Cuba in a large armed protest (Fernández Robaina 1998a; Helg 1995; Rolando 2010, 2011, 2012).[4] This protest was presented to the media as another Black revolutionary act, immediately conjuring up the specter of the Haitian Revolution. The protest was violently repressed over a period of three days, culminating in the murders of three thousand to six thousand Black Cubans (Fernández Robaina 1998a; Helg 1995; Rolando 2010, 2011, 2012). The result was a silencing of discussions concerning race that would shape intellectual thought and political action in Cuba through the 1920s and signified the end of organized Black radicalism until the mid-1990s (Helg 1995; Rolando 2010, 2011, 2012).

It is thus ironic that only later, through a resurgence of Cuban nationalism, were Blacks symbolically, albeit problematically, brought back within the fold of the nation. By the end of the 1930s the U.S. presence in Cuba had manifested through capital investment and corporate ownership in the tourist and sugar industry, Cuba's largest sources of profit. Blacks were heavily discriminated against in U.S. businesses and constituted much of the underpaid working class.

As Cubans of all races began to resent their poverty as well as U.S. discrimination and cultural and economic influence, they began to embrace all that was considered "Cuban" in a reactionary move to look inward and understand themselves in relation to the rest of the world, especially the United States. Cubans increasingly felt that they needed to seek independence from their neocolonial predicament.[5] The result was the emergence of a new national myth that Black Cubans were the "true Cubans," who had started the process of developing a genuinely *Cuban* culture. Black Cubans were also presented as the ones who suffered the most under Spanish colonialism and U.S. neo-colonialism. It was Blacks who felt U.S. imperialism the most, as they were barred from working due to the racist U.S. social policies that dominated the Island (de la Fuente 2001; Moore 1997). Black Cubans went from being seen as potential traitors or agents attempting to subvert the viability of a stable Cuban nation to being seen as those who actually represented the nation, albeit in a highly "primitive" and romanticized fashion.

Even with this newfound positive valuation of Blacks and the African-derived elements of Cuban culture, however, white Cuban interpretations of the Black situation and estimation of Black Cubans still dominated racial discussions. Despite this move to nationalize blackness, it was difficult for Blacks themselves to speak out about their racial situation because of the ever-present threat of being called racist or unpatriotic. This tension reemerged in 1990s cultural debates concerning whether or not hip hop was Cuban or foreign and therefore anti-Cuban and counter-revolutionary. For white Cubans, racism was packaged as an economic situation and a social problem that would be corrected once U.S. imperialism ended. In this vein, many writers equated the situation of Blacks with the situation of poor whites and hence as symbolic of the Cuban nation. Ironically, the racial situation in Cuba was thus framed not as an issue pertaining to Blacks but as something pertaining to all Cubans. It was this understanding that dominated thinking about race and nation when the 26th of July Movement came into power in 1959 and continued after Fidel Castro became the domestic and international face of the Cuban Revolution.

Race and the Cuban Revolution

After the Revolution, the state claimed that it would eliminate racial inequality through its materially based redistributive programs and policies. By the end of the 1960s it publicly classified the race problem as solved. All Cuban citizens were thereby officially pronounced equal in society, at least in the eyes of the state. Organizing around any identity other than Cuban was prohibited, leaving Afro-descendant Cubans with no way of challenging the ongoing effects of internalized racism among Black youth or critiquing Cuba's culturally based racial classification system.

Between 1965 and 1968 those deemed antisocial, bourgeois, and possibly counter-revolutionary were sent to forced labor camps called Military Units for the Aid of Production (UMAP) (Arguelles and Rich 1984; de la Fuente 2001). This included Afro-Cuban religious practitioners, Jehovah's Witnesses, hippies, rockers, and those suspected of being homosexual. Though the camps were eventually closed in the late 1960s due to internal and international pressure, the targeting of Afro-Cuban religion and culture during this period further entrenched prerevolutionary cultural norms that viewed Afro-Cuban culture as marginal, criminal, and socially deviant (de la Fuente 2001). By the mid- to late 1960s the Cuban state pushed to homogenize revolutionary discourse and to eliminate elements that the leadership felt would be detrimental to the revolutionary process (Camnitzer 2003; Sweig 2002). This homogenization of discourses resulted in state rhetoric and policies that asserted that there were no women, Blacks, whites, gays, feminists, or any other identities: there were only Cubans. The imposition of this hegemonic discourse stifled any criticism—or even basic discussion—of experiences and realities that did not fit into this model.

Gender and Sexuality during the Revolutionary Period

After the Cuban Revolution in 1959, the state undertook what Fidel Castro described as a "revolution within the Revolution" to ensure women's equal rights (Bunck 1994; Fleites-Lear 2003). In an effort to rectify the social, economic, and political inequality faced by women, Cuban women began participating in national projects that sought to eliminate class and racial inequalities (Bunck 1994; Fleites-Lear 2003; Smith and Padula 1996). The result of these efforts, however, was the institutionalization of prerevolutionary cultural discourse surrounding reproduction and women's role as mothers, but now combined with revolutionary discourses that framed women as workers, revolutionaries, and militants (Smith and Padula 1996).

During the early years of the Revolution, numerous debates arose about what types of work women should undertake in the public sphere. The state commissioned studies to figure out what jobs were appropriate for women (Smith and Padula 1996). The revolutionary leaders wanted to ensure that women were not given jobs that might jeopardize their roles as mothers and wives. These dynamics yielded a contradictory experience for women after 1959 that is captured in the logo of the Federation of Cuban Women (Federación de Mujeres Cubanos: FMC) The image is of a fair-skinned female revolutionary fighter with a gun slung across her back who is holding an infant. The message: women now have control over their reproduction, but they are also still largely responsible for what they reproduce. In comparison, photos of the revolutionary male tend to show him with a gun in positions of political and economic leadership or a headshot of the male revolutionary subject as friend, protector, and thinker. As demonstrated by the FMC logo, official discourses surrounding femininity and women's revolutionary citizenship continue to be tied to women's reproductive capabilities (Smith and Padula 1996).

At the core of the image of the revolutionary was a notion of morality: revolutionaries were white, heterosexual, male, and deeply moral subjects who cared for and defended their nation (Bejel 2001). This nationalist imagery, combined with Cuba's highly racialized society, has created a situation in which women exist politically and imaginatively only as feminine, heterosexual subjects. Contemporary Cuban citizenship is constructed around the image of the militant revolutionary fighter in such a way that to be a citizen is to be a revolutionary. Revolutionary discourses surrounding femininity yield a feminine subject whose representation as a revolutionary is dependent upon her sexual relationship to men. For example, during the 1970s the state noted the continued difficulties faced by women. Domestic violence was a significant social problem. Women were expected to be subservient to their male partners and to their families. They also continued doing the overwhelming majority of the domestic care-giving work. In response to these issues, in 1977 the Ministerio de Justicia republished *The Woman in Socialist Cuba*. The book was designed to inform women of the legal obligations and social services available to them as women. The introduction to the book stated:

> Esos objetivos, sin embargo, no pudo alcanzarlos sino después del triunfo de la Revolución. De esa manera quedó demostrado, con claridad meridiana, que sólo la abolición de la propiedad privada sobre los medios fundamentales de producción y la construcción del socialismo, crean las bases para la realización de la igualdad de todos los ciudadanos y, consecuentemente, la igualdad real de derechos entre el hombre y la mujer.
>
> En este libro se recogen las normas jurídicas que plasman las medidas adoptadas por Revolución, dirigidas a la protección de la mujer, la maternidad, el matrimonio y la niñez.
>
> These objectives, nonetheless, could be reached only after the triumph of the Revolution. In this way it has been demonstrated, crystal clear,

> that only the abolition of private property as the fundamental means of
> production and the construction of socialism will create the basis for the
> realization of equality for all citizens and, consequently, the real equality
> of rights between men and women.
>
>   This book recognizes the juridical norms that shape the means adopted
> by the Revolution, aimed at protecting women, maternity, marriage, and
> children. (Ministerio de Justicia 1977, 1)

While the introduction affirms the liberation of women as an integral part of Cuba's socialist revolution, it also affirms the need to protect women, maternity, marriage, and children. Despite the construction of women as militant, revolutionary citizens, the state did not seek to protect the rights of women as autonomous subjects who were targets of systemic violence (at the level of culture). Instead the state sought to protect women by protecting the social norms surrounding femininity and affirming a socialist morality that firmly located women in terms of maternity, marriage, children, and their conjugal relationships with men.

From the late 1960s through the late 1970s homosexuality was deemed a decadent bourgeois social ill by the revolutionary Cuban state (Arguelles and Rich 1984; Lumsden 1996). Between 1965 and 1980 the revolutionary government considered homosexuality to be a form of immorality that could corrupt youth and enforced preexisting social decency laws that criminalized homosexual acts (Arguelles and Rich 1984; Lumsden 1996). In 1971 the state mandated that known homosexuals not be allowed in educational, cultural, and other institutions that were in direct contact with revolutionary youth. In the case of women's rights organizations, by 1970 known lesbians were not allowed to join the country's only women's rights association: the state-run FMC. This exclusion lasted until the late 1980s (Smith and Padula 1996).

Existing research on sexuality in Cuba largely focuses on heterosexual women and gay male sexuality; analyses of homosexuality have tended to focus on a universalized "gay experience" (Almendros and Jiménez-Leal 1984; Arguelles and Rich 1984). Additionally, print accounts of homosexuality in Cuba in the 1980s and 1990s were written by men who acknowledged that their work did not focus on the experiences of lesbians, which are hard to access (La Fountain–Stokes 2002; Lumsden 1996).

Independent films offer some representation of lesbian experiences (*Not Because Fidel Says So* [1988], *Looking for Space* [1994], *Gay Cuba* [2000]). These films capture the changes in state policy concerning homosexuality between 1980 and 1996, when the state began to target homophobia within Cuban society in order to address the HIV/AIDS crisis of the 1980s and early 1990s. The state sought to address the crisis by reducing the social stigma around homosexuality and undertaking a massive sexual education program that targeted men who had sex with men (Acosta et al. 2003; Grupo OREMI 2005). The result of these state policies has been more public space that is inclusive for gay male Cubans.

T Con T: Lesbian Lives in Contemporary Cuba (a forthcoming film in which members of the CUHHM group Las Krudas CUBENSI are interviewed) is the first film to focus exclusively on lesbians in Cuba. *T Con T* offers more insight into the issues facing lesbians, as it focuses on the efforts to create a lesbian community while also exploring the decreased economic independence of women after Cuba's economic crisis in the 1990s. The women in the film contrast the increase in gay male public space over the last twenty years with the continuing invisibility of lesbians and their lack of safe space. Gay male domination of nonheteronormative space is linked to the ways in which heteronormativity intersects with machismo to create a particularly vitriolic and isolating experience for Cuban lesbians (Arguelles and Rich 1984).[6]

I define Spanish-speaking Caribbean machismo as a racialized sex/gender system in which the experiences of men are generalized to a larger human experience (which differs from the rejection of any personality traits considered to be "feminine," as under Anglo-patriarchy). Women are excluded from the public sphere in this sex/gender system.[7] Their subjectivity is restricted to a feminine subjectivity in which they are primarily sexual objects of men. As such, a gay male and a transgendered person assigned male at birth are included in the public sphere. Though their sexual desire and gender performances face social sanctions, they are still able to represent their experiences as "human" by virtue of being designated "male" at birth, even if their experiences are considered representative of a flawed masculinity (Allen 2011; Saunders 2009a; Smith and Padula 1996). Likewise, a heterosexual female prostitute may face social sanction and violence but is still seen as a viable or at least visible subject within the public sphere because she performs a form of femininity in which she is sexually available to men.[8] In contrast, however, the very idea of a lesbian is virtually inconceivable for many (Acosta et al. 2003; Más 2003; Grupo OREMI 2005; Saunders 2009a). Lesbians are often understood as disgusting or even as a source of violent anxiety because their complete rejection of sexual availability to men renders them culturally unrepresentative and invisible (Grupo OREMI 2005; Saunders 2009b, 2011). Additionally, women who reject the narrowly defined "feminine" gender role that women are expected to use to represent their subjectivity are seen as man-haters and potential lesbians.

Several factors seem to make it difficult for women, particularly Black lesbians and self-identified feminists, to challenge the social ills that they face. Throughout the Caribbean and much of the world feminism is associated with imperialism. This belief has a basis in some of the historical actions of European and North American feminists. For example, during the hemispheric struggle for universal suffrage during the 1920s and 1930s, feminists from the United States argued that Latin American women were not ready for universal suffrage and that they did not understand the responsibilities of participating in an electoral public (Stoner 1991, 113). During the early twentieth century, white feminists from the United States fought against suffrage being expanded to the racialized and by extension inferior populations of women of Latin America and the Caribbean (Stoner 1991). As a result, this history added to negative perceptions of feminism and its rejection as a legitimate discourse for social equality in postcolonial and neo-colonial societies.

Another factor is that postcolonial and neo-colonial Caribbean states tend to conflate morality, sexuality, and gender. M. Jacqui Alexander (1991) argues that managing sexuality through legislating morality has affected the effectiveness of subsequent organizing against heteronormativity. In the case of Trinidad and Tobago, Alexander links this move to legislate morality to colonial rule and to the postcolonial state's attempt to legitimize itself: the postcolonial state uses Victorian notions of civilization as a tool to discipline and regulate the social order. By conflating gender and sexuality with a notion of morality, feminists and other women-centered activists cannot only focus on gender or women as a means of challenging social inequality: they must also focus on morality. Like Trinidad and Tobago, Cuba also implemented morality laws that sought to implement social order through the conflation of gender, sexuality, and morality.

The 1975 Family Code (Ministerio de Justicia 1975) promoted monogamous heterosexual marriage as an ideal (Bunck 1994; Fleites-Lear 2003; Smith and Padula 1996). Other social policies enacted a few years before the publication of the Family Code delineate the state's stance on morality, gender, and sexuality. The revolutionary state attempted to undertake social policy aimed at addressing the colonial and neocolonial legacies of social inequality, but its heteronormative stance on morality has reinforced preexisting social inequalities concerning gender and sexuality. By enforcing previous colonial and neocolonial penal codes that criminalized homosexual acts, the revolutionary state reentrenched colonial constructions of morality as a euphemism for heterosexuality (Alexander 1991).[9]

For example, as I have argued (Saunders 2009a, 2009b), the state's race-blind, merit-based policies have had some effect in promoting Black Cuban women to professional positions such as doctors and lawyers. The economic downturn, however, severely affected the state's ability to maintain a centralized economy and by extension continue its material equality programs. This has posed a key problem for lesbians: cultural norms concerning femininity and increasing material inequality have resulted in a lack of safe public space for lesbian socializing. These women do not have the social, cultural, or political capital necessary to challenge their marginalization. Wealthy white women who own or rent their own homes limit black lesbians' access to white-dominated women-only space. For many Black women who are forced to live with large families in cramped apartments, public space for socialization is limited.[10]

In my analysis (Saunders 2009a) of the beginning and ending of the Havana-based, state-sponsored group called Grupo OREMI (the group has since reformed), I addressed the ways in which sexuality is racialized and gendered in Cuba. The state's efforts at ending homophobia have been successful in decreasing homophobia among queer subjects assigned male at birth, while the social acceptance of lesbians actually decreased. I argued that OREMI's emergence and eventual dissolution by the state is intertwined with a racialized sex/gender system that continues to impede Black lesbians' ability to participate fully in Cuban society as autonomous subjects. This is intertwined with the ways in which racialized heteronormative constructions of femininity are replicated in Cuba's lesbian population, in which lesbians of all races overwhelmingly eroticize hegemonic white femininity. Thus in Cuba's racialized sex/gender system Black lesbians are constructed as masculine or mannish by virtue of their race and regardless of their actual gender expression. Hegemonic forms of femininity are so strictly policed within the lesbian community that Black women who identify on the femme end of the butch/femme spectrum have a hard time finding butch partners. At parties that are predominantly white, and even at Black and mulata parties, women tend to approach Black women with the expectation that they will find a butch partner or a "johnny." Some women have commented that they end up feeling sexually and emotionally unfulfilled because they are expected to be the emotionally distant and sexually dominant partner by virtue of being Black.

The laws that directly equate homosexuality with perversion have been repealed in the state's recent efforts to create a more inclusive environment for gay citizens. But one article concerning appropriate sexuality that is based on a notion of morality was only recently modified. According to the 1999 penal code, someone who violates article 303 must pay a fine of 100–300 pesos or $4–$13 U.S. This article is divided into three parts: section (a) states that anyone who sexually harasses another person will be fined; section (b) states that anyone "offending good customs through improper exhibitions or obscene acts" will also be fined; and finally, section (c) states that the circulation of pornographic materials or any other materials that pervert or degrade good customs will also be fined. These laws are still used by police to fine gay, especially lesbian, couples who hold hands or kiss in public. This policing of sexuality reinforces a notion of national and collective social obligation that is based on the supposedly moral duty of maintaining a stable heterosexual family, which in turn is naturalized as the basis of a "healthy" nation. But it also reinforces notions of gender, specifically femininity. Although today Cuba offers free sexual reassignment surgery for transgender people and boasts that the state no longer supports a policy of policing public displays of non-normativity, Cuba's LGBT population still faces stops and questioning by the police (see fig. 2.1). This is not unique to Cuba and happens in many societies, but it is important to point out that culturally entrenched expectations concerning heternormativity still affect the everyday lives of Cuba's LGBT population.

The Special Period: The 1990s

The collapse of the Soviet Union created an economic crisis for Cuba in the 1990s, which not surprisingly affected Black Cubans the most (de la Fuente 2001; Fernandes 2006; M. D. Perry 2004). The economic changes and the generational pressures of the 1980s resulted in a legitimacy crisis for the Cuban state, which no longer had the political and economic support of the Soviet Union. Cuba was forced to devise a new way to obtain economic resources for its population. It was necessary to develop an ideological and political project to achieve national ideals and, most importantly, maintain stability. The government took a two-pronged approach, liberalizing both social restrictions and the economy.

As part of the economic liberalization, previously guaranteed social welfare programs were cut. Food rations and state-based incomes were decreased, while the state allowance for private businesses and foreign direct investment was increased. A privatized tourist sector was created that quickly attracted foreign currency and financed a dollar-based dual economy. Cuban citizens were paid in Cuban pesos, while tourists were sold Chavitos (as they were called in the 1990s and early 2000s: Cuban Convertible Currency). The currency was pegged to the dollar at a 1:1 ratio. The exchange rate was 26 pesos for 1 Chavito from the 1990s until approximately 2005. Within the dual tourist economy, however, 1 peso was treated as 1 Chavito for Cuban citizens. A Cuban citizen might pay 5 pesos to enter a theater, but a foreigner would pay 5 Chavitos. A beer in a local restaurant might cost 1 peso, whereas a beer sold in a commercial restaurant would cost 1 Chavito. Chavito stores also began to emerge alongside stores that continued to sell products in pesos. The stores that sold in pesos often had shortages, and eventually many staple goods were only available for purchase in Chavitos.

With the liberalizing and privatizing of the economy, Black Cubans began to face more public discrimination; they were the first cut from jobs and the least likely to be hired within the lucrative foreign currency–driven tourist industry. Black Cubans were usually employed by the state and thus paid using the weak Cuban peso. They were also the least likely to receive remittances from family members abroad, as the early generations of immigrants included few Black Cubans. The economic downturn demonstrated that Black Cubans continue to live in a highly racialized society where the majority of the population holds negative views about Afro-Cuban culture, social conduct, and physical appearances (de la Fuente 2001, 322–323). The post-Soviet economic downturn created a rupture in which racist ideologies reemerged, both publicly and materially.[11]

Material disparities between Black and white Cubans began to increase. White Cubans had greater access to the tourist sector's informal economy, while Blacks were prevented from even talking to foreigners or staying at hotels. While I do not know of any formal laws forbidding Black people from entering the hotels, until recently laws stipulated who could stay at tourist hotels: only tourists or "non-Cubans." The racialized enforcement of these policies continues to this day. For example, I was not allowed to enter hotels during my time in Cuba. If I did, I was harassed by doormen or denied service (for instance, not being allowed to use the internet services available to the general public). In order to avoid constant harassment by security guards and city police, I stayed with friends or rented rooms from friends of friends and often refused to meet visiting colleagues at their hotels. Hotel guards would not hesitate to grab me and try to force me out of the hotel physically. After hearing some protest in English, they usually registered with shock that I was U.S. American and would then let me enter. Whenever a group of Black Cuban friends and I tried to go to large hotels such as the Havana Libre to eat or visit the bar, however, we were either not allowed to enter or not allowed to eat in the restaurant. White Cubans could freely visit these spaces. This is one of the interesting ways in which discourses operate in contradictory ways: revolutionary national discourse declared Black Cubans to be the "real Cubans," but only Black Cubans were targeted for enforcement of the policy that Cubans could not stay in hotels.

The liberalization of the economy during the Special Period also created a major ideological rupture on the Island. Rodolfo Rensoli, one of the founders of the Cuban Underground Hip Hop Movement, reflected on some of the ideological mistakes made during the early revolutionary period in an interview in Havana in 2005:

> Durante el periodo después la revolución, nos dábamos cuenta de cuánto el exterior podía servirnos para abrir el diapasón de apreciar muchas cosas. Nosotros asumimos la teoría marxista, nos creíamos que teníamos las herramientas e la solución de todos los problemas y nos estábamos perdiendo muchos avances culturales que se estaban gestando por el mundo que son revolucionarios. Le puedes aplicar a todo ese el marxismo, y decir que desde el punto de vista del marxismo eso también le pertenece al marxismo. Pero todas esas corrientes tienen una propia idealización para sí misma y así se veía.

>> During the period after the revolution, we didn't realize how much the outside could help us open the field to appreciate a lot of things. We took on Marxist theory, we believed that we had the tools and the solution to all of the problems, and we were losing a lot of the revolutionary cultural advances that were gestating in the world. You can apply that Marxism to everything and say that from this point of view of Marxism that also pertains to Marxism. But all of these currents have their own idealization for themselves, and so you see it.

Here Rensoli discusses one of the key ideological crises facing Cuban artists, intellectuals, and politicians (fig. 2.2). Cubans had become so insular and had so reified Marxist theory as a means to achieve Martí's ideals that they did not participate in many of the ideological changes happening globally. A common critique that emerged during the Special Period was that the emerging ideological currents in other parts of the world would have been useful in helping Cuba to move forward in its revolutionary processes. But it took the Special Period and the fall of the Soviet Union to wrest the nation out of its ideologically based hemispheric isolation. This process forced the Cuban state and intelligentsia to consider ideological alternatives to existing Marxist orthodoxy.

During the economic crisis, the majority of Cuba's population was becoming increasingly impoverished, while the turbulent political culture of the Island offered few redistributive opportunities in the way of economic and political empowerment. This reality was contradicted by government discourse, which stated that the government was providing economic welfare and social security to address the historical effects of race and class and was thereby creating the conditions for all citizens to participate fully and equally in society. Younger

Figure 2.2.   Rodolfo Rensoli (*right*) on a panel with psychologist and LGBT activist Norma Guilliard (*left*) at the 2010 Hip Hop Symposium, the first to be held since 2005. (Photo by Tanya L. Saunders)

generations of Cubans, including Rensoli, feel that by silencing critical discussions that did not use an orthodox Marxist material discourse the state limited the production of alternative discourses that would have provided useful innovative tools to continue the evolution of Cuba's post-1959 social experiment. But the measures used to analyze the successes of the Revolution were constructed using Eurocentric notions of social advancement. Given the silencing of alternative critical discourses during the Soviet period, those who sought to advance the interests of the revolution by challenging Eurocentric notions of morality (such as heteronormativity) and human expression (such as notions of "high culture" and "low culture") were limited in their ability to press for ideological and social change. This created what some call a "stalled Revolution," in which the revolutionary process ceased to produce innovative ideas, while the world and Cuban society continued to change. The result was a disconnect between hegemonic state ideology and reality. Yet it is precisely this disconnect between official discourse and reality that has made cultural politics so central to Cuba's post-1959 context.

Culture, Politics, and Social Change after 1959:
The Emergence of Cuba's Politicized Cultural Sphere

The emergence of Cuba's cultural sphere, what Ana Belén Martín-Sevillano (2008) refers to as a "nascent civil society," is largely a result of a number of political moves by the Cuban state and the corresponding pushback by generations of Cuba's politicized cultural workers. Cuba's revolutionary leaders and artivists were invested in cultivating Cuba's politicized cultural sphere as part of the process of political activism and democratic empowerment. These political actors did not see political activism in material terms, solely as a product of classes competing for control over the means of economic production and distribution. They did not accept the economy as the sole (re)producer of society and primary avenue of social change. Instead these revolutionary actors also recognized the significance of the superstructure: they viewed culture as a key site for the reproduction of society and therefore a potential propeller of social change. Thus Cuba's cultural sphere constitutes a nascent civil society.

The initial years after the Cuban Revolution brought a notable increase in artistic production and even, it seems, artistic freedom (Craven 2006; Howe 2004; Martín-Sevillano 2008). The state immediately created various art institutions aimed at supporting and enfranchising artists, while giving the general public greater access to artistic productions as participants, creators, and critics. When the revolutionary government came into power, artists and intellectuals were challenged to socialize culture, in essence to socialize ideological production (Camnitzer 2003; Craven 2006; Howe 2004, Moore 2006). In 1959, for example, the state created the Casa de las Américas, which was to become one of the regional centers of artistic production for several years and is still widely respected. The state also created the Instituto Cubano del Arte e Industria Cinematográficos (Cuban Institute of Cinematographic Art and Industry: ICAIC), which led to a proliferation of Cuban film by the early 1960s and established Cuba as a key player in cinema and one of the best places in the world to produce and learn how to produce film.

The Bay of Pigs invasion in 1961, however, served as a major reality check for the new revolutionary utopians (Howe 2004). The invasion created the basis for Cuba's strategic alliance with the Soviet Union as a means of military and economic protection from the United States and ushered in a series of state justifications for limiting democratic freedoms (Howe 2004; Martín-Sevillano 2008; Sweig 2002; Thomas 1971). As part of the Cuban government's alliance with the Soviet Union, the government began to incorporate prerevolutionary Communist hardliners into the state as heads of political, economic, and

cultural institutions. Many of them detested the "unorthodoxy" of Che Guevara and Fidel Castro, who were very much influenced by the ideas of Martí
and Simón Bolívar and other Latin American/Caribbean ideologies. The hardliners sought to impose a Stalinist ideological orthodoxy on the Island instead
(Camnitzer 2003; Sweig 2002). All ideological and cultural production was to
be used to serve a very narrow vision of what constituted social inequality and
what social change should look like. Those who challenged this new orthodoxy
faced outright censorship through arrest, harassment, and social exclusion. Desiderio Navarro (2002) describes the following key contradiction at the heart of
the state's efforts to encourage citizens to participate in Cuba's revolutionary
process as critical actors: "In the bosom of Cuban socialism, Marxist criticism,
among other forms of criticism, is expected to be less sociological, that is, *to be
less Marxist or to cease to be Marxist*" (195; emphasis in the original). The Revolution encouraged the development of a critical revolutionary subjectivity but
at the same time sought to restrict revolutionary praxis.

In the year of the Bay of Pigs invasion, an uproar broke out over the government's censorship of the film *P.M.* (1961), a documentary by Orlando Jiménez
and Sabá Cabrera Infante, shown on the TV show *Lunes de Revolución*. The
film, according to the state, idealized social life in prerevolutionary Cuba. During the public debates that ensued, Cuban artists and intellectuals pointedly
asked the new revolutionary state: "What kind of Revolution is this? Is this a
Revolution that supports freedom of expression or one that restricts freedoms?"
In his famous response, "Las palabras a los intellectuales" (Words to the Intellectuals), Castro ([1961] 2011) replied: "For [those who support] the Revolution;
everything. [For those] against the Revolution; nothing." In short, only those
who supported the revolution *as defined by the state* would have access to all
of the rights and benefits that it guaranteed. Conversely, those who did not
show wholehearted support for the new state would receive nothing and could
be subject to a lack of support that amounted to formal censorship. More omi-
nously, Castro argued that Cuba might prove a tough place to live for artists
and intellectuals not fully supportive of or indifferent to the Revolution. This
policy marked the beginning of state intervention in civic, political, economic,
and private life, which resulted in the censorship of Cuban citizens by the state
and by themselves.

Three years later, writing from Bolivia, Che Guevara offered an alternate
view in *Socialism and Man in Cuba* ([1965] 1989). According to Guevara, poor
education had led to mass disempowerment for many of the potential actors
who could be involved in social change on the Island. People needed to develop
the critical consciousness needed to understand how their reality was a product

of larger historical processes and thus begin to envision alternative possibilities for social change. Guevara went on to argue that humans need to be given the ideological tools necessary to make critical connections among feelings, everyday experiences, and the material world around them. An educational system that socialized cultural production was necessary to create the framework necessary for organic intellectuals to emerge. Guevara was adamant that freedom of expression should never be repressed, even if the result was artistic production that represented "vulgar" or "bourgeois" thinking.

Socialism and Man in Cuba and "Las palabras a los intellectuales" are important pieces for an initial understanding of the tensions within the Cuban state between those who shared a more utopian vision of artistic production and those who valued restriction.[12] These ideological tensions played out both within the state and within Cuba's art worlds. The result of these internal divisions, to the ire of many Soviet leaders, was that Cuba did not *consistently* impose a form of artistic realism (Craven 2006). Cuban artists, intellectuals, and other citizens continually challenged the state and revolutionary leadership when it attempted to impose this model or to deny its many contradictions. Unfortunately, as both the Revolution and the Cold War progressed, research institutions and resources for intellectual and artistic production were increasingly influenced by Soviet hardliners in the state and would remain so until Abel Prieto became the minister of culture in 1997 (Howe 2004).

For many Cuban artists and intellectuals, socialist realism represented a stifling of free speech and a barrier to radical social change. While socialist realism was not officially imposed during this period, the state certainly sometimes explicitly attempted to impose firm restrictions on Cuban artists and intellectuals. On April 27, 1971, the poet Heberto Padilla's forced public confession of treason indicated to all Cubans, and to the intellectual world outside of Cuba, that a socialist-realist aesthetic was expected and would be enforced.[13] There was a public outcry on the part of preeminent scholars and writers at the national and international level, protesting the treatment of Padilla. The hardliner elements of the state were forced to ease their approach somewhat, but the damage had been done. Padilla, like many other artists and intellectuals in Cuba, left the Island. For many during the 1970s and early 1980s, exile was preferable to constant harassment and possible imprisonment (Howe 2004; Martín-Sevillano 2008). The year 1971 marked the end of widespread public artistic and intellectual experimentation, which would not reemerge until the 1980s (Borges-Triana [1970] 2009; Howe 2004; Martín-Sevillano 2008).

The 1970s was a period of tightened bureaucratic control that was manifested in stricter standards for cultural production. The Declaration of the First

National Congress on Education and Culture, held in 1971, established the political and ideological criteria for staffing universities, mass media institutions, and artistic foundations. These policies included barring homosexuals from these institutions and tighter control on literary contests to ensure that judges, authors, and topics conformed to revolutionary ideology (Howe 2004; Lumsden 1996; Navarro 2002). The Cuban state continued to institutionalize the cultural sphere, while at the same time decentralizing cultural production. The earliest institution created to oversee macro-level cultural production was the Consejo Naciónal de Cultura (National Cultural Advisory: CNC) in 1961 (Moore 2006), which was initially part of the Ministry of Education. During the 1960s and early 1970s the CNC established world-renowned cultural institutions such as the Unión de Escritores y Artistas Cubanos (Union of Cuban Writers and Artists: UNEAC) and socially radical programs such as the Movimiento de Aficionados (Aficionados' Artistic Movement) (Moore 2006).

The goal of Cuba's Movimiento de Aficionados was directly to involve as many people as possible in the arts. Some of its most visible examples were neighborhood mural projects and the formation of theater and dance troupes, choruses, and amateur music ensembles (Moore 2006, 85). The import of the Aficionados movement can be understood only relative to the more conventional trajectory for Cuban cultural professionals. Once they begin attending secondary and postsecondary institutions, Cuban students typically are expected to attend political rallies, become members of the Communist Youth organizations, and participate fully in political life. They also are sent to work in Cuba's rural communities as sugarcane cutters as part of their sociopolitical preparation. Those who complete these obligations and express a properly "revolutionary" subjectivity have access to all of the state's institutionalized mechanisms for career advancement. In the case of cultural production, they have a highly rewarding arts career, receiving material and institutional support to disseminate their work. It is important to note, however, that not all of Cuba's professional artists are ideological automatons: numerous artists are simply pragmatic about their participation within these structures. Once in positions of power, some individuals also support projects or artists who are critical of social life and the state.

The Aficionados movement, in contrast, encouraged collective composition, downplayed the role of the "star," and was so morally driven (believing that art was created for free dissemination among Cuban citizens) that amateur artists rarely took money for their work (Moore 1997). Hugh Thomas notes that artists faced numerous tensions, given the state's coercive encouragement of ideological incorporation, homogeneity, and self-censorship, on the one hand, and the artists' and intellectuals' impetus toward challenging efforts at censorship or incorporation, on the other. Thomas (1971) writes the following about the effect of Cuba's art policy:

> Against this should be set the fact that the regime has spent a great deal on artistic promotion, and it can fairly claim to have brought poetry, ballet, music, traveling libraries and theatre to the countryside of Cuba. . . . But new popular music seems to have died and Cuba which, during the "bad old days," was for so long a source of new music and dances, from the conga, rumba, mambo and habanera to the chachachá, has not had any new rhythms to which to dance or to export. (1464)

Hegemonic state-run art institutions imposed a European aesthetic. Popular music, however, continued to be produced in the "informal" arts spaces supported by the state's decentralized approach to artistic literacy at the grassroots level. The Aficionados' Artistic Movement coincided with mass grassroots literacy and health education campaigns of the 1960s. These campaigns drastically reduced illiteracy and infant mortality and were integral in improving many of Cuba's material well-being indexes. The Aficionados' Artistic Movement was an integrated part of Cuba's educational agenda and just as important as Cuba's health programs, which indicates the central importance of artistic literacy in Cuba's revolutionary project. The movement brought art into marginal, poor communities and into the countryside by developing the educational and material basis necessary for broader-based artistic production. During the 1960s and 1970s, several of Cuba's most famous poets and musicians were factory workers, children of working-class families, or illiterate before the massive educational campaigns, including José Yañes, Eloy Machado, and Nancy Morejón, who was the daughter of dock workers (Craven 2006).

Numerous complaints arose as a result of the socialization of culture and the downplaying of the "star" or "professional artist." While a lot of impressive art emerged from the movement during the 1960s, a lot of substandard art was produced as well. Artists and intellectuals tried to encourage the state to pursue a process of standardization and a system of mass dissemination (Moore 2006). Between 1963 and 1967 the state sponsored a series of lectures, known as the Popular Music Seminars, as a means of educating the "masses" in music theory and history (Moore 2006). It hoped that this would help to stimulate people's desire and ability to produce more socially critical and aesthetically appealing art. As a result of artists' protests, the number of professionalization schools available to Cuban citizens increased. Shortly thereafter a system of pay was instituted (Moore 2006). The pay that artists received was based on their level of formal education and the social value of their work. To the dismay of many artists, many of the incomes remained stagnant throughout the 1980s (Moore 2006). As part of the standardization process, the determination of the "value" of art or the artists' social significance was not based on their popularity, influence, or how much they contributed to Cuban society. Instead it was tied to levels of institutional degrees and whether or not bureaucrats found the work to be aesthetically pleasing. Thus artists who did not have a high level of degree-based education or were considered to have produced work of little social value (even if embraced by Cuban citizens) were not paid well or given additional resources beyond those guaranteed to all citizens (Moore 2006). The result was that some artists who were nationally and internationally renowned were paid less than obscure classical music instructors (Moore 2006).

Alternatively, the Casas de Cultura (locally run cultural spaces at the neighborhood level) were established to ensure that all of those with or without "talent" (as termed by the Cuban state), regardless of their material circumstances, would have an opportunity to participate in sociocultural production at the national level. In fact, the politics involved in the selection process of the Casas de Cultura privilege those who support revolutionary ideology and the revolutionary political agenda. The Casas de Cultura are only one of nearly fifty institutions affiliated with the Ministry of Culture and are also home to numerous groups and associations that work at the community level. While they provide a venue for the state to target talent, Casas de Cultura and organizations such as the Asociación Hermanos Saíz (AHS) serve as institutional options for young Cuban artists who could not or decided not to enter into state professional institutions as well as other community members who want to engage in cultural productions. These spaces are controlled by local actors and supported by other locally run institutions and often support cultural activities that conflict with national ideology and cultural policy.[14] Thus, even though the Cuban state and larger Cuban society may have found homosexuality "repulsive" during the late 1980s and early 1990s, events such as drag shows were locally supported by the Casas de Cultura (one example is the film *Mariposas en el andamio*, an independent film about an early 1990s drag performance released in 1996). Thus the state at times implicitly supports projects that are critical of its larger ideology. Some of these activities occur in poor, violent, and intensely marginal areas where people carry out events despite objections from officials. Events may simply take place without any state-level attention. Or state support of an event may represent policy and ideological changes at the local and national levels.

State-run institutions, such as the Ministry of Culture, were created as a result of Soviet influence and given the mandate to streamline bureaucracy and standardize national institutions (Moore 2006). The ministry was designed to be a centralized organization that would establish ideological uniformity among independent cultural organizations and state-supported institutions.[15] The Ministry of Culture describes its cultural policy as follows:

> En las condiciones históricas en que vivimos, donde predomina la dominación hegemónica sobre los medios de comunicación y se imponen modelos culturales alienantes; la política cultural Cubana se ha orientado, por una parte, a propiciar la participación de nuestro pueblo en los procesos culturales y su acceso a lo mejor del arte Cubano y universal y, por otra, a garantizar la activa intervención de los escritores y artistas en el diseño y la práctica de esa política. Los creadores Cubanos, comprometidos con nuestra Revolución, han tenido y tienen un peso decisivo en la proyección nacional e internacional de los valores de nuestra cultura.[16]

> In the historical conditions in which we live, where hegemonic domination predominates through the means of communication and imposes alienating cultural models, Cuban cultural politics have been oriented, on the one hand, to foster the participation of our people in cultural processes and their access to the best of Cuban art and universal [art], on the other, to guarantee the active intervention of writers and artists in the design and practice of that politic. The Cuban creators, committed to our Revolution, have had and have a decisive role in the national projection and international [projection] of the values of our culture.[17]

At least in terms of its stated aspirations, then, the overall focus of Cuba's cultural policy is to ensure that the individual participates fully in the sociocultural development of the Cuban people. The ministry was largely encouraged by the Soviets as a means of controlling cultural production and expanding the state's ideological influence. But it has been the Ministry of Culture and its institutions, such as the *Unión de Escritores y Artistas de Cuba* (Union of Writers and Artists in Cuba: UNEAC) and the Casa de Las Américas, that in different moments have provided some level of protection for critical artists who draw negative attention from the state.

The numerous possibilities for cultural participation at the national and grassroots level have helped to develop a sphere of human expression and social critique that has come to have some influence on hegemonic discourses and public policy at the state level. In this context of ideological production, alternative worldviews, and alternative visions of democratic praxis, the activism of the Cuban Underground Hip Hop Movement, one of Cuba's critical artistic spheres, plays a significant political role in social change. The generation of Cuban youth who reached adulthood during the 1970s and 1980s placed further pressure on the Cuban state for constant, albeit slow and uneven, change (Fernandes 2006; Howe 2004). These highly educated citizens came of age during what many considered a stalled revolution: their parents experienced large-scale social change, in some ways for the better, in other ways for the worse. But the revolutionary process had since slowed, and the children of this generation were the first not to see any benefits of revolution. These youth soon joined the critical voices of those resisting efforts to implement a Soviet version of homogeneous socialist realism. The perspective of these young visual artists and writers involved in the emergent noninstitutionalized artistic and intellectual production scenes in the cultural sphere was "to go 'beyond art' in order to bring it directly to bear on society's problems, without making even the smallest artistic concession" (Navarro 2002, 191). These artists were publicly critically engaging social problems that people only discussed outside of the public sphere in places beyond the view and ear of the state.

The 1980s marked a non-institution-based explosion of critical intellectual activity that centered on social criticism of the problems persisting in revolutionary society (Fernandes 2006; Martín-Sevillano 2008; Navarro 2002; Zurbano Torres 1994). These artists acted out, at times literally, the ideal of art as a revolutionary weapon of resistance (Martín-Sevillano 2008). Artists and intellectuals began to locate their work within Cuban society at large as a means of spurring social discussion about how to rectify persisting social inequalities. As such, these artists amplified the many whispers concerning the state and the difficulties of everyday life that had yet to be addressed, or that intensified as a result of state inaction, circulating within the Cuban public sphere (Armony 2005; Camnitzer 2003; Craven 2006; Dilla Alfonso 2005; Navarro 2002). Cuban music and literary critic Roberto Zurbano Torres (1996) writes the following about the height of this period:

> La tendencia sociológica que marcó los finales de la década del ochenta ha ido atenuándose en la medida en que esas subjetividades antes silenciadas van legitimándose en un campo literario cada vez más libre de prejuicios estéticos e ideológicos. . . . El espacio poético cubano de los últimos diez o quince años ha sido un campo de batallas estéticas e ideológicas donde han logrado coexistir los más diversos estilos, temáticos y conceptualizaciones que expresan la cambiante realidad histórico-social y la movilidad del horizonte utópico e ideológico de esta etapa. Espacio donde se legitiman esos sujetos sociales que se erigen—cada vez más definidos y diversos—en este espacio de la cultura cubana.

The sociological tendency that marks the end of the 1980s has been the
increase of the means by which those subjectivities, before silenced, have
been legitimating themselves within the literary camp that has become
increasingly free of ideological and aesthetic prejudices. . . . The Cuban
poetic space in the last ten or fifteen years has been a field of aesthetic
and ideological battles that have resulted in the coexistence of diverse
styles, themes, and conceptualizations that express the sociohistorical
changes and the mobility of the utopic and ideological horizon of that
period. [This was a] space that legitimized these social subjects that
stand—each time more defined and diversified—in that space of Cuban
culture. (10–11)

The 1980s was a decade of legitimation for perspectives and subjectivities,
at least within Cuba's cultural spheres, that had been previously silenced by
revolutionary ideology. The ideological challenges that occurred during this
period broadened the utopic and ideological framework of revolutionary ideology. The effect was the recognition and inclusion of diverse subjectivities, ideologies, themes, ideas, worldviews, and ways of being, even if that recognition
only took the form of state tolerance (Borges-Triana [1970] 2009; Craven 2006;
Fernandes 2006; Martín-Sevillano 2008; Moore 2006; Zurbano Torres 1996).
The changes that occurred affected nearly every area of cultural production,
including film (Chanan 2004); music (Borges-Triana [1970] 2009; Moore 2006);
literature and poetry (Martín-Sevillano 2008; Zurbano Torres 1994, 1996); and
visual arts, such as theater, painting, and sculpture (Camnitzer 2003; Craven
2006; Fernandes 2006; Martín-Sevillano 2008).

But critical areas of ideological production continued to be heavily influenced by the state's political discourse. During the 1990s, for example, the government attempted to rein in critical intellectuals through the restriction of exit
visas and other forms of "politics by omission" (Armony 2005). Artists based
in central Havana, for example, would be offered performance spaces outside
of the city that were difficult to access; the bureaucratic hurdles for the publication of manuscripts were increased; and numerous other forms of informal
repression were employed (Navarro 2002). As a result, artists often worked independently of Cuba's institutionalized artistic structures. Some of these artists
worked independently because their choice of aesthetic or topic was judged by
government officials, instructors, or others within Cuba's cultural institutions to
be far from exemplary or to be in poor taste or "lacking in talent." Other artists
rejected Cuba's institutional structures and felt that working outside of the state
cultural apparatuses would allow them to have greater artistic freedom. The

Cuban alternative music scene and subsequently the Cuban Underground Hip Hop Movement developed out of this context.

Music-Based Activism: The Cuban Alternative Music Scene

Sujatha Fernandes (2006) uses the term "artistic public spheres" to describe "sites of interaction and discussion among ordinary citizens generated through the media of art and popular culture" through which critical art cultures are produced (3). Fernandes is primarily interested in thinking through how Cuba's artistic communities have effected changes on the Island. She focuses specifically on how artists have used the market both as a way to sustain themselves during the 1980s and 1990s and as a way to mobilize the material and political support necessary to challenge the hegemony of state discourses through transnational networks. According to Fernandes, artistic public spheres emerge at the convergence of individual artists' interests, state interests (cultural policies), and market interests (cultural production for consumption). She describes how the Cuban state was able to protect artistic production from being dependent on market interests. Through increased access to a multinational consumer market, Cuban artists were then able to make strategic use of this space between the state and the market for social critique that is still very much a part of the public sphere.

I would expand Fernandes's analysis further to say that critical arts *movements* have been produced in this process: many of these critical art cultures are organized social movements and artivist collectives working for social change. I am interested in groups of artists who have mobilized to work for social change, not just to create a space for critique that aligns with market-driven consumptive/profit interests. These critical arts movements have their origins within artistic public spheres, particularly those associated with music. Music is an understudied element within arts-based social movements, in which concert venues function as meeting halls and the concert itself is the call to order and the political meeting. Theories concerning the relationship between art and social change primarily focus on literature and visual arts (Camnitzer 2003; Chanan 1986, 2004; Craven 2006; Fernandes 2006; Howe 1995, 2004). But music, especially popular music, is a particularly interesting area to analyze, as concerts can bring hundreds of thousands of people together to listen to the ideas of a small number of performers.

Cuban music critic Joaquín Borges-Triana (2001, [1970] 2009) seeks to write critical music cultures into the country's history. He notes that Cuban alternative music is an operative category and coins the term CAM (Cuban Alternative Music) scene to capture a history of generational activism and pressure for social change. Borges-Triana argues that the CAM scene is not simply a passive product of globalization; the exchange of information, ideas, and identities is not unidirectional: ideas and worldviews circulate across geopolitical borders. CAM was produced, beginning in the mid-1980s, through the critical interventions of musicians who were themselves the products of their own complex identities and those of their publics. The critical political discourses and identities embedded in Cuban music reflect the social and political realities of the country, particularly issues such as material inequality, racism, sexism, heteronomativity, the suppression of religious practices and beliefs, and a host of other subjectivities and identities not critically addressed by state discourse. As such, the CAM scene serves as an entry point into the subject positions of those producing this music and forming the basis of an artistic movement (Borges-Triana 2001, [1970] 2009).[18]

The CAM is composed of a number of different genres, including hip hop, rock, jazz, and Nueva Trova (a protest music that emerged in Cuba in the 1960s). But the one common element that characterizes all alternative music is its challenge to established revolutionary cultural institutions and their efforts to homogenize Cuban citizens, their experiences, and their needs. CAM presses for the recognition and acceptance of the numerous particularities of Cuban society (Borges-Triana 2001). For Borges-Triana, the cultural movements that began in the 1980s were born at the margins of what was considered legitimate. These cultural expressions were foreign, literally and figuratively, to centralized state power and centralized state discourse. These cultural movements, including the nascent alternative music scene, challenged the homogenizing tendencies of the revolutionary state's cultural politic. According to Borges-Triana, the CAM scene is a result of the dialectic between the universal and the national, between tradition and the vanguard. As Fred Moten (2003) argues, even this division between traditional and the avant-garde is racialized and infused with Western European notions of modernity. The notion of an avant-garde excludes Black people: it is Eurocentric and associated with Western European notions of modernity. Hence there was an attempt to write Blacks out of complicated music like jazz (see Kofsky 1975).

CAM does not reject the egalitarian ideals of the revolution; indeed, it works to further revolutionary ideals through its advocacy of multiple discourses in the service of social equality. The alternative music scene does addresses one central critique of the revolutionary cultural aesthetic: that the revolution's hegemonic discourse of unity and sameness, originally constructed to ensure equality and defend against U.S. aggression, implicitly supports older pillars of Eurocentric artistic expression and epistemology by limiting the criticism of revolutionary discourse and social policy. The effect is that the classism, racism, homophobia, and other forms of social inequality associated with prerevolutionary institutions continue to be unaddressed in many areas of social life. CAM musicians argue that there is no one experience of oppression but multiple experiences that require multiple discourses aimed at challenging oppression (Borges-Triana 2001; Camnitzer 2003; Craven 2006; Navarro 2002; Vitier 2002; Zurbano Torres 1996).

The Aficionados' Artistic Movement, discussed above and undertaken by revolutionary leaders, facilitated the development of CAM as a grassroots artistic movement, which encompasses a number of genres. Hip hop, one of the key movements in the alternative music scene, captures many of the social changes that have occurred in Cuba since the mid-1980s, such as the development of social institutions to represent the voices of Cuban youth, thus allowing competing ideologies to be publicly articulated. The boom of rap in the 1990s paralleled the boom in the popularity of other music genres such as salsa, reggaetón, rock, and a renewed interest in Nueva Trova. Salsa and reggaetón embrace "fun": music that is socially uncritical, that is not politically correct, and that embraces sensuality and materialistic desires. The revolutionary leadership initially discouraged fun music because of its uncritical, nonpolitical, and possibly "immoral" orientation (Moore 2006).

Cuba's alternative music scene is racialized and classed, with each of the music scenes drawing from various subject positions to present and critique social life. For example, Nueva Trova is known as the folk, hippy, all-inclusive music scene. This scene is also racially and sexually diverse, socially progressive, antisexist, and antiracist. The subject position with which the artists and public identify, however, is a progressive, middle class, white liberal perspective that embraces a notion of "multiculturalism," in which all would be included in Western European notions of modernity and not oppressed by rampant global capitalism. The incorporation of the Nueva Trova movement into revolutionary institutional structures in the late 1960s and 1970s truncated some of the radical potential of the movement, particularly its antiracist discourse. Over time, Nueva Trova has evolved into an overwhelmingly white, "light" mulat@, or upper-class Black phenomenon. Shows are still transgressive to a certain degree, as Nueva Trova events constitute one of the few nonheteronormative public spaces in Cuba. But the inclusivity of Nueva Trova is tempered by apparent privileging of and nostalgia for whiteness as a universal sign for civility, humanity, and cosmopolitanism.

In Cuba rock and roll is known as a music culture that draws poor and working-class whites, mulat@s, and very few Blacks (though the artists, many of whom are able to afford their instruments, come from a wealthier material situation). The scene is associated with white supremacy, excess, and the embracing of the counterproductive and countercultural (participants are known as rockeros or freakies). Rock music has had a difficult history in Cuba. It came to Cuba during the late 1960s and became popular during the 1970s and 1980s. It was the first countercultural movement of the post-1959 era (Manduley López 2001). It continues to be associated with gays and drugs. Because much of Cuba's rock originated in Spain, the United Kingdom, and the United States, rock was also understood as profoundly foreign. This supported the state's discursive classification of rock as music that is ideologically corrupted, promotes capitalism, and encourages the ideological reproduction of the social ills and perverse desires associated with European capitalism and U.S. imperialism.

One final type of music that is also a part of Cuba's alternative music scene is Cuban experimental music. It is important to consider this music in terms of delineating Cuban artivism and the way in which the cultural sphere functions differently in Cuba, in comparison to Western European capitalist economies, as a space of deliberation and critique. The Havana-based experimental music group called Grupo OMNI is key here and functions as a nexus for all of Cuba's contemporary alternative music scenes. The group produces a number of artists in all of the music genres, who are actively involved in community-based organizing and education within the arts. Through their work, Grupo OMNI artivists see themselves as creating breaks or ruptures within the realm of representation and aesthetics:

> El performance es, para nosotros, una actitud que propicia la manifestación constante del estado creativo, pero también es la manifestación artística que mejor nos caracteriza, y a través de la cual podemos conjugar todas nuestras posibilidades creativas. A través de él asumimos elementos del cuerpo, de la oralidad, la poesía, la escritura en su aspecto visual, la danza-teatro, la música, el canto, y toda la creación plástica, los que enfáticamente proyectamos en espacios urbanos, aunque también en teatros y galerías. En fin, que el performance es como la vida y a través de él adoptamos una conducta cívica de intervención en los asuntos y espacios públicos de la Nación.

> Performance is, for us, an attitude that supports the continuous manifestation of the creative state, but it is also the artistic manifestation that best characterizes us and through which we are able to conjure with all of our creative possibilities. It is through him that we assume the elements of the body, of orality, poetry, writing in its visual aspect, dance/theater, music, song, and all of the visual arts that we emphatically

project in urban spaces, although also in theaters and galleries. In sum, that performance is like life and through him we adopt a conduct of civil intervention in the public affairs and spaces of the Nation.[19]

This quotation frames the vision of the generation of Cuban artivists who came of age in the 1990s and 2000s and helps to contextualize the emergence of the CUHHM. This generation of Afro-descendant artists identifies with the role of performance in subject formation and social change. In the text OMNI refers to art and performance as "él," the pronoun used for describing people or beings, thus ascribing a spiritual element to art and its ability to bring forth life, that is, the birth of the subject and the engaged citizen. Through art performers are able to make an intervention where they are, locally. David, a member of the group OMNI, is part of the CUHHM generation (figs. 2.3 and 2.4). In his artwork he incorporates West African and African American (regionally speaking) cosmologies and ways of knowing. The body, orality, poetry, writing as a visual art, dance/theater, music, song and all of the visual arts are key tools of subject formation and action. David's invocation of the civic dimension of art and its relationship to the "public affairs and spaces of the Nation" harkens back to arguments made by Weheliye in his discussion of diasporic citizenship and subjectivities. Weheliye (2005) argues that music, as it is transmitted through different sound technologies, provides alternative spaces for the articulation of "'diasporic citizenship' and offers avenues for present-day black musical artists to envision and sound their multiple sites of political and cultural membership" (15).

During the early years of the CUHHM, people referred to it as Nueva Trova

Figure 2.3. David of Grupo OMNI with his family during an independent performance arts event in his apartment in Alamar. (Photo by Tanya L. Saunders)

Figure 2.4.   David of Grupo OMNI performing at the Puño Arriba awards in 2013.
(Photo by Tanya L. Saunders)

because that was the only existing framework available to understand it: like the
socially critical Nueva Trova artists of the 1960s, hip hop also had an antiracist,
anticapitalist, and anti-imperialist ideological bent. Its location "among the
people," its protest tendencies, and its status as a nonincorporated independent
music genre were obvious points of similarity. In both genres, racism is a social
ill that the artists seek to address. The two genres share the ideals of the Revolution and work to see that they are achieved. Both forms of music also challenge the aesthetic debates that would describe them as "low culture," threats
to established institutional and aesthetic structures. Unlike Nueva Trova, however, hip hop speaks from a Black subject position, instead of the white middle-
class subject position commonly associated with Nueva Trova. As such, it rejects
Nueva Trova's celebration of white liberal ideologies centered on multiculturalism. Instead, hip hop is a racialized critique centered on embracing all aspects
of blackness and African cultural legacies—physically, ideologically, and culturally. Hip hop, until approximately 2007, was considered one of the most critical
of the contemporary art forms and is associated with a younger generation that
radically challenges Cuban society to recognize and critically address the way in
which a crucial issue such as "race" continues to oppress and marginalize Cuban
citizens. Cuban artists and intellectuals also considered hip hop to be the face

of the new Black social movement in post–Special Period Cuba, which would foreshadow the changes to come during Cuba's post Special Period transition.

In its early years (circa late 1970s–late 1980s), Cuban hip hop was based primarily on Cubans' imitation and enjoyment of the new music culture from the United States. Through hip hop, new generations of critical youth in the United States could ideologically address many of the social issues undertaken by the 1960s generation without suffering the institutional backlashes that the 1960s social movements experienced (Kitwana 2002). The spread of this form of music to Cuba is part of a long history of cultural exchange. After the 1959 Revolution, U.S. socially conscious activists, scholars, and artists continued going to the Island and participating in intellectual, cultural, and political exchanges. For example, New Afrikan revolutionary Nehanda Abiodun and former Black Panther leader Assata Shakur now have political asylum in Cuba. In 1999 and 2002 Danny Glover and Harry Belafonte, who have gone to Cuba numerous times, met with Fidel Castro to advocate for state support for the CUHHM. Other artists, activists, and scholars who have visited include Randall Robinson, Fab 5 Freddie, Tricia Rose, Jesse Jackson, and recently Jay-Z and Beyoncé. Contrary to much of the narrative concerning the emergence of the Cuban Underground Hip Hop Movement, however, the movement did not begin with the arrival of African Americans who approached Cubans to host international hip hop festivals. The emergence of the CUHHM was not a result of passive Cuban actors who—in an anti-imperial cultural context—somehow were passive consumers of U.S. race discourse. The opposite occurred.

For example, in 1999 Alan Ket, the founder of New York's *Stress Magazine*, centered on hip hop and social justice, received a handwritten letter from Cuba from the Cuban underground hip hop producer and independent journalist Ariel Fernández. He outlined a major Cuban hip hop project and requested help in order to make it happen. Fernández had found a discarded copy of *Stress Magazine* in Havana. Given the social justice orientation of the magazine, he decided to contact the editor, so that the world could learn about an arts-based social movement well underway in Cuba. Steve Marcus, Alan Ket, and others working at *Stress Magazine* took a trip to Cuba to see if the letter and the movement was legit. What they found was an arts-based social movement. Responding to the requests of those within that movement, they worked to mobilize the technological and media resources that Cuban artists felt would be integral in gaining national and international attention.

As a result of the work of independent artists, activists, and producers like those at *Stress* the Black August Hip Hop Project and U.S. college students would become integral in supporting artists in the evolution of the CUHHM.

Indeed this cultural exchange involved not only U.S. African Americans but hip hop artivists, activists, scholars, and intellectuals from throughout the larger African diaspora. Artists, scholars, and activists influential in the development of hip hop in Cuba came from places such as Puerto Rico, Brazil, Somalia via Canada, Jamaica, and Venezuela. Furthermore, since the 1980s, Cuban citizens with illegal antennas, satellite TV, and cable connections have continuously received radio signals and TV images from Miami, Jamaica, and even as far away as the U.S. Virgin Islands and Haiti. Importantly, socially critical hip hop artists from abroad have also viewed the accomplishments of the Cuban Revolution in a favorable light, so performing in Cuba has become the hallmark of demonstrating a socially critical or revolutionary political orientation.

The issues discussed within Cuban hip hop and the question of whether or not it constitutes a (Cuban) art form soon captured the attention of Cuba's press. Articles about Cuban hip hop began to appear in leading revolutionary publications such as *Bohemia, Revista Salsa Cubana, Cultura y Revolución, Juventud Rebelde, Trabajadores,* and *Jiribilla.* The sheer numbers of Afro-descendant people who listened to hip hop and the number of self-described underground hip hop groups caused the government to take note and treat the movement as a legitimate cultural and, by extension, political force. The emergence of hip hop in Cuba terrified the state. At one point, around the year 2000, researchers recorded that at least five hundred self-described hip hop groups and activist collectives considered themselves to be a part of the CUHHM (Perry 2004). The presence of so many groups of people who described themselves as part of a Black cultural and political movement explicitly seeking to hold the state accountable for its promises of equality restoked historicized fears of Black political mobilization on the Island. As the next chapter details, these fears were well founded: the CUHHM developed into one of the most exciting arenas for Black political mobilization in recent Cuban history.

3

La Revolución dentro de la Revolución/
The Revolution within the Revolution

Hip Hop, Cuba, and Afro-Descendant Challenges to Coloniality

Grizel Hernández Baguer, vice-president of the Cuban Agency of Rap at the time of our interview in Havana in 2005 (and currently the director of the Cuban Institute of Music), spoke about the critique of racism and sexism:

> Lo que me llama la atención siempre es que es una mirada que no es ne-gativa. Que es una crítica siempre de frente, enfrentando los problemas de negros, los problemas femeninos de la mujer, los problemas de que si la policía los para, que si la delincuencia. O sea, esa crítica fuerte, pero no destructiva. Es la crítica de que ésta es nuestra sociedad, éstos son nue-stros problemas y ellos los están diciendo y vamos a arreglarlos. Entonces, esa es su manera de decir, su manera de comunicar, su manera de plantear la realidad. Siempre lo he visto de esa manera y siempre he defendido el discurso del hip hop y del rap por ahí. Porque ellos son muy listos precisa-mente al decir las cosas, no es el contra del proceso revolucionario, sino lo contrario, es como para perfeccionar ese proceso. Y siempre lo he visto así, que su exposición es muy positiva.

> What always drew my attention is that it is a perspective that is not nega-tive. That it is always a direct critique, confronting the problems of Blacks, the feminine problems of women, the problems if the police stop them, about delinquency. Or better, it is a strong critique, but not destructive. It is the critique of what our society is; these are our problems and they are saying it and we are going to fix them. So this is their way of saying, their way of communicating, their way of presenting reality. I have always seen it in this way, and I have always defended the discourse of hip hop and rap. Because they are very smart in telling it like it is, and it is not against

the revolutionary process, but the opposite, it is a way to perfect this process. And I have always seen it like this, that their expression is very positive.

Etián ("Brebaje Man," a CUHHM MC) told me in Havana in 2013:

A mí me han pasado incidentes racistas fuertes. Yo una vez venía caminando por la calle Jovellar, eso es por la Universidad de La Habana, y había muchos policías. Iba a haber una actividad, pero se suspendió. Y había muchos policías, muchos. Y . . . yo iba para Karachi. Y uno me dice "Carnet de identidad." Y yo le digo "Cómo no. . . ." "Mire," él lo coge y me dice: "Ven para el carro." Yo me acerco al carro. En el carro estaba él y tres más. Grandes y fuertes. Él no era tan grande ni tan fuerte, pero los otros sí. Aparte había cuatro aquí, y mil por allá. El averigua, uno, dos, tres, oye [ininteligible], no tienen antecedentes, no tienes problemas. "¿Usted, qué hace?" "No, yo soy músico, soy rapero," "Ah, okay." "¿Ya terminó?" "Sí, no tienes antecedentes ni nada. El problema es que, yo te pido el carnet porque un negro, caminando a esta hora, por la calle Jovellar, de eso, a un robo con fuerza, no va nada, ¿entiendes?" Bueno, mi hermana, mira, yo me siento muy conectado con la paz del mundo, principalmente en los momentos en los que la paz se hace imprescindible. Hay momentos en los que uno tiene que tener paz, si es inteligente.

Really racist incidents have happened to me. I was walking down Jovellar street. That's near the University of Havana. And there were a lot of police officers, a lot. There was going to be an activity, but it was suspended. There were a lot of police officers. And I was going to Karachi, and one guy says: "Show me your ID." And I say, "Of course. Here it is." And the guy says, "Come to the car." I get closer to the car. That police officer and three more were inside the car. Big and strong. He wasn't that big or strong, but the other guys were. Besides, there were four here, and like a thousand over there. He calls . . . one two three, hey [unintelligible], "No, he has no record, he has no problems whatsoever." "Oh, okay. And what do you do?" "I'm a musician, a rap musician." "Oh, okay." "Are you done?" "Yes, you have no record. The problem is that I ask for your ID because Black guy, walking at this time of day, down Jovellar Street, I know that there is going to be a robbery." Well, sister, listen. I feel really connected with peace in the world. In the first place, in those moments where peace is paramount. There are moments in which you need to have peace, if you are intelligent.

In her interview excerpt Grizel Hernández Baguer notes a key aspect of Cuban underground hip hop: the artists honestly talk about Cuban realities, one of which is continued racial discrimination in Cuba. In Etián Arnau Lizaire's interview he recounts two racist encounters with police. There has been significant academic and media interest in the Cuban Underground Hip Hop Movement over the last decade (Armstead 2007; Baker 2006, 2011; Fernandes 2003, 2006; Joffe 2005; Pacini Hernández and Garafalo 1999; Perry 2004; West-Durán 2004). The CUHHM has garnered much international attention because of underground hip hop artists' public criticism of the numerous social difficulties that many Cubans face. It is even more impressive that the CUHHM artists' invocation of transnational Black solidarity challenges the invisibility of the African diaspora throughout the region. The racialized critique of the CUHHM challenges a key hegemonic ideology in the region: the myth that racism is an issue of individual prejudice, not a systemic, culturally and materially based problem. Additionally, the CUHHM offers a pro-Black, antiracist critique in a country that once hailed the elimination of racism within its society. CUHHM artists link racialized oppression to the legacies of colonialism, imperialism, and rampant global capitalism. They seek to make a cultural intervention against social oppressions that they believe are rooted in ideology and not easily resolved by redistributive policies.

In the mid-1990s, articles about Cuban hip hop began to appear in major revolutionary publications such as *Bohemia, Revista Salsa Cubana, Cultura y Revolución, Juventud Rebelde, Trabajadores,* and *Jiribilla.* The sheer numbers of Afro-descendant people who listen to hip hop and the growing number of publicly recognized underground hip hop groups caused the government to take note and to treat the movement as a legitimate cultural and, by extension, political force. The emergence of hip hop in Cuba terrified the Cuban state. In about 2000 researchers recorded at least five hundred self-described hip hop groups and activist collectives that considered themselves to be a part of the CUHHM (Perry 2004). The presence of so many groups of people describing themselves as part of a Black cultural and political movement aimed at holding the state accountable for its promises of equality restoked historicized fears of Black political mobilization on the Island. As it turns out, these fears were well-founded: the CUHHM developed into one of the most exciting arenas for Black political mobilization in recent Cuban history.

But while much of the published work (Baker 2006; Fernandes 2006; Pacini Hernández and Garofalo 1999; Perry 2004) on the CUHHM has noted the racialized and economically turbulent context in which Cuban underground hip hop emerged, very few published essays have theorized about the CUHHM's ideological relationship to transnational Black cultural movements and, most importantly, how the movement represents and articulates a challenge to coloniality (but see Fernandes 2003; Perry 2008). Afro-diasporic social movements against coloniality challenge the underlying logic of Western modernity, which fails to recognize the humanity of all Black people, especially Black citizens living in Western democracies. As discussed in the introduction, the continued racial oppression of nonwhites reveals that the equality, prosperity, and freedom promised by Western modernity within capitalist, socialist, and democratic discourses are a myth (Gilroy 1993a; Jameson 1984). This chapter reviews some of the literature specifically on the CUHHM, noting to what extent scholars have highlighted artists' radical critiques of race, gender, sexuality, and coloniality. I then turn to interviews with artists and an examination of their lyrics, in order to address the political and ideological interventions that the artists chose to make as activists.

One of the most prominent themes in literature on the CUHHM is the tension between the movement's link to global capitalism, modernity, and local cultures and identities. Cuban artists commonly use global consumer networks as a way to get their work out to a larger audience and avoid the state monopoly on the culture industry (Fernandes 2006). The state controls these institutions as a way to make a profit and to control discursive production so that artists have to decide whether they want to make ideological compromises in order to access the state-dominated market. Thus through the usage of global markets Cuban artists have been able to make some money in order to remain critical and survive (Fernandes 2006). But this situation also exposes a contradiction between the production of art for social change (advocated by the state) and the artists' need to feed themselves and to become known. The ability of CUHHM artists to produce music that is socially critical is connected to their use of transnational networks to obtain the materials that they need to produce music. Thus the terms "underground" and "commercial" take on dual significance within a Cuban context. Though the state may provide sound equipment and other resources for underground artists, the term "underground" refers to socially critical music produced by artists who refuse to conform to the ideological dictates of the Cuban state or the global consumer market as a means of disseminating their music. Hence they are able to maintain a sense of authentic social critique in comparison to artists who go commercial and change their music to appeal to a global audience or to the Cuban state's mass media institutions.

Describing the social significance of the CUHHM's emergence within this sociopolitical context has been a central focus of scholars focusing on the CUHHM. Alan West-Durán (2004) argues that the CUHHM is a form of protest in which hip hop artists are marginal actors within Cuban society who "were themselves those demoralized disorganized elements of society at one point, or still live among those marginalized sectors where this demoralization constantly surrounds them. They are using rap as a form of social pleasure and action for the expansion of civil society" (16). Cuban music critic Joaquín Borges-Triana (2009) directly challenges the reduction of contemporary Cuban popular music, such as hip hop and rock, to a form of globalization or cultural imperialism on the island: "Ocurre que la recepción . . . es intrínsecamente local en el sentido de que es el resultado de la acción de individuos específicos singulares y que emplean los recursos a su alcance para producir sentido y apropiárselo o incoporarlo en sus vidas" (It happens that the reception [of foreign music]. . . is inherently local in the sense that it is the result of the action of specific individuals who are situated in singular, uniquely specific sociohistorical contexts and employ the resources at their disposal to produce meaning and to appropriate or incorporate it into their lives" [13]). Borges-Triana argues that actors in local contexts use the resources at their disposal to produce meaning in their lives, national and transnational music scenes being one of those resources.

Similarly, in their analysis of Cuban underground hip hop, Deborah Pacini Hernández and Reebee Garofalo (1999) argue that CUHHM artists employ hip hop as a tool to negotiate their difficult daily realities. Like Borges-Triana, myself, and many of the artists and cultural critics that I have interviewed, they consider the CUHHM to be a continuation of Cuba's post-1959 radical music cultures, specifically Nueva Trova. What became the underground hip hop movement emerged from a conscious decision to use hip hop as a medium for social critique. Along with Robin Moore (2006), Pacini Hernández and Garofalo link the emergence and later cooptation of Nueva Trova, a 1960s radical music scene, to the institutionalization of the cultural sphere by Cuba's "protest state."

This relationship between culture and the state is a thorny one. The Cuban state's investment in the CUHHM is often presented as an effort to co-opt and appropriate hip hop as a means of stifling the social critique that is part of it. Geoff Baker (2005), however, offers a particularly nuanced take that notes the Cuban state's interest in appropriating hip hop precisely *because* of its association with social critique: "The nationalization of protest music has not entailed the purging of resistant elements, but instead the highlighting and exploiting of facets that correlate to the ideology of what may be considered a 'protest state'" (399).

Baker argues that the Cuban rappers and state representatives draw on a "shared rhetoric of revolution and resistance to U.S. hegemony" (102). The Cuban protest state has institutionalized a hybrid discourse combining a Eurocentric worldview drawn from socialism and elements of non-European (counter)cultural discourses. This discourse also converges in the Americas with multiple worldviews, one being the Black radical tradition, which draws primarily on African epistemologies and collective memories of resistance to various forms of colonial exploitation. Given that the Cuban revolutionary state is anticapitalist, anticolonialist, antiracist, and anti-imperialist, the competing discourses of Black modernity in the Americas are largely compatible with those of the state. Yet that compatibility is limited. The CUHHM's critiques conflict with the discourse of the Cuban state when it highlights the enduring inequalities of class, race, gender, sexuality, and coloniality in the region.

But Baker, among others, has questioned the extent to which the CUHHM should be understood through the lens of race. In 2011 Baker reviewed *A Short Radiography of Hip Hop in Cuba* (2004), at that point the only film about hip hop in Cuba produced by a Cuban director, Ricardo Bacallao. Baker (2011) argues that the film left out much of the internal debate that occurred within the movement and reductively presented the CUHHM as an instance of Black Cuban culture being usurped by whites. Additionally, Baker (2011) calls into question Bacallao's own authenticity (the validity of his perspective) by saying that the director "was not heavily immersed" within the hip hop scene:

> A polemical film, it contributes to the debate on race but somewhat bends reality in order to make its overarching point, since (as happens with academic analyses) the urge to see Cuban Hip Hop through a race lens entails overlooking significant nuances (for example, the music accompanying the opening titles of this film about "Black culture" in Cuba is provided by Edgar González, a White rapper). (310)

In essence, Baker argues that a racialized analysis prevents a nuanced approach to understanding social life in Cuba. I would argue precisely the opposite. First, however, it is important to note that Ricardo Bacallao is a filmmaker who grew up in the 1990s and participated in Cuba's critical arts scene. He was very much a part of Cuba's alternative music scene, although he mainly associated with critical experimental artists such as Grupo OMNI. Additionally, because the CUHHM was a source of national debates concerning race during the 1990s, Bacallao is far from an interloper with no sense of the important polemical debates occurring within his own country.[1]

To be sure, any analysis of the CUHHM or Cuba in general is ill served by an effort to read it as a one-dimensional narrative of simple racial oppression — particularly if that racial oppression is conceptualized, as it so often is, through the lens of U.S. racial dynamics. Far from preventing a nuanced analysis of life in Cuba, however, the lens of race is integral to understanding culture in the Americas. The concept of race contains the long history of social angst and negativity concerning African corporality as well as African culture and intellectual thought and is a fundamental cultural logic of the Americas. As Evelyn Brooks Higginbotham (1992) argues, it is the "metalanguage" through which we in the Americas understand the world and social phenomena. As such, to ignore race would be to ignore one of the primary ways (subtly or not) in which Americans understand and experience reality. While Baker (2011) gives some attention to the racial discourses circulating within the movement, his focus is primarily on U.S.-Cuban relations and does not situate Cuban hip hop discourses within their regional context. I would argue that his rejection of race makes sense *insofar as* it is a rejection of an exceptional, U.S. understanding of race imposed upon the Cuban context. Academic work critiquing U.S. Black identity as "essentialized" is actually doing the work of flattening and essentializing U.S. understanding(s) of race (homogenizing the various regional experiences of more than 40 million people: in which blackness in Biloxi, Mississippi, in Baltimore, Maryland, and in Denver, Colorado, varies in profound ways). I would also contend that such an argument unfairly characterizes Bacallao's film, which actually offers a more sophisticated and properly national and implicitly regional analysis. Bacallao's discussion of whiteness is contextualized within a broader discussion of the "colonial gaze." Indeed, the film talks about as much about coloniality as it does about whiteness. Put another way, the film actually discusses coloniality *when* it discusses whiteness. It is this critique of coloniality that makes the CUHHM truly radical and distinct, yet it has received far less discussion by scholars.

The chapter on Cuban underground hip hop, "Fear of a Black Nation: Local Rappers, Transnational Crossings, and State Power," in Fernandes (2006) is an excellent overview of the CUHHM that both converges with and diverges from my analysis. On the one hand, Fernandes (2006) offers a sophisticated understanding of the transnational significance of racialized discourse in hip hop:

in countries such as Cuba, Brazil, Columbia, and Venezuela, as well as in several African countries such as Senegal, South Africa, and Mali, black communities draw on African American rap music to address local issues of race and marginality, however differently those relationships may be constituted. *The importance of transnational flows based on race, particularly as promoted by the more black nationalist African American rappers, must be viewed somewhat independently of global cultural flows related to the popular music industry.* (92; emphasis added)

Fernandes's crucial point here is that not all "global" is the same when talking about hip hop and not all "global blackness" (specifically as a sign of difference) is the same when we talk about global Black identity politics. In other words, blackness as a sign has important local, regional, and global variations. I seek to highlight this point in taking a hemispheric approach to blackness(es) in the Americas.

Fernandes also offers an insightful critique of the problematic way in which Cuba and the arts are often presented in Western academic scholarship. She takes issue with the one-dimensional portrayal of Cuba as a repressive totalitarian state. As she rightfully points out, most European and North American theorists like Jürgen Habermas cannot conceive of public spheres as existing in countries classified as "socialist," authoritarian, or highly bureaucratic. The problem is with Eurocentric definitions of "public sphere" and "politics" that obscure the more diffuse and permeable role of culture in countries like Cuba. Fernandes instead uses the term "artistic public spheres," which I think is an incredibly useful way to think about the role of the arts in Cuba and any "democratic" society, socialist or capitalist, for that matter. Her work resonates with that of Martín Sevillano (2008), who argues that Cuba's cultural sphere functions as a nascent civil society. When we actually focus on the critiques occurring in Cuba's cultural spheres, we are also able to bring into the conversation Cuban citizens whose voices are often drowned out in larger geopolitics and shift the focus away from the state and formal political organizations (and the lack thereof) as the sole indicator of local realities.

Fernandes also writes about the feminist intervention that women artists have made within the CUHHM. She discusses the difficulties that women artists face, in terms of not having the same access to the opportunities for music production and promotion as male artists. Indeed, as I argue in the conclusion of this book, the women artists within the CUHHM are the most "underground" of any of the CUHHM's artists in a sense. They tend to have to produce and promote their independent CDs more than their male counterparts and are even more limited in terms of their access to the limited resources of the movement. Fernandes points out that women artists within the CUHHM were among the first publicly to discuss the issues facing Cuban women after 1959. As Fernandes notes, CUHHM feminists are linked to a larger transnational network of global feminists, third-wave feminists, and Black feminists who are in conversation with each other through hip hop.

My analysis diverges from Fernandes's argument on the issue of race. In her discussion of blackness and identity, Fernandes draws on the work of Latin American scholars who emphasize the "fluidity" of racial identity politics in

Latin America and the Caribbean. Reviewing this literature, Fernandes (2006) writes:

> Race relations in Cuba differ considerably from experiences of race in the United States. . . . To talk of "blacks" or "race" in Latin America is problematic because race relations have not been historically perceived as primary markers of identity . . . while discourses of racial fraternity in Cuba minimized claims for justice made by blacks, the more *fluid* understanding of race that such discourses made possible also opened up avenues for the participation of blacks in mainstream cultural life. (88–89; emphasis added)

Such scholars are making precisely the point that I seek to emphasize: the importance of understanding race within the historical, colonial, and regional context of the Americas. All too often, however, efforts to differentiate the specificity of how race functions in the Americas outside of the United States swing to the opposite extreme: if U.S. race is a rigid binary structure of Black and white, then race outside the United States is so fluid that it no longer matters. Additionally, using an intersectional approach to understanding identity is important here. There is an assumption that Black U.S. Americans who may give primacy to their racial identity do not also see themselves as U.S. Americans: the idea that U.S. patriotism is not as important as racial identity, which is an impressive misreading of Black U.S. politics. That is, in Cuba people are Cuban first and Black later, while in the United States people are Black first and U.S. American later. In reality both forms of identification, in both contexts, are at moments primary modes of identification at the same time (along with other identities such as gender or sexual identities). At other moments, depending on the context, one identity may be salient, with its meaning depending on that moment in national and local history.

As discussed in chapter 2, a Black, African, or Afrocentric consciousness did not come to Cuba with hip hop; nor has Cuba been isolated from the discourses of liberation circulating around the Black Atlantic (Brock and Castañeda Fuertes 1998). CUHHM artists locate themselves as part of the African diaspora. Their music and lyrics address issues that they face locally and globally as part of marginalized Afro-descendant populations in the Americas and identify with the liberation movements of the African continent. Some Cuban artists use hip hop as a vehicle to represent a Black radical consciousness that has long existed on the Island, which openly reemerged into the larger public sphere during the 1990s. If we contextualize the CUHHM within the ideological circuits of the African diaspora, it becomes clear that the movement is not simply the imitation of hegemonic, globalized music cultures emanating from the United States. Cuba's Afro-descendant challenge to modernity is a struggle over cultural hegemony (Hall 2008). It is about changing the balance of power through challenging the configuration of cultural power in order to fundamentally alter society through an ideological revolution (Hall 2008, 287). The vision of the new society draws upon explicit and residual African worldviews. These countercultures and competing visions of Western modernity are a transnational conversation with other African and Afro-descendant populations who are participating in a circuit of ideological exchange throughout the Americas and Africa. These particular ideological exchanges are based on recent and distant memories of Africa, cultural affinities, enslavement, resistance, racial oppression, and material inequality—and, in the case of Cuba, direct military aid and training to support anticolonial independence movements.

The CUHHM's critique of coloniality focuses on how one particular axis of power, racialization (itself a process colonial in origin) is structured and how it reproduces/forms social inequalities related to gender, sexuality, and class. In this chapter I examine the central critiques and knowledge-practices of the movement. The path to ending racialized social inequality begins with a recognition by some sectors of Cuba's Afro-descendant population that "race" and "racism" do exist and are at the center of many of the difficulties that they face daily, especially after 1990. CUHHM artists argue that members of Cuba's Afro-descendant population should embrace their blackness (corporality) and their African culture and history (culture and consciousness). Both of these are central to their experiences as Cubans via their centrality in the formation of the Cuban nation and Cuban culture but have been denied or devalued in the process of racialization. This process of consciousness-raising will not only improve the self-esteem of the some sectors of the Afro-descendant population but will help people to feel a greater sense of connection to Cuban society once they realize that Black Cubans have actually been central to the formation and development of the nation. For others, this process allowed for the public articulation of Black identity politics that had been privately passed down in their families for generations. Finally, for many of the artists, once Cuba's Afro-descendant people understand that they are of value and importance in Cuban society, they will be spurred to act for change. This spark to spur social change via antiracist activism, however, is not centered on Black Cubans per se. It is reflective of a larger Cuban experience that encourages *all* Cubans to work for social equality.

Looping It: Cuban Youth and U.S. Hip Hop

With the intensification of the economic crisis during the 1990s, Havana's urban landscape changed and began to reflect the decimated urban landscape of New York City (specifically the Bronx) during its 1970s economic crisis. At this time CUHHM artists began to identify more with their U.S. counterparts. As the government liberalized its economy in the 1990s, tourism and cultural exchanges increased markedly. Cuban youths of African descent, fascinated by the images of hip hop that they had been receiving since the late 1970s, actively requested recordings of hip hop music videos and tapes from foreign visitors. Additionally, foreign and Cuban students who attended the Instituto Superior de Arte (Superior Institute of Art: ISA), located just outside of Havana, had access to cable television. These students shared copies of videos and music with their peers on the Island. As noted in chapter 2, because of the political orientation of the foreign artists, activists, and scholars who have visited the Island since 1959, Cuban youth and Cuban artists were primarily exposed to socially conscious hip hop (Fernandes 2006).[2]

When the first hip hop videos and songs began arriving in Havana, most Cuban listeners did not know English. The artists I interviewed commented that they related to the music because something in the sound resonated with them. When they started seeing the music videos, the urban and rural landscapes reflected their environments in Cuba. Cuban youth felt that the artists looked like them, moved like them, and sounded like them. After a while, Cuban youths wanted to make their own contribution to hip hop culture and began to study hip hop intently in order to start creating their own distinct version. In our interview in Havana in 2011, Etián Arnau Lizaire, one of the founding members of the Cuban underground hip hop group Explosión Suprema, described the emergence and development of his group during this period (fig. 3.1):

> '95 vino la idea más bien, la idea vino en el '95 porque fue cuando empezó el rap Cubano y a nosotros el '95, pero nosotros salimos a escena en el '98, tres años después fue que ya salimos a escena, pero esos tres fueron terribles, esos tres años fueron rapiando en las gua guas, rapiando en los restaurantes, porque siempre fuimos excéntricos, siempre fuimos personas muy, muy excéntricas, llegamos a los lugares y queríamos que la gente se estuviera [arriba] de nosotros, llegamos ahí y la gente no nos hace caso. [Smiles] "Yo, que esto y lo otro" y parar los lugares y ponernos a rapear en lugares eso de madre, y sacar a la gente, y todavía "No, ¿qué grupo son ustedes?" "No, no somos ningún grupo" hasta que llegaron al nombre "el grupo."

Figure 3.1. Etián "Brebaje Man" Arnau Lizaire performing at the Puños Arriba Awards, Havana, December 2013. (Photo by Tanya L. Saunders)

> In '95 the idea really began, the idea came in '95 because it was when Cuban rap began and to us, it was '95, but we came on the scene in '98, three years later was when we were already on the scene, but those three years were terrible, in those three years we were rapping on the buses, rapping in restaurants, because we were always eccentric, we were always very, very, very eccentric people, we arrived at places, and we wanted people to be all over us, we arrived there, and no one paid us any attention. [*Smiles*] "Yo! this and that" and we would stop by places and we would rap, it was crazy, and to take it to the people, and still, "No, what group are you all?" "No, we're not any group" until they called us "the group."

Many of the future underground hip hop artists arrived at the music in a similar way: something about the music culture struck them, and they were moved to create. Future B-boys and B-girls made up dance moves as they imitated what they saw others doing, what they saw on video, or what they imagined would be a great dance move. Alexis "DJ D'Boys" Rodríguez once commented that people were constantly being arrested when hip hop first arrived in Cuba, because they claimed public space by dancing in the streets, restaurants, parks, wherever, and ran afoul of the police (Alexis Rodríguez, personal communication, 2012). People rapped nonsense, made up words, repeated English words that they did not understand. They were rapping on street corners and battling each other wherever a potential audience existed. As people became invested in creating *Cuban* hip hop, circa 1995, hip hop would become a way for future CUHHM artists to challenge and change the ideologies that shaped their realities and to continue the affective element of hip hop: to help others to feel where they are "coming from" in their lyrical analysis of their lived experiences. Odaymara Cuesta Rosseau, of the underground hip hop group Las Krudas, told me about the themes of their music: "We are not talking about something new, but it's something that people have forgotten, or are kind of aware of but forget, or things that make people think . . . 'I have heard this somewhere before. But I don't remember where I heard it'" (Odaymara Cuesta Rosseau, personal communication, 2006).

In our interview in Alamar in 2010 Etián "Brebaje Man" Arnau Lizaire described the first time that Explosión Suprema emerged as a hip hop group, conscious of itself as a group:

> nosotros salimos con una escenografía, salimos con árboles, eran cosas muy locas, me entiendes, hicimos esto y . . . antes del concierto estuvimos fumando, fumando, fumando y . . . en el monte, no, en el monte ante llegar al lugar y empezamos a arrancar matas, y llegué con este, yo fui con un palo, el palo era un árbol [*makes the gesture of holding a small tree with roots hanging and leaves in front of his face*] así y cuando ya vi, hacía así, y en la punta hacía así, era una cosa así, ojos rojos, el portero de la discoteca: "¿Pa' donde tú vas?" "No, yo voy a cantar." "¿Pero que grupo es?" "Explosión Suprema," el otro amigo mío con un palo y un pantalón por aquí arriba, el otro por abajo y los botones de la camisa disparejos así, y los ojos rojos y el otro con un sobrero y una roca [*makes the gesture of a big rock being carried under his arm*]. "¿Y ustedes quiénes son?" "Nosotros somos Explosión Suprema, ¿entiendes?" fue la primera presentación de nosotros, ya la echamos y la gente se quedó como quien son esos tipos de esa onda, y empezamos a darnos cuenta que teníamos.

> we went out there with stage props . . . we went out there with trees, it was something really crazy, understand me, we did this and before the concert were smoking, smoking, and smoking and . . . in the woods, you know, in the woods before going to the place and we began to rip up plants, and I arrived with this . . . I went with a stick, but the stick was a tree [*makes the gesture of holding a small tree with roots hanging and leaves in front of his face*] like this and when I saw it was like this, and in my fist like this, it was a thing like . . . red eyes, and the doorman of

the discotheque asked: "Where are you going?" "No no no, I'm going to sing." "But what group is it?" "Explosión Suprema," my other friend with a stick, and a pants leg up, the other down, and the buttons of his shirt disheveled like this, and the red eyes, and the other with a big rock [*makes the gesture of a big rock being carried under his arm*]. "And you, who are you?" "We're Explosión Suprema, understand?" It was the first time we presented ourselves, and they listened to us, and the people were left with the image that we were some guys on this kind of trip, and we began to realize what we had.

The image that Arnau Lizaire invoked is the image of the *cinmarrón* (runaway). Unlike the Mambies (Cuba's nineteenth-century independence fighters), the *cinmarrón* is the "other" revolutionary in Cuban history: the maroon. Maroonage in Cuba or any other part of the Americas was never only about escaping enslavement. It was about rejecting the imposition of a foreign social order. Thus the image of Explosión Suprema coming from the woods covered in dirt, with red eyes, and one guy holding an uprooted small tree and a rock certainly invoked the image of the *cinmarrón*, rejecting the imposition of a European worldview. These images, these histories, and the African religious traditions practiced by the overwhelming majority of CUHHM artists point to revival and public appreciation of histories, cultural values, and traditions that were marginalized in Cuba's cultural sphere before and after 1959.

Both Odaymara and Etián are referring to what Raymond Williams (1977) calls the archaic and residual within culture:

> The residual . . . has been effectively formed in the past, but it is still active in the cultural process, not only and often not at all as an element of the past, but as an effective element of the present . . . certain meanings, and values which cannot be expressed or substantially verified in terms of the dominant culture, are nevertheless lived and practiced on the bases of the residue—cultural as well as social—of some previous social and cultural institution or formation. (122)

As Odaymara Cuesta Rosseau and Etián Arnau Lizaire note, they began incorporating themes into the music that people were familiar with but did not necessarily remember where they came from. Sometimes the artists themselves needed to take time to reflect on what they had done in those moments. These images and the presence of Black and mulat@ youth invoking them also reminded many that Cuba is as much an African society, with a vision of modernity influenced by African cosmologies, histories and cultural legacies, as a European one. The engagement of memory and structures of feeling as a means to maintain a collective consciousness and spur individual and collective change is a product of the diaspora's continuous transnational circuit of knowledge, a key affective element experienced by many who would become hip hop heads.

Alexis "DJ D'Boys" Rodríguez spoke with me about the interest of Cuban youth in hip hop during the formative period. DJ D'Boys is the founder, director, and producer of the project L3y8 (El Vedado's neighborhood hip hop collective named after a street corner in the borough). He was also the manager of the Almendares Park and amphitheater in Havana. While working at this park, DJ D'Boys would also host hip hop festivals and events. The artists included in the L3y8 collective were Los Paisanos, Los Aldeanos, Kumar, DJ Leydis, DJ Yari, and an international artist from Aruba called Inti Mc. Before joining hip hop, DJ D'Boys was part of the Nueva Trova movement. He explained that he got his start in the hip hop movement as a break-dancer. DJ D'Boys told me in our interview in Havana in 2005 about his decision to learn about underground hip hop after practicing in the parks and making up background music with his friends in the 1980s:

DJ D'Boys: Después fuimos buscando más información, porque sabíamos que había más información. Había algo más grande en esta cultura. Y ya descubrimos, me entiende, cuáles eran los cuatro elementos de la cultura, cuáles eran sus nombres. Ya sabíamos que el bailar el break dance, se llamaba B-boy, el que canta, se llamaba MC, el que escrachaba se llamaba DJ y descubrimos el elemento del grafiti, mediante una película que se llamaba *Wild Style*.

Tanya: ¿Cuál sería?

DJ D'Boys: No sé, mi inglés es muy malo, pero bueno Wildstyle, Estilo Salvaje, puede ser algo así. Y es de grafiti y empezamos a tener conocimiento de esa cultura. Ya en los años '91, '92, producto ya del bloqueo de los EU con Cuba se empiezan a dificultar mucho más las cosas, como alimentación, para conseguir el dinero, hay muchos problemas y bueno como que ese movimiento de hip hop se empieza como que a morir un poco. Siempre quedaron dos ó tres. Pero después en el año '94, finales del año '94 empiezan, salió un grupo de jóvenes haciendo grupos de rap increíbles y gracias al grupo, a este Proyecto Uno, que son los primeros que hicieron el festival de hip hop, ahí fue que de nuevo comenzó a coger fuerza la cultura de hip hop en Cuba y salieron muchísimos grupos de hip hop, como Grandes Ligas, Obsesión, Júnior Clan.

DJ D'Boys: Afterward we were looking for more information, because we knew that there had to be more information. There was something bigger about this culture. And there we discovered it, you understand me, that there were four elements of the culture, and what their names were. We already knew how to break dance, they are called B-boy[s], the one that sings they call MC, the one that scratches they call DJ, and we discovered the element of graffiti from a movie called *Wild Style*.

Tanya: Which was it?

DJ D'Boys: I don't know, my English is really bad, but OK, *Wildstyle*. [Translates *Wildstyle* into Spanish: *Estilo Salvaje*], it could be something like that. And [that was] the graffiti, and we began to have knowledge of that culture. It was already in '91, '92, a product of the U.S. blockade with Cuba, things became harder to come by, like food, how to get money, there were many problems and the hip hop movement began to die a little. There were always two or three. But after the year '94, at the end of '94 a group of youths began to come out with a group producing incredible rap, and thanks to this group, to this group Proyecto Uno, that were the first to create the festival of hip hop, and it was there that the hip hop culture of Cuba began to gain force and a lot of hip hop groups came out like Grandes Ligas, Obsesión, Junior Clan.

During the 1980s, Cuban youth were imitating hip hop, but during the late 1980s and early 1990s artists started to feel that there had to be more to the music. After researching the origins of hip hop, they learned about the form and structure of socially conscious hip hop, which they came to understand as a culture. By the mid-1990s, during the height of the Special Period, the first generation of Cuban underground hip hop artists emerged and had a huge impact locally and nationally. DJ D'Boys talked about how difficult life had become during the Special Period. The United States intensified the blockade, which further stressed Cuba's economy after the Soviet collapse. Life became increasingly hard for Cuban youth, both socially and economically. Once people learned more about hip hop, and its relationship to Afro-descendant populations living in the United States, Afro-descendant youths started to educate themselves about the history of African and Afro-descendant people in Cuban history. Randy Acosta said the following about this transition in our interview in Havana in 2005:

Entonces ya como que se hizo más importante arreciar el trabajo ese underground. Empezamos a investigar y a comentarnos. Ahí fue realmente, pienso yo, cuando el Pikky dejó Los Paisanos que, por lo menos yo, Randy Acosta, empecé a realmente a amar el hip hop, a entender qué cosa era el hip hop, a asumirlo como una forma de vida, a acercarme más a los comienzos como fue realmente. Y me di cuenta que esto era mi vida, que yo estaba enamorado realmente del hip hop y dentro del hip hop la vertiente underground, subterráneo. Ahí empezamos a comentarnos y siempre me gustaron los ritmos más serios. Entonces, no una forma, no por prejuicios ni nada, pero entonces ya dejé de escuchar un poco a Easy-E y a estos grupos que en ese momento eran los más comerciales.

Bueno fue sencillo yo me di cuenta que los ritmos con los que ellos cantaban y algunas veces cuando amigos me traducían las letras me di cuenta de que tenía que ver con mi realidad, me entiendes. Me di cuenta de que mi vida realmente no era una fiesta. Mi vida no es una fiesta y no solamente mi vida, sino la historia de mis similares. Porque ya cuando uno está en el hip hop el compromiso no es solamente contigo, va más allá de tu persona. Ya es un compromiso con tu familia, con la comunidad, con gente que te están mirando, que te están estudiando, te están siguiendo y están esperando un ejemplo, están esperando lo mejor de ti. Y es como que tú no los puedes defraudar a ellos. Ya como que llega un momento como que tú no eres tú, tú te debes a otras personas.

Las revoluciones son eso, unos adelante se sacrifican para que los demás atrás tengan cosas más grandes. Yo me di cuenta que esto era amor, esto era una cosa que ya yo lo llevaba por dentro, que era inevitable y ya cuando aprendí a controlarlo, empecé a dejarlo salir, en forma de letra, en forma de presentación, en forma de cada gesto que yo hacía, en cada actitud ante la vida. Ya el hip hop corría por mis venas. Y como yo lo entendí, entonces comencé a transmitírselo a otras personas que no estaban claros, como te digo con la letras, en conversaciones, en entrevistas, con actitudes, dando apoyo.

So we did the most important thing in order to undertake this underground work. We began to research it and to inform ourselves. That was really when, I think, when Pikky left Los Paisanos that, at least for me, Randy Acosta, I began to really love hip hop, and to understand the thing that was hip hop, and to undertake it as a form of life, and to get closer to what it was really about when we began. I realized that this was my life, that I was really in love with hip hop and within hip hop the path to the underground. There we started to inform ourselves and I always liked the more serious rhythms. So, not out of prejudice or anything like that, I began to stop listening to Eazy-E and the other groups that were more commercial from that moment.

So it was really simple, I began to realize that the rhythms with which they sang. And sometimes when friends translated the lyrics for me, I realized that it had something to do with my reality, understand me? I realized that my life really was not a party. My life is not a party and not only my life, but the history of those similar to me. Because already when you are in hip hop, the commitment is not only to yourself, but beyond that between you and another person. Already it is a commitment to your family, to the community, with people that are looking at you, and that are studying you, and that are following you as an example. Already there arrives a moment when you are not you, you have to be you for other people.

Revolutions are like that, some that are ahead sacrifice so that those behind can have better things. I began to realize that this was love, that this was something that I carry within myself and it was inevitable that when I learned to control it, I began to let it come out, in the form of letters, in the form of presentation, in the form of every gesture that I did, in every attitude in life. Already hip hop coursed through my veins. And I began to understand it, then I began to transmit it to other people that were not clear about it, how would I explain it, it with lyrics, conversations, in interviews, with attitudes, giving support.

Drawn to the rhythms, the beats, and the general feel of the music, Acosta researched the music and asked friends to translate the lyrics, as every underground hip hop artist I spoke to did. Whatever they did not understand, they found a way to translate the text and shared this information with others. Once Acosta and others realized what the artists were saying, their suspicions were confirmed: the connection they felt with the artists and the music was that they shared similar hardships and both had a difficult life. Acosta comments on another shared realization among the artists: once they understood the music as an art form they felt a commitment to it and a responsibility to their communities. They realized that they did not want to produce art that was detrimental to the advancement of their communities. As activists, working for social change (within a revolutionary movement), they realized that they had a responsibility as conscious actors to set the best example for others that they could. For these artists, hip hop is revolutionary. Etián Arnau Lizaire, talking about the emergence of Explosión Suprema, reflected on the energy of this historical transition in our interview in Havana in 2010:

y empezamos acá underground, y aquel tiempo era en casete y casi siempre era más backgrounds americanos y Ariel y nosotros empezamos con backgrounds americanos montar cosas y empezamos a crecer y a crecer—¿qué hacen?...salimos a la escena con backgrounds norteamericanos y vimos que la gente no nos aceptó del todo pero no nos rechazó, la gente se quedó así como que en una historia diferente. Nosotros salimos con una escenografía, salimos con árboles, eran cosas muy locas, me entiendes, hicimos esto.

> and we began there underground, and in that period it was on cassette and we almost always had more American backgrounds and Ariel and us, we began with American backgrounds and we began to grow and to grow and then what did they do?...so we came on stage with North American backgrounds and we saw that people did not accept everything from us, they did not reject us, people stayed there like it was a different [moment in] history...we came out [onstage] with some stage props, we came out with trees, with crazy things, you understand me, we did this.

Here Arnau Lizaire is discussing a moment of transition, when artists began to reflect and think about what they were going to do with hip hop. The artists could tell that part of the U.S. Americentric nature of how Cuban artists were performing hip hop, via the beats, did not completely resonate with their Cuban audiences. But the Cuban artists were already incorporating local imagery and historical references. As he says toward the end of this quotation, the way that they came out onstage, the stage props that they used, reminded people of a different time. He is referring to *cinmarrones* (runaway slaves) who hid in the mountains of Cuba in the colonial period.

Alexey of the CUHHM group Obsesión discusses how important hip hop has been in developing a completely different subjectivity. Before hip hop, he says that he did not know where he would be. If not for hip hop, he would have been in jail or in the United States. Like all of the hip hop artists with whom I spoke, Alexey says that the racial theme is important. Many Cubans either do not realize that they often experience discrimination and micro-aggressions because they are socially interpellated as Black or mulat@ or know that they are Black or mulat@ but don't want to be considered Black. He had not realized how much the lack of a Black identity and lack of knowledge about the role of Black Cubans in the independence of the nation had affected him psychologically.

Alexey commented that several additionally important events happened as artists began to take hip hop seriously. The first was a course on Black Cuban history given by Cuban scholar Tomás Fernández Robaina. Fernández Robaina is also a senior archivist and researcher at Cuba's National Library who has been integral in researching and cataloging Cuba's Black history. The next event was the availability of the Spanish version of *The Autobiography of Malcolm X* in Cuba. Cuban youth identified with Malcolm X's quest of self-discovery: he started out in one of the most marginal situations that they could imagine, as a Black man who was marginalized within a racist society and further marginalized through his criminal activities. Starting out at the lowest point, in prison, he began a path of self-education that led to his emergence as an international civil rights figure. Another event that was formative for many Cuban hip hop artists was the series of courses offered by exiled U.S. American New Afrikan revolutionary Nehanda Abiodun in her apartment. These classes centered on racism, racial identity, and the history of transnational Black Nationalist movements. Abiodun eventually ended the courses at the "request" of the Cuban state.

As Arnau Lizaire and DJ D'Boys note, the initial years were a period of excitement. Most of the groups understood that they had not yet developed their own aesthetic, style, and contribution, but they kept trying anyway. During his interview, Arnau Lizaire mentioned Ariel Fernández, who used to cut and splice cassette tapes together in order to create different beats for the artists. They did not have the high-tech beats system, turntables, or mixers that most DJs used for a seamless transition between records to create new sounds. Instead Cuban artists did this by hand, using old cassettes, tape, a boom box, and a pair of scissors. It is important to note here that they were only using U.S. beats in the beginning, while most people were listening to Cuban music and not to much foreign music. Here we see the early signs of artists who were excited about the aesthetic but also realized that something else was missing: their own distinctive take. Regardless of how strange or U.S.-centric some of the novices were in their artistic production, people were respectful and continued to support the groups' artistic development.

The Development of a Movement:
Redefining Art, Negotiating the Cuban State

From this beginning emerged a group of underground hip hop artists who are now part of a new generation of utopian critical artists and intellectuals. The goal of their work as artists and activists was to challenge hegemonic discourses locally and globally and contribute to "a revolution within the Revolution": the liberation of socially marginal communities, particularly Black and mulat@ people. Their work centered on consciousness-raising as a means of encouraging Cuban citizens to work for their own empowerment. In their music, theater, and hip hop performances, CUHHM artists attempt to interrupt hegemonic systems of representation as a means to expand revolutionary discourse to include the citizenship demands of socially marginal groups.

Here is track 6 of "Hip Hop y pensamiento" (Hip Hop and Thought) from the album *Asere #2* by 100% Original from the compilation CD *Cuban Agency of Rap*:

(Coro)	(Chorus)
Revolución en Cuba tiene un nombre:	Revolution in Cuba has a name:
hip hop	hip hop
. . .	. . .
No sé qué sería de mi si no hago	I don't know what would have been of me
este hip hop	if I didn't do this hip hop
. . .	. . .
Rompiendo las barreras	Breaking the barriers
de tu conciencia	of your consciousness
. . .	. . .
Y los ministros de cultura digan	And the ministers of culture say
Ahí si hay hip hop	Yes, there it is, hip hop
. . .	. . .
Acontecimiento histórico de esta	A historical account of this
generación	generation
. . .	. . .
No cuento con la radio ni con la	It isn't found on the radio
televisión	or the television

This song reflects a common sentiment of many hip hop artists and participants: they don't know where they would be without hip hop. The song argues that hip hop is a revolution. Based on everyday experience, hip hop serves as a tool to deliver a message to the people. For the MC, hip hop is a way to express feelings as well as educate and strengthen listeners by preparing them mentally to understand and challenge the oppression that they face. As artivists argue, hip hop gives life: it offers meaning. Through understanding your situation, you can work for a solution. The MC argues that one day hip hop is going to be recognized for its revolutionary contribution to uplifting society. This validation is going to come when the director of the Ministry of Culture recognizes the social importance of hip hop and that it is an art form. That is when the artist can claim, "Yeah, there it is!" That will indicate that hip hop has reached the highest cultural level, as 100% Original says, "where there is no other." This is a legitimacy claim that hip hop has cultural and political relevance in the area of representation, political interests, and ideological production: it is not marginal and "uncultured." Regardless of whether or not this happens, artists are going to continue their devotion to the movement.

By 2005 the movement had become so organized that CUHHM artists began to think about how best to present their ideological orientation. Thus CUHHM leaders presented the "Cuban Underground Hip Hop Declaration" at the First International Hip Hop Symposium, held in Havana in 2005. Like the declaration of their Nueva Trova counterparts of the 1960s, the artists argued that music and song should be located within community activism. The CUHHM artists rejected art in its consumer-oriented commercialized form, seeing music as a tool for community empowerment. For these critical artists, songs are to be used to spur fundamental change at the level of collective consciousness as a means to challenge societal problems. The "Final Declaration of the First Symposium of Cuban Hip Hop in 2005" is another example of how the CUHHM is embedded within a larger politicized cultural sphere that serves as Cuba's nascent civil society. The declaration captures the spirit, aims, and social tensions of the previous generation of socially critical musicians and also reflects the movement's initial equation with Nueva Trova in the national media:

DECLARACIÓN FINAL DEL
PRIMER SIMPOSIO DE HIP HOP CUBANO

. . . Durante estos días revisamos, cuestionamos y fortalecimos la identidad de un nuevo movimiento cultural en Cuba, cuyas características no se agotan en una sola manifestación artística, ni únicamente en sus propósitos estéticos, sino también en los sociales. Razón que ha hecho difícil la ubicación del movimiento en el entramado institucional de la cultura cubana. Este I Simposio ha demostrado las múltiples limitaciones de las formulas y respuestas institucionales creadas para encauzar el movimiento y nos pronunciamos por encontrar los espacios que puedan propiciar, desarrollar y promover TODAS las expresiones culturales del Hip Hop en nuestro país. Dicha búsqueda tendrá lugar a través del dialogo responsable, anti burocrático y creador con las instituciones más cercanas a nuestros propósitos—Asociación Hermanos Saíz, Agencia Cubana de Rap, Instituto de la Música (incluyendo sus centros provinciales), UNEAC y Cultura Comunitaria.

Durante estos días disfrutamos el orgullo de un discurso propio, de un saber diferente que no se coloca de espaldas al conocimiento académico ni a las visiones tradicionales de la cultura, sino que les exige profundizar, actualizarse y comprometerse más. Los talleres de Construcción de Genero, Educación Popular, Orientación Civil, Break-Dance y Grafiti permitieron desmontar textos y prejuicios, compartir técnicas artísticas y otras cualidades estéticas del Movimiento así como incorporar nuevas herramientas para el trabajo en la comunidad, con la comunidad y para la comunidad. En estos días pudimos confirmar que nuestros propósitos son compartidos no solo por raperos, grafiteros, djs y bailadores de hip hop; sino por muchos investigadores, periodistas, profesores, fotógrafos, maestros, funcionarios, pintores, estudiantes, niños, poetas y amigos que nos han acompañado. El evento propicio la búsqueda compartida de nuevas formulas y estrategias que nos permitan interactuar con diversos sectores de público: es nuestra petición mayor a la política cultural cubana, pues los actuales diseños organizativos y promocionales de esa política no toman en cuenta la complejidad de nuestro movimiento.

El Simposio de Hip Hop Cubano se convierte en un proyecto que pretende—a través de todo el año y de toda la isla—sistematizar una mirada crítica, autocrítica, creadora y comprometida de todas y cada una de las artistas cubanas y cubanos del hip hop, que han demostrado su identificación con los presupuestos emancipatorios y sociales de la Revolución Cubana.

> Leído y aclamado a las 7 P.M. del 27 de noviembre del 2005,
> En la Casa de la Cultura de Plaza de la Revolución.
> Ciudad de la Habana, Cuba.

THE FINAL DECLARATION OF THE
FIRST CUBAN HIP HOP SYMPOSIUM

. . . During these days we reviewed, questioned, and strengthened the identity of a new cultural movement in Cuba, whose characteristics are not exhausted in a single artistic expression, or only in aesthetic purposes, but also in social purposes. That is why it has been made difficult to locate the movement in the institutional fabric of Cuban culture. This First Symposium has shown the many limitations of the formulas and institutional responses created to curtail the movement and we speak to find spaces which may lead to the development and promotion of all cultural expressions of hip hop in our country. That search will be held accountable through dialogue, antibureaucratic and creative, with the institutions closest to our purposes, such as the Asociación Hermanos Saíz, the Cuban Agency of Rap, the Institute of Music (including its provincial centers), UNEAC, and Cultural Community.

During these days we enjoyed the pride in our own discourse, a different knowledge that does not rest on the shoulders of academic knowledge or in a traditional vision of culture, but demands in-depth study, to bring ourselves up to date and to commit ourselves to become more involved. The workshops on the Construction of Gender, Popular Education, Civil Orientation, Break-Dance, and Graffiti enabled us to take apart texts and to dismantle prejudices, [and to] share artistic techniques and other aesthetic qualities of the Movement as well as incorporate new tools for work in the community, with the community and for the community. In these days, we were able to confirm that our goals are shared not only by rappers, graffiti artists, DJs, and hip hop dancers but by many researchers, journalists, teachers, photographers, teachers, civil servants, artists, students, children, poets, and friends who have accompanied us. The event enabled the sharing of the quest for new formulas and strategies that will allow us to interact with various sectors of the public: it is our biggest point of contention with Cuban cultural policy, the current organizational designs and promotional policy of this politics that does not take into account the complexity of our movement.

The Cuban Hip Hop Symposium has converted into a project that tries—during the whole year and throughout the Island—to systematize a critical perspective, self-critical, creative, and committed to all and to every one of the Cuban artists and Cubans of hip hop who have demonstrated their identification with the emancipatory and social proposals of the Cuban Revolution.

> Read and approved at 7 P.M. on November 27, 2005
> in the Casa de la Cultura de Plaza de la Revolución.
> Havana, Cuba.

This declaration hailed the emergence of Cuban underground hip hop as a social and cultural movement. It was partially in response to the state's last-minute cancellation of the International Hip Hop Festival in 2004. International artists from all over the world, from Canada to Brazil, arrived in Cuba expecting to participate in a festival, only for it to be canceled at the last minute. This left the international artists looking for money after they had paid for their tickets but suddenly found themselves without a place to stay (per their participation in the festival) in Cuba. The cancellation resulted in a meeting with the leadership of the Cuban Underground Hip Hop Movement artists at the Teatro Amadeo Roldán (figs. 3.2 to 3.5).

In 2000 the state-sponsored youth cultural association called Asociación Hermanos Saíz took over control of the Hip Hop Festival from Grupo Uno, the founders of the festival and the group credited with being among the founders of the CUHHM. The process of co-optation of the Hip Hop Festival by a state-run institution is what Ricardo Bacallao is critiquing in his film. The state is co-

Figure 3.2. Odaymara Cuesta Rosseau (*left*) and Michael Oremas (*right*) at the CUHHM meeting at the Teatro Amadeo Roldán, Havana, 2004. (Courtesy of Sahily Borrero)

Figure 3.3. Producer Pablo Herrera (*left*) and Alexis "DJ D'Boys" Rodríguez (*right*) at the CUHHM meeting at the Teatro Amadeo Roldán, Havana, 2004. (Courtesy of Sahily Borrero)

Figure 3.4. Irak of the group Doble Filo at the CUHHM meeting at the Teatro Amadeo Roldán, Havana, 2004. (Courtesy of Sahily Borrero)

Figure 3.5. Grupo Uno member (founder of the Cuban Hip Hop Festival) and cultural producer Rodolfo Rensoli (*right*) at the CUHHM meeting at the Teatro Amadeo Roldán, Havana, 2004. (Courtesy of Sahily Borrero)

opting something that was understood to be a space where Blacks and mulat@s could engage in antiracist social critique, making interventions in the silences concerning race, specifically Blackness, within hegemonic state discourse. The "usurpation" (as several artists state in the film) of the Hip Hop Festival was seen as step in the disempowerment of Black youth. The cancellation of the 2004 International Hip Hop Festival was viewed by many as the continuation of a process that began with Grupo Uno, who were also at the 2004 meeting held at the Teatro Amadeo Roldán. Cuban photographer Sahily Borrero commented that the general feeling at the meeting to discuss the cancellation of the International Hip Hop Festival was sadness.

The artivists defined themselves as being independent of state institutions, though a division had emerged within the movement: some artists had pressed for state incorporation as a successful strategy via the creation of the Cuban Agency of Rap, while others resisted state efforts at institutionalization. CUHHM artists argue that their knowledge-practices, ideologies, and discourses, the histories that they are uncovering, and their vision of culture are not found in hegemonic academic literature. They contend that their work and their goals not only are shared by other artists and artivists but are also of interest to everyone, including researchers, teachers, journalists, and civil servants. Like many of the artivists before them, the artists embrace the emancipatory ideals of the Cuban Revolution, while stressing that embracing the ideals of the Revolution is not the same as uncritically accepting state policy and contemporary Cuban culture. These artists seek to work toward the ideals of the Revolution through critique and independent mobilization as critical participants in the revolutionary process, even if this means sometimes running into problems with the state. The symposium addressed a broad range of issues, including the social construction of gender and sexuality (again highlighting that this was a broad-based cultural movement). Using hip hop, the artivists sought to create new tools for community mobilization and support, developed by local communities for local communities. As the artivists state, "our biggest point of contention with Cuban cultural policy" is that it "does not take into account the complexity of our movement," making it clear that they are a part of a broad-based, arts-based social movement.

This becomes evident when we reflect on the four elements of hip hop: graffiti, MCing, DJing, and break-dancing. Typically DJs have such a wealth of knowledge about local and global music cultures that they function as historians of local culture, of histories encoded in music, and often as local ethnomusicologists. Graffiti engages in cultural documentation and knowledge production within the visual arts, while break-dancers vividly engage the corporality of cultural knowledges and experiences. The MCs deliver their discourse, knowledge-practices, and insights through spoken word. Much of the literature cited so far has not focused on important elements of hip hop such as graffiti and break-dancing.

Joseph G. Schloss (2009) highlights one understudied element of hip hop culture: B-boying and B-girling. He notes that battling is important in B-boying and B-girling and generalizes this importance to hip hop. Schloss argues that this reflects the diversity of hip hop as a critical space: it encourages criticism. B-boying and B-girling remind us that a central element of hip hop is challenging the mind/body separation and invite us to return to the body as a site and producer of knowledge, a store of experience and history. Those who are involved in hip hop as a social movement also recognize a fifth element, as noted by Afrika Bambaataa, one of the pioneers of hip hop and the founder of the Zulu Nation. This fifth element is knowledge, culture, and understanding—often grouped together as consciousness.

The Zulu Nation argues on its website that a central element of hip hop is social change through promoting peace, love, and positive change within the individual and among the community.[3] Through hip hop, people can communicate with each other, learn from each other, and have fun together in a way that brings joy and happiness, decreases negativity, and encourages positivity through faith. Thus hip hop has a spiritual element. Additionally, artivists refer to hip hop as consciousness, as knowledge, as wisdom, as a means of obtaining insight and awareness. The pursuit of knowledge is what encourages artivists and others in the hip hop public sphere to learn about their history and world history as well as to work harder for social change. In the case of the Black and Latin@ youths participating in hip hop when it emerged in New York, one focus was on learning about and embracing their African heritage. Like other Black music cultures, hip hop would become the contemporary sphere of ideological exchange and critique for Afro-descendant populations in the Americas.[4] These perspectives on hip hop have been an important element of the exchanges of African Americans, Cubans, Brazilians, and many hip hoppers within the diaspora. Those in the United States who share a socially conscious orientation to their theorization of hip hop also have tended to share a diasporic perspective concerning hip hop.

Diasporic Currents within Cuban Underground Hip Hop

In 2008 I organized the El Proyecto Cuban Underground Hip Hop Conference at Lehigh University—the first event to bring together members of the

CUHHM living in Cuba and in the diaspora. At that event Monifa Bandele, the coordinator of the Black August Hip Hop Project, discussed the transnational circulation of Black music cultures and the idea of a transnational cultural and ideological feedback loop:

> And I want to say that it is a two-way street: Ariel talked a lot about African culture coming from the U.S. influencing what is going on in Cuba, Eli talked about reggae, I mean . . . if you go back to the 1950s and it was really the Afro-Cubans who came to the U.S., that really put in place, put in motion the understanding the reclamation of African spiritual traditions, and African religion, through Santería through Yoruba, and it had a tremendous impact in the communities that then produced the children of hip hop and in talking about claiming one's African identity and here you have the African gods right from the continent through Cuba infusing into U.S. culture and growing in a way that fed organizations from the East, a lot of organizations in California, like the one called US, the Black Panther Party, all these organizations tap into the presence of Afro-Cubans and the spiritual and traditions that they brought, so also I just wanted to emphasize that it is a two-way street, it's not just hip hop, it's not just reggae, it's not just culture as far as entertainment culture, but also culture in terms of spirituality that it also is exchanged, and oh boy, Brazil and Venezuela too? Then you're just like talking on a whole other level, but again Cuba being able to maintain and preserve the very sacred African tradition and then share it within the Cuban diaspora in the West also fits differently into everything that we have been talking about.

Bandele is referring to a conversation in which Ariel Fernández, the influential CUHHM producer, DJ, organizer, and scholar, discussed the impact of U.S. cultural production on the rest of the world.[5] In response to Fernández, the Puerto Rican filmmaker and hip hop documentarian Eli Jacobs-Fantauzzi commented that other Black cultural movements that did not originate in the United States have also had a profound impact on the world, including the United States. He gave reggae as an example. Bandele then commented that African Americans are not involved in a unidirectional exchange. She pointed out that there is a feedback loop with immigrants from the diaspora moving and traveling to the United States and influencing worldviews there. Bandele posited that including all of the cultural and ideological exchanges within the Americas results in something much more complicated than just commercially based cultural exchanges.

The Black August Hip Hop Project, of which Bandele is a coordinator, is credited with helping hip hop in Cuba to become a social movement (though my research shows that hip hop in Cuba was becoming an arts-based social movement long before the arrival of the Black August Hip Hop Project). The Black August Hip Hop Project is affiliated with the Malcolm X Grassroots Movement (MXGM), a Brooklyn-based pan-African activist organization. Members of the movement self-identify as New Afrikans. They write:

> The term "New Afrika" reflects our Pan African identity, our purpose, and our direction. Although we come from distinct ethno-linguistic groups in Africa and the African Diaspora, our shared oppression and the interdependence of our liberation redefines our borders. We are New Afrikans and we are a Nation. We will be free. Toward that end, MXGM will work to honor the legacy of our ancestors, for our own progress and for future generations. Let us surface the New Afrikan Nation for ourselves, all Afrikans and all humanity by proudly calling ourselves . . . New Afrikan![6]

This statement is a hallmark of what Ifeoma Nwankwo (2005) calls Black cosmopolitanism and is an example of the types of social movements that Agustín Lao-Montes (2007) argues are possible and that exist, united by various forms of Afro-diasporic identification. What is interesting here is that the term "New Afrikan" refers to all of the African diaspora and all of humanity. This is a way of claiming blackness as a marker of humanity and group membership. The strategy is reminiscent of the Haitian Revolution, in which all citizens of Haiti were declared "Black." Here blackness functions as an anticolonial subject position that highlights the liberation of the Afro-descendant body (exploited, abused, and tortured as a key commodity within the emergent transnational economic and social order) and redefines these experiences of oppression as central to Western notions of human liberation. As such, MXGM decenters the experiences of white, male, European, bourgeois subjects—who were oppressed by the anciens régimes and whose liberation serve as the ideological basis for a Eurocentric vision of Western modernity—and puts oppressed Africans and their descendants in their place. The liberation of New Afrikans that the MXGM refers to is universalized to human emancipation.

Acknowledging the heterogeneous origins of the African diaspora in the Americas, the MXGM argues that the shared oppression experienced by members of this diaspora forms the basis for transnational identification. The key goals of the MXGM are to recognize the continued colonial condition of Africa and its diaspora, to promote self-determination and recognition, and "to affirm our connection to the landmass on which our ancestors toiled and bled; to affirm our connection to land from which all wealth and health flows." Finally,

MXGM wants "to be able to act as a resource, example, and sanctuary for oppressed people everywhere."[7] Similarly, as part of the larger MXGM, the Black August Hip Hop Project describes its mission:

> The Black August Hip Hop Project strives to promote human rights though supporting and influencing the global development of Hip Hop culture. By facilitating exchanges between international communities where Hip Hop is a vital part of youth culture, we promote awareness about the social and political issues that affect our global communities.
>
> Our vision is to bring culture and politics together and to allow them to naturally evolve into a unique Hip Hop consciousness that informs our collective struggle for a more just, equitable and human world.[8]

The Black August Hip Hop Project seeks to challenge the separation of culture and politics in order to influence the consciousness of communities where hip hop is present throughout the world. CUHHM artists themselves have a transnational perspective in their activism. The group that would come to appreciate hip hop was diverse.

For example, DJ D'Boys, like many of the artivists in the CUHHM, is a formally trained musician and visual arts student from El Vedado, a middle to upper middle class borough in Havana. While many other artists were from "el gueto" (the ghetto), the Cuban Underground Hip Hop Movement also included a significant number of people who were middle-class and affluent before the Special Period. Given the "classless" context of Cuba, these seem like the best terms to use in describing the combination of social sensibilities and access to material resources and social status, although I could also refer to them as "Cuba's revolutionary class." Nonetheless, what attracted this diverse Afro-descendant population to hip hop was the pro-Black antiracist critique embedded in much of early U.S. hip hop, which also included a Black feminist critique. Reflecting on the time when he organized the first hip hop festival in our interview in Havana in 2005, Grupo Uno co-founder Rodolfo Rensoli described his surprise at how many Blacks and mulat@s showed up at the first festival in a housing project on the outskirts of Havana called Reparto Bahia:

> Mira . . . El hip hop . . . Cuando yo estoy haciendo el primer festival de Rap, de pronto se me acerca, casualmente la mayor parte éramos negros los que estamos organizando eso, el amigo aquí y yo, y se me acerca Mery Matamoro que es uno de dos hermanos que fueron que asumieron esta idea de hacer el Festival y me dice: oye . . . te están gritando por abajo vivan los chardos. Aquí se le dice chardos a los negros. Y yo me quedé así

y lo vi muy peligroso . . . porque yo estaba acostumbrado a participar de ambientes mixtos de negros y yo no tenía conciencia de cuantos, grandes masas de negros se sentían muy marginaos y habían encontrado un lugar de expresión libre.

Además, vi blancos ahí también, porque tú sabes que aquí se ha mezclado más la cosa que en otros lugares. No se realizó el desarraigo social ese tan radicalmente dividido. Pero de pronto me doy cuenta que sí, de que le estoy dando oportunidades a muchos muchachos negros que no tenían otros espacios donde hablar sus propios intereses, sus propias perspectivas y con una alta cultura y con un alto lirismo. Y por ahí me fui porque siempre tuve consciencia del problema. También por mi padre, por mi mamá y por las experiencias que tuve de niño.

> Look . . . hip hop . . . When I was doing the first Rap Festival, suddenly it dawned on me that most of us organizing it happened to be Black; a friend and I approached Miguel Matamoros, who is one of two brothers who had the idea of doing the festival, and he said to me: "Listen . . . they are yelling below 'Long live the chardos!'" Here they call the Blacks "chardos" [a derogatory term for Black people]. And I stayed right there and saw it as very dangerous. Because I was accustomed to participate in environments mixed with Blacks [and other races] and I had no awareness of how many of the large masses of Blacks who felt very marginalized and had found a place of free expression.
>
> In addition, there were also whites there, because you know that here things have been mixed more than in other places. You don't realize with so much uprooting that things were so socially divided. But suddenly I realized that, yes, I am giving opportunities to many Black youths who had no other spaces where they could speak to their own interests, about their own perspectives, and with a high culture and high lyricism. And there I went because I was always aware of the problem from my father, my mother, and the experiences that I had as a child.

For many Black youths, hip hop offered a moment and communicative structure for the public articulation of forgotten and residual discourse invoked symbolically through hip hop beats and images (themselves residual African and Afro-diasporic discourses). In this quotation, Rensoli states that he was surprised that almost all of the festival attendees were Afro-descendant and that he primarily participated in racially mixed social environments. This comment refers to a central aspect of post-1959 social spaces: because of the Cuban state's imposition of a raceless discourse in Cuba, many Black Cubans did not grow up with a racial identity and all social spaces were forcibly integrated. Public discussions of persistent racism were discouraged (see chapter 2), and those who publicly discussed racism were seen as potentially counter-revolutionary or as the true racists (de la Fuente 2001; Helg 1995).

The raceless discourse that emerged in Cuba implied that the state did not see race. It seems also to have meant that the state did not see Black people. Cuba had become so discursively raceless that Blacks were not included in history courses and in national media. Many Black Cubans, who received at least a partial secondary education after the Revolution, grew up without knowing about the social, political, and cultural contributions of Africans and Black Cubans to the nation. Those who do not attend a university are largely ignorant about the role of Black Cubans in founding the nation.

Nonetheless, while the lives of some Cubans were structured by hegemonic revolutionary discourse, many Cubans had a racialized consciousness. Though their lives were dominated by a raceless discourse in the public sphere, at home parents passed on stories about Blacks in Cuban history and reminded their children to watch out for racism and self-hate. Racist discourses continued informally and subtly, publicly reemerging during the economic downturn. Black parents taught their children that their bodies (such as dark skin and African hair) were beautiful. They taught their children to be wary of people who tried to tell them that they were uncivilized or backward because of their physical appearance and cultural practices. By drawing upon collective memory and connecting it with contemporary experiences, CUHHM artists spurred the (re)emergence of a public Black identity politics and activism among Black and mulat@ youth.

The following sections examine how several of these artists reflect on these issues, as a way to highlight some of the themes that arose in my larger data set.

Alexey

Alexey of the group Obsesión said in our interview in Havana in 2006:

> Y pienso que también en la vida cultural de las personas interesadas en el hip hop puede influir muchísimo. Es un arma para eso, para interesarte políticamente no solo de tu país, sino a nivel mundial. Pienso que el hip hop que hace falta hoy es un hip-hop integral culturalmente. Cuando digo integral culturalmente no estoy remitiéndome solamente a conocer cuáles la particularidades de tu país, sino interesarte por las particularidades que tiene, Irak, Germania, qué hay en Filipinas. Entiende. Eso hace que tu historia sea más integral. En la medida que tú puedes entender cómo fun-

ciona, cómo funciona no, entender todas las particularidades que tiene el hip hop en todas las comunidades posibles. . . . tu propio país . . . barrio . . . escuela. . . . El hip hop son tantas cosas. Y ya te digo, salgo y es el aire que respire. . . . Es un arma para que la gente se conozca mucho mejor como individuo, deudor que aporta a la sociedad. Porque a veces pensamos que estar consciente de los problemas que tenemos en solamente eso, o sea lo que quiero decir que es bueno estar consciente de los problemas que tenemos, pero la pregunta es ¿qué vas a hacer por es? Más allá de este gobierno u otro, la pregunta es qué vamos a hacer es ¿qué vamos a hacer nosotros? En ese sentido el hip hop juega un papel bien importante . . . eso es . . . y así inconscientemente o conscientemente va creciendo una cultura, una manera de ver la vida, de asumirse. . . . Actualmente contextualizando no son los mismos problemas los de Colombia, que los de Brasil, o los de Cuba. Cada cual encuentra en el hip-hop una repuesta, aunque sea en un solo punto, es diferente en algunos modos.

> And I think that also in cultural life people interested in hip hop can influence a lot. It is a weapon for that, to interest you politically not only in your country but on the world level. I think that hip hop, what it lacks today is a hip hop that is culturally integrated. When I say culturally integrated I am not focusing only on the particularities of your country but that you be interested in the particularities of Iraq, Germany, and the Philippines. Understand? This makes it such that your history is much more complete. To the extent that you can understand how it works, not how it works, but to understand all of the particularities that hip hop has in all kinds of communities . . . your own country . . . neighborhood . . . school . . . Hip hop is so many things. And as I said, I go out and it's the air that I breathe. . . . It's a weapon for people to know themselves much better as an individual, as a debtor who contributes to society. Because sometimes we think about the problems we have and only about that, or, better put, what I want to say is that it is good to be aware of the problems that we have, but the question is what are you going to do about it? Beyond this government or another, the question is what we will do . . . is what are we going to do ourselves? In this sense hip hop plays a very important role . . . this is . . . and it's like this, unconsciously or consciously, it goes creating a culture, a way of seeing life, of lifting oneself up. . . . Actually contextualizing, the problems of Brazil, Colombia, and Cuba are not the same. Everyone who encounters in hip hop a response, albeit at a single point, it is still different in some ways.

In this quotation, Alexey elucidates his global perspective on the political and social significance and potential of hip hop. For him, hip hop can help people understand the problems that they face in their own country, neighborhoods, and community-based institutions as well as help people understand the realities of those living in other countries. There is not just one hip hop or one reality expressed by hip hop, Alexey argues, even though some points are shared. For Alexey, as for nearly every CUHHM artist that I interviewed, hip hop is his life. Hip hop helps him to understand reality and to realize that he has a purpose, to contribute to the betterment of society. Alexey says that the point of hip hop is not only to be aware of the problems that a society faces but to ask what people are going to do to address those problems, regardless of the government that is in power. For Alexey, hip hop is a revolution: it is independent of all institutions and has its own vision and political agenda.

Alexey also points to the way in which hip hop addresses social issues at multiple levels, often simultaneously: at the global, national, local, and community levels. The artivists seamlessly move across micro and macro points of view as they analyze everyday life at the local level and connect them to larger systemic issues at the cultural, national, regional, and global levels.

Michael

Michael, a member of Junior Clan and the CUHH group EPG&B, co-wrote the song *Internacionales* (International) that they recorded:

Lucha, hermano, haz tu revolución	Fight, brother, start your revolution
. . .	. . .
la mala nutrición estatal es	the state's malnutrition is
lo más abundante	the most abundant
escribir, fascinante,	to write, fascinating,
discutir es revolucionar la mente	to discuss is to revolutionize the mind
. . .	. . .
Ningún desarrollo para nosotros,	No development for us,
ellos nos mienten a nosotros,	they lie to us,
esto es protesta, cultura,	this is protest, culture,
hip hop.	hip hop.
. . .	. . .
Hablar de las calles cubanas,	To talk about Cuban streets,
prisiones cubanas, verdades cubanas.	Cuban prisons, Cuban truths.

(*translated by Ariel Meilich*)

In this song Junior Clan and EPG&B talk about the problems in Cuba via a larger discussion about the problems that people face globally. Junior Clan and EPG&B directly challenge state discourse, arguing that Cubans died for the revolutionary struggle in Angola, but the revolutionary struggle at home needs to be taken care of. How many people are struggling, while one class of people has no problems? In the song Michael calls for Cuban citizens to wake up and directly challenge the problems at home. The central point is that their perspective is international. They are calling for a global revolution for all the people who are struggling because of the material interests of a small elite.

In 2005, during a conversation with Michael at the apartment of New Afrikan political exile Nehanda Abidioun in Bahía, Michael explained that in the song "Internacionales" he is naming the contradictions of the revolutionary elite and linking them to the contradictions of the elite of the larger world, such as people who espouse equality but seem to be hoarding all of the material wealth for themselves, while others have very little to eat. Michael says that the Cuban government turns a blind eye to the problems of violence and material inequality facing people in poor communities. When he talks about global revolutions in the song, he does not mention the Soviet Union or any European revolutions, only anticolonial revolutions: the Cuban Revolution (which symbolically represents the revolutionary impulses of much of Latin America and the Caribbean) and the Black U.S., Asian, and African revolutions. This reflects the anticolonial challenge to persistent coloniality, manifested by rampant global capitalism that is characteristic of the revolutions in the geopolitical south. Most importantly, it mirrors the transnational, anticolonial vision of the Cuban Revolution. Michael's song is a reflection of the internationalist revolutionary vision of the Cuban Revolution: the artists are revolutionary subjects critiquing the limitations of the Revolution. The Junior Clan and EPG&B and the CUHHM are examples of revolutionary subjects who were raised to be revolutionary critical actors. But they are encouraged (in some cases forced) to be *less* critical when they act as critical subjects. Black revolutionary subjectivity is also formed by the Cuban state's support of anticolonial struggles in Africa, which generations of Black Cuban soldiers, doctors, and other military and civil personnel were sent to support.

Nonetheless, Michael's worldview, which is informed by the nation he grew up in, is another example of the ways in which a global revolutionary perspective is in conversation with the global (anticolonial) perspective of antiracist Black radicalism of many leaders in the Americas and on the Continent. Michael also undertakes a material-based analysis of social inequality: he frames the difficulties facing Cubans in terms of a class struggle in which one economic

Figure 3.6. Producer Alexis "DJ D'Boys" Rodríguez (*left*) with Questlove (*right*) of the Roots, Havana, 2002. (Courtesy of DJ D'Boys)

Figure 3.7. DJ Leydis (*left*) after performing a set with Erykah Badu in Oakland, California, 2009. (Courtesy of DJ Leydis)

Figure 3.8. (*Left to right*) Alexis "DJ D'Boys" Rodríguez with Black Thought of the Roots and Michael Oremas of the Junior Clan, Havana, 2002. (Courtesy of Alexis "DJ D'Boys" Rodríguez)

class is completely disconnected from the realities of the average Cuban citizen. Michael is asking average Cubans to wake up and realize that they need to be working for social change at home (figs. 3.6 to 3.8).

Yompi

Yompi, part of the Junior Clan and like Michael, is based in El Cerro, one of the poorest boroughs in Havana. He expressed the following thoughts in the form of spoken word poetry in a 2005 interview in Havana:

> Bueno, dice así. Es un espoking word que dice así hip hop es quién soy. La voz universal reclamando un mundo mejor. El sentido común y la reflexión de los jóvenes de barrios. La esperanza de los pobres, la valentía y la rebeldía invocando libertad. El negro respeto, la paz, la unidad, el enemigo de la guerra. La lucha por la revolución de todos los pueblos buscando un mundo mejor. Hip hop soy yo, un símbolo de resistencia para mantener limpia la conciencia. Y hablando palabras, ¿que estás haciendo tú cerca de esto? . . . No te das cuenta que el mundo está en ebullición, de mal en peor. Y la solución está en nosotros mismos, cambiando esta mala forma de pensar, de actuar.

> OK, it's said like this. There is a spoken word [poem] that says it like this: hip hop is who I am. The universal voice reclaiming a better world. It is the common feeling and a reflection of the youth from the hood. The hope of the poor, the valiant, and the rebellious invoking their freedom. The Black [person is] respected, the peace, the unity, the enemy of war. Hip hop I am, a symbol of the resistance in order to maintain a clean consciousness. And speaking words, what are you thinking about this? . . . Don't you see that the world is boiling, from bad to worse? And the solution is in ourselves, changing this bad way of thinking, of acting.

Yompi describes his skin as ebony and has shoulder-length dreadlocks. He says that he has experienced a lot of racism. Before hip hop he could not understand what was happening to him; he just felt a general malaise. But with hip hop he was able to gain a better sense of self, to understand what was depressing him, to develop a sense of purpose in life. Through hip hop Yompi learned how to be successful as a conscious Black man and to support Black Cuban youths by helping them understand the racial prejudices that they face.

Yompi argues that liberation and working for a better world start at the metaphysical level of spirit and consciousness. This is reflective of what numerous scholars characterize as a key part of African epistemology: an African world-view focused more on the needs of the collective. Osumare (2007) writes: "The Africanist aesthetic in hip-hop becomes an all-encompassing system of values that is instrumental in bringing forth good form, play on the self, and an ethical responsibility to one's community" (27). This worldview also has its own metaphysical orientation, which gives primacy to the unity of the realms of the spiritual *and* the material. This produces forms of liberatory politics and actions different from those that may emerge from a Western European epistemology, especially in countries that maintain an African consciousness, which is a key element of African and Afro-descendant emancipatory politics. Thus maintaining the unity of the mind and spirit, the body and a collective consciousness, is the key to total liberation. In his quotation Yompi invokes the sublime messages circulating in socially conscious hip hop. He embodies hip hop as a consciousness and a worldview. For Yompi, hip hop is a symbol of resistance because it focuses on developing a clear consciousness as a path to collective liberation.

The themes that the music of the Junior Clan address have a social message for the community, young people, and the world. Their messages support women, all Black people, and all African people. The artivists believe that they can help the world through hip hop. It gives the lives of the artivists a sense of meaning and helps them develop a framework in which to understand the world and their particular situations. But it also helps them to be conscious of their subjectivity as human beings and their existence as Afro-descendant people who have been targeted for physical, psychic, and subjective invisibility, if not elimination. The message embedded in cultural norms is not lost on the subconscious of Black and Afro-descendant people, particularly youths: Black people are worthless, invisible, insignificant, unproductive, lacking in creativity and intellectual potential, ugly/physically unappealing criminals who should be detested. Such an ideology embedded in cultural praxis and resulting in social, material, and affective marginalization has an effect on the mental health of those who are visibly associated with blackness (through the shape of a nose, hair texture, or any hint of Africanness: see chapter 4). In sum, the CUHHM is about privileging Black subjectivity in all of its forms: nonheternormative, feminine, masculine, young, poor, and so forth.

Cuban Youth/Black Radical Aesthetics: The Symbols and Ideologies of the CUHHM

The following sample of the images that circulate within the CUHHM shows several key elements within the movement: how and why the CUHHM artivists connected to their 1970s and 1980s peers in New York City materially. Both populations had limited access to material resources and were able to produce living culture and knowledge from little material means. The CD covers and inserts also feature diasporic imagery, including shirts and fashions showing the CUHHM's identification with much of the African diaspora globally. The images of Cuban national heroes and national history demonstrate the Cubanization of hip hop: the emergence of Cuban hip hop. The images also highlight global concerns, such as the destruction of the environment, indicating that this hip hop movement is concerned with issues that affect humanity, the earth, and the spirit.

Figures 3.9 through 3.11 are images of the *Cuban Hip Hop All-Stars* CD produced by Ariel Fernández Díaz and Pablo Herrera Veitia. The design of the CD was completed by Steve Marcus, a New York-based freelance artist.[9] Figure 3.9 shows a young Black youth dressed in B-boy gear, which was made fashionable in New York City. Behind him is a fist, representing Black Nationalist imagery and the Black struggle generally. The B-boy gear and the Black Nationalist movement are products of the intellectual and cultural exchanges of Afro-descendants throughout the Americas. The needle of the turntable and soundboard behind him is placed on top of his heart, which looks like a record. This illustrates the importance of hip hop in expressing what is felt and lived.

Figures 3.10 and 3.11 depict the process of colonization. Figure 3.10 shows the Spanish colonizers on a slave ship, which has come to represent trauma and the beginnings of global European-based capitalism (Gilroy 1993a; Quijano 2000). Two are wearing crosses, indicating the Catholic Church's complicity in the colonizing process. In front of them indigenious people kneel on a beach. The souls leaving their mouths represent the colonial genocide of indigenous populations. This image melts into the image of the slave ship. One of the enslaved is glancing at a dying indigenous person on the beach. This illustrates the connection between the colonial genocides of the indigenous people and the slave trade. The masses of people piled onto the slave ship are thinking of Africa. This picture is melded with the American and Cuban colonial elite: white and light-skinned wealthy people are drinking, smoking, and thinking about money (fig. 3.10 right). This alludes to the emergence of the neocolonial class in Cuba. They are eating well and thinking about profit, while poor people scramble behind the table for crumbs and think about food (fig. 3.11). A church with a cross is in the background, symbolizing Catholicism's support of neocolonialism.

To the right of the poor people is an image of Che Guevara. For many Cubans, this symbolizes the ideals of the Cuban Revolution. Behind Che are fire, Kalashnikov rifles, pigs (associated with the Bay of Pigs), cars, and the American flag

Figure 3.9. Album cover: *Cuban Hip Hop All-Stars, Vol. 1* (Papaya Records, 2001). (Courtesy of Steve Marcus)

with dollar signs in the stars, symbolizing American greed, aggression, and imperialism (fig. 3.11 right). The Kalashnikov rifles are often used to symbolize revolutionary struggle and also invoke the presence of the Soviet Union, specifically the Cold War, in Cuban revolutionary history. In later copies the word "Censored" appears just below the chains at the base of the American flag. This alludes to several forms of censorship. One is the censorship resulting from Cuba's global isolation via the economic embargo. The other is the market censorship that all underground artists face for their social critique. At the end of the narrative depicted in the insert, the United States represents the contemporary incarnation of the colonial agenda. This insert reminds viewers that blackness is also a relational identity: its emergence is linked to the genocide of in-

Figure 3.10.   First section of album insert for *Cuban Hip Hop All-Stars, Vol. 1* (Papaya Records, 2001). (Courtesy of Steve Marcus)

Figure 3.11.   Second section of album insert for *Cuban Hip Hop All-Stars, Vol. 1* (Papaya Records, 2001). (Courtesy of Steve Marcus)

digenous populations who share the experience of suffering that has its origins in profit-driven, European, regionally based capital.

For many artists, the images of 1970s and 1980s New York looked like poor parts of Havana. Some artists reference the video *The Message* by New York–based artists Grandmaster Flash and Melle Mel (circa 1983), to point out how 1970s–1980s Bronx looked like boroughs in Havana during the Special Period.

In the music video *The Message* Grandmaster Flash and Melle Mel are out on the streets of their neighborhood. They are utilizing the Black public sphere, where they talk about the difficulties facing their communities: unemployment, crime, limited opportunities. While the artists are standing on the corner speaking to friends at the end of the video, the police pull up and immediately force them into the police car, seemingly for no other reason than being Black men standing in public. Other images in socially conscious U.S. hip hop include Afros, braids, African clothing, and inexpensive casual clothing.

The music video *Jodido Protagonista* (2003) by Cuban artist Randy Acosta contains similar images, including him getting his hair braided. This is about embracing his identity: Black hair is seen in Cuba as "bad hair," undesirable and ugly. Acosta is not only getting his long, kinky hair braided but is respecting and caring for it by getting it styled. In another scene he is also standing out in the street talking. In one section of the video Acosta uses parentheses to highlight a uniformed officer. He talks in the song about being harassed by police for being a young Black man who does not overdress as a means of making the larger society feel comfortable with his presence. There is an image of a child holding up a justice sign at the end. It is clear that Acosta is not only talking to fellow Cubans and representing their experiences but talking to the global hip hop community.

The CD cover of *Jodido Protagonista* is representative of the do-it-yourself aesthetic of underground hip hop. Acosta is considered one of the "most underground" hip hop artists. While living in Cuba he produced his music independently, relying heavily on his one-gigabyte, secondhand laptop computer to mix his beats and make his videos. His CD cover is a photocopied photo of him rapping, though he looks as if he is actually lecturing to the public. He is wearing urban street-wear, indicating that his knowledge is from the streets, not based on detached, canonized academic theory, which often excludes the lived experiences of the Afro-descendant populations. This CD cover is one of the many sophisticated independent covers produced by CUHHM artists. It is simple: a cheaply made photocopy is cut and placed into a very inexpensive plastic CD cover (materials given to Acosta by scholars, artists, and activists who came to Cuba). His CD, like those of most independent artists such as Las Krudas CUBENSI, the Junior Clan, Los Paisanos, and Anónimo Consejo, was burned at home or by friends. The photocopied CD cover is actually an insightful marketing strategy; he uses the "low-quality" aesthetic of the photocopy and the image of him rapping to deliver a very complicated message: Randy Acosta is a man of the streets. His CD targets members of the Black public sphere, delivering knowledge based on Acosta's own experiences. This CD cover helps him to sell himself as one of the most authentic underground artists within Cuba's Underground Hip Hop Movement—and the marketing strategy has worked.

To reduce these aspects of Cuban underground hip hop (such as the young man dressed in B-boy gear) to "African American culture" disconnects African Americans from the rest of the Americas and erases a long history of cultural, intellectual, and insurrectionary exchanges. It also implies that Cuban people are uncritical subjects who lack agency: that they are not participating in cultural exchange but are simply uncritical recipients of culture. As evidence to the contrary, consider, for example, that B-boy fashion actually started in Jamaica, only to be made popular in New York City by Jamaican immigrants (Rose 1994). The burgeoning scholarship on hip hop music, culture, and aesthetics has traced the genealogy of the Afro-diasporic origins of hip hop images (Chang and Herc 2005; Neal 1999; Rivera 2003; Rose 1994). Nevertheless, the designer of this cover is letting the public know that this is a CD of *Cuban* hip hop. On his shirt and his hat the B-boy is wearing the Cuban flag, which is also incorporated into the background. Here the artist invokes the geopolitical and cultural (ideological) context that he/she is representing.

Other CD covers address the relationship between modernity and blackness by using different symbols linked to contemporary exploitation. La FabriK (a play on the word *fábrica*, which means "factory") is a collaborative, independent production of the CUHHM groups Obsesión and Doble Filo. The CD is targeted to "you," the listener: the person who lives for the particular kind of knowledge and insight available in La FabriK's music. The dedication side of the insert reads: "To our parents, to the Cuban Hip Hop Movement, to the people that have been waiting for this, and to you." The dedication is to die-hard hip hop fans, who live for the next CD. In my interviews with CUHHM artists, I learned that many of the newer generations of CUHHM artists were initially fans. Frequently the artists told me stories of how they were on a road to self-destruction. Some tried to leave Cuba illegally on dangerous rafts. Others felt suicidal; before hip hop they did not understand why they felt that way. Receiving an education via underground hip hop lyrics on CDs, however, helped fans understand their situation. These future artists started realizing that they had internalized racism and that they felt disconnected from Cuban society because it culturally discouraged embracing all forms of African aesthetics, including African bodies. Thus, as fans, they started looking forward to the next CD because the CUHHM educated them about their history and their current social context. It taught them about themselves, embraced African aesthetics, and proudly displayed them in public space.

The CD cover of La FabriK is a rejection of industrialization itself. Behind the backdrop of a factory and a red, toxic-looking sky, a Black fist (a reference to Black Nationalist rebellion), a peace sign, and a middle finger (symbolizing a "Fuck You"). The last hand is an open palm symbolizing "Stop!" These images represent messages about the destructive nature of modernity, a request for peace in the face of the environmental destruction caused by industrialization, and a rejection of the drive for endless profit that results in the destruction of all forms of life.

The fight for Mother Nature is of both practical and religious concern. Respecting and protecting nature is a central tenet of Yoruba and indigenous religious traditions. It is also a challenge to the legacies of colonialism through which nature and bodies were commodified.

In my interview with the Junior Clan, the group articulated the connections of environmental rights, freedom of expression, and human equality as central elements of the CUHHM's discourses. For artists such as the Junior Clan, environmental rights, the challenge to racial discrimination, the fight against all kinds of racisms (which, for the CUHHM members, include homophobia and heteronormativity), and the fight against the commercialization of the arts market in Cuba are intertwined with human emancipation. They reject war in favor of peace and free collaboration between peoples (a key element in the struggle for equality, freedom, and the elimination of social ills). For the CUHHM artivists, the struggle for equality is a fight against all of the ways in which people, their creative energies, and nature have been commodified and degraded for the sake of profit.

Another effect of these CD covers is to deliver political messages encouraging independent grassroots work within an individual community. They encourage those marginalized youth from economically depressed communities, who live in an economically depressed and "defamed" nation, to take pride in where they are from, to embrace their Black Cuban ancestors' contribution to the nation, while embracing their existence as Black people. If CD covers do not make these messages clear, however, they are also indicated through style of dress.

Underground hip hop artists wear a lot of red, black, and green, colors reflective of pan-Africanism and Black Nationalism. T-shirts also serve as a means to convey and reinforce self-education and Black consciousness. In one CUHHM concert, Michael Oremas wore a black T-shirt that said "Power to the People," showing the images and names of Black Panthers Huey Newton and Bobby Seale. At the same concert there was another reference to pan-African and Black Nationalist ideology: Yompi of the Junior Clan wore a T-shirt that said "The Black Revolution." The artists also wore army fatigues. Combined with the revo-

Figure 3.12.   Odaymara Cuesta Rosseau of Las Krudas CUBENSI, drumming.
(Courtesy of Sahily Borrero)

lutionary imagery of the Black Panther Movement, this was impressive, especially considering that these images were being deployed within a revolutionary
context. They reemphasized the theme of "a revolution within the Revolution."
The "revolution within" is the challenge to the racist, sexist, and homophobic
colonial legacies that continue within Cuban culture (Saunders 2009b).

In figures 3.12 to 3.14 members of the CUHHM group Las Krudas CUBENSI
are wearing dashikis and dreadlocks. Their style is the rejection of hegemonic,
Eurocentric standards of beauty in which Black women are encouraged to
straighten their hair and wear tight, revealing clothing in order to show that
they are sexually available to men. Las Krudas and their stage presentation are
discussed in further detail in chapter 7.

Figure 3.13. Odalys Cuesta Rosseau of Las Krudas CUBENSI, singing. (Courtesy of Sahily Borrerro)

Figure 3.14. Olivia Prendes Riverón of Las Krudas CUBENSI, singing. (Courtesy of Sahily Borrerro)

Figure 3.15.   Graffiti artist NoNo12 in front of a mural in her apartment building in El Vedado, Havana, 2006. (Photo by Tanya L. Saunders)

Graffiti is another medium through which CUHHM artists seek to educate the masses. One of the themes of the Havana-based graffiti artist NoNo12 is Cuban history, specifically the history of transnational anticapitalist, antiracist, and anti-imperialist struggle. In figure 3.15 NoNo12 stands in the archway of her apartment building. In the foreground the word "Underground" is written in English on the left side of the arch, with a basketball painted behind the letter "U." This is a reference to the urban U.S. origins of the art form. To the right is the African

Figure 3.16. Graffiti artist NoNo12. (Courtesy of Sahily Borrero)

blessing "Aché," which is a key phrase in Afro-Cuban culture and religion. This is symbolic of the African influence in underground hip hop. In the background is a silhouette of José Martí sitting on the lettering "Apostle." He is sometimes referred to as the apostle for foretelling the development of U.S. imperial ambitions. Here NoNo12 combines the past and the present and draws on cultural elements that have been influential in the formation of Cuban underground hip hop as a revolutionary and critical art form, firmly rooted within its own history as well as being located within regional and global social movements (fig. 3.16).

Concluding Thoughts

The ideological intervention of the CUHHM artivists is not only reflected in Black identity politics, lyrics, clothes, music, dance, videos, and other visual media. Knowledge-practices and ideological production are also seen in the language used by the artivists. The participants that I interviewed comment that the CUHHM is the only critical arts scene in which they have heard the term "activist" used to describe their work. The artists' self-identification as activists and the specificity of their activist politics often go unnoticed outside of Cuba's unique political context. For example, track 3 of the album *La FabriK* contains an interlude skit ("Vamos a ser juntos siempre") in which several artists meet with a representative from a North American hip hop magazine. The artists are excited about the opportunity to be interviewed by the magazine and seem to assume that the interchange will actually be a conversation. The artists think that they will have an opportunity to express their political investments, interests, and concerns and to discuss their reality as artists and activists living in Cuba. The interview (in which the interviewer speaks with a North American accent, with no attempt to pronounce the Spanish words correctly) does not go as planned, however, for the artists at least:

Interviewer: Buenas tardes. Um . . . Yo soy Stephanie Miller [*Good afternoon, I'm Stephanie Miller*] . . . Y yo estoy trabajando con *Hot and Spicy Magazine* [*And I am working with* Hot and Spicy Magazine].

Artists: ¿Cómo? [*What?*]

Interviewer: [*Repeats*] *Hot and Spicy Magazine . . .*
[*Artists seem confused.*]

Interviewer: . . . no tenemos mucho dinero para hacer una ummm una presupuesto [. . . *you know that right now we don't have a lot of money to make a, um, contribution*].

Artists: Eh eh [OK OK] [*The artists begin to talk about their thoughts about the project.*]

Interviewer: [*interrupts*] Pero cuando el proyecto salió nos vamos a tener muchos beneficios y vamos a ser juntos siempre. [*But when the project comes out we are going to have a lot of benefits and we are going to be together always.*]

Artists: [*Murmurs*]

Interviewer: [*Again interrupts artists and speaks louder in order to continue her thought.*]

Artists: [*Murmurs*]

Interviewer: [*Interrupts artists and speaks even louder, completely drowning out the voices of the artists in order to continue her thought.*] . . . entonces tengo unas preguntas [*so I'm going to ask you some questions*] . . . I'd like to ask you . . . Disculpa en español, sí. Ummm . . . Yo quiero saber desde cuando hay rap aquí en Cuba [*Sorry in Spanish, yes. Ummm . . . I want to know since when has there been rap here in Cuba?*].

Artists: . . . [*Begin to speak about their work but are abruptly interrupted by the next question.*]

Interviewer: ¿Existe censura en sus textos? [*Is there censorship in your texts?*]

Artists: . . . [*Begin to answer the question with a nuanced answer but are abruptly interrupted by the next question.*]

A friend of Lou Piensa (of the Montreal-based hip hop group Nomadic Massive) who was visiting Cuba at the time plays the interviewer in this piece. As the clip ends, we hear the artists begin to laugh because their Canadian friend has done such a good job imitating the interviews that so many artists have had to endure. In the mock interview, a woman from a magazine called *Hot and Spicy* talks with the artists. Given her accent, she is probably North American.

The name of the magazine indicates that the reporter represents a highly commercialized and seedy hip hop magazine. She says that she is poor and has no money to offer the artists for the interview. Again this is a common trope used by independent researchers and those seeking to make a profit from their interactions with the artists. The artists, trying to get an advantage from every possible moment of artistic dissemination, will often take their chances with people that they know are highly likely to profit from Cuban artists' work, without recognizing them in credits. Additionally, the artists know that they are taking a chance with someone who could possibly misrepresent their words. But they continue with the interview anyway.

The simulated interview reveals the biases and imbalances that Cuban artists face in typical interviews. The reporter claims to be interested in understanding the artists' lives and experiences. The artists initially are very excited, because people don't often care enough to ask them about their thoughts on their experiences and their social context. Once the interview begins, however, the interviewer bombards the artists with questions about repression and about the Cuban government. The artists are not given an opportunity to respond and are never asked questions about *their* experiences. The interview follows the typical trope of going to Cuba to find repression. This is an example of how Cubans' attempts to represent themselves globally are truncated because the nation has been categorized as a Soviet-style totalitarian state and is discursively and economically alienated from the global community.

This simulated interview is an example of a central frustration of CUHHM artists when it comes to news coverage of the movement: their activism is centered on knowledge practices, but that is completely ignored when the interviewer sets the parameters of the discussion and refuses to permit the artists to speak or offer their knowledge or, most importantly, to articulate their context. The very discourse used to initiate the discussion is oppressive. The artists are not white Cuban dissidents who feel that they have been wronged by having numerous privileges (formerly taken for granted) revoked. These artists are speaking from another history and have a perspective on culture that differs from and critiques the views of the Cuban state *and* Western liberal capitalist democracies.

The usage of particular language can itself result in a miscommunication and misrepresentation and be used as a tool to disempower participants and then impose dogma. This leaves the respondents struggling to try to alter the balance of power by bringing to awareness the differences in the nuances and ideas embedded in language so that they can have a simple conversation. Sometimes the respondents just give up, used to being silenced when their voices are not heard.

In the case of this interview, the reporter already knew what perspective she wanted to represent: when an informed, nuanced alternative perspective was about to be articulated, it was cut short and ignored.

This chapter addresses the emergence and development of the CUHHM as a sphere of racialized social critique that offered primacy to the development and public articulation of a post–Special Period Black identity politics. Cuba's racial classification system is centered around three racial categories/identities: Black, mulat@, and white with numerous intermediary categories describing someone's closeness to blackness or whiteness. In order to begin to engage the intervention the movement has made into racial identity politics and anti-Black racism, it is important to think about the significance of whiteness and mulat@-ness as subject positions with material significance. Part of this project entails a more nuanced analysis of terminology and how language is used within its own cultural and regional context. Thus the next two chapters address the specific histories and meanings evoked by racial categories and discourses and the CUHHM artivist lexicon, respectively.

4

Whiteness, Mulat@ness, Blackness
Racial Identities and Politics within the Cuban Underground Hip Hop Movement

The song "El negro cubano" (The Black Cuban) by Soandry del Río is performed by the group Hermanos de Causa:[1]

El negro cubano quiere ser igual que el blanco	The Black Cuban [man] wants to be the same as the white [man]
porque cree que lo oscuro es atraso y lo claro adelanto	because he believes that dark is backward and light is advanced
. . .	. . .
Negro, entiende asere	Black man, understand, homie,
que el mundo es también tuyo	that the world is yours also
tu color y tu pasa son parte de tu raza	Your color and your kinky hair are part of your race
y tu raza y tu pasa tienen que ser tu orgullo	and your race and your kinky hair have to be your pride
negro, tienen que ser tu orgullo	Black man, you have to be your pride

(Translated by Ariel Meilich)

In this song Soandry, artivist and member of the CUHHM group Hermanos de Causa, speaks directly to the internalized racism of Black Cubans. The Black Cuban wants to be the same as the white Cuban, to the extent that he has internalized racism: he thinks lightness of skin is civilized, while associating blackness with backwardness. Soandry also addresses a key aspect of Black corporality: hair as a primary marker for blackness and the presence of stigmatized Africanness. He argues that the Black Cuban should embrace his body, embrace his race, embrace his hair. Those primary markers of shame and stigma, manifested in racist jokes, should be a source of pride. Soandry ends the song by arguing that Black Cubans should also remember that the world is theirs.

Etián "Brebaje Man" Arnau Lizaire talked about Cuba's racial classification system in an interview in Havana in 2010:

> Y eso aquí funciona así: aquí hay racismo del blanco para el negro, principalmente. Del negro con el blanco no se ve mucho: existe, pero no se ve mucho. Del blanco con el negro, del negro con el blanco. Entonces están los mestizos. El mestizo ... mira al blanco desde abajo, o sea, mira al blanco de abajo para arriba, y mira al negro de arriba para abajo. ¿Viste eso? El mestizo nada más que se ve un poco más claro. Dice, "Bueno, no soy más claro que este, no ... ¡Pero soy más claro que éste!" Wow, entiendes, se crea una mecánica ahí, rara. Una mecánica rara. Para mí, el racismo, en todas sus direcciones, es una cosa, para mí, verdaderamente estúpida. Vaya, yo, a mí me da risa. A mí me han pasado incidentes racistas fuertes.

> And this here it works like this: there is racism from white people toward Black people, in the first place. You don't see much racism the other way around. It exists, but you don't see much of that. From white people toward Black people. So, there are the mestiz@s, mixed. The mestiz@ looks up at white people from below, or rather, looks at the white from below to up above, and down at Black people from up high to below. Did you see that? The only difference is that mestiz@s, are a little bit "lighter." And he says, "Well, I'm not lighter than this guy ... but I'm definitely lighter that that guy! Wow!" So there is a strange mechanism going on there. A strange mechanism. For me, racism, in every direction, is something that is really stupid. It makes me laugh. I've had problems because of racism, strong incidents.

Much of the book focuses on Black identity and identity politics in post–Special Period Cuba. The text also situates contemporary Cuban Black identity and identity politics as being in conversation with Black identity politics throughout the Americas. There is significant feedback among the countries around the Caribbean, including the U.S. South and Brazil. In talking about racialized social structures, where racial identities and hierarchies are imbued with coloniality, however, it is important also to consider the other racial classifications of Cuba's racial hierarchy and racialized social structure and economy. This chapter seeks to contribute to the small but emerging body of literature that analyzes the social and material significance of whiteness as invisible in Cuba. The silence concerning them implicitly supports the naturalization of whiteness and mulat@ness as an invisible, unmarked subjectivity, as opposed to markers of power dynamics that are central to the reproduction of Cuban society.

I begin here by discussing whiteness, mulat@ness, and blackness in Cuba and then turn to activist social movement discourses. I offer reflections throughout on the specifically regional but also transnational meanings of race in the Cuban context. The chapter ends with a discussion of the way in which my particular approach to race challenges existing scholarly tendencies in studies in and of the Americas. As Mark Q. Sawyer (2005) notes, Cuba has multiple racial classifications. As a result of Cuba's racial history, the mulat@ category symbolizes Cuban multiculturalism. Although social benefits are associated with mulat@-ness, the economic costs indicate that mulat@ness is a *kind* of blackness, as CUHHM writer, producer, and DJ Ariel Fernández argues later in this chapter. I focus on these categories as the primary nodes in Cuba's racial classification system, while exploring the various ways in which they co-constitute one another.

Whiteness

Olivia Prendes Riverón of the group Las Krudas CUBENSI is socially interpellated and classified as a white woman in Cuba. Olivia is staunchly antiracist. The particularity of her antiracism has its basis in the history of Cuba's anticolonial and anticapitalist social movements (Ferrer 1999; Moore 1997). It should not be assumed that her antiracism is the same as the antiracist consciousness of white U.S. women: that would mean analyzing her identity out of its particular context. While she has her own perspective on the experiences of Cuban women, she has worked closely with fellow Las Krudas members Odaymara Cuesta Rosseau and Odalys Cuesta Rosseau (known as Wanda) to center their activism on elucidating the experiences of Black women (figs. 4.1, 4.2). When Olivia speaks about the difficulties facing Black women, she is acutely aware of the privileges that she has received as a white woman in Cuba. She is very careful not to speak *for* Odaymara and Wanda, both of whom are Black. Olivia tends to focus on her intersectional experience as a poor lesbian who (though white) grew up materially poor and in a marginalized and isolated Afro-descendant nation. When people question her about the particular experiences of Black women, she says that they should talk to Odaymara or Wanda.

In a 2005 interview in Havana, I pointedly asked Olivia about her racial identification and what that meant for her participation in the Cuban Underground Hip Hop Movement:

Tanya: Yo tengo otra pregunta. Me has dicho de la historia de Krudas desde las hermanas, pero ¿para ti cuál es la historia tuya dentro de este grupo?

Figure 4.1. Odaymara Cuesta Rosseau (*center*) and Olivia Prendes Riverón (*right*). (Photo by Tanya L. Saunders)

Figure 4.2. Olivia Prendes Riverón (*left*) and Odaymara Cuesta Rosseau (*right*). (Photo by Tanya L. Saunders)

Por ejemplo, hablas mucho sobre negritud o cosas negras, pero ¿tú cómo te identificas, como una mujer negra o qué?

Olivia: Mira, para mí . . . , o sea yo respeto mucho la afrodescendencia y yo sé perfectamente que no soy afrodescendiente. Yo soy una mujer latina y yo siento que puede en algún momento haber en mis raíces algo que me una de alguna manera a cualquier parte de la tierra. Pero yo nací en Guantánamo, que por densidad de población es la provincia de mayor cantidad de población afrodescendiente. Y desde niña estudié y viví entre gente negra y sentí mucho respeto, a pesar de que mi familia no se enseñó a respetar.

Tanya: Por ejemplo.

Olivia: No, mi familia es una familia de personas que casi todas sus amistades son blancas, o se casan entre blancos y blancas, su descendencia es casi siempre blanca. O sea, mi mamá tenía once hermanos, de los once hermanos, uno tuvo un hijo con una mujer negra y ese muchacho negro se crió con mi mamá. Ese es como el único hombre negro que hubo en mi familia hasta donde yo crecí ahí. Todas las demás diez personas se casaron entre blancos y tuvieron hijos blancos o algo así. Mi mamá y mi papá se considera mi papá blanco y mi mamá se considera blanca. Yo me miro al espejo y veo mi nariz y veo mis facciones y me veo y me siento como diferente a muchas personas blancas que tienen rasgos finos, algo así. Yo tengo mis rasgos anchos y mi pie grande y, no sé, siento que hay algo así como dice Lala que pudiera haber, quién sabe en alguna parte de las Islas Canarias que están tan cerca de África. Entonces, yo tampoco que gusta decir que soy mestiza, porque eso no me gusta, pero tampoco nunca diría que soy blanca, jamás.

Tanya: ¿Por qué?

Olivia: A mí me gusta el término aborigen, porque nací aquí en esta isla que está apartada del mundo, encerrada dentro de su propia soledad y para mí soy un poco una aborigen, una nativa de aquí de Cuba. Y me identifico también mucho con la gente que llegó aquí de alguna manera antes o después de la colonización, qué importa. De hecho, mi familia por parte de madre no tiene sus raíces en España directamente, se pierden las raíces ahí en los montes de Guantánamo. Así que pueden ser indígenas, quién sabe.

Tanya: Explícame la importancia o el papel de raza en la música de hip hop.

Olivia: Mira, cuando nosotras empezamos a hacer música, yo estudié teatro y estudié actuación, y tenía como mucha iniciativa para escribir y para protagonizar los performance y mis mujeres, Krudas, me educaron a mí en una conciencia de respeto al protagonismo de la raza negra dentro del hip hop y al equilibrio en cualquiera de los casos del discurso entre, por ejemplo, lo que pudiera representar yo con esta piel tan pálida y lo que representan ellas como mujeres negras. Entonces para mí fue una escuela, Krudas ha sido una escuela de respeto y de ceder protagonismo todo el tiempo, porque hip hop es a nuestro ver, de la única cultura contemporánea, las poquísimas culturas que tiene protagonismo para las razas oprimidas, en este caso fundamentalmente la raza negra. Yo pienso que todas las personas blancas que gusten de hip hop o hagan hip hop tienen que tener eso muy consciente y dejar a un lado sus necesidades de ser protagonista para sentir como la necesidad de hacer, como de ceder todo el tiempo el protagonismo a quienes son dueñas y dueños de esta cultura.

Tanya: I have another question. You have told me the history of Krudas from the sisters' [perspective], but what is your history within this group? For example, you talk a lot about blackness or Black issues, but how do you identify, as a Black woman or what?

Olivia: Look, for me . . . or better, I really respect Afro-descendants and I know perfectly that I am not Afro-descendant. I am a Latina woman, and I feel that in whatever moment to have in my roots something that for me is from whatever part of this earth. But I was born in Guantanamo, that by density of population is in the province with the largest Afro-descendant population. And since I was a child I have studied and lived among Black people and I feel a lot of respect for those whom my family taught me not to respect.

Tanya: For example.

Olivia: No, my family is a family of people almost all of whose friends are white, or they marry within white men and women, and their descendants are almost always white. Or better, my mother has eleven siblings. Of those eleven siblings, only one had a child with a Black woman, and that little Black kid grew up with my mother. This is the only Black man that has been in my family until I grew up there. The rest of the ten siblings married within whites and had white children or something like that. My mother and father, they considered my father white and my mother considers herself white. I look at myself in the mirror and I see my nose and I see my features and I see myself and I feel myself to be different from white people who have fine features, something like that. I have my high arches and my big foot and, I don't know, I feel that there is something that, as Lala says could be, who knows in some part of the Canary Islands that are so close to Africa. So I don't like to say that I'm mestiza, because I don't like this, but I will never say I'm white. Never.

Tanya: Why?

Olivia: For me, I like the term *aborigen*, because I was born here on this Island that is apart from the world, enclosed in its own loneliness and for me I am kind of an aboriginal person, a native of here, Cuba. And I identify as much with the people who arrived here in different ways before and after colonization. What does it matter? So my family, on my mother's side, has its roots in Spain directly, and she lost them here in the mountains of Guantanamo. So that way they could be indigenous, who knows.

Tanya: Explain to me the importance of race in hip hop.

Olivia: Look, when we began to make music, I studied theater and I studied production, and I had a lot of initiative to write and to organize performances and my women, Krudas, educated me about consciousness in respect to the protagonism of the Black race within hip hop and to balance whatever discourses within, for example, that which I would represent with this skin so pale and that which they represent as Black women. So, for me, it was an education, Krudas have been an education in respect to and to cede the protagonism all the time, because hip hop is our way of seeing, of the only contemporary culture, of the few cultures that are centered on the protagonism of oppressed races, and in this case fundamentally the Black race. I think that all the white people that like hip hop and that do hip hop have to have more consciousness and to leave aside their need to be the protagonist, to feel the necessity to do it, always to yield protagonism to the ones who are the owners [women and men] of this culture.

In this quotation, Olivia claims U.S. *latinidad* as a way to disidentify with Cuban whiteness. For Olivia, her racial identity is a complicated issue in relation to her racial classification. She grew up in Guantanamo, Cuba, in what is known as the Black and most Caribbean part of the Island. It is the part of Cuba where the 1912 massacre, often referred to as a "race war," occurred. This was where the Cuban Wars of Independence started when landowner Carlos Manuel de Céspedes freed his enslaved workers, the area that Black independence fighter Antonio Maceo liberated from Spain. This part of the Island is also only ninety miles from Haiti. Olivia argues that she is fully aware that she is not Afro-descendant. She also is fully aware that she grew up embedded in Black culture—that is, she did not grow up embedded in hegemonic "Cuban" culture, associated with the lighter-skinned part of the Island that is only ninety miles from the United States.

Olivia rejects her classification as white for three reasons. First, she rejects whiteness culturally—she is not European. She is a "creature," she sometimes says, from the mountains of an isolated island in the Caribbean. She and her partner Odaymara sometimes like to use the term "aboriginal" as a way to point to the uniqueness of Cuban subjectivity. Here they use "aboriginal" instead of "indigenous," which would represent a particular subjectivity and historical experience. Second, Olivia notes that she rejects whiteness because physically she does not look European. Invoking the African history of Spain, she argues that perhaps she is displaying the African roots of her mother's side of the family, who are from the Canary Islands. She also says, however, that people "consider" her father white or describe him that way. Olivia later specified that he was *javao*, a mulat@ category that indicates near whiteness or acceptability into the realm of whiteness (see the next section on mulat@ness). The most questionable part of her manifestation of a family history of miscegenation seems to come from her father, who did not appear to be European enough to be outright classified as white. She also rejects whiteness because of the racism that it represents, in a place where so few people can claim gringo-style whiteness.[2]

While some artists who are socially accepted as white are critical of whiteness, others embrace a raceless discourse typical of revolutionary and prerevolutionary nationalist discourses concerning race, while acknowledging that racial prejudice exists. Other artivists, like many who are accepted as white and may even self-identify as white, live in the space between whiteness and mulat@ness. Sawyer (2005) argues that another aspect of Cuba's racial social structure is based on perceived racial status. Thus an aspect of Cuba's racial classification system functions as a "pigmentocracy." Race matters in determining someone's status in society, and miscegenation has actually created more steps in Cuba's racial hierarchy. Sawyer uses six primary racial classifications: *blanc@, javao(á), trigueñ@, mestiz@,* mulat@, and *negr@.* There are more racial classifications between mulat@ and *negr@* (Black), which define how close someone is to being Black, while the racial classifications between white (*blanc@*) and mulat@ indicate proximity to whiteness. These categories between whiteness and blackness can be classified as a mulat@ or a non-Black, Afro-descendant category. Sawyer notes that although mulat@ness affords some social mobility, it does not mean faring better economically than Black Cubans.

When I asked some of the artists about this finding, I was met with a lot of disbelief. The artists felt that it was impossible that people who fall within mulat@ness were not economically benefiting from racial privilege. Sawyer's work was completed in the early 2000s. Fifteen years later, with the intensification of economically liberalization policies, perhaps the artists are picking up on some dynamics that were not captured just after the effects of the Special Period.

Figure 4.3.   Lourdes "La Cinmarrona" Suárez, 2013. (Photo by Tanya L. Saunders)

Lourdes "La Cinmarrona" Suárez is an example of someone who identifies as mestiza and, given her family background, lives between whiteness and mulat@-ness (fig. 4.3). Unlike Olivia Prendes Riverón, who can speculate about the possibility of African heritage in her family, Suárez's immediate family has Black ancestors. I asked about her thoughts on the role of race within the CUHHM in Havana in 2013:

> Aparentemente yo soy blanca, tú me miras y "ah, ella es blanca," no, es una gran mentira, soy mestiza, ¿entiendes? Porque vengo de un padre negro, de un bisabuelo recontra prieto y tengo seriamente . . . la raza ahí está mezclada porque viene también parte de España . . . o sea la música no tiene color de piel, no tiene raza. La raíz tuya es la que dice cuál es tú música, con cuál música tú te identificas. Y nosotros tenemos una raíz negra, por excelencia, tenemos una raíz árabe también que también es negra, porque el árabe no es negro ni de ojos azules.

> > Apparently I am white, and you look at me and say "ah, she's white," no, it's a big lie, I am mestiza, understand? Because I come from a Black father, from a Black great-grandfather and I have sincerely . . . the race that is mixed there because part comes from Spain also . . . or, better, music does not have a color of skin, it does not have race. Your heritage is that what

tells you what is your music, with which music you identify. And we also have Black heritage, par excellence, we have Arab heritage also that is also Black, because the Arab is neither Black nor blue-eyed.

Here Suárez begins to discuss the lie of whiteness in an Afro-descendant country and culture. She, like Olivia Prendes Riverón, is very much aware of how people classify her in larger Cuban society, despite the way in which she herself may identify and classify herself. Thus people who are classified as white within larger social relations are also aware of how they are perceived, despite how they would like to identify themselves. Recognizing the reality of her cultural history and genealogy, Suárez identifies as mestiza because of her known Black ancestry, but she looks white and is accepted as white. In comparison to Prendes Riverón's discussion of her father, who could be considered white, Suárez talks about her father and her great-grandfather, who are Black. She is conscious of her social classification as white. She is aware, however, that because of her family history the truth is that she falls within mulat@ness, on a racial continuum of blackness. Her artistic name "La Cinmarrona" (the [female] maroon) reflects her identification with her African ancestry, via the image of the Cuban Black revolutionary and liberatory figure of the runaway slave. Suárez also argues that those who appear to be white, including Spaniards from southern Spain and Arabs, who are mestiz@, are also Black. Here she argues that people may not see African ancestry in their skin color but can feel it in terms of the cultural legacies that speak to their soul and spirit.

Suárez's comments also support the thoughts of Cuban scholars such as Joaquín Borges-Triana (2009): Cuba's music scenes do not confer identities on all of their participants but are a major site of social mobilization for people who already have shared identities. This occurs even if they are not conscious of their identification as in some cases or develop an identification as a result of hearing shared experiences being represented within these music scenes. Suárez goes on to say that the flow and the music are part of the orality and musicality passed down to and between Afro-descendant people. Thus hip hop is an Afro-diasporic culture. This shared orality manifested by the flow of African American hip hop artists, Suárez argues, in addition to the discussion of the struggle for liberation, helped Cubans to feel a connection to hip hop. In her longer interview she also talks about Cuba being a Caribbean country, locating the Caribbean as an African, Black, and Afro-descendant space.

The positioning of Cuba as a Caribbean country (which it is) is important here, especially in the analysis of Cuba's racial structure. It shows the limits to the applicability of the way in which whiteness is understood in Latin America, in the analysis of how race is understood within a Caribbean context. Here I turn again to Sawyer (2005): based on his empirical work, Black Cubans believe that other Blacks are attractive and whites tend to find other whites attractive. According to Sawyer, this challenges much of the research that comes out of Latin America, which is used to argue that Black Cubans have largely internalized Eurocentric standards of beauty. Further research on how Caribbean whiteness and blackness are lived and experienced is also needed, in order to situate Cuba within its regional context and avoid reducing it to having more in common with Argentina or Mexico than with Jamaica or Haiti.

The particularities of Caribbean whiteness are also present in Olivia Prendes Riverón's discussion of her experience. She talked about how she was raised in a family where some family members taught their children not to respect Afro-descendants—the very people she grew up around, and the very people she sees when looking in the mirror. But the lightness of her skin, her straight hair, and the place where she grew up allow society to keep secret the possibility that she is also Afro-descendant. Olivia discusses how nearly all of her family members married other whites. To her knowledge, the only Black person in her family is her cousin, who was raised by Olivia's mother. In the end she refuses to identify as white or to even say she is white, both because of her experiences and perceptions of the contradictory nature of Cuban whiteness and out of nationalistic solidarity with Black Cubans and her intense desire to fight all forms of social oppression.

In recognizing the power and privilege associated with whiteness, Olivia Prendes Riverón also learned from her experiences within the CUHHM and from her friends and chosen family within the movement. She noted in our interview quoted above that it has been pointed out to her that as a (white) person raised with social privilege she has to watch her impulse to speak *for* Black people and to take up so much space and visibility that she ends up dominating discourse and space. Olivia argues that those whites who participate within the Cuban Underground Hip Hop Movement have to be aware (despite of their best intentions) of a historical tendency to dominate public space and to co-opt forms of creative expression that were designed to express the experiences and realities of Blacks in Cuba—hip hop being a prime example of a contemporary music culture centered on the Black experience in Cuba. "Cooptation," "appropriation," and the idea of whites stealing from Blacks have a slightly different connotation in Cuba than in the United States and in England, for example, as noted by the Cubanist and musicologist Robin Moore (1997) and Cuban scholar Alejandro de la Fuente (2001).

Figure 4.4.   Mikel El Extremo (*center*) at the Puño Arriba Awards, Havana, 2013.
(Photo by Tanya L. Saunders)

The knowledge of a familial history of miscegenation is central to national discourse and integral in the identification of who is "white" in Cuba versus who is "foreign." This is also central to the process of transculturation,[3] in which bodies and cultural practices are rendered white or whitened in the process of becoming accepted as part of "national culture." Those classified as white are empowered to reaffirm their social position within Cuba's racial structure as well as the social location of those classified as Black or nonwhite. One of the ways for people to distinguish themselves as culturally white is to redefine African cultural legacies as Cuban or non-Black—to appropriate or, as Bacallao argues in his documentary *A Short Radiography of Hip Hop in Cuba* (discussed in chapter 3), steal Black culture. This is also why Bacallao refers to the "white gaze" in the film as a "colonial gaze." This process of cultural appropriation, assimilation, transculturation, theft, or whatever other term Cubans may use to describe it is linked to a longer colonial process in which Cuba's non-European (culturally or physically) whites embedded in the white supremacist social hierarchy—itself a colonial legacy—attempted to address the "Black problem."

This structural dynamic allows antiracist whites in the CUHHM, like Mikel El Extremo (figure 4.4), Edgar (of the group Doble Filo), La Cinmarrona, Olivia Prendes Riverón, and others to fight alongside mulat@s and Black Cubans. They realize that "anti-Black racism is the fulcrum of white supremacy."[4] These artists still work to challenge racialized social inequality without speaking *for* those classified as nonwhite, while other whites reproduce social inequality through appropriation. This is discussed in detail in the concluding chapter and is now a concern for many "old-school" Cuban artists.

Mulat@ness

The figure of "La Mulata" is considered to be the physical embodiment of white and Black/African and European racial and cultural union, representing the Cuban nation (Kutzinski 1993). She also represents what many scholars claim to be a fluid racial category in which, depending on how "European" (a reference to race and style) biracial people appear, they can participate in white-only spaces and predominantly Black spaces. La Mulata serves as a way to dismiss white Cubans' historically based fears of a national race war, in which the large African and Afro-descendant population would take over the Island and establish a Black republic like Haiti (Arroyo 2003; Fernández Robaina 1994; Ferrer 1999; Helg 1995).

Cuba's white elite began to imagine a national racial union and an end to race, represented by the mulata's mixed-race body. Vera Kutzinski (1993) argues that La Mulata symbolizes the sexual availability of Black female bodies to white men. Hence, according to Kutzinski, the mulata represents sexual and gender deviance by virtue of her race. Her Africanness makes her a hypersexual woman who supposedly seduces honorable white men to act on their "deviant" sexual desires. In Cuba's racialized sex/gender system, the idealized woman is white, representing purity, honor, and motherhood, and is considered the natural and appropriate object of sexual desire. The mulata is tolerated by virtue of being partially white, but she represents a fallen woman because of her African ancestry. At the other extreme is the opposite of white femininity: the Black woman.

The Black woman represents absolute sexual and gender deviance because of her race. She is considered to be so unfeminine that she is perceived as masculine or even as a deformed male, with the physical characteristics of a prostitute described in nineteenth- and early-twentieth-century sexological literature (with large genitalia and an insatiable sexual desire and libido, potentially a rapist of men and women) (Helg 1995; Kutzinski 1993). La Mulata is also queer. As Siobhan Somerville (2000) notes, early definition of the sexual invert (later called a homosexual) was someone who had interracial sexual desire (Arroyo 2003; Kutzinski 1993).

Studies such as Jafari S. Allen's work addressing Black and mulato gay and bisexual men and *transvestis* (men who dress as women and pass as women but typically do not identify as transsexual women) and my work addressing lesbian and bisexual women have analyzed the erotics of Black and mulat@ racial classification and identification through an examination of the significance of race and racial identity within queer communities in Cuba. This work offers a perspective on how racial identities are internalized and enacted in the making of sexualized subjects; sexuality is at the core of identify formation.

Allen's book ¡Venceremos? (2011) is a much-needed and long-overdue text that addresses the relationship between the erotics of Black racial identity formation, Cuban cultural politics, Cuban state discourse, and actual lived realities. It is an excellent contextualization of queerness within Cuba's longer racial and gender history. Allen's chapter entitled "Discursive Sleight of Hand: Race, Sex, Gender" offers a queer reading of the way in which *mestizaje* functions as a whitening discourse in Cuba. Allen (2011) notes how celebrated white Cuban intellectuals, specifically Fernando Ortiz with his notion of transculturation, are complicit in encouraging the acceptance of *mestizaje* as a cultural fact and cultural ideal: "the celebration of mestizáje is the celebration of Black holocaust" (48):

> The process of transculturation takes two phases: one is deculturation, or the loss of culture, and the other is neoculturation. The former is the loss of a group's original culture(s), and the latter is the adoption of a new culture that is born of contact with other culture(s). Rather than seeing transculturation in terms of a value-free cultural process, therefore, I want to consider it as another sort of imperial or (neo)colonial project. Although it takes place in the margins of the Caribbean and Latin America, this recasting of *mestizaje*, seeking as it does the production and maintenance of more "whitenesses" at the same time that it reserves the privileges of masculinity, is no less a (neo)colonial project. (47)

Here Allen is referring to the way in which African elements are taken up and signified as something else (as mulat@ or creole culture) and thus rendered invisible, while European elements are highlighted and embraced as positive cultural attributes. This aspect of Cuban cultural appropriation (see chapter 2) reflects Rensoli's comment at the beginning of the book: Cuba defines itself as a mestiz@ nation, an identity that is wrapped up in European humanist discourse. It gives the illusion of being inclusive but includes elements of difference. Cuba was never a mestiz@ nation: in terms of cultural legacies, it is largely an Afro-descendant/Afro-diasporic nation. Thus people of African descent are defined out of existence within their own nation.

In the chapter entitled "The Erotics and Politics of Self-Making," Allen highlights the way in which discourses concerning *mestizaje* play out in the erotics of queer self-making in describing the transformation of Octavio into the *transvesti* Lili:

> Though he and his mother share a rich brown skin color, Octavio cannot even imagine being a tobacco-colored woman. Thus, Octavio's transformation from man to woman is attenuated by *color drag* from negro to mulata. Octavio must extend the suspension of disbelief that a man can be(come) a woman, to a tobacco-colored man be(com)ing a mulata. First, liquid foundation makeup and powder two or three shades lighter than Octavio's skin color is applied. Lili draws lips covering only two-thirds of Octavio's actual lips and brushes on—"never draws on"—eyebrows that accentuate eyes that are *"poco* China" (a little "Chinese looking"). A straight wig, or "wet-and-wild" hair extensions, braided at the base and then combed out and spritzed with water for the appearance of natural curls, *bring out* the phonotypical features that suggest mulatáje. (78–79; emphasis in the original)

Octavio could not even imagine that becoming a beautiful woman meant that he could be a beautiful dark-skinned woman. His feminine transformation, his feminine drag, also required what Allen calls "color drag." This involved eliminating anything culturally associated with Black femaleness (changing hair texture and skin tone). As Ariel Fernández says later in this section, mulat@ness is a kind of blackness. I would add it is another kind of blackness, one that is rendered invisible. Thus for Black *transvestis* the process of transforming into femininity lies in racial transformation as well.

The perception of Black women as the embodiment of masculinity is internalized by Cuban women, including lesbians and *transvestis*: Black women are not as desired as white and mulata women because they are interpellated as men, as unfeminine and not beautiful. Black women are encouraged to manage perceived female masculinity or hypersexuality by straightening and elongating their hair, losing weight, and wearing clothing that minimizes the visibility of their bodies.

When I first arrived to Cuba, younger, thinner, and with straight hair, I was referred to as a mulata. When I began going to Cuba heavier and with an Afro, however, I was referred to as *negra*. As scholars have noted, racial classifications in Cuba are based on a combination of physical attributes. The comments that I experienced in public could be understood as reinforcement of my racial classification in Cuba. Women explicitly drew attention to the physical characteristics that framed my blackness and then offered suggestions on those characteristics that I could potentially change for the better and possibly change my racial classification—although not to a classification that falls into the realm of whiteness—but changes that could help me enter into the realm of nonblackness.

In the same way that whiteness is linked to coloniality, it is also important to understand the colonial roots of another persistent aspect of Cuba's racial structure: "mulat@cracy." This term refers to the way in which the idea of *mestizaje*, represented by the image and racial category of the mulat@, serves in discourse as a way to render invisible Cuba's African corporal and cultural heritage. The existence of the mulat@ affirms the ideology of racial intermixture and of a national culture that is increasingly less Black or African but is close to being white. Mulat@ness offers some segments of the population marginally better social access in some areas and what is culturally perceived as greater social acceptance. As many mulat@s argue, however, they continue to face racial discrimination, with no evidence in the post–Special Period that they benefit economically from their mulat@ status (Sawyer 2005). Some who are classified as mulat@ may experience feelings of marginalization because they are not completely accepted by either Blacks or whites. Some mulat@s identify with blackness, while some identify with whiteness or nonblackness (by rejecting African culture and physical characteristics).

An incident recorded in my 2004 field notes reflects on the experience of being mulat@:

I was sitting in Las Krudas' apartment when Alejandra walked in.[5] Odaymara and Olivia were in the kitchen preparing a vegetarian dinner, Marta and I were playing chess. Alejandra is a queer woman: she kept herself skinny so that her chest would remain flat, she had a beard, dark brown loosely curled hair, and was cinnamon colored when tan. I often wondered if FTM [female to male transsexual] had existed as a possibility within the lesbian community at this point in Cuba, if she would be a transman.

We were talking about my work in Cuba, about being Black. Odaymara came out of the kitchen to participate in the conversation at times, Olivia stayed in the kitchen, Marta stayed quiet. Alejandra weighed into the conversation, at times interrupting Odaymara. After listening to Alejandra talk for a while, I said to her, "Yeah, I hear what you're saying. But I have a question, you're talking about being Black, right?" She responded yes. "OK," I said, "remember, I'm not Cuban, and the racial system in the U.S. is different. But here in Cuba, are you considered mulata?" She paused and smiled; I saw a twinkle of recognition in her eye. At that moment, Marta smiled and giggled, I heard Olivia say, "OOOOOOhhhhh!!" loudly and shift in her seat. Odaymara laughed loudly. "No, no no," Alejandra began saying, while smiling. Odaymara came running out of the kitchen. "Nooohhhh!" Odaymara said to Alejandra. "Tell her. Tell her," Odaymara said, laughing while waving a wooden sauce spoon at Alejandra. "Tell her what it's like for you, 'Black woman,'" Odaymara said, laughing while returning to the kitchen. Alejandra broke down, "Look. Yes, I'm a mulata. But there's no difference between mulat@s and Blacks." Odaymara returned to the room. "Nooo. You mean to tell me that there is no difference? Ay chica, there is! You mean to tell me that if a Black person and a mulata. . . ." They began to compare experiences. Alejandra began to talk about some of her experiences with racism. At one point in the conversation, people showed their Cuba identification cards. Their mulat@ status was actually noted on their Cuban identification cards! I remembered another point when another friend showed me her Cuban identification card and under race the word *tribueña*—a term for a deeply tanned looking Afro-descendant person with straight Black hair and "European" features—was written. Marta, also mulata, shifted on the bed and sighed during the conversation. At moments, Alejandra agreed with Odaymara about her having more social privileges than a Black woman, but at the end of the conversation Alejandra commented: "But look, at the end of the day, I'm not white. I'm not always treated with respect like white people are. At times, I am treated the same as a Black person. But remember, I face challenges from both sides, I also have challenges from Blacks who do not like me because I'm not Black, they assume that I want to be with whites, or they resent that I can move through space a little easier than they can. But I'm still discriminated against. I'm still not white." Odaymara nodded, "It's true," she said, going back to help Olivia finish dinner. That conversation was one of the most interesting conversations I'd had in Cuba. It was then that I realized the importance of trying to understand what a "mulat@" is.

The position of the mulat@ in Cuban society is empirically under-researched, as are the position and experiences of being Black in Cuba. Nonetheless it is an importantly symbolic and tenuous subject position within Cuba's racial hierarchy. In another first, the CUHHM was one of the few spaces that openly discussed interracial dating and mulat@ identity in Cuba.

The following is an excerpt from a popular song "Achabon Cruzado" by Joel Pando Heredia, performed by Amenaza (1997), which directly addresses the question of mulat@ness, a hot topic that emerged early on in a movement that many saw as a Black social movement:

También soy Congo,	I am also Congo,
también fui esclavo,	I also was a slave
también mi esperanza sufre para aquellos que el racismo no ha acabado,	Also my hope suffers for those that racism has not ended,
soy rumba, Yoruba Andavo,	I'm rumba, Yoruba Andabo,
y no acabo hasta ver lo mío multiplicado,	and I will not stop until I see that which is mine multiplied,
no ves que soy pinto, achavon cruzado,	don't you see, I'm painted achabon cruzado[6]
negro como el danzón,	Black like *danzón*,
el són cubano,	Like Cuban *son*,
negro como esta mano,	Black like this hand,
negro como mi hermano,	Black like my brother,
negro como Mumia	Black like Mumia,
y negro como muchos blancos más quién lo diría y no me cuentas,	Black like many whites but only those who would say it and don't you tell me,
desafía, raza mía . . .	challenging, my race . . .
(Dijeron, dijeron, dijeron)	(They said, they said, they said)
Dijeron negro pero a mí no me contaron.	They said Black but they don't count me.
Dijeron blanco pero en ese clan no me aceptaron.	They said white but that clan doesn't accept me.
Uh-huh.	Uh-huh.
Dijeron tantas cosas,	They said so many things,
soy el ser que nadie quizo,	I'm the being that nobody wanted,
lo negro o lo blanco,	the Black or the white
el grito de un mestizo.	the cry of a mestizo.

(*Permission given by Joel Pando Heredia/Translated by Ariel Meilich*)

In this song the singer Pando from the group Amenaza directly addresses the critiques in the movement of the time concerning race and more specifically Pando's status as a mulato. The origins of the song have to do with Amenaza's status as one of the most talented CUHH groups before 1998. The members of the group were mulat@ and white, though one of the artists who fell within the realm of whiteness could be classified as *javao*. From the perspective of Black artists, the members of the group had never experienced racism. So there was an unspoken ambivalence toward the group. In response Amenaza, known for singing songs about girls and partying, decided to make an intervention into the discourses concerning race within Cuban Underground Hip Hop. In the song

Pando addresses his contradictory experience as a mulato. It is an in-between space where others are always trying to tell him what his identity is, what his subject position is, and to which racial group he belongs. In his experience, he is never fully accepted anywhere. In the song he claims "the Black experience" and argues that mulat@s also suffered the traumas of slavery. Pando also has to live with the pain of seeing those that he loves and cares about, people who are close to him, dealing with racism. He even challenges the legitimacy of whiteness and the difficulty that mulat@ness poses to Cuba's racial structure when he says, "Black like the whites who will admit it, challenging, my race [my race is a challenge]." Within the Cuban Underground Hip Hop Movement, it is common for people who are socially classified as mulat@ also to identify as Black. The discourse surrounding a mulat@ claiming a Black identity centers on three points: an antiracist solidarity in which the person identifies with the struggle of Black family members or an intimate partner; a cultural embracing of blackness through religious traditions and other forms of an African cultural heritage; and a rejection of whiteness, specifically white supremacy, given their own experiences of racism and in-betweenness.

I asked Ariel Fernández about this at the El Proyecto Conference at Lehigh University in Bethlehem, Pennsylvania, in 2008:

Tanya: I was asking if more or less, you could talk a little bit about the relationship between being Black and mulat@ and the identity that mulat@s have within the hip hop movement.

Ariel: I understand. She is talking about different types of blackness. Different stages [aspects] of blackness, you know, I mean, I think blackness really is a political action, or a political statement I mean, I definitely think that color of the skin definitely makes things more difficult in life, especially for someone who is darker than me, and it's the most difficult thing, I mean that, I am not 100 percent Black, you know what I mean, and I realize that. I've got Black blood and I've also got white blood, you know what I mean, and in my case it is very interesting because I'm not interracial because [of] a rape case, I'm interracial because a Black woman who was my mother decided to marry a white man who was my father, you know what I mean, but at the same time my father was white, who wished to be with my mother, you know what I mean, race is a really complicated thing.

... but at some point when I see myself that I am Black but also white at the same time, and I ask myself, if I have to choose a side of who I am, that needs more work to get done, if I need to decide which side of my identity needs to get more justice, needs to get more recognition, needs to get more fought for, you know what I mean, I choose my Black side because I recognize there is more work to get done for Black people than white people right now, you know what I mean, I mean for me to call myself Black is not only recognizing the blackness that is in me but also saying where is the part of me that I stand for? You know what I mean, and I think that's a political action and a political context that you make a decision: this is the cause that I want to take, you know what I mean, this is the fight that I'm going to do, you know what I mean, so I mean we are discussing how Black you are, at some point, it makes sense but it's not really what defines your blackness, you know what I mean, and that's how I see that, and for me it is difficult because sometimes, you know what I mean, because I talk so specially about blackness and sometimes people say why are you talking so specially about Black you're not so dark Black, you know, that's difficult! Because sometimes I have more pressure to talk about blackness with people who are more Black than me but you know to be aware that, you know, what is your stage [your platform] to talk about being Black, you know what I mean, what are your limitations and what is your privilege too, you know what I mean, and you handle it, and you fight and you choose the battle, you know what I mean.

In this quotation Fernández, one of the formative members of the Cuban Underground Hip Hop Movement, argues that embracing a Black identity means embracing a political identity. He challenges the stereotype of "mulat@-ness" being solely a product of violent rape—a product of a perverse or undesired sexual encounter—to argue that his existence was the loving choice of his parents. This is something that Pando discusses in the song "Achabon Cruzado." One of the ways in which mulat@ness is stigmatized and is also used as a way to stigmatize all interracial sexual relations as being perverse and violent. This reduces the African body to an object of violence or the illicit seduction of white men (in the case of women) and reinforces the discourse of Black violent aggression and sexual undesirability. In other words, in addition to carrying the stigma of being Afro-descendant, mulat@s have also come to symbolize rape.

Fernández also argues that he chooses to identify with blackness as a way to fight against racism, to support the part of his family that is still being oppressed. He notes his privilege as someone who is light-skinned, which indicates that he is multiracial. Fernández argues that he recognizes that people with darker skin have it tougher and also recognizes that hip hop is a movement centered on addressing the experiences of Black people, who do not have the ability to choose their racial identification or have limited tools to navigate it. In acknowledging this, Fernández, like Olivia Prendes Riverón, notes the importance of people who are not Black being aware of their privileges and making sure that they respect the space open to those who are classified as and live as Black people to be able to articulate and express their experiences and needs. Those who are not classified as Black have to know when to cede the stage and to understand their limitations when they join Blacks in an antiracist struggle.

The themes of history, choice, and in-betweenness were key throughout my interviews. In order to obtain a better idea of how to identify who is mulat@, I asked several artists and music officials how one describes a mulat@. Grisel Hernández Baguer, the former vice-president of the Cuban Agency of Rap, said the following in our 2005 interview in Havana:

> No sé cómo explicarte eso. Como diríamos viene de atrás, de hace mucho tiempo. . . . A ver yo creo que eso es un problema del caribe como tal, porque puede pasar en Brasil . . . en Jamaica, Dominicana, Puerto Rico. Como mismo puede ser mulata con un pelo bueno, como dirían pelo más lacio, o con un pelo más malo. O más trigueñita o más . . . tú eres así no estás muy definido. No sé explicarte, eso es un problema. A ver, se dice que mulata es la mezcla de todas las razas, del indio, del chino, del negro y los españoles. . . .
>
> Una sopa, un asopao, como dice Fernando Ortiz. Entonces tú sabes qué pasa. Que para los blancos, no pensaba te digo ahora, la mulata es el fruto, no sé como decir. Es como aquella cosa que se creó en el caribe. Es una cosa que no es ni europea, ni africana, no es del indio, ni el indígena latinoamericano, no es el negro africano, no es el blanco europeo. Es un producto caribeño. Entonces es la cosa aquella intermedia. . . . Pero creo que son patrones que todavía quedan de racismo, de mentalidad racista. Es como el medio, para el negro un poquito más adelantado y para el blanco también, no es el negro, es un poquito más adelantado. Es una cosa social ahí que es así, que ya es tan natural así que. . . .
>
> Fíjate tú te has dado cuenta y nosotros vivimos con eso y sí yo me doy cuenta, sé que eso pasa, pero no soy consciente de eso. Es una cosa natural, te das cuenta, no sé cómo decirte. Como mismo hay mulatos que son muy racistas y rechazan a los negros porque yo soy más clara, y los negros, bueno, qué se cree este, se cree que es blanco. Es un problema que llega a ser un problema en algunos momentos y en otros momentos no es un problema.

> I do not know how to explain that. As we say it comes from way back, from long ago. . . . Let's see, I think that's a problem in the Caribbean as

such, because it can happen in Brazil . . . in Jamaica, Dominican Republic, Puerto Rico. You can be a mulat@ with good hair, that's what they call straighter hair, or with a bad hair. Or *trigueñita* [darker], or more like . . . you are like this, you're not too defined. I don't know how to explain it to you, it's a problem. Let's see, it is said that the mulat@ is a mixture of all races, Indian, Chinese, Black, and Spaniard. . . .

A soup, a stew, as Fernando Ortiz says. Then you know what happens. That for white people, I haven't thought about it, I'll tell you, the mulata is the fruit, I don't know how to explain it. It's like the thing that was created in the Caribbean. It's something that is neither European nor African, not Indian or Latin American, it's not from Black Africa, it's not white European. It is a Caribbean product. So it's that intermediate thing. . . . But I think that they are guardians of what remains of racism, of a racist mentality. It's like halfway there, for a Black person that is a little more advanced and for white people too. It's not Black, but a little more advanced. It's a social thing there that is like that, and it's so natural already, so . . .

Just look at this: you have realized the situation, and we live with it, and yes, I realize it, I know that this happens, but I'm [also] not aware of it. It is a natural thing, you realize, I do not know how to explain it. Like there are mulat@s that are very racist and reject Black people because they see themselves as being "lighter" or paler, and the Black people, well, they say, "What does this girl think? That she is white?" It is a problem that can be a conflict sometimes and at other times is not even a problem.

Here Dr. Hernández Baguer points out several important aspects of mulat@ subjectivity: mulat@s have limited ability to choose how to negotiate their blackness. Some may say that mulat@s have the ability to choose to be white. I would argue, however, that the choice that mulat@s have is to choose not to be Black: they cannot choose to be white. By living in the liminal space of not being Black, mulat@s are able to enjoy some of the social, though not always economic, privileges afforded to those who are not Black, as blackness is the fulcrum of race thinking and racism in the Americas. Hernández Baguer also points out that some physical characteristics are associated with mulat@ness: she uses the common term *adelantado* (advanced). She refers to Fernando Ortiz's notion of Cuba as an *ajiaco* or stew—where all of the different distinct cultural flavors and races blend together to make that which is Cuban. All of these are allusions both to the national myth of racial mixture and to the notion of racial advancement through whitening. All of these ideologies are playing together at once in Hernández Baguer's attempt to describe and contextualize what is mulat@.

The multiplicity of types of mulat@s, classifications that function also as racial categories, gives the impression that racial identity and classification are flexible. But it is important to note that multiple classifications function as racial categories on ID cards, which allude to different kinds of blackness or whiteness. Some people have defined racial classifications which would fall under the category mulat@ on their identification cards (for example, *javá, trigueña*). It takes learned scrutiny to be able to notice and classify the slightest variations in different physical characteristics in classifications that can place people on a path where they are labeled according to the perceived level of racial intermixture. This indicates just how important and how highly valued whiteness is. For example, Hernández Baguer looked at me and commented that I am not that easy to classify. She paid attention to the texture of my hair, which a lot of people ignore when I wear locks or an Afro. Nonetheless, my racial classification changed as my hair changed over the years of doing research in Cuba. When I first arrived in Cuba at the age of twenty I was referred to as a mulata. People sometimes made specific racist remarks about Black people. When I returned with an Afro, however, I was referred to as Black (*negra, negrita*). During this interview I had dreadlocks. As she scrutinized my hair texture and skin tone, Dr. Hernández Baguer's assessment was that I was not easily classifiable as Black. While she went through this analytical process as she tried to answer my question, she commented that she was fully aware that people were operating within racist ideological structures. But at the same time she was unaware of it, because it is naturalized.

The ways to assess who is mulat@ and who is not, says Hernández Baguer, are so subtle and subconscious that people do not even realize that they are doing it. Trying to explain this to someone else is very difficult. Hernández Baguer is not the only one to talk about racism among mulat@s in society and within their own families. As she notes, everyone is fully aware of the historical nature (the coloniality) of Cuba's racial structure. Nearly every time people talked about mulat@ness they began to frame what a mulat@ is by referring to a longer historical context, often the colonial period. For example, MC La Yula, who is socially classified as mulata and identifies as Black, talked about being mulata in our interview in Havana in 2005:

> Los mulatos eran cuando un español estaba con un esclavo o una esclava y surgió el mulato. Pero ese mulato ya no era esclavo, ya ese mulato era para la parte blanca, porque eran los jefes, me entiendes. Entonces ese mulato no era ni esclavo ni español. Simplemente le daban su valor a su color. . . .

Sí, pero es que la gente se basa mucho en los tiempos de antes. Hay muchas personas que todavía, hay muchos blancos que todavía piensan que están en el tiempo de los españoles y siguen tratando al negro como lo que es, es un esclavo. Sin embargo, hay millones de negros que todavía se sienten esclavos y dejan que los blancos los pisoteen. Me entiendes. Eso es lo que realmente uno tiene que tener por encima de lo que es la humanidad. El color no importa, porque tienes la cabeza que yo, tienes los mismos ojos que yo, la misma nariz, la misma boca, la misma forma de pensar, es diferente, pero es una sola. Se piensa porque el ser humano piensa, el animal no piensa, pero el ser humano sí piensa . . . nosotros no deberíamos ser racistas, ni los blancos de los negros, ni los negros de los blancos, ni los blancos de los propios blancos, ni los negros de los propios negros.

> Mulat@s were born when a Spanish man or women joined with a male slave or a female slave. Out came the mulat@. But this mulat@ was not a slave, and this mulat@ was part white, because they were the bosses, do you understand me? So this mulat@ was not a slave or a Spaniard. They always gave value to color. . . .
>
> Yes, but people base a lot on what happened in the past. There are a lot of people that still . . . there are a lot of white people who think that they are in the time of the Spanish and they continue treating Black people like slaves. Nevertheless, there are millions of Black people that still feel themselves like slaves and allow white people to trample them. Do you understand me? That's what you must have really above you, humanity. The color is not important, because you have a head like me, you have the same eyes as I do, the same nose, the same mouth, the same way of thinking, it [humanity] is different, but there is just one. You think because human beings think, animals don't think, but human beings think . . . we should not be racists, not white people owned by Blacks or Black people owned by whites or Black people owned by Black people.

La Yula argues that the racial tensions and classifications come from the colonial period. During this time, Spaniards, creole whites, and mulat@s were free. Africans and creole Blacks were enslaved or equated with being treated as if they were enslaved, even if they were free. The mulat@s were not white and did not enjoy equal privileges with whites. They were part white, however, which had some value: they had social recognition as being human in the way that a Black person was not. La Yula says that a lot of whites still think that they are in the time of slavery and treat Black people as if they are enslaved. She argues that people should get over this colonial mentality, because that relationship is something that happened in the past. People should move beyond the legacies of the colonial system.

While talking about her classification within mulat@ness in our interview in Havana in 2005, DJ Leydis discussed the complicated race dynamics within her racially mixed family:

Tanya: Tengo otras preguntas. OK, primero como tú sabes soy de los Estados Unidos y allá solamente tenemos blancos y negros y algunos asiáticos y algunos los latinos, pero aquí yo creo que tú eres ¿mulata?

DJ Leydis: Aquí es difícil. La gente dice que soy mulata, otros que soy javá, que viene siendo como mestiza.

Tanya: ¿Qué es javá?

DJ Leydis: Mestiza. Pero aquí no hay cultura, no sé la gente. . . . Como por ejemplo, se dice que no hay racismo y sí hay racismo. Hay racismo porque en lugares . . . he llegado a lugares de buenos trabajos, trabajos buenos y es difícil ver a un negro trabajando. Entonces aquí a algunas personas de mi color tú no puedes llamarle negra, pero no creo que exista un negrito más claro o un negrito menos claro o un negro fuerte. No creo que cuando se creó el mundo se creó el negrito menos claro, el negrito menos fuerte, se creó negro, blanco, amarillo o los chinos o no sé. . . . Pero sí, aquí la gente vive sus problemas con la raza. No es negro, no es blanco, es mulatito, javaíto.

Es duro porque el mayor racismo es entre nosotros mismos, entre los propios negros. Porque el racismo de blancos para negros eso ha sido mundialmente siempre me entiende. Decir que un blanco siente racismo por un negro eso es normal. Yo creo que para mí eso no. . . . Pero sí te duele cuando lo ves entre los propios negros. Por ejemplo, muchas personas de mi color sienten racismo por una persona que es más negro que ellas. Como yo que soy más clarita podría vivir, quisiera haberme buscado para tener a mi hija a alguien de mi color para adelantar un poquito la raza a ver si me sale . . . me entiende todas esas cosas.

Tanya: ¿Qué es la diferencia entre mulata y javá?

DJ Leydis: Javá, bueno las mulatas. . . . Normalmente yo siempre he tenido el conocimiento de que las verdaderas mulatas son aquellas personas, tal vez las personas más oscuritas que yo, pero bueno que su pelo no es tan malo. Bueno cualquiera de mi color con un deril [derriere] es una mulata. Pero yo no soy una mulata, yo soy una mezcla de blanco con negro, creo que soy una mestiza. Aquí en Cuba se llama javá. Pero estoy muy orgullosa

por a veces dicen: coño . . . un javao una cosa así. Javao es malo, sabrá Dios
. . . siempre esos dichos que se tienen aquí en Cuba, pero no me interesa.

Como vengo de mezcla blanco con negro casi siempre existe el racismo
me entiende. Estuve, mientras no fui dueña de mí propia para decidir mis
cosas, creo que tuve una ideología, hay que estirarse el pelo y todas esas
cosas. Cuando fui descubriéndome que . . . para ser, por ejemplo, si yo me
consideraba alguien agradable, alguien bonita entiende. Muchas veces yo
llevaba pañuelo yo llevaba turbante yo decía que . . . sigo siendo honesta
con las personas. Quiere decir que aunque no enseñe mi pelo no soy más
fea sigue siendo la misma persona. Fui descubriéndome que el pelo no era
realmente me hacía más bonita o más agradable y entonces dejé mi pelo
como se dice libre. No quise hacer trenzas, no quise hacer moñas, no quise
hacer más na'. . . . Y ahora vivo orgullosa y feliz de los drelos [dreds] que
llevo.

Tanya: Como te dije, es posible que, puede aparecerte una pregunta un poquito tonta, pero es para entender más. Generalmente hay mucha gente
que dice que no hay razas, que hay solamente cubano. Si esto es normal
¿cómo es posible que la gente diga que hay racismo? porque podría ser
una cosa u la otra. . . .

DJ Leydis: Yo por ejemplo te lo puedo decir porque yo vengo de una familia
por parte de padre que todos son blancos y mi familia por parte de madre
son negros, negros. Y no quiero hablar fuera de mí, voy hablarte de mí.
Existe el racismo. . . . Porque no me lo dice, pero sé que lo siente, que le
molesta y lo sentí cuando decidí tener una hija con una persona negra
como yo, pero él no lo ve así. El no me dijo porque haces esto, pero lo sin-
tió y cuando nació Erykah. Todos los niños nacen blancos pero, cuando va
a ser negrito desde ya se pone negro.

> Tanya: I have some other questions. OK, first of all, as you already know, I'm
> from the USA, and over there we only have white people, Black people,
> and some Asians, and some Latinos, but I believe that here you are . . .
> mulata?
>
> DJ Leydis: It's less straightforward here. People say that I'm mulata, others
> say that I'm *javá*, which is like being mixed.
>
> Tanya: What does *javá* mean?
>
> DJ Leydis: Mixed. But here there is no culture like . . . I don't know about
> people. . . . For example, it is said that there is no racism here, but there
> is. There is racism because in some places . . . I've had the opportunity to
> work in good places, to have good jobs, and it's hard to see a Black person

working. So, here you can't call some people of my color "Black," but I don't think that there are Blacks, lighter Blacks, or darker Blacks. I don't think that when the world was created there was the lighter Black one, the less Black. It was that Blacks, whites, and yellows or Chinese were created, and that's it, I don't know. . . . But yes, here people have their problems with race. It's not Black, it's not white: it's *multatito, javaíto*.

It's hard, because the greatest racism is among ourselves, among Black people. Because white racism toward Black people, that has been the case worldwide, do you understand? To say that a white man feels racism toward a Black man, that's the norm. I think that to me, that's not. . . . But it really hurts when you see it among Black people. For example, many people of my color feel racism towards someone who is darker than they are. I, for example, I'm lighter, I could go by, so I wish to find someone of my color, to "improve" my race a little bit . . . see what I mean?

Tanya: What's the difference between mulata and *javá*?

DJ Leydis: *Javá*, well, mulatas. . . . Normally I've always understood that the real mulatas are those people, maybe people darker than me, but well, with not such bad hair. Anyone of my color with a *deril* [derriere] is a mulata. But I'm not mulata, I'm a mix of Black and white, I think I'm a mestiza. Here, in Cuba, it's called *javá*. But I'm really proud, because sometimes they say: shit . . . a *javao* or something like that. *Javao* is bad, God only knows . . . those are always the sayings we have here in Cuba, but I'm not interested.

As I'm a mix of white and Black, the possibility of racism is always there, do you understand? As long as I wasn't self-aware to decide about things, I think I had an ideology, you have to stretch your hair and all those things. When I started to discover that . . . to be, for example. . . . If I considered myself someone pleasant, someone nice, get it? Many times I used to wear a scarf, and a turban, and I said that . . . I'm still honest with people. That means that I'm uglier because I don't show my hair . . . I'm still the same person. I started to discover that hair really didn't make me prettier or more pleasant, so I let my hair free, we could say. I didn't want any braids or bows, I didn't want anything. . . . And now I live proud and happy about the dreadlocks I have.

Tanya: As I said, it is possible that . . . well, this may seem like a stupid question, but it's just in order to understand a little bit more. Generally a lot of people say that there are no races, that there are only Cubans. If that's normal, how is it possible that people say there is racism? Because it could be one thing or the other. . . .

DJ Leydis: I, for example, I can say so because I come from a family in which,
on my father's side, they are all white, and my mother's family, they are
all Black, Black. And I don't want to talk about others, I want to talk about
what I think. Racism exists. . . . Because it is not expressed, but it is felt,
it bothers, and I felt that when I decided to have a daughter with a Black
person like me, but he doesn't see it that way. He didn't ask me "Why are
you doing this?" he just felt it when Erykah was born. Every kid is born a
white kid, but when the kid is expected to be Black, she is Black already.

DJ Leydis's discussion of race politics in her family sheds light on a lot of
the complicated dynamics that happen within families in Cuba. In this interview Leydis talked about the racial division within her family. Her father is
prejudiced, but he is married to a Black woman. Before she begins to discuss
his reaction to her decision to have a child with a Black Cuban, DJ D'Boys, she
mentions how her father treated her friends. He would not let them ride in his
car, for example. She mentioned that she could tell that he was disappointed
that she decided to marry a Black man, but he did not say it—such an explicit
statement would be an articulation of racist thinking in a society and a familial
situation that claims *mestizaje*. Additionally, DJ Leydis talked about how she
internalized the ideologies concerning blackness and beauty. Hair is a major
issue in self-esteem, aesthetics, and deciding who is an acceptable, beautiful person. At one point she had internalized the ideology of straightening her hair.
For many mulat@s, straightening their hair can propel them closer to whiteness
and in some cases drastically improve their social privileges or reclassify them
as white or as acceptable in being almost white. For Leydis, this is a complicated
situation. She loves her dad but talks about her father's prejudice, which most
Cubans share, regardless of their racial classification.

DJ Leydis had to unlearn a lot of the internalized ideologies concerning
beauty and self-worth. One of the central ways that she did this was to embrace
her hair, just respect her hair and let it be. The process of rejecting the impulse to
force herself to alter her hair chemically because larger society told her that her
hair is bad hair began with her participation in the CUHHM. As in the case of
many of the Cubans that I interviewed, the very language available to describe
race is imbued with racism. This attests to how ingrained it is in Cuban thought:
Cubans talk about "good skin," "bad skin," "good hair," "bad hair" when talking
about race and racial politics. The usage of the word "bad" to describe the physical attributes attributed to African corporality is so normalized in everyday language that "bad" functions both as an adjective and as a prefix to indicate that
the speaker is talking about anything "African." Leydis also describes what type

of mulata she is classified as in Cuban society: *javá*. She is very light-skinned, has a very slight frame, and is about five foot two. Though she is a mulata, with one white parent and one Black, the lightness of her skin classifies her as Javá.

Blackness

In our interview in Havana in 2005, La Yula summarized the multiplicity of racial identifications within mulat@ness, why some mulat@s chose to identify as white or as Black:

Tanya: ¿Te identificas como negra?

La Yula: Sí, yo me identifico como lo que soy, pero yo soy negra. Mis hijos son negros y mi esposo es negro. Blanca no soy, porque primeramente el color que tengo no es blanco, mi color es entre el negro y el blanco. Y entre el negro y el blanco están los mulatos. Es decir, que como mis padres sus mulatos, yo soy mulata, yo soy negra también.

Tanya: De verdad.

La Yula: Claro.

Tanya: Porque yo estoy aprendiendo sobre las diferencias . . . , no diferencias, pero no puedo pensar en una palabra mejor para decirlo, pero las variedades entre las razas o las personas de aquí, por ejemplo, en los Estados Unidos solamente hay blancos y negros y asiáticos. Pero aquí es blancos, mulatos, negros, . . .

La Yula: Trigueños, javaos.

Tanya: Pero, ¿no eres trigueña?

La Yula: Soy entre trigueña y mulata, como que mis padres son mulatos, pasan por trigueños o pasan por mulatos.

Tanya: Y para ti, he oído que los mulatos pueden decidir más o menos si quieren ser negros o blancos. ¿Esta es una mentira o qué?

La Yula: Los mulatos pueden decidir . . . , sí, sí. Pueden lo mismo decidir yo soy negro que yo soy blanco.

Tanya: Verdad.

La Yula: Claro, claro, porque cuando no es el color es el pelo y pasan por ahí.

Tanya: Y por qué te dices que eres negra.

La Yula: Porque yo soy negra, porque no soy de piel obscura, pero soy negra. Yo soy criolla. Yo no soy blanca, no soy ni africana, ni soy asiática. Ni soy africana ni soy asiática, soy criolla. El criollo tiene un color impermeable, cualquier color. [*Laughter*]

Tanya: Entonces, para que yo pueda entender bien. ¿Cuál es la diferencia entre una persona como tú, porque he conocido trigueñas, o mujeres que se aparecen como tú, que me han dicho soy blanca? ¿Cuál es la diferencia?

La Yula: Ah, bueno ellas quieren ser blancas. La diferencia no es ninguna. La diferencia es que hay negros, blancos y mestizos. Hay tres. Las personas hablan por hablar y dicen por decir. Cada cual tiene su color. Pero hay personas que dicen ser blancas, porque se tiran al blanco, porque son un poquito claras. Y hay personas que son negros y dicen que son mulatos, pero son negros, no son mulatos. Eso es como lo quiera la persona.

Tanya: ¿Por qué dicen...?

La Yula: Ah, porque les gusta decir así, les gusta defender su yo, yo soy así y soy así.

Tanya: Interesante.

La Yula: Yo en mi caso soy negra, porque en mi familia hay negros. En mi familia blancos, blancos no hay, nada más que mi bisuabuela que era gallega. Pero de ahí mi abuela estuvo con un mulato y se mezcló. Y yo estoy con un negro ahora y mis hijos son de mi color, pero tienen de él también, pero es negro ... mi esposo es negro, yo estoy hablando del contexto ahora, no estoy hablando del futuro ni del pasado, yo estoy hablando del presente. En el presente mi esposo es negro y mis hijos son negros y yo soy negra.... Desde que empezó la entrevista, Tanya, me ha hecho la pregunta y le he dicho que yo soy negra, que no soy blanca. Porque tú sabes qué es lo que pasa. Porque la gente tiene miedo que se forme algo y antes decían: No los negros pa' los negros. Tú sabes que antes los españoles eran blancos, los esclavos eran los negros.

> Tanya: Do you identify yourself as Black?
>
> La Yula: Yes, I identify as what I am, and I'm Black. My children are Black and my husband is Black. White I'm not, because first, I have the color that is not white, my color is between Black and white. And between Black and white are the mulat@s. That is, as my parents were mulat@s, I am mulata and I'm Black too.
>
> Tanya: Really?
>
> La Yula: Sure.
>
> Tanya: Because I'm learning about the differences.... I cannot think of a better word to say, but the varieties between races or the people here ... for example, in the United States there are only white and Black people, Asian. But here you have white, mulat@, Black....
>
> La Yula: *Trigueños, javaos.*
>
> Tanya: But aren't you *trigueña*?

La Yula: I'm between *trigueña* and mulata, as my parents are mulat@s, they pass either as *trigueñ@s* or mulat@s.

Tanya: And for you, I have heard that mulat@s can decide about whether to be Black or white. Is this true or what?

La Yula: The mulat@s can decide . . . yeah, yeah. They may as well decide if they are Black or white.

Tanya: Really?

La Yula: Right, right, because if it's not their hair, it's because of their skin color and it goes on from there.

Tanya: And why do you say you are Black?

La Yula: Because I am Black, I'm not dark-skinned, but I'm Black. I am Creole. I'm not white; I'm neither African nor Asian. I'm not African or Asian, I'm Creole. The Creole has a waterproof color, any color [*laughter*].

Tanya: So that I can understand, what is the difference between a person like you . . . because I've known *trigueñ@s*, or women who are like you, who have told me "I'm white." What is the difference?

La Yula: Oh, well they want to be white. There is no difference. The difference is that there are Blacks, whites, and mestiz@s, mixed. There are three. People talk just to talk and say things just to say things. Each has its own color. But there are people who claim to be white, and they throw themselves at whites, because they are a little lighter. And there are people who are Black and say that they are mulat@s, but they're Black, they are not mulat@s. It's just the way the person wants.

Tanya: Why do they say . . . ?

La Yula: Ah, because they like to say it like that, they like to defend themselves, I am like this and I'm like this.

Tanya: Interesting.

La Yula: In my case I am Black, because in my family they are Black. In my family, there are no white people, no more than my great grandmother who was *gallega*, from Galicia. But then my grandmother was with a mulato and she mixed. I am with a Black man now, and my children are of my color, but they have his Black color as well, because he's Black . . . my husband is Black and I am talking about the context right now. I am not talking about the future or the past, I am talking about the present. In the present my husband is Black and my children are Black and I am Black. . . . From the beginning of the interview, Tanya, you have asked me the question, and I have told you I am Black, I am not white. Because you know what happens? Because people have fear, they make up something and before they say: "No, the Blacks for the Blacks." You know that, before, the Spanish were whites, the slaves were Black.

Like all racialized systems in the Americas, the boundaries defining who is classified as what create trouble or problematic ruptures where racial categories become unstable: their artificial, socially constructed nature becomes visible. In Cuba, as in racialized societies throughout the Americas, the racial categories are understood as distinct and are policed in everyday interactions. Given the colonial history of Cuba, in order for these racial classifications to work and have power, the way in which someone is classified and treated in society and self-identification are very important. The variations in identification give racial classifications their seemingly fluid nature. People who reject complicity in anti-Black racist ideology by embracing a Black identity, African physical characteristics, African cultural practices, and even marrying "Blacker" face various forms of affective and material social sanctions. People classified as mulata, *trigueña*, *javá*, and so forth may have various reasons to choose to identify as Black.

In the case of La Yula, part of the reason is that she married a Black man. She is mulata and comes from a family of mulat@s, so she is racially mixed and is therefore treated differently, but most importantly her husband and children are Black. DJ Leydis's identification with Blackness is the result of a process of learning to love herself as she is. She rejected the pressures to straighten her hair, which would indicate that she disliked her African hair and sought to reject her blackness in an effort to move more toward and embrace her whiteness. Ariel Fernández's identification with blackness is based on a recognition of his experiences with racism and choosing to fight for the rights of the side of his family that faces the most social oppression: his Black relatives.

The racial identification of all of the people I interviewed who are socially interpellated as Black or mulat@ and identify as Black resulted from a realization that they are Black and that they have experienced various levels of racism based on their racial classification. If racism is defined in terms of racialized social prejudices and discrimination that have material effects, then racism openly returned to Cuba after the Special Period, while racial identities from the prerevolutionary period continued throughout the revolutionary period. Some people developed their racial identity and understood its social relevance through family members, daily interactions within the larger public sphere, and their own personal experiences or engagement with a consciousness-raising group such as the Rastafari or hip hop movements. Usually it was not something that someone said within these movements that captured the attention of the youths who would become hip hop artivists. It was something about the images that they saw and the beats and rap flow that they heard that sparked them to think and to learn more about themselves and their reality and to do something about it.

Because of the Cuban state's imposition of a raceless discourse and the forced integration of all social spaces, many Black Cubans did not grow up with a racial identity. As discussed in chapter 3, public discussions of persistent racism were discouraged and were seen as potentially counter-revolutionary (de la Fuente 2001; Helg 1995).

In a manner that only appears contradictory, CUHHM artists often critique the Cuban Revolution and the revolutionary state by redeploying its own revolutionary discourse. CUHHM artivists are critical of the state yet support many of the ideals of the Revolution. When they highlight the contradictory aspects of the Cuban state's own discourse, however, they are encouraged and in some cases coerced to be less critical ("less revolutionary") (Navarro 2002). The frustration with the Revolution is particularly intense among the Black middle classes. When I interviewed Michael Oremas of the Junior Clan, he pointed out that in part the CUHHM is a middle-class Black struggle. It took a while for me to understand what he meant by this, but his point became clearer after conversations with other Black Cuban artivists, cultural critics, and professionals.

The 1990s produced a major trauma for a class of Black Cubans who were firmly integrated into what could be called Cuba's revolutionary class. These people had access to Cuba's educational institutions and were part of the revolutionary professional class (doctors, state officials, lawyers, professional artists and academics, the diplomatic corps, and so forth). For the generation that came of age in the 1980s, after Cuba was given preferred trade status by the Soviet Union, it seemed that the racist attitudes of a few individuals did not affect the ability of Black Cubans to be successful in a merit-based social structure. This class of Cubans, specifically Black Cubans, lived an existence free of institutionalized racism. Therefore it made sense to believe that Cuba was fundamentally different from the United States and other countries with large Black populations. A central aspect of racism is the ability of racists to act on their prejudices through the mobilization of micro-aggressions that truncate other people's ability to participate fully in society as materially enfranchised humans.

If Black Cubans who were part of this revolutionary class were called a racial slur as a kid, that was easily ignored: they would succeed if they studied hard and did well in school. In that period there also seemed to be no material differences between races. This supported the idea that what Blackness meant in Cuba was fundamentally different from what it meant globally. For those who lived this Black revolutionary class existence, this reality was formative in the development of their identity and subjectivity. Some Cuban citizens had a different skin color, and people could make jokes about that, but in the end the experience of blackness was only about skin color and not much else. The cultural framing of blackness as a sign for African cultural legacies was also disrupted. Through the Revolution's framing of Cuba as an Afro-European nation, in contrast to the self-definition of the United States as a European nation, some African cultural legacies of Cuban culture were seen as a part of Cuban culture and not a marginal one at that. They were to be celebrated as part of Cuba's discourse of *mestizaje* and the nationalization of mulat@ness (racial and cultural intermixture) as a unifying ideal for the Cuban nation.

For those Black Cubans who grew up as a part of this revolutionary class, the Special Period was a traumatic experience. The reemergence of a racialized class structure created a new situation where the youths of the Black revolutionary class were suddenly confronted with a racialized social structure in which lighter-skinned and white individuals suddenly had the economic "freedom" to discriminate as a result of the state's liberalization politics. The liberalization of the Cuban economy included allowing remittances from abroad and created a dual (dollar-based) economy.

Thus lighter-skinned and white Cubans on the Island began to receive dollars from family members abroad (the first waves of immigrants from Cuba were light-skinned and white). In this context having Black skin began to take on a different meaning, and many of the youths of the Black revolutionary class were forced to struggle to figure that out. Black identity and identity politics were based on a person's economic class and actual location on the Island, especially for those from poor and crime-ridden neighborhoods. Identity politics also depended on whether or not families passed down Black Cuban history and identity in private. Hence hip hop ended up functioning as a Black public sphere in Cuba. A disparate group of people came together to think about and address the newest major economic and subsequently political shift in Cuban history, which directly impacted all Cubans who were visibly of African descent.

Hip hop spurred the public articulation of a Black identity politics for some and the formation of a Black subjectivity for others. The irony is that the development of the CUHHM reinvoked longtime, culturally based fears of a Black political revolution that had the power to destabilize the Cuban state. Rodolfo Rensoli notes that at an early stage the state was fearful that the CUHHM was a cover for a Black Nationalist movement. "They assumed that we wanted to make a 'Black Power [Movement]' against the official power [the state] and now they are starting to see that we are about something else. But how is it, if my people [fellow Cubans] are still part of the problem, that they won't be the center of what I discuss?" (interview in Havana in 2005).

The point is that CUHHM artists' antiracist critique and Black identity politics are inherently revolutionary. As Rensoli puts it, racism is still a problem, so as a critical artist he is going to focus on the people and issues that negatively affect his life. The concern of an impending Black revolution on the Island, however, is linked to the reality that African worldviews and cultural practices continue to be a competing cultural power in Cuba. The non-Western ideological orientation of Cuba's larger population has not been colonialized. CUHHM artists have incorporated cultural themes, music, and religious symbols that are understood to be culturally Cuban and African in origin. These cultural legacies are marginalized in Cuba's public sphere. Artists have publicly embodied/displayed/articulated these cultural legacies as a means to stimulate the public's consciousness as a way to help all Cubans to remember their history, collective work, and collective worth. For Cuba's Eurocentric elite, these cultural symbols are linked to residual discourses that describe African culture as the degenerative non-European elements of Cuban culture.

I call for engaging with a hemispheric understanding of blackness that locates identity firmly in the colonial history of the Americas and the transatlantic slave trade but also considers how this identity plays out regionally and in various local contexts at different moments in history. As such, I agree with Marc Perry's (2008) assertion that "diasporic rather than U.S. understandings of Blackness are in the end instrumental in fashioning critical expressions of a Black Brazilian self. The emphasis here is on dialogic engagements rather than reductive appropriations of Blackness" (641). Understanding the Black self within American nations requires a dialogic engagement with how blackness functions and is articulated and experienced in various contexts and historical periods throughout the Americas. As noted, my views both converge with and diverge from those scholars who would emphasize the fluidity of race in this region.

When we talk about race and racism in Latin America and the Caribbean, we are not necessarily talking about them in U.S. terms simply by virtue of using the language of race, which is a Western (read: American) construct, regionally speaking, with origins in the transnational slave trade in the Americas. But neither are we talking about racial categories and identities so fluid and dynamic that they essentially do not matter. The tendency has been for scholars to focus far too much on the sign (the language of race and racism) without examining what people *do* with that sign, how they speak through the language of race both to maintain and to challenge regionally based systems of power that center on racialized and gendered social hierarchies that support white supremacy and continued European cultural and hegemony in the region. Those who would deny the possibility of talking about race in the region truncate the ability of marginalized populations to develop their own language to articulate and make sense of their particular experiences with race and racialization (as in the case of Bacallao) are dismissed as irrational.

Concluding Thoughts

Throughout this book I strive for a balance thus far missing from most of the discussions of the CUHHM and its context. I seek not only to highlight both the regional and historical specificity of Cuba but also to locate the country and the movement within a system of ongoing transnational cultural and political exchanges that constitute the African diaspora and a hemispheric Black public sphere. The CUHHM, one might say, is distinctly and specifically national, regional, transnational, and global all at the same time, with race operating differently at each one of those levels. Keeping all these analytical strands together is the real challenge of understanding the Cuban Underground Hip Hop Movement. I began this chapter with Soandry's song "El negro cubano." The title of this song is translated "The Black Cuban," but it could also be understood as "The Black Cuban Man," because male gender pronouns are sometimes used generically in Spanish to include women. It is important to note the male-centeredness of this discourse in order to understand the interventions of women artists in the Cuban Underground Hip Hop Movement.

5

"Never Has Anyone Spoken to You Like This"

Examining the Lexicon of Cuban Underground Hip Hop Artivist Discourses

Often the lyrics of CUHHM artivists point in two directions at once: back to a history of language and speaking that has marginalized certain members of Cuban society and forward to a new vision of reclaiming words and space through art and music. This chapter highlights the ways in which Cuban underground hip hop artivists seek to rework the discourses that describe and shape Cuban society and speak to audiences too long left unaddressed and without a voice. Because the stakes of cultural political struggles are contested meanings and their effects, it is important to examine the diverse ways in which key terms and concepts resonate among the artists of the CUHHM. I am in no way claiming that the language practices of the artivists are homogeneous or unanimous. My point is that in their lyrics, their art, their performances, and their everyday lives Cuban hip hop artists confront the awareness that certain terms are loaded with particular cultural weight but as such are also sites for powerful rupture and reconfiguration.

Social movements that are based on material distribution and identity politics use different language structures and terminologies to advocate for their movement's interests and to express what the movement is trying to achieve. Cuban citizens' integration of politics and culture is manifested within the social movement terminology used by underground hip hop artists. Cynthia A. Young (2006) specifically engages the terminology used by the "U.S. Third World Left," noting that the usage of "Third World" in and of itself represents an effort to invert the very geopolitical, economic, and social hierarchies that the term inscribes. Taking its cue from the French revolutionary term the "Third Estate," which was used to describe those at the bottom of the economic ladder, "Third World" demonstrates the feedback loop among socially marginalized communities within the West and communities impacted by Western colonialism.

Importantly, the development of this discourse did not happen in isolation. The activists and cultural workers that Young engages in her work are very much a part of a broader, transnational conversation about social inequality and social change. Young focuses on how these intellectual exchanges and the empowerment and mobilization of these social movements occurred through film, literature, and other art forms, with global movements for decolonization greatly influencing U.S. activists. U.S. activists of color absorbed literature, films, ideologies, and political movements that originated in the so-called Third World, including Cuba, to create new vocabularies and aesthetic forms calling for social change in the United States. Cuba has had a profound ideological impact on African American (and global) notions of revolutionary struggle and social equality, and the CUHHM is also integrated into this feedback loop.

In this chapter I examine the terminology used by CUHHM artivists, noting the various ways in which words and concepts are reworked and redeployed. Cuban hip hop artists alternately draw upon and subvert meanings that originated in other times and places, always insisting on specifically regional or Cuban articulations. This list is not exhaustive, but it usefully highlights that understanding how important Cuba's racial identity and artivist language politics are as actors within cultural movements defines their contexts and names what they seek to change:

- Revolution, Revolutionary
- Activism, Activists
- Poverty, Marginalization
- Underground, Commercial

In my many interviews and conversations, I noticed that certain terms in Cuba have a dual meaning. One meaning may be reminiscent of liberal discourses concerning freedom and equality, while the other may be reminiscent of a rejection of Western European notions of modernity or a conversation with Martían or socialist discourses that has some convergence with West African religious-based notions of community and community support (Vidal-Ortiz 2005). Examining the regional lexicon of the movement provides insight into the agenda of the artivists who interrogate and employ terminologies as a means of articulating and defining the terms of their own political struggle.

Revolution/Revolutionary

Artivist definitions of revolution have three central elements: aesthetic change (of which religion and notions of the beautiful and the good are a part), profound social change that results in a more just and egalitarian society, and revolution as a process not an endpoint. Society and people continuously change, along with our understandings of justice, equality, and the beautiful. Cuban psychologist Yesenia F. Selier (2005, 2010) discusses the theme of CUHHM terminology and significance to the movement:

> ¡Hip Hop, Revolución! es por ejemplo uno de los lemas recurrentes de las agrupaciones de rap en Cuba. Enarbolado por el dúo "Anónimo Consejo" en 1998 produjo un impacto extraordinario dentro de la comunidad. Su director, Sekuo, en entrevista a la revista *Movimiento* (2003), dice al respecto: "Esta expresión logró cambios en el Movimiento hasta en la forma de vestirse, de cómo tratar nuestra estética y no fuimos nosotros los únicos que comenzamos a usar guayaberas y pullovers del Che. ¡Hip Hop, Revolución! Es el concepto de tomar las cosas como son y revolucionarlas. Es aportar para salvar todo cuanto nos pueda afectar como movimiento sociocultural y como sociedad en todos los sentidos. Comenzó a definir nuestra cultura e ideología hip hop y estos son tiempos de definiciones. . . . Revolución es definirse ser consecuente con tus principios ante cualquier situación. Es un modo de vida que hay que enfrentar y asumir. Hemos asumido este término como una revolución de pensamiento, de forma de escribir, de expresarse y representar el hip hop y la vida."

> Hip Hop Revolution! is one of the recurrent slogans of rap groups in Cuba. Started by the duo Anónimo Consejo [Anonymous Council] in 1998 it had an extraordinary impact within the community. Its director, Sekuo, in an interview to the magazine *Movimiento* (2003), explains: "This expression achieved changes in the Movement even in the way of dress, how to treat our aesthetic, and we were not the only ones that started using guayaberas and Che T-shirts. Hip Hop Revolution! It is the concept of taking things as they are and revolutionizing them. It is to contribute to save all that we can affect as a sociocultural movement and society in every sense. It began to define our culture and ideology, hip hop, and these are times of definition. . . . Revolution is to define yourself to be consistent with your principles in any situation. It is a way of life that must be faced and undertaken. We have taken on this term as a revolution of thought, of how to write, of expressing yourself and representing hip hop and life." (Selier, 2005, 11)

Selier writes about three areas where the artists make an intervention, which I believe highlight some of the movement's overall goals for social change. They are rooted in the continuation of African cultural logics in Cuba, which are in large part tied to the cosmologies and worldviews passed on within the African-based religious traditions present in Cuba and rooted in revolutionary ideology. For example, a part of Sekou's definition reflects revolutionary discourses, specifically in Fidel Castro's speech "Words to the Intellectuals," where he argued that you have to take a side in a revolution. That side should reflect what you stand for. Sekou also talks about aesthetic interventions. This was one of several arts-based social movements that turned style into political discourse. That may seem totally innovative to some, but it actually is a part of everyday life for Cuba's visibly Afro-descendant population, particularly those who practice West African–based religious traditions. In her work on racial identity in Cuba, Selier (2005) noted that people (specifically Black Cubans) who wear religious necklaces or any other clothing indicating African religious practice could not find a job (though at present this seems to be changing). Aesthetics *as* political discourse is very important for people in a majority-Afro-descendant nation (culturally speaking), who want the right to express their ways of thinking and being in the world, without the imposition of European cultural aesthetics. As mentioned throughout this book, the majority of the artists in the CUHHM practice some form of Santería and/or Ifá. This is also a point highlighted by Selier that resonates with my observations. Much of CUHHM music is filled with references to Orishas (African religious figures), including references to Olofin (God). When Sekou argues that hip hop is being used to define a culture and ideology, this is a direct challenge to the imposition of Western European cosmologies and worldviews on a population that is not in the majority European descendant but majority African descendant (culturally and physically). A goal of the CUHHM is to revolutionize consciousness, as a way of changing society.

For CUHHM artists, a revolution is a continuous process without an end point. Alexei of the group Obsesión spoke about the revolutionary process in our interview in Havana in 2005:

Es como el concepto de la revolución, la revolución no es una cosa que puedes decir . . . fue, esto es la revolución. La revolución es como espiral no . . . tú tienes que ir, limando las cosas, viendo qué errores tienes para ir cerrando el círculo y cerrando el círculo para ir construyendo, sí ir construyendo, nunca paras . . . desde el mismo momento que no somos perfectos como humanos, la revolución no puede parar, nunca puede parar. Es lo mismo que pasa con el hip hop me entiende. . . . Decimos hip hop, decimos revolución. Es cambio, pero no pienso que se pueda resumir en esa palabra. Son muchos elementos digamos "esto es hip hop," "esto pude ser hip hop." El hecho de que mi mamá me dé un consejo muy bueno es hip hop para mí. El hecho de que un pintor más allá que no sea garitero, por ejemplo, esté haciendo su pintura y con eso [holds up a pencil] diga que los pueblos tienen que unirse, para mí eso es hip hop me entiende . . . porque yo amo eso y es mi propósito de vida que los pueblos del mundo se unan. Si tú desde tus zapatos tú estás limpiando zapatos y estás cantando una canción a favor de que se vaya Bush, eso es hip hop para mí me entiende. . . . Entonces hay quien tenga su concepto muy cerrado de las cosas que apoyarían o no, al hip hop. Yo pienso que en la medida en que podamos enriquecer ese concepto, de cuanta gente está aporando a este concepto de liberación, de libertad, en fin de enriquecimiento humano, eso es hip hop.

> It is like the concept of a revolution, the Revolution is not something that you can say, "Ha! This is the revolution!" The Revolution is like a spiral, right, you have to go, highlighting things, looking at the errors that you have to go closing the gaps and closing the gaps in order to keep constructing, if you keep constructing, you never stop. . . . From the same moment that we are not perfect as human beings, the Revolution cannot stop, it can never stop. This is the same thing that happens with hip hop, understand me? We say hip hop, we say Revolution. It is change, but I don't think that you can summarize this word. There are a lot of elements we say "this is hip hop," "this could be hip hop." If it just so happens that my mother gave me some really good advice, that is hip hop for me. If it should happen that a painter that's out there, that's not a graffiti artist for example, is painting and with this [holds up a pencil] it says that communities have to come together, then for me, this is hip hop, understand me? Because I love this, and it is the reason for my life, that all people come together. If you, from your shoes, you are cleaning shoes and you are singing your favorite song that says "Bush should go," this is hip hop for me, understand me? So there are those who have a very narrow concept of what things to support or not concerning hip hop. I think that the way in which we can enrich this concept of liberation, of liberty, in the end is an enrichment of humanity, this is hip hop.

In this quotation Alexey defines hip hop as revolutionary because it brings people together to work for the common good, while giving people insight and the impulse to understand the world in a different way. He comments that sometimes problems need to be addressed; he is referring to the "Rectification process" undertaken from 1986 throughout the 1990s, when the state recognized the past "errors of the Revolution" and sought to correct them during the revolutionary rectification period, 1987–1990 (Selier 2005). Very few of these groups on the Island, even the contemporary dissident groups, are working to overthrow the government as much as they are working for change and pressuring the state and society to change. This is something that is shared by much of Cuba's politically active citizenry and has two different strains.

On the one hand, Cuba has a well-known, publicized, and financed dissident population fighting for the freedom to organize and directly challenge the hegemony of the state and its silence on the profound social issues that persist and are unaddressed by state policy. They also fight for a civil society independent of the state and for free and open multiparty elections. Within this population some are fighting for a liberal capitalist democracy, while others are challenging the repressive actions of the Cuban state as a means of challenging it to live up to its promise of a democratic socialist state. On the other hand, some actors are focused on other areas of social change within Cuban society—the state is not the only source of power and social inequality on the Island: Cuban culture is another. Some actors are not worried about the state as much as they are worried about changing other things that have more of an effect on their day to day life. The ripple effect means that these actions will eventually change all of society, including the state. The idea is that through working for change in the areas where it is necessary do so the revolutionary process can continue to move forward. This is not to say that critical artists who are choosing to work in other areas of social life reject the work of dissidents while they uncritically embrace the Cuban state. All of these things are needed if Cuba is going to continue its process of self-definition: all of these actors are in conversation with each other.[1] But the most important thing to note is that a revolution is a process of social change, and a revolutionary is a person who actively participates in this process in any way possible.

Activism, Activists

Within the "old-school" underground hip hop movement, the artists referred to themselves as "activists." I had never heard artists (even socially conscious ones) call themselves activists in the United States, so that their creative production was understood as activism. In the United States socially conscious artists who are also activists are often involved in activities outside of their artistic production. The artistic production is generally not seen as central to their activism or as constituting activism in and of itself. Cuban artivists take a different perspective.

Graffiti artist NoNo12 explained how she got involved in the CUHHM in our Havana interview in 2005:

Ya lo hacía porque tenía revistas y cosas pero no pensé que lo que yo hacía, esas letras que eran precisamente eran graffiti. Hasta que ya me fui instruyendo un poco más y no me dio pena, porque me gusta mucho el hip hop. Entonces me integré y era un activista más en el movimiento. Y vi que no había ninguna graffitera, no hay nadie. Entonces, yo empecé en El Almendares: No, yo quiero pintar, yo quiero ir ahí. Y más o menos hacía cositas. . . . Pero ya me estuve ahí, ahí hasta que traté de lograr mi propio grupo con otro muchacho. . . . Pero yo seguía haciendo mis cosas solas y quería ser alguien en el movimiento hip hop. Antes de rapear. Hasta que ya me fui más o menos organizando, informándome sobre las cosas. . . . Y así fue como me fui perfeccionando y aquí estoy.

> I was already doing it because I had the journals and things but I did not think about was what I was doing, that these letters were graffiti. I kept learning more, and I still didn't realize it, because I liked hip hop so much. So I joined the movement and was a participant in the movement, just another activist in the movement. I say that there weren't any graffiti artists, there wasn't anyone. So, I began in the Almendares Park: No, I want to paint, I want to go there. . . . But I was there [working alone], there until I tried to make my own group with another guy. . . . But I was still doing my solo stuff and wanted to be someone in the hip hop movement. Before rapping, until now I got more or less organized, learning about things. . . . And that was how I went ahead perfecting things and here I am.

NoNo12 talks about becoming an *integrante* (participant) in the movement. She was already painting as a hobby and eventually decided to become a graffiti artist, as there were few in the movement. Early on, when she started reading graffiti magazines, she still did not recognize that what she was doing as a visual artist was graffiti. She kept painting, learning more about graffiti, and at the same time she really enjoyed the emerging hip hop movement. She became involved in the movement in the late 1990s then joined the movement as more of an activist. In this interview NoNo notes two things. First, she wanted to become more involved in the leadership of the movement. In order to do that, she needed to decide through which element of hip hop she would make her contribution. While she was deciding this, she entered into the movement as an organizer, as one of many activists who were working in the hip hop movement but who were not necessarily artists themselves. She looked around and realized that no one was doing graffiti, that people were only focused on being an MC and that there were very few DJs as well. It was then that she realized what she could contribute to the movement by being a graffiti artist.

DJ Leydis had a similar experience. She realized that there was a need for DJs, and that this could be her contribution to the movement. The following excerpt from my interview with DJ Leydis in Havana in 2005 is an example of how the term "activist" is incorporated into the hegemonic discourse within the CUHHM:

Tanya: Primero cuéntame tu vida como rapera.

DJ Leydis: ¿Cómo, mi vida artística?

Tanya: Sí.

DJ Leydis: Bueno, yo no me quejo de mi vida artística, ha sido muy bonita y he descubierto muchas cosas en la música y en el mundo de hip hop. Primeramente empecé como una muy buena activista del movimiento, '97, '98 por ahí, apoyando a Grandes Ligas, un grupo muy bueno que es vecino por aquí del 1910 [house number]. Entonces apoyando a los Hermanos Saíz, en los festivales fui siendo parte del movimiento organizativo, fui teniendo mis credenciales ante de hacer algo. Como que me fui motivando, porque yo quería . . . cuando vas metiéndote adentro quieres ser más y más y no te basta con ser una activista. Y yo creía que podía ser algo más y también la música me gustaba mucho y creía que la cultura del DJ no estaba explotada, solamente el MC. Ni siquiera en las instituciones tenía conocimiento de más nada, solamente el MC, el DJ, el grafiti, no existía.

> Tanya: First tell me about your life as a rapper.
>
> DJ Leydis: About my artistic life?
>
> Tanya: Yes.
>
> DJ Leydis: All right, I don't have any complaints about my artistic life, it has been very beautiful and I have discovered a lot of things in music and in the world of hip hop. First, I began as a really good activist of the movement, '97, '98, around then, supporting Grandes Ligas, a really good group that is a neighbor here at 1910 [house number]. So by supporting los Hermanos Saíz, in the festivals, I was gaining my credentials before doing something. Since I was so motivated, because I wanted to be . . . when you are going to get yourself involved in something you want to be more and more and it's not enough to be an activist. I believed that I could be something more and . . . the music, I liked it a lot, and I really loved that DJ culture was not exploited, only the MC. No one in any institution had an idea of anything; only MC, DJ, and graffiti did not exist.

DJ Leydis also points out that she was an activist in the movement. Her activism was one of the ways in which she gained the credentials that helped her to become a leader and central contributor in the movement via artistic expression. Many of the CUHHM artists began as activists: people responsible for helping to organize community events and seminars supporting artivists and undertaking any role that would help the movement expand and reach a broader public. All of this was central to showing commitment to the movement, that you had your own critical, socially conscious discourse, which ensured that the movement would continue to be an agent of change. Through community activism, particularly as an artivist, the future CUHHM artivist would be invited to perform at public events. It is in this way that artists such as Las Krudas CUBENSI, who were established street theater performers, were invited to participate in the CUHHM. They were not yet activists in that movement but were arts-based activists in their own right. The leaders of the CUHHM also thought that Las Krudas could provide an important critical perspective concerning gender and sexuality that was largely absent from the movement at that time.

Responsibility to the larger community and the use of hip hop as a tool for social change are a tangible reality in the lives of the artists. The following is an excerpt from my field notes (Havana 2005):

I remember one day, while I was at Alexis's [DJ D'Boys'] apartment, the phone rang. Alexis put the phone to his ear, smiled, and looked at me awkwardly, perplexed. He listened silently. He put the phone to my ear for a few seconds to listen—there was a kid passionately rapping on the other end. Alexis returned the phone to his ear and continued to listen. Suddenly and excitedly, Alexis began speaking. He gave the boy his critique on the phone. I heard the kid excitedly saying "uh huh, uh huh!" At the end, Alexis told the boy that he had talent, that he should keep practicing and maybe one day soon Alexis would invite him to perform on stage. The boy got really excited: "Really! Thank you! Thank you!" the boy shouted and quickly hung up. I imagined the boy getting right to work on his next rhyme. I pictured him, sitting on the side of a tattered bed, hunched over a worn notebook in a small Havana apartment. The kid probably used every single white space available on its pages; you had to be sure to use every scrap of resources well, there were no materials to be wasted.

After Alexis hung up the phone, he looked at me with a curious look on his face: he was partially embarrassed, partially taken aback. "You see, Tanya," he said, "Lately, I've been getting more and more calls like that. I pick up the phone and a kid starts rapping. These kids don't have anything else. Hip hop gives them a purpose, they want to try and become like us . . . and that is a lot of responsibility. We have to be here, Tanya, to encourage and support our youth so that they choose a better life." I asked him who the kid was. "I don't know," he said. Somehow I'm sure that he will eventually find out.

The kid who called was probably from Alexis's neighborhood. Alexis, like several producers in barrios all over Havana, had a neighborhood-based arts collective that organized educational events. In his case, he organized cleanups of the Almendares Park in Havana. On the park cleanup days, kids received lessons on environmental sustainability and learned about the park's eco-system, which taught them to appreciate nature and take responsibility for their environment. All of the arts-based activities, symposiums, and other events empowered youths to act in their own best interests, to care for themselves and others. It also taught children to be responsible, to work hard, and to strive to improve themselves and their communities. Hip hop is consciousness, the artivists argue; anything that supports consciousness, self-empowerment, and the desire and the will to work for a better society is hip hop. And consciousness and knowledge are the key to change.

But not everyone can become an artivist. Alexey of Obsesión once commented that one of the hardest things for a lot of the artists is when they meet people who have been activists in the movement and want to become a part of the movement's leadership as a DJ, MC, B-girl/boy, or graffiti artist but who do not have very much talent, despite trying their hand at every element of hip hop (in terms of performance). The leadership tries to support them, to consider different ways in which they could still contribute to the movement as a symposium organizer, producer, or something else. For these artists, activism and being an activist mean consciously orienting their work toward the goal of social change. Given the organizational structure of the Cuban Underground Hip Hop Movement—where the artivists are the faces and the voices of the collective movement—participants in the movement refer to themselves as activists because that is what they are.

Magia, also of the group Obsesión, said the following in our interview in Havana in 2006 about when artists started to realize that they were activists:

También había un evento teórico en los Festivales que eran los Colóquios y que nos fue dando una dimensión un poco más amplia de toda esta repercusión que iba a teniendo el hip hop dentro de la sociedad. Nos hizo un llamado en el sentido ese de que sí teníamos que tener una responsabilidad cuando nos subíamos a la tarima y decíamos algunas letras, en qué medida repercutía en las personas. A partir de ese momento fue bueno como esperar. Hay que pensar un poco más lo que tú quieres hacer, lo que quieres decir, lo que quieres proyectar. Fue como eso, no. No sé exactamente lo que he hecho dentro del movimiento de hip hop yo creo que, o sea, tendría un poco sentarme y decir específicamente. . . . He hecho muchas cosas, además, de rapear, creo que ambos desarrollamos algo muy inconsciente que fue el activismo. El activismo fue algo inconsciente dentro del movimiento. Yo lo llamé así hasta que fuimos a los Estados Unidos por primera vez y que supimos, o sea, que eso era un activismo un poco ya consciente.

O sea, no lo supimos hasta que no llegamos en el 2001 a los Estados Unidos cómo era que se llamaba ese tipo de trabajo y cómo era que podía realizarse un poco más conscientemente con la comunidad, empezando con la comunidad del hip hop. Pero en ese tiempo, antes, ya veníamos realizando ese tipo de trabajo que en aquellos tiempo no lo llamábamos activismo, sino que decíamos bueno esto es lo que a nosotros nos toca hacer. Había un grupo de gente que tenía un sentido de organización, que sabía que había que organizar a nuestra gente. Sabíamos que teníamos que establecer un diálogo entre las instituciones y el mismo trabajo que se hacía, que nosotros hacíamos. Hay que entender que aquellos tiempo no había una aceptación del género como tal. O sea, habían mucho lugares en que sencillamente no aceptaban el hip hop como género, o sea el rap, como en aquel momento se llamaba.

> Also there was a theoretical event in the festivals that was the colloquiums and that gave us a broader dimension in which [to understand] the broader impact of hip hop within our society. It was a call to us in the sense that, yes, we must take responsibility when we take the stage and when we say our lyrics, to what extent it had repercussions in the people. As of that moment it was good to hope. But it is necessary to think a little about what you want to do, what you say, what you want to project. It was like that, right. I do not know exactly what I would have done within hip hop movement, I believe that, that is to say, I believe that I had to sit with myself and to say specifically. . . . I have done many things, in addition to rapping, I believe that we both developed something very unconscious that was the activism. The activism was something unconscious within the movement. I named it when we went to the United States for the first time and we knew it, that is to say, that this was activism, and we became a little more conscious.

That is to say, we did not know it until 2001, when we were in the United States and learned that it was what they called this type of work [activism] and how you could become more conscious with your community, beginning with the community of hip hop. But in that time, before, we were already doing this type of work though we did not call it activism, but we said, good, this is what we were called to do. There was a group of people who had a sense of organization, who knew that our people needed to be organized. We knew that we had to establish a dialogue between the institutions and the same work that they did, that we did. It is necessary to understand that at those times this genre was not accepted as such. That is, many places simply did not accept hip hop as a genre, that is to say rap, as it was called at that moment.

Magia talks about when she and fellow group member Alexey became conscious of the word "activism." She notes that underground hip hop artists were already focused on social justice work. They were working within their communities as well as becoming more conscious of the social impact of their work as hip hop artists. It was not until their trip to New York in 2001, however, that they encountered the word "activism" and decided that the term reflected what artists were doing within their own community. In exploring what activism meant within the United States, Magia and Alexey also started to realize that successful activist work meant organizing and working within their own institution as well as working with other institutions, including state institutions. Magia says that some people within the movement had a great sense of organization and moved to organize a hip hop journal, entitled *Movimiento*. They created a purpose and mission for the movement and sponsored symposiums as an educational component. These actors challenged established institutional structures for the recognition of underground hip hop as a revolutionary art form and pressed for the creation of the Agency of Rap, so that artists would have an established mechanism within the state institutional structure to pursue the interests and needs of the movement.

Magia also makes reference to the period in which underground artists began to realize the utility of using the discourse of activism to describe their movement. It seems that 1998–2003 was a time of rapid ideological development for the underground hip hop movement. During this period, Cuban artists and intellectuals, with greater access to the ideological changes that had happened within the Americas since 1970, were heavily engaged in accessing, discussing, digesting, and critiquing the works of theorists such as Michel Foucault, Stuart Hall, Paul Gilroy, bell hooks, and Judith Butler. There was a push to look externally to find developments in social theory as a means to contribute to global intellectual and ideological exchange as well as to rethink approaches to equality at home.

Another factor contributing to the development of activist discourse may have been the exchange of ideas with the African diaspora outside of Cuba—for example, with people in New York City—but also with members of the African diaspora who visited Cuba, such as Brazilian artists Nega Giza and MV Bill. Underground youth increasingly began to engage Black radical activists with political asylum in Cuba. Additionally, for the majority of the first generation of underground artists, the visit of activists such as Danny Glover and Harry Belafonte to the Island helped them to think critically about their actions and the potential power of the movement. Magia and other artists commented that the significant contribution of those meetings was when Glover and Belafonte at one point said: "It's not enough just to hope and want change. What are you going to do about it? You can't accomplish anything without a plan."

Underground hip hop has become a mechanism through which artists make an intervention into issues not commonly recognized or publicly discussed after 1959. Artists may also take on an activist role in an established area where artists are fighting for change and offer their perspectives as a way to amplify the public's and other artists' views on an experience. For example, many women are addressing what it means to be a woman, particularly a Black woman, from multiple perspectives and from the intersections of multiple social experiences and social identities. Central to the movement's knowledge-practices, its consciousness raising, is addressing poverty and marginalization.

Poverty, Marginalization

The following excerpt is from my field notes in Havana in 2005 (two days after Hurricane Katrina):

> The phone started ringing late in the afternoon. Everyone was worried, and surprised. They wanted to make sure my family was OK, but also, people were REALLY surprised. I was waiting to interview Yompi. There came a frantic and loud knock on the door. I ran downstairs to open it. It was Yompi. I opened the door, his eyes were wide. "Tanya, I cannot believe it!! I didn't think the United States would do something like that?! No one can believe it! They won't even let the Cuban doctors come in and it's only a 15 minute flight." "I told you," I said, feeling really sad that I was right. "But I don't understand! It's the United States! How could they

just let people die like that?! I mean we have hurricanes all the time in Cuba, and no one dies—well not thousands and the U.S. is so rich! How could the United States let all of those people die! It's such a rich country! Is it really still that racist? I can't believe it!" "They're all Black people and poor whites. All of them people who don't have a lot of power," I said morbidly. "I see that now," he said, staring at me with wide eyes. "I mean the Cuban government always puts propaganda on the TV about the United States, and we're so used to it that we just ignore it. No one really believes it. But wow . . . I can't believe that the U.S. would let something like that happen to its people. I'm so sorry, Tanya, it must be so hard to watch that from here," he said. We walked upstairs for the interview. After the interview I knew I needed to rush, there was going to be a fundraiser to help Hurricane Katrina victims and I wanted to make it to the organizational meeting in time. . . .

I arrived at the meeting at Joseph's apartment. At least ten to fifteen of Cuba's hip hop leadership was there. Magia called the meeting. She explained what had occurred in the States. Everyone had heard and there was some discussion, some disbelief. "We decided to have a fundraiser, maybe a concert, where people can bring stuff, and we can send clothes and other necessities here from Cuba, out of solidarity, so that we can help people who are less fortunate than us," Magia said. Everyone agreed, and the discussion began about what we should do. At one point, a person bought up a major concern: "Everyone is horrified by what happened. But you know how Cubans are. We have to be careful. If we ask for donations, for shirts, we don't want people to give the shirt on their back." I looked at the speaker perplexed. I thought they were joking. Everyone agreed, and the discussion continued about how to frame the request for goods. After several minutes I realized that they were serious. There are people here who literally have only one shirt, but they have a house and food. And they would actually not think twice about giving up their last shirt, because "at least they had a place to sleep and some food."[2]

For underground artists, there are two sides to defining and understanding poverty. One way is to analyze poverty in material terms, while others reject a materially based analysis of poverty. But all of the artists seem to associate poverty with personal attributes, such as having a poor conscience, being badly educated, or lacking high self-esteem and respect for themselves or their community. Again I would like to note that the period I am talking about is about 1995 to 2006. In recent years, with the liberalization of the economy and cuts in the social welfare net, material poverty has reemerged in Cuba, such as food shortages and a cholera outbreak in 2012—the first in about fifty years, according to several CUHHM artists. Nonetheless, despite the reality of material poverty returning to the Island, both conceptualizations of poverty exist among artivists.

For example, in a 2005 interview in Havana Alexis "DJ D'Boys" Rodríguez and Mikel El Extremo gave similar accounts of poverty: someone can be materially poor but not spiritually or culturally impoverished; alternately, someone could be wealthy but spiritually or culturally impoverished. Alexis said the following:

> Ahí no hay diferencia. Dentro de la pobreza está lo underground y lo marginal. Ya con eso está dicho todo. Hay underground, hay, está lo marginal y la pobreza. La música no puedes venderla, pues es una música de mucha conciencia, me entiendes. Y hay más amantes a la música underground que a la comercial. Aunque tú no lo creas, como en el mundo siempre hay más pobres que ricos. Los que oyen música comercial son los que nacieron en cunas de oro y lo tienen todo y no están para oír una historia de pobreza, porque no conocen eso. Me entiendes. No es importante, me entiendes.
>
> Es importante HH [hip hop] y underground. Para mí es importante que siga creciendo pues eso es lo que va a hacerme, es como una lucha, una lucha de que algún día yo tengo fe, me entiendes de buscar la igualdad de todo el mundo. Porque todos somos iguales, tú tienes un poquito más un poquito menos, pero todos somos iguales. Que puedes tener mucho, pero a lo mejor no tienes salud y la salud no se da con dinero. Y yo soy pobre, pero tengo mucha salud. Yo te puedo ayudar a ti. El respeto para todos los underground, el respeto para los marginados, para todo el mundo.

> There is no difference. Within poverty is that which is underground and that which is marginal. And with this everything is said. There is underground, there is that which is marginal and poverty. [Underground] music, you cannot sell it, because it is a music of much conscience, you understand me? And there are more lovers of underground music than there are of the commercial kind. Although you do not believe it, as in the world always there are more poor than rich. Those that hear commercial music are those that were born in gold cradles and they have everything and they are not ready to hear a history of poverty, because they do not know about that. You understand me? It is not important, you understand me?

What's important is hip hop and underground. For me it is important that it continues growing, that is what I am going to do for me, it's a struggle, a struggle through which someday, I have faith, you understand, to see equality worldwide. Because we are all equal, you have just a little bit more, others a little bit less, but all we are equal. You can have much, perhaps you do not have health and health does not come with money. And I am poor, but I have much health. I can help you. Much respect for all those underground and much respect for the marginalized ones all over the world.

Alexis is saying that poverty relates to two types of experiences: being underground and being marginal. You can be materially poor but be underground—that is, conscious of your reality and choosing to live a productive life where you work for the betterment of yourself and your community. A marginal person, in contrast, because of poverty of consciousness, is isolated from society.

Olivia Prendes Riverón of Las Krudas summarized a central perspective on poverty within the CUHHM in our interview in Havana in 2006:

Tanya: Este tema de pobreza, éste es un tema que es muy importante para el hip hop. ¿Puedes explicarme cómo funciona esta idea de pobreza . . . ?

Olivia: Mira, para mí también Odaymara es una maestra porque ella siempre me rectifica, cuando yo digo que somos pobre. Porque no somos pobres. Y también es un término que hay que saber utilizar. No somos nada pobres, tenemos una gran riqueza, tenemos nuestra felicidad de estar juntas, nuestra cultura que es riquísima, nuestra inteligencia que es suprema, nuestra sensibilidad que es más valiosa que cualquier cosa, la vida que es algo grandísimo, nuestro amor, nuestra amistad, nuestra hermanidad con nuestra gente. Y yo pienso que hablar de pobreza en comunidad hip hop o en comunidades pobres en Cuba, habría siempre que especificar pobreza de qué tipo o a qué se refieren cuando hablan de pobreza. Hablamos entonces de otras cosas, hablamos de alcance económico menor o de poca economía, poco nivel adquisitivo o algo así. Pero el término pobreza no nos gusta para referirnos a nosotras, a nuestra gente. Nuestra gente no es pobre, nuestra gente no tiene economía, economía solamente.

Tanya: Explícame más, pues no estoy seguro si yo entiendo bien el dicho [palabra] economía.

Olivia: Dinero, capital, inversiones, manera de qué sé yo, de aquirir, consumir, de estar más cerca del mundo del consumo. Para el hip hop es difícil, porque el hip hop es un género que controversialmente tiene mucha poesía, mucha alma, mucho espíritu, mucha fuerza de comunidades que han sido desprovistas de economía y de poder adquisitivo, pero a la misma vez es una cultura que necesita de mucha tecnología, mucho equipamiento y entonces es algo ahí como una especie de contradicción hermosa que aquí en Cuba hemos sabido asumir de cualquier manera.

Ya te dije que al comienzo, cuando en el mundo entero ya la gente tenía compact disk, aquí en Cuba todavía teníamos cassettes y todavía escuchábamos la música con antenas de percheros, por eso no lo vas a poder traducir nunca. Nosotros hemos asumido todas nuestras carencias materiales de una manera hermosa y hoy día todavía sabemos que la lucha sigue siendo durísima por el bloqueo y por la falta de material que tenemos aquí para trabajar. Pero, el hip hop lo seguimos haciendo y la vida en la cultura hip hop seguimos ahí, de alguna manera seguimos respirando vivas y vivos.

Tanya: Para repetirlo, para ver si yo entiendo bien. Hay un sentido de pobreza que significa que no tienen acceso a la economía, y esto es algo que aplica a toda la gente en Cuba, más o menos. Pero, ¿cuál es el otro tipo de pobreza?

Olivia: El otro tipo de pobreza es el que tiene la gente que tiene mucho, a lo mejor, material, pero tan poco en el cerebro, en el alma que son super pobres.

Tanya: ¿Acá dentro en su alma?

Olivia: En su alma, en su amor, no sé, hay mucha gente que tiene poco amor, que tiene poca cultura no, que tiene una cultura super desviada, o no sé, la gente sexista, la gente clasista, toda esa gente es super pobre.

> Tanya: This theme of poverty, this is a theme that is very important for hip hop. Can you explain to me how this idea of poverty functions?
>
> Olivia: Look, for me also Odaymara is a great teacher because she always corrects me when I say that we are poor. Because we are not poor. And also it is a term that you have to know how to use. We are not poor, we have a great richness, we have our happiness of being together, our culture is the richest, our intelligence is supreme, our sensibility is more valiant than anything, life is something that is enormous, our love, our friendship, our kinship with our people. I think that to talk about poverty in the hip hop community, or in poor communities in Cuba, it would have to be specified what type of poverty you are talking about when you talk about poverty. So we talk about other things, we talk of being of limited economic scope, being of few economic means, minimal level of acquisition, something like that. But we don't like to refer to ourselves, to our

people, with the term "poverty." Our people are not poor, our people just
do not have economic means [literally, our people do not have economy].

Tanya: Explain it to me more, because I am not sure if I understand well the
word "economy."

Olivia: Money, capital, investment, a way to, I don't know, acquire, consume,
to be closer to the world of consumption. For hip hop it's difficult, because
hip hop is a genre that controversially has a lot of poetry, a lot of soul, a
lot of spirit, more force in the communities that have been deprived of
an economy and acquisitive power, but at the same time it is a culture
that needs a lot of technology, a lot of equipment, and so it is something
that is there like a beautiful species of contradiction that here in Cuba we
know how to overcome in whatever way.

Tanya: So to repeat it, to see if I am understanding this well. There is a sense
of poverty that means that you don't have access to the economy, and it is
something that applies to all people in Cuba, more or less. But what is the
other type of poverty?

Olivia: In your spirit, in your love, I don't know, there are a lot of people who
have poor love, that have very little culture, that do have a culture really
diverted, I don't know, people who are sexist, classist, all those people are
super poor.

Tanya: There within your spirit?

Olivia: The other type of poverty is one where people have a lot, the best material, and they have little in their head, in their spirit they are really poor.

Several things are happening in this conversation. Olivia Prendes Riverón
and her partner Odaymara Cuesta Rosseau, like the other artists, are socially
critical actors who grew up in a revolutionary context. The question of material
inequality is something that is very much discussed and debated in hegemonic
state discourse and through its politics. Questions concerning the relationship of
capitalism, imperialism, and coloniality are also constantly engaged in state institutions and policies (such as the Cuban government's foreign policy centered
on the support of anticolonial and anticapitalist social movements primarily in
Africa, Central America, and Latin America). They are also actors embedded in
Afro-Cuban/Caribbean religious and cultural traditions, as well as participants
in Cuba's critical arts movements which seek to address the question of social
inequality resulting from culture, specifically social consciousness and collective ideological orientation. These artists address a crucial area of social life
and a central node in power relations: culture as the power behind economic
production and social relations, which is often dismissed or simply goes unad-

dressed by state discourse and policy. The result is that poverty does take on a dual meaning for artivists: poverty is not only material but also spiritual and mental. You can create a situation where people have all the material resources that they need, and even have them in excess, and the people are still negative people, individually and collectively, who make life difficult for themselves and others around them.

It is for this reason that the artivists distinguish which type of poverty that they are fighting against and that people suffer from: working for change in both types of poverty, spiritual and material, is needed for long-lasting and fundamental social change. Mikel El Extremo explained this in our interview in Havana in 2005:

> Son gente, la mayoría de esos raperos son gente de barrio, son gente pobre. Estos son las raperos que no tienen poesía, que no tienen ritmo, que no son raperos los que me dan las ideas a mí. Ellos son prácticamente los compositores del sistema. Ahora yo estoy aquí sentado y viene uno y me dice: No, nosotros . . . y ta, ta, ta me dice una cosa. Ellos lo dicen sin consciencia. Hay personas que son muy positivos por una parte, por otra parte son muy negativos, tienen una mente muy rara. En la calle pasa eso muy a menudo. Gente que son muy, muy, muy radiactivos, muy elementos, sin embargo, tienen unos sentimientos muy malos. Que tienen unos códigos, unos valores, una hombría. . . . Hay mucha gente que tiene mucha más educación, tienen una vida mucho más holgada, sin embargo son personas que hacen más daño.

> > They are people, most of those rappers, they are people from the hood, they are poor people. These are the rappers that don't have poetry, that don't have rhythm, they are not rappers that give me ideas. They are practically the composers of the system. Now I here am seated and one might come to me and say to me: "No, we . . ." and ta, ta, ta says a thing to me. They say it without conscience. There are people who are very positive on the one hand, on the other hand are very negative, have a very strange mind. People that are very, very, very radioactive, very elemental, nevertheless, have very bad feelings. That they have codes, values, machismo. . . . There are many people who have much more education, have a comfortable life much more, but nevertheless are people who make more damage.

Like the differing perspectives on understanding poverty, similar differences occur between people's understanding of marginality when thinking about issues in social life. For many of the artivists, a marginal person can be someone who, for whatever reason, chooses not to be a part of society. A criminal is marginal and has a poverty of mind; someone who is a horrible person and ends up isolated within society is also marginal.

For most artists, however, the idea of marginal people actually existing in Cuba, outside of prison, is almost an impossibility, as the state had taken efforts to bring everyone into society through its social welfare programs and the socialization of culture. The effect is that people are understood to feel marginalized or to marginalize themselves through their own poverty of mind. Ideas surrounding poverty also map onto notions of marginality.

La Yula talked about being marginal in our interview in Havana in 2005:

De ser pobres, somos pobres. Realmente yo no pienso que aquí hay personas sean pobres, simplemente que uno tiene que desarrollarse, que explotarse a sí mismo . . . yo quisiera que hacer alguien en la vida, como qué, bueno como carpintero, o cualquier oficio que exista en la tierra. Lo que hay es personas que se estancan en sí, se encierran, se esconden, no se dan su valor . . . se siente que no es nadie. . . . Lo marginal es casi lo mismo. Para mí porque son personas que no se dejan ver, que piensan nada más lo negativo, lo negativo, lo negativo. Entonces, no hay en ellos algo positivo, eso lo cubre todo lo negativo. Porque toda una vida ha estado en casa que no tienen fin, que no tienen ni principio ni fin.

> To be poor, we are poor. But really, I don't think that here there should be poor people, only because you have to develop yourself, to exploit yourself . . . [someone who would say] I would like to be someone in my life, like a good carpenter, or whatever office exists in the land. There are people that stagnate, that enclose themselves, that hide themselves, they don't give themselves value . . . they feel that they are no one. . . . That which is marginal is almost the same thing. For me because there are people who don't stop to look, to think nothing more than negative [thoughts], negative things, negative things. So they are the ones who are not positive, who cover everything in negativity. Because all of [their] life they have been in the house and don't have any ends, they don't have a beginning or an end.

La Yula implies that being in poverty is the basis of being marginal. Among Cuban artists, to be marginal means to be outside of society, not to have access to an education, to be completely removed from society. In other words, embedded in notions of marginality are revolutionary discourses of social inclusion: everything that you would need to participate fully in society has been guaranteed and social discrimination is forbidden. Thus it is assumed that people who are marginal actually marginalize themselves by not participating in society or by committing crimes that remove them from society. If you are not criminal, you can't be marginal unless you make yourself marginal—though *feelings* of marginalization can be a term that people use to describe larger social dynamics such as racism, sexism, or heteronormativity.

Underground, Commercial

Conflicting ideological currents are also embedded within the notions of "institutionalization" and "commercialization" in Cuba. Hip hop artists seek to work with institutional structures that value and support their communitarian efforts. The organizations that are listed in the dedication of the Underground Hip Hop Symposium Declaration include the Asociación de Hermanos Saíz, the Unión de Escritores y Artistas de Cuba (UNEAC), the Cuban Agency of Rap, and the Casa de Cultura, all of which are quasi-institutionalized with the Ministry of Culture or are key grassroots-based institutions of Cuba's decentralized Aficionado movement. Though the movement is willing to work with state institutions, it will only work with those that will allow hip hop artists some degree of ideological autonomy. This autonomy at the grassroots level has allowed underground hip hop to emerge as a space for Black and mulat@ youths to express the social ills that they face. It is the internal structure of aesthetics, values, and the articulated goals for social and institutional change that makes underground hip hop a movement.

Cuban psychologist Yesenia F. Selier (2005) defines artists' perception of "underground": "ellos el apego a la realidad que viven y en un sentido más amplio y eminentemente político, representa una postura solidaria respecto a los oprimidos en otros lugares del mundo. Asumiéndose como underground un MC, o rapero, ratifica un compromiso ético, una responsabilidad social respecto a sus seguidores, de crear en ellos conciencia respecto a la realidad que los rodea" (their attachment to the reality they live and in a broader and eminently political sense, it represents a united stance on the oppressed elsewhere in the world. Presenting themselves as an underground MC or rapper ratifies an ethical commitment, a social responsibility toward their followers, to create awareness in them about the reality that surrounds them [3]).

Selier's observations about the term "underground" resonate with my own observations. Because Cuban hip hop artists see themselves as part of a global hip hop movement, they are aware of the differing economic contexts in which hip hop operates. For them, U.S. hip hop has become the prime example of what happens to hip hop once it has become commercialized within capitalist economic structures. The music is co-opted and does not operate as a nonconsumerist consciousness-raising mechanism. Terming a form of music "underground" refers not simply to whether the music is mass distributed by profit-driven institutions but also to whether the artist is delivering an empowering, socially critical, and uplifting message. It is believed to be best to stay away from profit-driven institutions, as the amount of money offered can sometimes corrupt artists and compromise their ethics.

As Yompi of the Junior Clan put it in our interview in Havana in 2005:

Para mi underground es aquella persona que tiene sentimientos de humano, de un ser humano. ¿Me entiende? Que aparte de pensare en él, piensa también en darle a los demás, ¿Me entiende? Porque uno puede tener su yo, pero lo que le rodea forma parte de él, pues es lo que lo hace vivir y sentirse que está viviendo, porque él sólo si se encuentra en un lugar que está solo y nadie lo rodea ni hay personas ni hay na', es un hombre muerto porque no tiene con quien comunicarse y entonces no puede tener en su proprio yo pensando que todo es para él y para él sin poderle dar nada a los demás. Entonces para mí underground significa eso, una persona humana de sentimientos, una persona que sea capaz de saber ayudar o dar mensaje en un momento determinado a las personas que lo necesitan.

> For me underground is that person that has feeling of humanity, of human being. You understand me? That, besides thinking of himself, thinks also about giving to the rest. You understand me? Because he can have his own me, but that with which he surrounds himself forms part of him, well, it is that thing that he does to live and to feel that he is living, because he is alone if he encounters a place where he is alone, and no one surrounds him and there are no people, there is nothing, he is a dead man because he has no one with whom to communicate, and then he cannot have his own thinking that all is for him and only for him without the desire to give something to the rest. So for me underground signifies this, a humane person of feelings, a person that has the ability to know to help or to give a message in a certain determined moment to the people who need it.

Underground describes an artist's work that is socially consciousness and empowering. Yompi argues that someone who is underground is socially conscious and wants to deliver a message that helps people. The underground artist is someone who is altruistic, who is not selfish, and who realizes that humans cannot survive alone. It is people who feel love and respect for themselves and for their fellow human beings and who devote their energy to helping to empower others. These themes are also addressed in Che Guevara's *Socialism and Man in Cuba* ([1965] 1989). Underground hip hop artists' understanding of "underground" is intertwined with Che Guevara's notion of a "New Man" as a socially critical actor, who feels love and helps improve the lives of all members of the community.

Though many underground artists consider reggaetón an example of commercialized hip hop or an example of a commercialized music that lacks social consciousness, as Alexey of Obsesión mentioned during a 2005 interview in Havana, no one should think of telling reggaetón artists that they should stop producing their music:

> También quizás tenga que ver, que ha influido en algo el reggaetón. Pero yo veo el reggaetón como que ayuda dentro del movimiento a desgastar. . . . O sea al principio, sí te confieso, al principio sí, pero esto es cosa de ellos y nosotros un poco incómodos. Pero después dijimos esto es una cosa que lo que tenemos que hacer es coexistir, tratar de que no . . . , de que a la gente si tú le pones reggaetón, reggaetón, la gente va a decir: bueno reggaetón. Pero si la gente puede escoger teniendo las opciones, bueno he ahí el problema. Que la gente pueda tener las opciones. Por supuesto estamos en contra de todos los mensajes esos raros que hay en el reggaetón. De igual forma también dentro del hip hop también debemos luchar con los mensajes esos que se dan inconscientemente. Porque si no queremos que los niños oigan determinados mensajes en el reggaetón, tampoco quisiéramos que nuestros niños oigan otras cosas en el hip hop que se están dando.

> > Also the fact that reggaetón has influenced some may have to do with it. But I see reggaetón as something that helps the movement to wear away. . . . In other words, at the beginning, if I may confess, at the beginning, yes, but that's their thing and we [were] a bit uncomfortable. But then we agreed that this is the kind of thing with which we have to coexist, to try not to [let it take over], that if you play reggaetón over and over to the people, they are going to tell you—OK enough already with the reggaetón. But yeah, if people have the option, therein lies the problem. Of course we are against all of the negative messages in reggaetón. But in the same way, within hip hop we should fight against all those negative messages that there are in reggaetón. At the same time, within hip hop we have also

had to fight with those unconscious messages. Because we don't want our
children to hear those other things that they are doing in hip hop.

Alexey argues that as parents and socially conscious actors underground
artists should continue to ensure that healthy music is available for their children, themselves, and the general public. For many underground hip hop artists, commercialized reggaetón encourages consumerism, self-disrespect, and
the devaluation of women. In more recent years, some have noted the socially
critical messages within reggaetón. Nonetheless, for many underground artists,
commercialized reggaetón is not critical and uplifting. Though underground
artists may be against the messages within commercialized reggaetón, however,
Alexey believes that underground hip hop and the more commercialized forms
of reggaetón have to coexist: underground artists are never in favor of censorship. He argues that those who do conscious hip hop must struggle to fight
against those negative messages, even though commercialized music may start
to outsell socially conscious music. In recent years, this has started to happen,
mainly as a result of the state's support of reggaetón, and the (sometimes not so)
passive resistance to the CUHHM. The ideologically contested relationship between retaining independent status within a Cuban context, commercialization
and institutionalization, and maintaining socially critical content of message
has certainly played out over the emergence and lasting effects of the Cuban
Agency of Rap.

The goal of the creation of a new Cuban institution in 2002, the Agencia
Cubana de Rap (ACR), was to help artists with commercialization and professionalization. By then artists were already popular independently of state-run
commercial cultural institutions. If artists wanted to have access to any markets
in Cuba, have the ability to travel abroad, or just have exposure as an artist, the
structure of the public sphere and the centralized economy necessitated that
they become members of an institution. As discussed in chapter 2, in order to
access Cuba's official artists' institutions and thereby have access to the national
media institutions and cultural markets, people were expected to conform to the
state's socialist discourse in their artistic production.

The creation of the Asociación Hermanos Saíz (AHS) allowed independent
artists to join a cultural institution and offered artists no pay but at least national
and international exposure. The reason why these artists were not included in
the state's pay structure for professional artists is that AHS was classified as an
aficionado institution—it was there only to support amateurs. In this way the
state both acquiesced in the 1980s youths' demands for more space for them to
express their generation's voices, which often conflicted with the hegemony of

the perspectives and discourses of the septuagarians and octogenarians now running the government. At the same time, the state could systematically slow the reach of the work of critical artists by not guaranteeing the salaries and professional-level resources needed to produce their art and to disseminate it, since they were not "professional" artists.

Additionally, state-run record companies during this time (1998–2006) would not offer contracts to CUHHM artivists, claiming that they were not selling out shows, though during this period they were. Some artists noted that CUHHM artivists were overrun by foreign record companies who were offering them contracts outside of the country. They felt that this reflected both informal interests at the state level—some state officials were making money by allowing foreign companies to offer contracts to Cuban artists, while at the same time limiting the dissemination of CUHHM artists by not offering contracts at home. Leaders of the AHS supported the creation of the ACR, feeling that the artists that were part of AHS were clearly not amateurs and that the movement had developed enough that it merited its own institution.

The goal of the creation of the ACR was to address the issue of access to the means of commercialization by serving as an official professional (and professionalizing) institution for CUHHM artivists. Susana García Amorós, who previously worked at the Instituto Cubano del Libro (Cuban Institute of the Book, a centralized editorial institution), was named as the director of the ACR. Although she was well known and well respected in Cuba's literary circles, some artists were not happy that she was not a musician, much less someone who knew anything about hip hop.

Many artists felt that this was another example of the state appointing an unqualified state official to head a Cuban institution, indicating the state's indifference to the artists and intellectuals within that institution. Some artists also felt that García Amorós was given the position simply because she was Black and dealt with race in her work as a literary scholar. This also intensified feelings that the state was not listening or taking the interests of the artists seriously. Magia, from the CUHHM group Obsesión, was appointed to be the head of the ACR in 2006.[3]

Hip hop artists' decision to incorporate themselves by supporting the development of the Cuban Agency of Rap is also linked to people's need to survive: profit-driven commercialization enables one person to take care of an entire family. Commercialization also provides a way to disseminate socially conscious and empowering ideologies. The racially conscious discourse in underground hip hop offers multiple ideological and material solutions to those who felt marginalized during the Special Period. During my 2006 interview in Havana with

DJ Leydis, she talked about the time when she first realized that non-Cuban "socially conscious" artists were using antigay discourse in their music, even to the point of advocating the murder of gay people:

> Y nunca la puede entender hasta que un día lo vi en vivo, y se cuando se terminó la música, él dijo en inglés perfecto: fuego a los homosexuales. Y tengo este disco y me gusta y me encanta esa música, pero la letra no la soporto, entiendes . . . si yo me pregunto, no. Debe ser algo extraño porque gente como ellos, que son tan buenos dando tanta educación en su música, no creo porque deben pensar así. Porque es el mundo, no y ellos hablan para educar el mundo.

> I could never understand it until one day I saw it live, and when they finished the music, he said in perfect English: fire to the homosexuals. I have this disc, and I like it and I love the music, but the words, I don't support it, you understand . . . if you ask me, no. It ought to be something strange that people like them who are so good at giving so much education in their music; I don't believe they ought to think this way. Because it is the world, right, and they talk about educating the world.

Leydis and other DJs refuse to play music that encourages violence or harm to other people. She says that she was really surprised that a group she likes — a hip hop group from Jamaica, which claims to offer socially conscious music, would come to Cuba and openly advocate killing gay people. She decided never to play the group again. During my visits to Cuba, I sat with Cuban hip hop artists, especially DJs, for hours translating music from English to Spanish. Cuban artists who are not fluent in English make their decisions to play the music of non-Cuban artists based on socially conscious symbols and the aesthetic of the artists in question, as judged by things like the album artwork and CD inserts. As in the case of the group from Jamaica, however, you can never be too sure about the message. For Cuban artists, even though someone like Kanye West may not appear to be materialistic, and neither does a socially problematic figure like 50 Cent, you can never be too sure that people have not appropriated underground symbolism to sell their music — after all, commercial artists did appropriate and commercialize hip hop.

The distinction of institutionalized versus noninstitutionalized refers to the way in which some hip hop artists define underground music in terms of its relationship to the state. Institutionalized hip hop is seen as suspect because the message of the songs is possibly co-opted to be representative of state interests. While it is true that the state dominates many of Cuba's material resources, specifically the market, and much of public space (it owns homes, cars, and performance spaces), the government does not control every aspect of daily life. In fact, the state depends on grassroots mobilization concerning everything from recording public/official meetings (though there is often a consensus at these meetings that the recorder will be turned off during critical discussions) to carrying out community-based projects. Because actors at the national and local levels are relied on to carry out particular tasks, numerous spaces and opportunities emerge for alternative discourses.

In essence, it is difficult for discourses to be policed, even within "official space." Official spaces can serve as alternative public spaces, depending on the context. Linked to this are varying levels of institutionalization: an artist who is not part of a state institution can perform in state-sponsored spaces, while other artists who belong to state institutions can deliver critical discourses in their artwork but will never be nationally distributed.

As artists work to ensure that the underground hip hop movement remains noninstitutionalized and underground, they are in effect negotiating the form that Cuba's reemergent Black public sphere will take.

– Public discourse and critique develop in the street, free of the state and the market.
– This provides an antiracist space in which the voices of Cuba's Black and mulat@ population are given primacy.
– Public discourse and critique are based on everyday experiences.
– Hip hop occurs in street corners, parks, Casas de Cultura, and other public places, so it is accessible to all members of the community.
– The movement focuses on consciousness-raising as a means to obtain the sublime.
– It offers a conceptualization of the sublime.
– There is a rejection of materialism, individualism, and other ideologies that fracture and disenfranchise the community.
– The movement is an effort to foster social change through democratic action at the grassroots level.

While some state institutions such as AHS and the Casas de Cultura offer space and material support for artists to undertake their projects, not all of these institutions operate uniformly across the Island. For example, the Casa de Cultura in Alamar offers a very different environment than the Casa de Cultura in Central Havana. Chapters of the AHS also offer different kinds of resources and support in various communities. The general effect is that since the origins of hip hop artists have depended on foreigners and their own local networks to obtain microphones, amps, turntables, speakers, computers, and other techno-logical equipment necessary to produce music. In fact, Vanessa Díaz and Larissa Díaz (2006) note that in the mid-1990s hip hop pioneer Ariel Fernández hand-cut and spliced cassette tapes and used rewired cassette players in place of turn-tables, as early hip hop artists did not have access to mixers (instruments that allow the DJ to change songs, overlap, or mix beats/songs with no noticeable break in the different musics used, unless the DJ creates one).

Because of material limitations in national structures of professionalization and dissemination, and because of the successes of the Nueva Trova movement with institutionalization, some hip hop artists pressed for the creation of the Agency of Rap, which was formed in 2003. This caused some ideological dif-ferences within the CUHHM. Some were concerned that underground hip hop was becoming incorporated like the Nueva Trova movement, a transition that they worried would end their ability to be an independent movement for social change. Through the usage of international networks, groups of underground artists began establishing their own underground studios (fig. 5.1).

Fernandes (2006) notes, however, that artists of the younger generations are more willing to negotiate with state institutions. One of the main reasons for this relates to the way in which marketing and commercialization are under-stood in Cuba. This is another example of how important language is when analyzing social life. In responding to a question about art in Cuba in a 2004 interview, Abel Prieto (then minister of culture) talked about the relationship between the market and Cuban art:

> I would say that in other places the market sets the rules; in Cuba, we only use it to promote our culture internationally. We think that the market is a great enemy of culture and true art. In fact, in the last decade, when an artistic manifestation appeared with a critical sense, the market has always tried to mutilate it. That is why we only approach the market as a means of promotion, but without making any concessions. Our cultural policy is not decided by the market as happens so many places, where the people may not know of a great writer or musician of their own country but know perfectly well the intimacies of Michael Jackson.[4]

In addition to the explicit market interests and profitability associated with commercialized music, some artists and intellectuals, like Prieto, think of mar-keting in terms of structures of mass dissemination.

I first learned of this view of commercialization in 2005 during an inter-view in Regla with Alexey of Obsesión. After our interview, Alexey, Magia, and I took a boat over to Old Havana. During the trip, we talked about Cuban hip

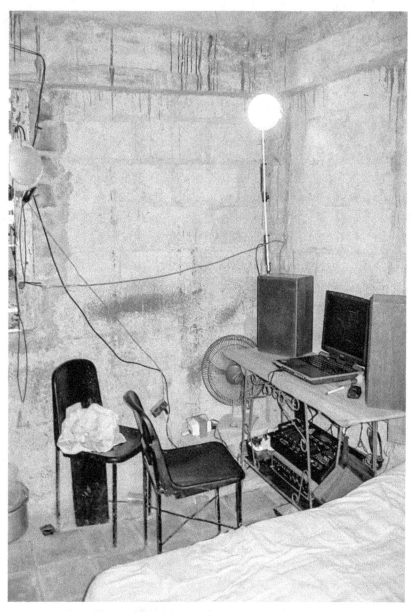

Figure 5.1. A community-run underground studio in a home. This room was the entirety of the home, which housed five people. I stood in the doorway to take this picture. This was one of several one-room houses that formed a square. In the center of the square (just outside of every home's doorway) was a communal hearth where people cooked their food over an open fire. A shared outhouse was just outside of the courtyard. Havana, January 2006. (Photo by Tanya L. Saunders)

hop and Black people in the United States. Once the ferry arrived at the dock, we started discussing Las Krudas and their work. As we walked along, Alexey got really excited when talking about how important Las Krudas are to the hip hop movement. "You know," he said, "they really should think about taking their music the commercial route." When I repeated what he had said, he smiled and said, "Yeah," as if there was no problem. I felt conflicted: how was it possible that an underground hip hop artist could support capitalism? He went on about how Las Krudas could reach many more people if they went commercial. He argued that their message was really important. I smiled and nodded. I felt that maybe I was missing something, because of this contradiction: an anticapitalist leader of a movement encouraging other artists to pursue profit? It just did not make sense until I came to understand that commercialism can also mean mass dissemination.

I heard other artists make similar comments about how they were being censored like early American hip hop artists. Given the history of censorship in Cuba, I wondered if they were discussing anything like the censorship that artists faced in the United States: in other words, was censorship based on a racist culture or on direct state intervention? It was only after a discussion with a colleague in 2006 that it began to make sense. He pointed out that the question facing artists in Cuba was not just about profit but about the ability to disseminate art through Cuba's state-run commercial institutions. It is the market that places a key role in censoring Black and Latin@ hip hop artists in the United States, but in Cuba it is the "taste" of individual officials that affects the ability to disseminate cultural work throughout the Island.

Some cultural workers in the United States who may produce very good music are passed over because it is assumed that their work will not sell. Others are encouraged to change their acts or to take on a different persona altogether in order to sell their work to the market. Hence cultural work loses its critical and expressive edge and people become alienated from their cultural work and from their spirit. The result is the constant recycling of uncritical, socially detached information that may have very harmful messages, though it is very marketable. For many Cuban artists, this is a way to create an oppressive society that is not moving forward to improve life for all people. Thus members of the newer generation of Cuban artists and intellectuals are attempting to negotiate with state institutions: they feel that their artwork must be geared toward the greater good if they want to participate in Cuban society as revolutionary artists and intellectuals. Access to the state's marketing institutions is important, even though, in a Cuban context, artists will not become as wealthy as Jay-Z or other multimillionaire American hip hop artists. While the opening of the economy and the decentralization of the state have led to alternative and even profit-driven capitalist discourses, the collective arts movements of the 1980s and 1990s have emerged as powerful counterdiscourses. This indicates that an independent, populist ideology still exists in Cuba concerning cultural production and its relationship to social change via challenging hegemonic culture as a central node of power in the maintenance and reproduction of social relations.

Concluding Remarks

The language that the CUHHM artivists use to describe their activism and their identities is unique among Cuba's contemporary music scenes. The terminology comes closest to another Cuban arts-based social movement, Nueva Trova. The examination of how artivists use language is important, because it helps scholars to understand more about the context of the artivists and the interventions that they seek to make. This is especially important given the overall context of Cuba after the Special Period: Cubans are developing new theories and new language to articulate their realities and develop relevant theories of social change. These artivists are revolutionary actors and are, interestingly, the results of Cuba's particular revolutionary process. As Che argued in *Socialism and Man in Cuba* ([1965] 1989), one of the goals of Cuba's cultural institutions, including its grassroots cultural institutions, was to create the conditions for organic intellectuals to emerge. Everyday Cuban citizens would be empowered through a process that included artistic literacy to be able to understand, critique, and express their lived realities and to develop new ideas and theories of social change. CUHHM artivists are consciously doing just that.

6

"I'm a Feminist, But I Don't Hate Men"

Emergent Black Feminist Discourses and Identity Politics within the Cuban Underground Hip Hop Movement

Magia MC said the following in our interview Havana in 2005:

El de la mujer es mucho más fuerte y más difícil de poder combatir. No siempre se le exige al hombre el ser bello.... Entonces, la mujer por ejemplo, arrastra todo ese sentido de la belleza. Debe tener buen cuerpo, de tener su cara bonita. Pero cara bonita a partir de la belleza europea, o sea nariz fina, boca fina. Entonces ya ahí estás como, bueno es una negra bonita. Yo pienso que no se ha aprendido a reconocer la belleza a partir de los prototipos negros, de negras que hay.... Que no necesariamente tiene que responder al prototipo de los modelos europeos, sólo que pintados de negro. Y entonces, en ese sentido yo pienso que nos queda mucho campo todavía.

> That which women face is much stronger and much harder to fight. Men are not always pressured to be beautiful. So woman, for example, is dragging with her this sense of beauty. She'd better have a good body and have her beautiful face. But a beautiful face based on European notions of beauty or a thin nose, a thin mouth. I think that she has not learned to recognize beauty based on Black prototypes, the Blacks that there are.... That it is not necessary to have to respond to the prototypes of European models that are only painted black. And so in this sense I think that we have a lot of ground to cover still.

The existence of Cuban women who publicly declare a feminist identity, a Black feminist identity, or a Black woman-centered identity politics to local and national audiences is an important development that highlights the profound changes that have been underway on the Island since the 1980s. Their presence within the Cuban Underground Hip Hop Movement specifically attests to its successful creation of a public space to address socially contentious issues such as the intersections of class, racism, sexism, homophobia, and heteronormativity. For much of the post-1959 period, self-identified feminists faced tremendous social and political sanctions and were often seen as divisive, counter-revolutionary man-haters. This chapter analyzes the heterogeneity of the women-centered discourses and identities of underground women MCs. Understanding the complex historical, cultural, and political context in which Cuban hip hop feminist praxis occurs is key. I attend to the different ways in which women within the CUHHM choose to identify themselves and how they negotiate the meaning of various identities. Not all women MCs self-identify themselves and their women-centered activism as feminist, though the number who do so has markedly increased since the debates discussed in this chapter, which peaked around 2006. As contemporary Cuban Black feminist identity was in formation from 1998 to 2006, however, women's feminist identification was overwhelmingly qualified as "Yes, I am a feminist, but I don't hate men." For these women, feminism was an ambivalent identity, all too often associated in Cuba with being socially divisive, man-hating, and unpatriotic. Some women performers' stance vis-à-vis feminism has changed over time, as in the case of one high-profile artist, Magia MC, who identified as a feminist in the late 1990s but had begun to reject a feminist identity by 2006.

In this chapter I examine the contradictions that emerge as women artivists, activists, and other participants in the CUHHM strive to articulate a feminist identity explicitly in solidarity with men. They talk about the concept of domestic violence in a few songs yet remain silent on the domestic violence that many of them face, often perpetrated by the very men who are included in women-centered space as a form of solidarity and revolutionary patriotism. While women MCs have articulated a feminist stance, they have also been limited in their ability to establish a discourse and feminist politics that truly challenge male supremacy both within the movement and within larger society. I conclude the chapter by discussing the effects of this limitation on the movement's ability to provide a safe space for all of its participants and the emergence of contemporary underground hip hop feminism in Cuba.

Gender, Race, State Policy, and Sexual Equality after 1959

Many of the ideological differences concerning the situation of Cuban women generally, and Black women specifically, reflect larger issues within Cuban society. Some of these issues are persistent, shared across multiple national contexts, such as domestic violence and restrictive cultural norms in which women are still valued according to their relationship with men (Allen 2011; Saunders 2009a, 2009b; Smith and Padula 1996). Others are specific to Cuba and its historical legacies of colonialism and socialist revolution. Paradoxically, one of the most difficult barriers that women in Cuba have to contend with is over fifty years of postrevolutionary state policy aimed at eliminating gender and racial inequality. After implementing material redistribution programs in the early 1960s, the Cuban state proclaimed that the problems of racism and sexism had been solved. The state now argued that it did not see gender or race, so the motives of those who continued to name these as issues were called into question. People who tried to discuss persistent racial or gender inequality or the need for women or Black Cubans, as groups, to empower themselves were seen as socially divisive, sexist, racist, or counter-revolutionary — accusations that resulted in socioeconomic sanctions and even imprisonment in some cases. Black Cubans and women could only make equality claims by using a raceless and genderless universalized citizenship discourse that in effect rendered their claims baseless or irrelevant. Although some women and racial groups benefited from the state's economic redistribution policies, these gains were paired with oppressive cultural norms and increased marginalization in other arenas, especially during and after the Special Period.

These larger contradictory sociopolitical dynamics were reflected in the early (1998–2006) feminist debates about Blackness and femininity within the Cuban Underground Hip Hop Movement. Women hip hop artists often struggled to negotiate the tensions of developing an emancipatory discourse for women alongside revolutionary-citizen discourse and Black woman-centered discourse. As discussed in chapter 2, revolutionary-citizen discourse privileges the roles and perspectives of men, naturalizes heterosexuality, and entrenches culturally based ideologies that confine women's contributions to motherhood and family. These discourses were taken up and repackaged as the post-1959 revolutionary ideology of the liberated "revolutionary" woman. After the Cuban Revolution in 1959, the state undertook what Fidel Castro called a "revolution within the Revolution" to secure women's equal rights (Bunck 1994; Fleites-Lear 2003). During the early years after the Revolution, there were numerous debates about what types of work women should take on in the public sphere. The state commissioned studies to figure out what jobs were appropriate for women (Smith and Padula 1996). The revolutionary leaders wanted to ensure that women were not given jobs that might jeopardize their roles as mothers and wives. These early concerns reflect some of the initial contradictions in revolutionary ideology that would shape the quest for women's equality after 1959.

Contemporary Cuban citizenship is constructed around the image of the militant (male, heterosexual) revolutionary fighter in such a way that to be a citizen is to be a revolutionary. Revolutionary discourses surrounding femininity yield a feminine subject whose representation as a revolutionary is dependent upon her sexual relationship to men. Additionally, the state's limitations on the public articulation of identities outside of a "Cuban" or "revolutionary" identity have restricted the production of discourses that women can use to address the complexity and heterogeneity of their experiences as women and as revolutionary actors working for social change. Women have had to use state discourses of universalism and gender invisibility to make claims for rights and to demand state initiatives aimed at social redress.

The Federation of Cuban Women (Federación de Mujeres Cubanos or FMC: Cuba's state-run women's rights organization and the *only* such organization recognized by the state) has produced texts such as *La mujer en Cuba socialista* (The Woman in Socialist Cuba, 1977) and *Código de familia* (The Family Code, 1975), published by the Ministry of Justice. These texts have sought to challenge persisting sexist cultural norms. Yet the logo of the FMC itself belies the limits of state-sponsored feminist critique and the resilience of racialized and gendered ideologies. The image is of a straight-haired, fair-skinned woman, dressed in military fatigues. She has a gun strapped to her back and a baby in her arms. Women's revolutionary status is thus tied to their reproductive capabilities, which are in turn symbolically linked to the defense of the nation.

The texts of the FMC similarly illustrate the contradictions within the state's discourse on women's liberation. For example, on the first page of *The Woman in Socialist Cuba* (Ministerio de Justicia 1977), the authors write: "This book recognizes the juridical norms that shape the means adopted by the Revolution, aimed at protecting women, maternity, marriage, and children." Likewise, *The Family Code* (Ministerio de Justicia 1975) promotes monogamous heterosexual marriage as an ideal (Bunck 1994; Fleites-Lear 2003; Smith and Padula 1996). While advocating for a shared division of labor within the home, key parts of the code further essentialize women and men as sexualized and gendered subjects. On the first page, under the heading "The Objectives of This Code," the authors emphasize the importance of maintaining a healthy conjugal relationship between a man and a woman. Together they form the unit responsible for providing care and a moral compass for children and the family.

The protection of "socialist morality" is a central theme in these documents. Though no explicit definition of morality is provided, the implicit framework for understanding it codifies previously existing racialized social norms concerning femininity and motherhood. The state began to delineate its stance on morality through social policies enacted a few years before the publication of *The Family Code*. At the 1971 Congress on Education and Culture, for example, the government mandated that homosexuals were not to hold positions that directly influenced the moral development of children. After the 1971 Congress, any known gay persons participating in Cuba's educational and cultural institutions lost their positions and LGBT students were prohibited from graduating from educational institutions. Penal codes were established for "public scandals" explicitly stating that public homosexual acts should be fined (Lumsden 1996). Further mandating heteronormative social relations, the FMC also prohibited known lesbians from joining its ranks until the 1980s (Smith and Padula 1996).[1] In short, state policy directives of the 1960s and 1970s reentrenched cultural norms concerning femininity, in which the liberation of women as moral and feminine subjects who desired men was encouraged, while challenges to gender and sexuality as structures of power were condemned as encouragement of immorality.

Women, the State, and Hip Hop Feminism

The state's limitations on any identity formation outside a "Cuban" or "revolutionary" identity has limited the production of discourses that women can use to articulate the complexity and heterogeneity of their experiences in Cuba. In Cuban society, women are restricted in their ability to access all of the social, economic and juridical rights associated with Cuban citizenship. Wendy Brown's (1992) description of the gendered welfare state is useful in understanding the situation of Cuban women vis a vis Cuba's large, Revolutionary welfare state. Brown posits that the welfare state depoliticizes the culturally-based ideologies concerning femininity by naturalizing women's work in the home and motherhood as a rite of passage. Furthermore, Cuban laws and welfare policies reinforce ideologies concerning femininity in which women are defined out of "citizen," and defined as feminine subjects. Therefore women are rendered to the unsafe, and constantly surveilled space of the home. The state and the public sphere, on the other hand, continues to be implicitly understood, as male/masculine space.

While the state presents itself as acting in the best interests of women, it further disempowers women through presenting itself as a non-gendered impartial guarantor of rights. As a result is difficult for women to challenge the supposedly gender neutral, impartial state. Nonetheless the state's discourse and policies prevent the politicization of life in the private sphere, which is culturally defined as beyond the reach of state intervention. Woman is defined as "citizen" based on her femininity, and is then unable to access the rights guaranteed to all citizens because she is a woman.

This is an outcome of how welfare policies and cultural norms together function to reinforce conflicting ideologies concerning the role and the position (at times literally the location) of women in society. For Black women the situation is more complex.

Feminists such as Cathy Cohen (2005) argue that heternormativity supports and reinforces institutional racism, patriarchy, and class exploitation. Cohen argues that the assumption that heteronormativity is equated with social privilege and homosexuality does not reflect the experiences of Black women, especially poor Black women, who are framed as deviant in a white normative imaginary. Cohen (2005) wants "to remind us of the numerous ways that sexuality and sexual deviance from a prescribed norm have been used to demonize and to oppress various segments of the population, even some classified under the label "'heterosexual'" (42). This is a struggle that many women artivists, activists, and other participants faced in the movement: being racialized as Black women, especially as poor Black women, does not guarantee them the same privileges of heterosexuality afforded to white Cuban women. Within the multiple racialized forms of social oppression that Black women face, it is an illusion for them to believe that they are included in normative sexuality (or, better put, that they should not reject their own investments in normative sexuality) because Black women are already understood to be sexually deviant by virtue of their race.

The threat of being called a lesbian, a man-hater, unfeminine, and, by extension, a bad citizen prevented stigmatized women's independent organizing to talk about their experiences and concerns linked gender and race. They almost always had to address these issues in front of men. Important issues concerning domestic violence within the movement, particularly the violent, sexist tendencies of male artivists, activists, and participants, did not get discussed. Many times it was the male batterers themselves who demanded, and received, access to women-centered spaces. Furthermore, the visibility of Las Krudas as the embodiment of sexual deviance caused a profound psychological rupture for both men and women within the movement. This unconsciously forced many straight women into feeling that they had to make a choice between their identities as women and Cuban citizens united for social change and being angry, man-hating lesbians who were divisive and rejected the ideals of the Revolution (aka individual rejection of participatory citizenship). Jorge Enrique, the editor-in-chief of the Cuban hip hop magazine *Movimiento*, spoke about the impact of the presence of Las Krudas onstage in our interview in Havana in 2013:

De hecho, en Cuba las expresiones gay siempre fueron más visibles en lo masculino. Incluso, esto es una cosa curiosa: el machismo dentro de lo gay. Yo me he puesto a pensar: ¿Jorge, machismo también dentro de lo gay?

¡Esto está jodido!, pero es real, porque de algún modo era más natural ver a un hombre gay, la gente decía: eh, mira a la loca esa, pero cuando se trataba de una lesbiana, ya el asunto era más chocante.

> In fact, in Cuba gay expressions were always more visible among males. Including, this is something curious, the machismo within gayness. I had to stop and to think: Jorge, machismo is also within that which is gay? This is fucked! But it's real, because in one way it was more natural to see a gay male, people would say: eh, look at this [effeminate gay male], but when they encounter a lesbian, already that's a subject that's more shocking.

In "Grupo OREMI: Black Lesbians and the Struggle for Safe Social Space in Havana" (Saunders 2009a), I discuss in greater detail independent data concerning perceptions of gays and lesbians showing that Cubans were far more resistant to the idea of a lesbian and were overwhelmingly likely to see lesbians as disgusting, dirty, uncouth, aggressive, unpleasant, and even antisocial. Even though some people had negative feelings about gay men, among least 30 percent of the sampled population gay men were likely to be seen as being nicer than lesbians and pleasant, sociable, and friendly. There were virtually no positive feelings toward lesbians. In fact, only 4 percent of the sampled population felt that lesbians and gay men were treated equally (Saunders 2009a). As Jorge Enrique notes, gay male sexuality is at least visible in the larger public sphere, while the presence of a lesbian is "shocking." This was a common theme in my interviews with Cuban artists, scholars, and activists, including people frequently using the description of their heads exploding when Las Krudas walked out on the stage and openly declared that they were lesbians *and* feminists (see chapter 7). While these theories certainly are useful in understanding the nexus of power affecting women in Cuba, it is also important to engage theory which reflects the major generational shift that has occurred for women in Cuba and in many parts of the world: hip hop feminism.

Black Music, Black Women, and Hip Hop Feminism

Cuba's hip hop feminists are part of a larger community of Cuban artivists who participate in a localized global hip hop movement. Global hip hop functions as a transnational, countercultural structure of communication and mobilization and as a transnational Black public sphere. Cuban underground hip hop artivists are not only producing music but also participating in global discussions of antiracist social change (Saunders 2012). Black women have historically been active participants in the Black public sphere, especially in the area of the arts (Davis 1998). The Cuban Underground Hip Hop Movement is no exception;

Black women have been foundational and constitutive members of the move-ment from the beginning. But at the same time their willingness to identify as feminists has been and continues to be tempered by their efforts to grapple with hegemonic discourses of femininity and revolutionary consciousness. By exploring women's participation in the CUHHM and their varied strategies for engaging with feminism, this chapter contributes to the emerging body of work examining hip hop feminism as a form of global feminist praxis.

The CUHHM emerged during the 1990s when the Cuban state faced a legiti-macy crisis, as generational pressures for social change increased and the loss of Soviet-based economic stability resulted in the post-Soviet economic downturn called the Special Period. This resulted in a decrease in the economic programs that buffered the material effects of culturally based forms of racism (Fernandes 2006; Perry 2004). Although hip hop is a male-dominated space, it has never been an exclusively male public space. As in other Black musical traditions, Black women have played a key role in Cuban hip hop from the beginning. Outside of the view of the larger public sphere, Black women have had equal participation in and at times even dominated Black music cultures (Davis 1998). Describing hip hop as a Black public sphere, Gwendolyn D. Pough (2011) argues that Black women have always been vocal members of the genre. She examines women's participation in hip hop as part of a new generation of Black feminist critique,[2] arguing that this generation has used hip hop as a way to engage issues such as sexism and homophobia in the larger public sphere. Similarly, Tricia Rose (1994) identifies hip hop as a key site of contemporary Black feminist critique.

Many in the larger public sphere are not aware of or do not understand the presence and influence of politicized Black women artists within hip hop, as Black music cultures and their leadership are often gendered (and marketed) as male and misogynistic by the music industry (Davis 1998; Durham 2007). As commercialized hip hop, particularly in the United States, became gendered and racialized as Black and male, it has also been racially sexualized as hyper-heterosexual and hyper-phallocentric. The presence of gays and lesbians is also erased from hip hop history and representation, though some scholars such as Keyes (2011) and Clay (2008, 2012) have acknowledged the presence of lesbian/bi hip hop/neo-soul artists, such as Queen Pen and Me'Shell Ndegeocello, dur-ing the early years of commercial hip hop.

There have been numerous critiques of how the oppositionality of hip hop has been commercialized and marketed to a larger public sphere obsessed with blackness as a form of social deviancy (Pough et al. 2007). As commercialization of the genre has progressed, women's critical voices and participation within hip hop have been narrowed to being male objects of sexual gratification and subjects who crave objectification. Some hip hop feminists have pointed out and protested Black male complicity in the sacrificing of Black women for economic gain (Durham 2007). But despite the ways in which commercialized hip hop has come to represent hip hop in the larger American public sphere, women still actively participate in both commercial and noncommercial hip hop. Tricia Rose, like Evelyn Brooks Higginbotham (1992), points out that the intersections of race and class encourage a form of solidarity across gender lines within the Black community, because race functions as a metalanguage, especially in the way gender and sexuality are understood. Racial solidarity results in cross-gender alliances within the Black community (including blackness within Latinidad) that are difficult to re-create between Black women and their white feminist and white lesbian peers. This difficulty is largely a result of dominant white, feminist, and lesbian discourses surrounding femininity and sexuality that marginalize nonwhite women's gender expression and sexuality. Black women involved in any aspect of hip hop are often portrayed by white feminists as women who have been duped or co-opted into being unconscious sexual objects of men (Pough 2011; Rose 1994). This erasure of Black women's creative agency within hip hop ironically obscures the important role and critiques of women artists within the Cuban Underground Hip Hop Movement.

The Hip Hop Feminist Debates: Critically Engaging the Work of Women MCs

Creating Space for Women and Afro-Cuban Ancestry in the CUHHM: Magia MC

Magia MC, the first hip hop artist to become director of the Cuban Agency of Rap, is the first woman MC to emerge with an explicitly Afrocentric discourse and identification within the Cuban Underground Hip Hop Movement (fig. 6.1).[3] The trajectory of Magia's relationship with feminism reflects shifts and debates within the CUHHM itself and illustrates the ambivalent, often strategic ways in which women MCs negotiate multiple identities and political commitments. Influenced in part by feminist debates within the movement between 1998 and 2003, Magia began identifying as a feminist during the early 2000s. But shifts within the movement and, most significantly, the growing popularity of Las Krudas CUBENSI (a group of "out" Black lesbian feminists: see chapter 7) spurred Magia to stop identifying as a feminist in approximately 2003. During a 2006 interview with Magia, I asked her what term was she using to define herself as a woman-centered activist who embraces blackness, as she no longer used

Figure 6.1. Magia MC.
(Photo courtesy of
Sahily Borrero)

"feminist."[4] She responded: "I don't know. The question of identity is something that I am struggling with very much at this moment." This notion of struggle was similarly echoed in interviews with other heterosexual women MCs, even those who identified as feminist but felt the need to qualify: "I'm a feminist, but I don't hate men." These formative debates concerning feminism and hip hop took place during the early years of the movement, approximately 1995–2006.

I started my 2006 interview with Magia by asking her to tell me about the history of hip hop in Cuba in her own words, to tell me about her history within the movement, and to talk about the themes that she addressed in her lyrics and why. Her particular story focuses on two key themes: her personal experiences in developing a Black consciousness and the tensions that she felt at the time in articulating a feminist identity, which ultimately led to her rejecting that identity.

Magia is one of the formative members of the old-school generation of the Cuban Underground Hip Hop Movement. Her entrance into the CUHHM was unique: it started when her husband, Alexey, began performing with a group called Obsesión in 1995. The group had about fifteen members. When Obsesión eventually fell apart, Alexey, upset about the imminent demise of the group, asked Magia to work with him as a duo with the same name. She agreed. She wanted to support her husband's vision even though she thought it was a little strange: she was looking forward to Alexey eventually working full-time and preparing for a family.

After Magia decided to form a duo with Alexey, she began thinking more about her role as an artist in the CUHHM. She knew that she wanted to address issues that were near and dear to her, such as her experiences as a Black woman. She felt that an antiracist perspective, centered on interrogating internalized racism, was one of the ways in which she could contribute to the emerging movement. In 2006 Magia explained when she first became conscious of how race operated in Cuba:

> Nos ayudó muchísimo las investigaciones que también estaba haciendo Ariel. Producto de eso también nos enteramos de este curso que estaba haciendo Tomás, o sea por la vía de Ariel, nos enteramos de este curso que estaba haciendo Tomás, que iba a empezar a hacer Tomás en la Biblioteca Nacional.
>
> Yo no sé si fue un poquito antes o un poquito después. Yo creo que fue un poquito antes que también leímos, nos ayudó mucho el libro de Malcolm X, la biografía de Malcolm X. Fue algo que nos ayudó muchísimo, o sea, a entender de qué manera uno lograba realizarse, uno mismo como negro, qué cosas tenían que asumir, y cuáles eran los valores, no o sea, todas esas cosas. Un poco como que era la ubicación, bueno éste es el camino, o sea el pensamiento en éste. Yo creo que lo que uno estaba buscando leer hace mucho tiempo para reafirmar cosas. Y el Taller con Tomasito nos dio una serie de elementos y fundamentos sobre la historia, sobre la situación racial aquí en Cuba. Bueno ahí vinieron temas como los pelos, que fue un tema muy importante para mí, aunque mucha gente lo ve como un tema muy . . . [*She shrugs and makes a waving motion with her hands, implying that it is not important.*]

>> It helped us a lot the research that Ariel was doing. What also helped us was the course that Tomás, or better through Ariel's guidance, we entered this course that Tomás was doing, that he was beginning to do at the National Library.
>>
>> I don't know if it was a little before or a little later. I believe that it was a bit before that also we read, it helped us a lot, Malcolm X's book, the biography of Malcolm X. It was something that helped us a lot, or better,

to understand that the way you could realize yourself, yourself as a Black person, that the things you have to take on, and things that were values [to embrace], and all of those things. I believe that I had been looking to read [these things] for a long time to reaffirm things. And the workshop with Tomasito gave us a series of elements and fundamentals about history, about the racial situation here in Cuba. But then there come the themes like hair, that was a very important theme for me, although people see it as very . . . [*She shrugs and makes a waving motion with her hands, implying that it is not important.*]

Magia developed a Black consciousness after several nearly simultaneous events: taking a course on Black Cuban history taught by national archivist Tomás Fernández Robaina, critically engaging the research of DJ, producer, and writer Ariel Fernández, and reading the autobiography of Malcolm X. These events occurred within a similar period for many of the youth who would become influential artivists in the Cuban Underground Hip Hop Movement. As a result of these formative experiences, Magia realized two things. The first was that she wanted to focus on being a Black person within Cuban society. She received affirmation of her suspicions that there was more to Cuban history than she had been taught: that Black people were indeed a part of Cuban history but had been rendered invisible in texts and the scholarship available to most Cubans, especially youths. She also began to embrace a Black identity as an identity with sociopolitical meaning: as she puts it, "there were values [to embrace]." Through her work in the CUHHM as an MC and organizer, Magia decided to address persistent racism in Cuban society and the silences in Cuba's educational system concerning race. She also wanted to help Black youths to develop self-esteem and a sense of national belonging by learning about and identifying with Black historical figures and their own ancestors.

Magia's second realization was that she wanted to strengthen her ideas concerning what Blackness meant for her, not just as a Black person, but as a Black woman:

Por ejemplo, comencé más o menos a tener una idea sobre la participación por ejemplo dentro de mí, dentro de la cultura . . . en los coloquios donde a nosotros nos daba . . . mucha picazón de investigar, de buscar, que sé yo. Y también no solamente como mujer, sino también como mujer negra dentro de una sociedad que posteriormente . . . fueron cosas que me fueron a mí dando elementos para poder tanto fortalecer mis ideas, como mi perspectiva a la hora de desarrollar un proyecto, a la hora de hacer un tema, a la hora de hablar.

> For example, I began more or less to have an idea about my participation
> in the culture [the hip hop movement] . . . in the colloquiums that he
> [Tomás Fernández Robaina] gave us . . . it really spurred us to research, to
> look for, whatever, and not only as a woman, but as a Black woman within
> a society that until then . . . They were things that gave me the elements
> to have the power to strengthen my ideas, my perspective when it came
> time to develop a project, and the time to perform a song, when it was
> time to speak.

Magia felt that taking the time to research what it meant to be a Black
woman and to reflect on what it meant for her would prepare her to make her
own intellectual intervention when she became an MC. As she asked herself,
"Who am I?" she realized that "I should be thinking about racial problems to
answer that question." Magia spoke about her work with Alexey:

O sea, lo veo como una situación donde la sociedad tiene mucho que ver.
Lo mismo ocurre con el problema racial. O sea hay un texto que es uno
de los que estamos defendiendo ahora que es con relación a que en el sis-
tema educativo no existe una . . . no hay un tratamiento sobre este tipo de
tema. O sea que el niño chiquito pienso que en la escuela sí debe haber
algo, algún tipo de educación que lo conlleve a sentirse orgulloso porque
es negro, a saber que existen líderes negros que han luchado por la revolución, que han luchado, que existen doctores, que existen maestros. Yo
pienso que es algo que el niño debe ir desarrollando desde que está en la
escuela, un poco para poder sentir el orgullo ese de que: Bueno soy negro
como fulano y negra como mengana. . . . Pero todavía estamos arrastrando,
yo pienso que todo este racismo desde hace muchísimos años. Es algo que
está muy internalizado, que uno nace con eso y que a veces es difícil ir
limpiando de esas cosas, no. . . . Hay temas en nosotros que no van a faltar,
es el tema de la racialidad, el tema de la mujer, es el tema quizás del amor,
porque son temas que de cualquier modo es el tema de la violencia domés-
tica. Son temas que de cualquier modo no se han resuelto todavía en nuestra sociedad y nosotros los vamos a tratar desde diferentes puntos de vista.

> Better put, I see it as a situation where society needs a lot. The same with
> the racial problem. Or better, there is a song that is one of the ones we are
> doing right now, that has to do with the education system that doesn't
> engage this type of theme. Or better, for a small child I think school ought
> to be doing something, some type of education that will help a child feel
> proud to be Black, to know that there exist Black leaders who have fought

for the revolution, who have fought, that there exist doctors and teachers. I think that it's something that children should continue developing from school so that they can feel a little pride and say: "Well, I'm a Black man like such and such and I'm a Black woman like so and so. . . ." But still we are struggling, I think that all of this is racism that has existed for many years. It something that's very internalized, and you are born with this and at times it's difficult to get rid of these things, right. . . . There are things that we are always going to do, the theme of race, the theme of women, sometimes the theme of love, because they are themes that at whatever moment could be about domestic violence. They are themes that for whatever reason have not been resolved still in our society and we're going to try and engage them from a different perspective.

Magia and Alexey are committed to focusing on several key themes in their music: race, Black history, and self-esteem. During the early years of the Cuban Underground Hip Hop Movement, Magia did not articulate a specifically feminist identity. Her work was primarily focused on addressing the question of race. During her interview, she spoke about how her Black consciousness developed. As a child, she loved to comb her hair and make ponytails—despite having to straighten her hair with chemicals in order to do so. She mentioned the scarring from the chemicals and how there is a place on the back of her head where her hair does not grow now as a result. She used the example of the pain she went through to straighten her hair to illustrate how racism is so internalized for many young Black girls and women who do not critically reflect on the excessiveness of this effort to conform to racialized beauty ideals. Through participating in Cuba's critical artistic and intellectual spheres she first began to reflect on her own experiences and to realize how much they were linked to the silences surrounding race.

In giving examples about her own internalized racism as a youth, Magia also mentioned some of the perspectives on Africans that she had as a child and teenager. These were common prejudices of many young Black Cubans who were taught to reject, detest, and attempt to hide their African heritage. For example, she remembered thinking that the clothing of Angolans living and working in Cuba was "funny." She also remembers being younger and wanting to have surgery to make her lips thinner. She said in 2006:

Que me hiciera esconder la bemba. [*She narrows her lips to show how she used to contort her lips continuously to make them look thinner, without thinking about it.*] Y, o sea, era una negra, yo fui una negra que crecí con eso. Yo creí queriendo que mi pelo fuera lacio y, no te digo, deben haber ahí imágenes mías con el pelo lacio.

> That made me hide my lips. [*She narrows her lips to show how she used to contort her lips continuously to make them look thinner, without thinking about it.*] And, better put, I was a Black girl, and I was a Black girl who grew up with that. I believed that I wanted my hair straight, didn't I tell you, there ought to be some images here with my hair straight.

Magia talks about how Black women's bodies are not culturally accepted as naturally beautiful. Not surprisingly hair is a common theme in Obsesión's music. Here are the lyrics of their song "Pelos" (Hair, by Alexey Rodríguez Mola and Magia López Cabrera):

Pelo suelto y carretera	Hair free flowing in the wind
No hay desrriz	There is no frizziness
Me di cuenta que pa' que	And I realized for what?
Si yo no naci así	If I was not born this way
El hombre que me quiere	The man that loves me
Me acepta como soy	Accepts me as I am
Africana y pal carajo	African and what the hell
¡¡A donde quiera que voy!!	I'm going to go where I want
Hoy mi naturaleza	Today my naturalness
Rompe patrón de belleza	Breaks the norm of beauty
Que no me vengan con que pa' lucir más fina	Don't come to me with this in order to be more beautiful
Hay que plancharse la cabeza pa' versar más femenina	I have to straighten my hair to be seen as more feminine
Óyeme no Nananina mis códigos determinan	Listen to me no Nananina [unattractive TV character] determines my codes
Iéndose por encima de todos esos esquemas se encaracola	Going above all frameworks
Mi pelo y es postura ante la vida	My kinky hair is my posture in life
Una doctrina	It's a doctrine
Que consolida esta imagen que te vengo dando	That consolidates this image that I am giving
Conmigo duermen 400 años soñando con el hasta cuando	Within me they slept 400 years with it until
El procedimiento te estira el pelo lo hace mentiroso	The method that you use to style your hair is a lie

Opacando lo que naturalmente es hermoso.	Hiding what is naturally beautiful

Coro:
¡¡Pa' rriba los pelos!!
¡¡Que crezcan los dread locs!!
¡¡Al que le guste bien y al que no, también!!
(*se repite*)

Chorus:
Stand up for hair!!
May dreadlocks grow!!
To all that you like and don't like!! It's all good!
(*Repeat*)

Según decreto ley cencuenti yo [decreto-ley 150]
a mi concierto y aprende que
tu pelo es malo solo cuando muerde
Si no quieres el que tienes entonces
Dámelo no lo mereces
Sigue quemándote el cráneo
Deja que pasen dos meses
La verdad en forma de raíces aparece

The second directive of the law 150 [cencuenti] yo
In my concert and I learned that
Your hair is bad only when you butcher it
If you don't want what you have,
Then give it to me! You don't deserve it
Go ahead burning yourself on your scalp
Just leave it alone for two months
And the truth in terms of your heritage will appear

Siempre,
A veces recibo raras miradas
De quienes creen que para estar bien arreglada
Necesito tener la moña estirada
Lo nuestro es nuestro y habla por nosotros
Ahí va mi idiosincrasia capilar
El aire no me despeina como a pilar

Always
At times I receive strange looks
From those who believe that in order to be put together
You need to have your hair straight
What is ours is ours and speaking for us
There goes my idiosyncrasy capitulating
The air does not make my hair fall out like a pillar

Veo al caminar un mar de tindas
Que no venden muñecas negras
Pero esa es otra historia que contar.

Walking I see a sea of stores
That don't sell any dolls
But this is the history that I want to tell you

Coro
¡¡Pa' rriba los pelos!!
¡¡Que crezcan los dread locs!!
¡¡Al que le guste bien y al que no, también!!

Chorus:
Stand up for hair!!!
May dreadlocks grow!!
To all that you like and don't like!! It's all good!!

(se repite)	*(Repeat)*
Identidad siempre dispuesta	Identity is always available
Orgullo sale a la palestra	Pride comes out of the lecture
Obsesión dice y demuestra	Obsesión says and shows
Convicción en talla extra	Conviction, extra on point
Entonces	So
Sales o entras	Leave or enter
O lo escondes	Or hide it
O lo muestras	Or show it
O te pierdes	Or you lose yourself
O te encuentras	Or you encounter yourself
Tu piénsalo que yo mientras	You think about it and meanwhile I
Seguire en la pelea	Will continue with the fight
De a partir de lo que somos	Departing from what we are
Entonces	So
Lo que sea.	Let it be.
(Coro se repite)	*(Chorus/(Repeat)*

Obsesión began performing this song around 2004. In the lyrics Magia asserts her natural beauty. She argues that straightening your hair because society believes it to "look more beautiful" is crazy. Why is it logical to change something so natural as hair texture to look more beautiful—an idea based on society's ideals? Your hair is the texture that it's going to be naturally, so it doesn't make sense to alter nature to fit a socially imposed standard of beauty. Magia and Alexey link this standard of beauty to 400 years of "sleep" (colonialism). Obsesión argues that the culturally accepted aesthetic is also a colonial product. Through the song, Magia and Alexey speaks to the corporal reality of blackness and the ways in which it is managed, dismissed, and devalued by those embracing racialized notions of beauty. Magia comments, for example, on how this invisibility is reinforced daily when she speaks of seeing a sea of stores without a single Black doll. The song ends by challenging members of the audience to show their pride, to embrace themselves and their hair.

"Hair" speaks directly to Black identity politics. In *AfroCubanas*, the first book focused only on Black Cuban women written by Cuban women and published in Cuba, Cuban scholar Carmen González Chacón (2011) writes: "Una de las libertades más tangibles observadas en la féminas dentro de la cultura hip hop, sin dudas, ha sido la emancipación de los pelos" (One of the most tangible liberties observed by the women within hip hop culture, without a doubt, has been the emancipation of hair) (181). In this text she discusses the oppression that women, particularly Black and mulata women, face. She calls Afro-descendant men to task for buying into an artificial and unrealistic standard of beauty that further damages the self-esteem of Afro-descendant women. González Chacón refers to the economic costs of straightening and maintaining straight hair and cites Magia's frequent discussion of how hair-styling chemicals damaged her hair and scalp. The internalization of racist aesthetics, González Chacón argues, comes at a price.

Obsesión urges its audience to embrace their own bodies and identities, but Alexey and Magia also try to integrate this into their own practice, first by simply being themselves. Magia explains how the duo, by openly embracing their African cultural heritage, began to address the nuanced ways in which race shapes even the most subtle aspects of daily life:

> Y por ejemplo, ya en el año '96, '97, ya nosotros estábamos hablando del tema este de Siguaraya,[5] que aparecen en "Un montón de cosas." No era exactamente el tema de Siguaraya, como título "Siguaraya," pero sí era un tema que tenía que ver con la negritud.
>
> Entonces, ya era como vestigios de que uno iba empezando a despertarse y yo pienso que lo primero no fue yo reconocerme como mujer negra, lo primero fue el reconocimiento a los ancestros. El reconocimiento de que tenía abuelos negros, de que mi mamá era negra también, de que ellos como que merecían como un homenaje por todo lo que hicieron, por ser nuestros abuelos. Entonces la canción de Siguaraya es como una conmemoración a los ancestros de nosotros. Entonces ahí está presente el problema de la negritud, vista como reconocimiento a los ancestros. Yo pienso que eso fue lo primero que nosotros nos pudimos cuenta. Después, bueno ya así fue como más: Bueno ahora, quién soy yo y qué es lo que estoy haciendo ahora mismo. Que es lo que yo pienso ahora mismo sobre este problema racial.

> And for example, already in '96, '97, already we were talking about the theme of Siguaraya, that appeared in "Un montón de cosas." It was not exactly the theme of Siguaraya, like the title "Siguaraya," but yes, it was a theme that had something to do with blackness.
>
> So already there were vestiges of beginning to wake up, and I think that the first thing was not me recognizing myself as a Black woman, the first thing was to remember the ancestors. The recognition that I had Black grandparents, that my mother was Black also, that they merited homage

for all the things that they have done, for being our grandparents. So the song "Siguaraya" is like a commemoration of our ancestors. The issue of blackness is present, seen through the recognition of the ancestors. I think that this was the first time that we could express it. Afterward, well, it was more like: OK, now who am I and what is it that I'm doing right now? What is it that I think right now, about the race issue?

The act of recognizing your ancestors rejects the culturally based Cuban ideological mandate of imagining yourself as being of European, specifically Spanish, descent. Recognizing your ancestors takes on important symbolic/cultural significance as hip hop artists publicly draw from African and Afro-Cuban culture and religious traditions, something that was discouraged during much of Cuban history, including after the Cuban Revolution. Magia was one of the first MCs to wear an Afro and to wear a dashiki and other clothing with an African aesthetic. Odaymara of Las Krudas commented that when she first started going to hip hop concerts as an audience member, it blew her mind to see a Black woman onstage calling herself a feminist, wearing an Afro and African clothing. She said, "Can you imagine what that was like for us to see a Black woman on the stage with an Afro and talking about blackness?" (personal communication, 2006). When Magia began to MC, she delivered a message that filled a significant void: she became one of the first women to publicly to articulate an Afrocentric Black identity and politics within the movement. This public articulation of a Black identity and epistemology inspired future generations of MCs, including many who are women.

While Magia came to a critical understanding of race through music, however, her relationship with feminism has been much more ambivalent. She did not publicly articulate a women-centered or feminist identity when she initially began to MC. She expressed a revolutionary consciousness concerning gender, but this revolutionary discourse actually denies the relevance of race, class, and gender in Cuba, as noted above. I asked Magia to talk about gender and her work within the movement. She described how she began organizing concerts with only women from 1997 to 2000:

Las primeras cosas que yo hice, que fue organizar solamente un concierto de mujeres en La Madriguera.[6] En La Madriguera nosotros teníamos un espacio que era de Obsesión, era la peña de Obsesión, se llamaba Obsesión por el hip hop. Y ahí hacíamos las peñas cada mes. . . . Una de las cosas que nosotros realizábamos eran estos conciertos de mujer. Que nos parecía, en particular a mí, que eran muy importantes en el sentido de poder realizar la presencia de la mujer dentro del movimiento . . . también en aquellos tiempos participaba con nosotros, nos sentábamos y decíamos que no solamente era importante la mujer dentro del rap, sino también la mujer que pintaba, la mujer que hacía poema, la mujer que cantaba. O sea, todo tipo de mujer. La mujer que hacía teatro. Ahí estábamos todas representadas ahí de alguna manera. Y fueron los primeros pasos que quizás se dieron con este sentido de impulsar un poco el trabajo de la mujer. . . .

Y entonces la primera vez que lo hicimos, bueno a mí no se me olvida nunca. Estaba, había como una exposición, había una exposición donde Diamela, la fotógrafa. . . . Teníamos fotógrafos, teníamos gente que escribía artículos, teníamos que filmaba también, había diseñadores que no venían de escuela. Todas esas cosas estaban acompañando al movimiento.

> The first thing that I did was to organize concerts only for women in La Madriguera. In La Madriguera we had a space that was for Obsesión, that was called "Obsesión for Hip Hop." And there we had some battles every month . . . one of the things we did was these concerts of women [artists]. What we noticed, me in particular, was that it was really important to increase the presence of women in the movement . . . also during this time, we realized that we, we felt and said that not only was it important that women rap, but also women that painted [graffiti artists], that did poetry, that sang. Better put, every type of woman [artist]. Women that do theater. There we were representing all that were there in some kind of way. And those were the first steps that we did in order to support the work of women. . . .
>
> And so the first time we did it, I will not forget it ever. It was, it was like an exposition, it was like an exposition with Diamela, the photographer, we had photographs, we had people that wrote articles, that filmed it as well, we had designers who were not trained in school. All these things were accompanying the movement.

Magia's work to create a specific space for women was extremely influential within the movement. Many of the women artists who would become key figures in the early years of the movement, during the old-school period, began their work as hip hop artivists during these events. The spaces and events organized by Obsesión were specifically for women artists, but the artists' work did not necessarily have to be *woman-centered*. Many women artists would use these events as an opportunity to begin their careers—including Las Krudas CUBENSI, who were well-known as theater performers by this time and were also invited to participate in these events and in other CUHHM performances. Others included La Yula, Danay, DJ Leydis, DJ Yari, NoNo12, Explosión Femi-

Figure 6.2.   Cuban Hip Hop Symposium, Panel on Gender and Sexuality (2004).
(*Left to right*) Nehanda Abiodun, Odaymara Cuesta Rosseau, [unknown person],
Olivia Prendes Riverón, Magia López. (Courtesy of Sahily Borrero)

nina, Atómicas, and Diamela, one of two of the most important photographers/
documenters of the early hip hop movement, the other being Sahily Borrero.

It was during this period, with the growing popularity of Las Krudas, that
Magia's political investments as a woman were directly challenged. As the diversity of Black women participating in the movement increased, so did the diversity of opinions, perspectives, and political agendas. During the 2000–2006
period, debates concerning race expanded to include racialized critiques of gender and sexuality. It was clear that these issues had become a central discursive
intervention in the movement when the 2004 Cuban Hip Hop Symposium included a workshop and panel on feminism and gender equality (fig. 6.2). It is
important to locate this event and its significance in the context of Cuba—a
country where known feminists were arrested or economically marginalized in
the first thirty years after the Revolution.

During the early 2000s, Magia began incorporating a gendered analysis
in her music. She focused primarily on questions of domestic violence, racialized prostitution, and women's experiences in heterosexual relationships. The
issue of domestic violence is especially important in Cuba. I was told by some
researchers that violence against women reached near epidemic levels in the
1970s and 1980s, given the years of silence concerning sexism, and the state was

forced to address the issue. But scholars lacked state support to research the issue in order to suggest policy solutions to the problem.[7] In its more woman-centered songs, Obsesión focuses on the economic basis of women's oppression and addresses the effects of women's oppression on the family, specifically on children. In another popular song called "Le llaman puta" (They Call Her a Whore), Magia challenges the marginalization of women who are prostitutes by locating prostitution within a racialized economic context. The song highlights that sometimes prostitution is a strategic option for poor women, especially Black women who have become poorer as a result of the economic downturn. While critical of how racialized structures impact Black women, however, Obsesión's critique of gendered ideologies remained more implicit than explicit. Rather using than an explicitly feminist perspective, Obsesión still relied on a hegemonic revolutionary discourse in critiques of the problems facing women.

But as more women began to participate in the movement, Magia started to notice inequalities that shifted her orientation toward feminism. She described how this played out in the gendered dynamics of performance:

> Bueno, cuando un hombre sale tiene chance de mejorar en las peñas, donde lo invitan, presentaciones que sé yo. Cuando sale una mujer, sino sale la primera vez bien, en verdad se lo quite. Entonces, para mí es como eso. Si yo tengo un espacio donde quizás se estén presentado un grupo de mujeres que a lo mejor, sí es verdad, le falta calidad, le falta no sé qué, bueno entonces pueden ir mejorando. Te hace falta ir mejorando esto, te falta ir mejorando lo otro. Pero que no me hace a mí decir [*pauses*] bueno. Desde ese punto de vista antes yo decía, que sí, que yo era una mujer feminista.

> Well, when a man appears he has a chance to improve in the battles, where they invite him, presentations and whatever else. When a woman appears, if she doesn't come out well the first time, honestly they just take [future opportunities] from her. So for me, it's like this . . . if I have a space where maybe a group of women should be presenting that are the best, if they are missing something, if they don't have whatever, well then, they can continue improving. You are missing something, you have to keep getting better at it, if you lack something, keep getting better with that other thing. But it's not up to me to say it [*pauses*], well. From this point of view I said that yes, that I was a feminist woman.

Magia began to identify as a feminist when it became obvious that women were more harshly judged than men in the movement. Women were not encouraged to develop as artists, whereas men were nurtured, encouraged, and provided the space to improve their work as artists.

Magia explained what feminism came to mean for her:

> Yo en algún tiempo decía que yo era feminista porque yo defendía los derechos de la mujer desde mi punto de vista. Los defendía, así como yo defiendo las cosas. Defendía a la mujer que viene trabajando, haciendo su esfuerzo y que quizás no se le reconozca. O sea, eso era para mí, o es para mí como una meta. De una mujer que viene esforzándose, trabajando y no sé que y que realmente la gente no conozca que existe ese tipo de trabajo que está haciendo. En defensa de la problemática de la mujer, ya sea en la casa, ya sea en la calle, ya sea con esta situación de género, ya sea defendiendo algún tipo de fuerza, en el sentido de que por ejemplo en el hip hop se da mucho la fuerza de la mujer, pero fuerza en todos los sentidos. Fuerza en el texto, fuerza en los gestos, fuerza en la ropa y era un poco lo que aceptaba.

> I, at one time, said that I was a feminist because I defended the right of women from my point of view. I defended them, as I defend things. I defended woman's work, empowering herself and that maybe people don't recognize her. Or better, this was for me or this is for me a goal. A woman comes empowering herself, working and I don't know whatever else, and really people don't recognize the kind of work that she's doing. In defense of the woman issue, she who's in the house, on the street, the gender situation, defending some kind of strength, in the sense, for example, that hip hop gives a lot of strength to women, but strength in every sense. Strength in lyrics, in gestures, in clothes, and that which is little accepted.

Magia articulates a Black feminist epistemology: for her, feminism is a product of a lived experience, not a product of consciousness-raising in which women are made aware of and educated about oppression through formal educational institutions. From Magia's perspective, any woman who believes that women have the right to fight for their own self-determination is a feminist—even if she doesn't self-identify as one. She focuses on women acknowledging the previous generations of women, particularly Black women, who worked hard to ensure that their families, children, and communities were taken care of. This is a way of writing women, particularly Black women, into history as a means of recognizing their work in the present.

By 2004 more and more women artists were openly identifying as feminist or as women-centered socially conscious actors. Underground male artists, such as the Junior Clan and Anónimo Consejo, started recording songs directly challenging men to address issues such as domestic violence. Women who participated in the CUHHM were considered, and considered themselves, to be independent women "from the streets," who were strong and could hold their ground without needing the help of a man. The pace of change was slow, however: despite efforts to increase the representation of women, the numbers remained low and some of the performance dynamics remained problematic. As early as 2000 Obsesión was criticized for not hosting enough events for women, especially large public concerts. Only one to three major concerts a year were for women, and only then on days like Mother's Day or International Women's Day. In addition, there continued to be too few women onstage during typical concerts and artistic events, which were largely dominated by men.

Wanting more opportunities to participate in the movement, newer women artists began organizing their own women-centered artistic expositions. One example was the creation of Omegas KILAY, founded around the end of 2004. The acronym KILAY is derived from the names of the founders of the women's collective: "K" from the group Las Krudas, "I" from the group I and I, "L" from DJ Leydis (the first woman DJ in Cuba), "A" from the group Atómicas, and "Y" from DJ Yari (the only other woman DJ in Cuba until about 2008). Artists such as MC NoNo joined later (Prendes Riverón 2006). Omegas KILAY worked together to empower women artists through informal women-centered workshops, collaborative efforts, and concerts. They became frustrated, however, when they were restricted to hosting concerts only during specific events, often performing as part of a women's artistic expo a few times a year. Eventually several of the artists realized that if they were going to succeed as artists, they needed to leave Cuba and look for opportunities abroad. Las Krudas and DJ Leydis left in 2006, and DJ Yari in 2010. Many of these artists' calculations were based on the assumption—which directly contradicts revolutionary state discourse—that the rest of the world had progressed in the area of race and gender equality, while Cuba had not. It was during this time, as more and more women with woman-centered and feminist orientations were moving both into and out of the movement, that Magia and other women MCs began to qualify or in some cases even end their identification as feminists.

Challenging the Limits of Hip Hop Feminism:
Magia and Las Krudas CUBENSI

During this period, Las Krudas CUBENSI was a three-person group of Black, openly lesbian, feminist hip hop artists.[8] The members are sisters Odaymara

and Odalys Cuesta Rosseau and Olivia Prendes Riverón, the long-term partner of Odaymara. Las Krudas' entrance into the Cuban Underground Hip Hop
Movement in 2000 created a major rupture for many artists, especially those
who considered themselves to be progressive, forward-thinking revolutionary
actors who were part of the vanguard of "true" revolutionaries working to end
the social marginalization of stigmatized and racially oppressed groups. Magia
says the following about the work of Las Krudas and herself:

> Eso fue en el 2000, 2001 ellas iniciaban aquella carrera como raperas,
> pero ya venían haciendo un trabajo un trabajo como artistas plásticas. In-
> cluso creo que Las Krudas estaba en la asociación de artistas plásticas en
> la Asociación Hermanos Saíz. Y bueno, en aquellos tiempos las Krudas ha-
> blaban algo que mucha gente no se identificaban con esos textos, porque
> era como de vegetariano, o sea no come carne, que sé yo. Pero, a nosotros
> nos parecía que era un elemento más que se podía aportar al discurso que
> estaba trayendo en aquel tiempo el movimiento.

> It was in 2000, 2001 that they began their careers as rappers, but they
> came [to the movement] after having already done work as visual artists.
> Including, I think, that Las Krudas were a part of the Association of Visual
> Artists and the Asociación Hermanos Saíz. Well, at that moment, Las
> Krudas talked about something that a lot of people did not identify with
> in their lyrics, because it was something about being a vegetarian, or
> better not to eat meat or whatever. But, for us, it seemed like this was an
> element more than we could support the discourse that they were bring-
> ing to the movement at that moment in time.

Magia notes that Las Krudas came from a different background when they
first arrived on the hip hop scene as visual and performance artists. They were
initially seen as discussing issues that few people could identify with, like being
a vegetarian. At the same time, however, people also recognized that Las Krudas
had the ability to help deliver the movement's racialized critique of social inequality. Some even appreciated that they offered an LGBT critique that was
absent in the movement (Alexey, personal communication, 2005). For Magia,
however, the arrival of Las Krudas prompted her to reconsider what her pri-
orities were as an organizer within the movement. She describes how she saw
her role:

> Y entonces las acciones que yo he desarrollado y he hecho como artista,
> y quizás un poco como organizadora, tienen que ver cuidado un poco el
> espacio de la mujer dentro del movimiento, no solamente la mujer under-

ground, sino también yo se fijo más por la consecuencia, me fijo más por el esfuerzo que realizas para hacer tu obra, por el tiempo que le dedicas, por tu preocupación. Esas son cosas que me mueven, quizás, a poder ayudar a una persona a que salga. Y no tanto: A ver, qué tu estás diciendo, no eso no me cuadra, porque está fuerte. Me guío menos por eso. Independientemente que también defienda un discurso serio, consciente, no. Y eso me ha llevado a no ser tan, tan específica con un grupo de personas, sino quizás he estado un poco más pendiente al desarrollo del movimiento en general, no solamente al desarrollo del movimiento de mujeres.

> And so the actions that I have developed and have done as an artist, and maybe a little as an organizer, have to do with protecting, a little, the space of women within the movement, not just underground women, but I am also concerned about the consequences, I am more concerned about you do what you need to do for your work, about the time you dedicate, about your commitment. These are things that move me, and perhaps the power to help the person that's starting out. And not so much: "Well look, what you are saying, I don't like it, because it's so harsh." I'm not guided by that. Independently of whether they defend a serious discourse, or a conscious one, no [I don't care]. And this has bought me to not be so, so specific with a group of people, without maybe me having been a little more thoughtful about the development of the movement in general, not only the development of the women's movement.

Magia positions herself as guarding women's space within the hip hop movement. She explains that creating a space for women is important to her but is not her priority. She is about giving opportunities to those who want to get a start in the movement, whoever they are. She does not consider herself to be a judgmental person and at the end of the day does not really care about things like lyrics. The only thing that she cares about is whether or not artists are serious, committed to their work, and doing what is necessary to their goals as artists. She goes on to say that she supports *all* artists and is not interested only in the development of the women's movement within the hip hop movement.

When Las Krudas entered the movement, they advocated the creation of a woman-centered space for artists and all women in the CUHHM. They especially pressured Magia, as an established leader in the CUHHM, to work to create a space only for women. This posed a problem in the movement and, indeed, in the context of the country, where dividing into groups based on identity politics has been forbidden, interpreted as a challenge to official state discourse. Las Krudas challenged the epistemological structures that many of the artists took for granted: they were out, Black-identified lesbian feminists, who were also vegetarians in a country where being a vegetarian can mean eating chicken instead of pork for many. Las Krudas ate *no* animals, including fish — something that was virtually unimaginable to many people. Also unimaginable were women who did not define themselves in terms of their sexual relationship to men and who did not define their beauty using normative notions of femininity — including even the counterhegemonic discourse of Black femininity that was emerging within the Cuban Underground Hip Hop Movement. Las Krudas wore only pants, no skirts or long, flowy dresses. They also wore their hair in dreadlocks, which were very much not associated with femininity at that time of the late 1990s and early 2000s. Further compounding the association of Las Krudas' dreadlocks with masculinity was their rejection of other aesthetic devices such as heavy makeup or tight-fitting dresses to manage the masculinity associated with blackness and unprocessed hair.

Las Krudas' aesthetic choices symbolically expressed their rejection of hegemonic notions of femininity that defined women as sexually available to men — still prevalent with the CUHHM itself. Importantly, Las Krudas do not see themselves as masculine. Instead they position themselves as challenging culturally entrenched narratives associating feminism with man-hating, the rejection of femininity, and the embracing of masculinity. For some artivists and members of the CUHHM, this seemingly radical stance further supported their understanding of Las Krudas as an asset to the movement: they represented an aspect of femininity or women's experience that was more direct and raw or crude (*kruda*). As a result, many listened and tried to understand Las Krudas' perspective and appreciated the personal insight that they gained from the group's challenges to accepted notions of masculinity and femininity.

While some embraced the challenge and cultural intervention of Las Krudas, however, others reacted strongly against it. Las Krudas forced many women in the movement to work to reconcile a woman-centered politics with a desire to pursue it only within a culturally accepted framework. This threw into sharp relief the hesitancy of women within the movement to challenge dominant understandings of femininity and heteronormativity. Black women hip hop artists' investment in heteronormativity, as a normative expression of femininity, reinforced the social norms that form the basis of their oppression as racialized women. Many were not yet ready to interrogate heterosexuality as a racialized discourse. Furthermore, as noted earlier, the social bias against lesbians in Cuba is far more intense than the bias against gay men. As shown by a number of studies (Acosta et al. 2003; Más 2003), when asked what they think of lesbians, straight women describe them as being disgusting, aggressive, and uncouth.[9] This is largely related to how women understand femininity in Cuba and the ways in which masculine or lesbian women have been coded as threatening and unpatriotic. So a group of women who openly identified as lesbians to stand onstage, talk about menses, dress only in pants, wear dreadlocks, and encourage women to empower themselves independently of men caused women and men to confront their internalized understanding of gender, sexuality, and equality.

The question of negotiating internalized stereotypes of gender and sexual transgression with a feminist praxis was a tension that existed for the majority of the straight women artists, only a small number of whom ever visited Las Krudas in their home in Havana. The women who did visit always made sure to bring along their boyfriends or husbands. Women often found themselves having to negotiate culturally based stereotypes concerning feminism and sexuality. This prompted many to identify as feminist, but only with added qualifications. DJ Leydis, for example, explained to me in 2006: "Bueno, las feministas, yo me considero femenina y feminista sin recriminar a los hombres. No es mi lucha contra los hombres, no creo que además valga la pena luchar contra los hombres" (Well, the feminists, I consider myself feminine and feminist without reproaching men. I don't need to fight against men, I don't believe that it's worth it to fight with men). Because Las Krudas challenged men by directly calling them out on their sexism, they were seen as aggressive women who were attacking men—an image that other women in the movement took pains to avoid. Therefore, in expressing a feminist identity, Leydis and others made it clear that they were not like "other feminists" and that they embraced their femininity, instead of rejecting it as Las Krudas were presumed to have done.

Magia's orientation toward feminism began to shift around 2003, as Las Krudas became increasingly popular and influential within the movement. Las Krudas released their debut CD and started challenging heteronormativity in a way that was not passive and deferent to men. This was understood by many to be "unladylike." Magia was at once confronted with a history of cultural stereotypes that framed feminists as man-hating lesbian separatists. She described how her feelings about feminism began to change:

> Quizás yo le tenga un poco de miedo a . . . [pauses] quizás no, yo le tengo un poco de miedo a esa palabra. Porque creo que me encasilla, creo que, no sé, quizás es una historia que, ah, pues si tú eres feminista yo no sé cómo tú estás haciendo eso. Cosas así y nada. Por ejemplo, una de las cosas que me ha hecho a mí un poco sacrificar, por ejemplo mi imagen y yo no hablo de un sacrificio bueno, sino para mí es un sacrificio bueno, pero de cierto

modo he tenido que cohibirme, cohibirme no es la palabra, sino limitarme en escena y defender mi imagen.

> Maybe I have a little fear to . . . [*pauses*] maybe not, I have a little fear of this word. Because I think it imprisons me, I believe that, I don't know, maybe it's a history that, ah, well if you are a feminist, and I don't know how you're doing it. Things like that and that's it. For example, one of the things that I have had to sacrifice, for example, is my image, and I am not talking about a good sacrifice, but for me it is a good sacrifice, but in a certain way I have had to coexist, coexist is not the word, but to limit myself onstage and defend my image.

Magia found herself in a difficult situation. She worried that she would be considered "suspect" if she continued to identify as a feminist and became very conscious of how she negotiated her image within the movement. Additionally, she was not sure that she was ready to sacrifice the image that she had created and the influence that she had gained in order to fight for a set of issues, such as vegetarianism and open discussions of menses. These were not primary concerns for her political agenda. Magia started to feel imprisoned by the term "feminism." She wanted to have a clear idea of what she was supporting, if she was going to risk the power she had worked for in a male-dominated social movement.

In 2006 Magia ultimately decided that the term "feminist" was no longer being defined (by Las Krudas, in particular) in ways that she supported and stopped identifying as one:

> Desde ese punto de vista antes yo decía, que sí, que yo era una mujer feminista. Ahora yo le tengo un poco de miedo a esa palabra. Y quizás no me catalogo como una mujer feminista, pues no sé, porque quizás he aprendido o he conocido que personas que se hacen llamar feministas, pues defiende como que un círculo muy cerrado de cosas que no es exactamente lo que yo estoy defendiendo. Y entonces, como que hay límites en esas defensas y no es lo que yo quiero. Yo no puedo, por ejemplo, defender un grupo de mujeres separando al hombre. Yo quiero defender un grupo de mujeres integrándolas al mismo proceso, al mismo trabajo que quizás esté desarrollando el hombre en ese sentido.
>
> Yo no quiero defender una postura desde la mujer, pero respondiendo a los prototipos masculinos: de esto de fuerza. Yo puedo hacer esto, yo puedo hacer lo otro. Yo no quiero eso, y quizás viéndolo en ese sentido de mujer que se hacen llamar defensoras del movimiento feminista, pues

entonces, en ese sentido quizás no. Yo digo que yo solamente defiendo a la situación de la mujer, los problemas de la mujer, a la mujer como tal. . . .

Porque también vengo defendiendo que no tengo que ponerme pantalones para defender un discurso fuerte, para quizás estar en la misma escena donde están participando y ayudar a los varones y se ve igual de fuerte o más de fuerte.

> From this point of view I decided I was a feminist woman, but now I have a little fear of this word. And maybe I don't classify myself as a feminist woman, but I don't know, because maybe I have learned, or have known people that call themselves feminist, who defend a very closed definition of things that is not exactly that which I'm defending and it's not what I want. I can't, for example, defend a group of women separating themselves from men. I want to defend a group of women integrating themselves to the same process, the same work that maybe men are also developing in a sense.
>
> I do not want to defend a woman's posture, by representing masculine prototypes, of this kind of force. I can do this, I can do that. I don't want to do this, and maybe coming from this [specific] perspective of being a woman they call themselves the defenders of the feminist movement, well then, so in this sense maybe not. I say that I only defend the situation of women, the problems of women, the woman as such. . . .
>
> Because I also come defending [the interest of women] and I don't have to put on pants in order to defend a harsh discourse, maybe to be on the same stage where they [men] are participating and to help men and to see oneself as equal in strength or of more strength.

It is important to emphasize here that Magia is a strategic political actor. In her efforts to help build the CUHHM, she did not want to be reduced to a "female MC" and thus be limited to being a gatekeeper of all interests concerning women. At the same time, however, she did want to ensure space for a diverse set of experiences and perspectives. She has always tried to maintain a macro-level view of the movement. She and other organizers specifically targeted other artists within Cuba's politicized alternative music scene and invited them to participate in the Underground Hip Hop Movement. In this way she has worked to maintain her image as "organizer," not as a person who takes sides or who fights for a particular set of interests. It is within the context of this set of goals that frame her relationship with feminism and with Las Krudas specifically.

Nonetheless, it also important to recognize that Magia's efforts to negotiate all these tensions have not always had positive results for women trying to carve out an empowered space within the movement. When she became the first hip hop artist to be named president of the Agency of Rap, her position became more influential but also fraught with difficulty: she now had to mediate conflicts not only within the movement but also between the movement and the state. In 2010, for example, during a hip hop symposium in which images of gender and sexual diversity were included in the movement's discourse, Magia would not permit Las Krudas to hold women-only workshops discussing how to MC and how to become empowered, autonomous actors within the movement. Las Krudas and other feminists argued that women need these spaces to be able to develop as artists while not being intimidated by men. Now in a position of power to implement changes that could directly affect the development of artists, Magia chose not to allow the women-only spaces. As a result, I watched as men showed up at several of the workshops and proceeded to dominate the space. The members of Las Krudas found themselves increasingly having to try to manage men who were talking over the top of quieter women, many of whom were new MCs. Only after about two hours of negotiating the men's presence in one of the workshops were Odaymara and Olivia finally able to focus on educating women about what to expect when they began to MC. Specifically, they explained that during MC battles the women needed to be prepared for vicious verbal attacks from other MCs. Such attacks were and are part of the hip hop "battle"—people will say whatever they need to in order to embarrass and outwit an opponent. In the case of women MCs, however, the attacks are specifically gendered and sexualized, targeting their bodies and their femininity (or perceived lack thereof). The harassment takes many forms, from jabs about menstruation, how they smell, or having a dirty "pussy" to accusations of being sluts or man-hating lesbians—anything that could be used to insult an opponent who is a woman. The inability to secure a women-only space to discuss such issues was therefore highly symbolic.

Importantly, the relations between Magia and Las Krudas are instructive not because of what they tell us about the individuals involved or who is "right" or "wrong." Rather, they highlight tensions within the movement and indeed within Cuba more generally—tensions that flow in multiple directions. While Magia was challenged to take an increasingly women-centered approach in the movement, Las Krudas, for their part, were challenged to become aware of their audience and to become more strategic about when and how they raised a queer critique. In her interview Magia noted the ongoing struggle to develop a unified, "universal" Afrocentric discourse. Because so many artists focus on male heroes and ancestors, she tries to contribute to a universal discourse of gender equality by including both women and men in her discourse and focusing on ancestors generally. Las Krudas, in contrast, given their particular ideological intervention concerning a woman-centered approach, focus specifically on calling upon their female ancestors when remembering the past. Well aware of the critiques of her approach to supporting women, Magia maintains that women need to understand the difficulties of being an artist, work harder, and be more assertive themselves.

Multiple Feminisms, Multiple Realities: Cristiane MC

In my interview with Dr. Grizel Hernández Baguer in Havana in 2005 she discussed the range of feminist discourses within the Underground Hip Hop Movement. When I asked her what she thought it means to be a feminist for the women of Cuban hip hop, she responded:

Yo pienso, que por ejemplo, un discurso más feminista . . . , [pauses] si el feminismo es eso de tratar . . . [pauses] Pienso que las Krudas tienen un discurso más feminista, en el sentido de que son más duras en el trato de los problemas de la mujer. Y en esa comparación de la mujer, la mujer se trata así y el hombre como tal. Pienso que Magia, por ejemplo, su discurso es más feminista. Es más enfocado de otra manera. Cuando trata de las jineteras, lo trata más como un problema social, no como una visión de feminismo, la posición de la mujer, en otro tipo de discurso. Son las que más así he visto. A Cristiane la vi cantar hace tiempo con el niño, pero es otra problemática como tal. La vemos a lo mejor como la madre, es otro problema como ella quizás vea eso. Entonces te digo, he visto poco, no me he dedicado a oír, por eso me interesa hacer un disco de las mujeres para ver todas esas maneras de ver de la mujer, que creo que es interesante. Pero creo que las positivas me parece que es más en el estilo de las Krudas, por las veces que me parece haberlas visto. Pero me parece que son muy buenas. No conozco así. Doris Sei, que es de Instinto creo que es más light, va más así. Hay otra que son tres, EPG, son dos muchachas que a veces me recuerdan más al estilo del pop y la otra va más al rap. Es una mezcla ahí y que no acabo de entender el discurso. Pero bueno, he seguido las Krudas porque me gustan mucho y he seguido a Magia porque se gusta también. Y he seguido a Mariana en algunas, con Mariana es a veces difícil, pero me gusta también su forma de rapear. Me parece muy clara, una dicción clara. Cristiane me gusta, lo que pasa es que desde el punto de vista musical a veces es muy desafinada, porque la voz es muy penetrante y entonces, a veces me molesta, pero creo que tiene mucha fuerza. Ella lo que pasa es que con los dos niños. . . . Yo nunca tuve tiempo de hablar con ella así de cerca y un poco decirle esto.

Porque me parece que ella como artista ya de tantos años tiene que manejar más vocalmente eso, sin perder lo natural, lo espontáneo, pero ya para lo profesional ser un poco manejable, porque se va a quedar sin voz. Pero también me parece que tiene mucha fuerza como tal.

> I think, for example, a very feminist discourse . . . [*pause*] yes, feminism is this thing that tries . . . [*pauses*] I think that Las Krudas have a discourse that is very feminist, in the sense that they are the strongest in their treatment of woman and man as such. I think that Magia, for example, her discourse is very feminist. She is more focused in another aspect. When she talked about prostitution, she treated it as a social problem, not as a vision of feminism, the position of women, it's another type of discourse. They are the ones that I have seen the most. Cristiane, I haven't seen her sing much since she had her child, but that is another problem. They saw her more as a mother, and this is another problem maybe she has seen. So I tell you, I have seen little, I haven't been able to hear much, for this reason, I am interested in making a woman-centered disc, to see all the ways of seeing woman, I think this is something interesting. But I believe that the most positive, it seems to me, is more in the style of Las Krudas, from the times that I have seen them. But to me, it seems that they are very good. I don't know them well.
>
> Doris Sei of Instincto I believe is "lighter," she goes more like this. [*Physically imitates Doris's flow with gentle hand and arm movements.*] There are another three, EPG, they are two girls that at times I remember being more in the style of pop, and the other raps more, MC Maygori. It is a mix and I haven't been able to understand their discourse. But OK, I have followed Las Krudas more because I like them more, and I have followed Magia because I like her too. And I have followed Mariana sometimes, with Mariana it is at times difficult, because I like her form of rapping. It seems to me very clear, a clear diction. Cristiane I like, but what has happened from one point of view is that she is very disheveled, because her voice is very penetrating and then, at times she bothers me, because I believe she has a lot of force. What happened with her is that with the two kids, I never have time to speak with her to tell her this. Because to me she appears to be an artist that after years of having to manage more vocally, without losing that which is natural, spontaneous.

For Hernández Baguer, the discourses of Magia and Las Krudas are the most feminist and most positive discourses within the hip hop community. She views Las Krudas as "tougher" in their focus on women and how men and women should be treated, whereas she believes that Magia is more concerned with the larger social problems that women face. Hernández Baguer sees them as sharing a feminist discourse, but with each focusing on a different dimension of women's experiences. She goes on to elaborate, however: Magia's intervention in the case of prostitution is more focused on economic issues, as she did not explicitly talk about how men treated women, particularly prostitutes. Once again, the specificity of how gender is understood within Cuba's revolutionary discourse is key: Dr. Hernández Baguer describes the women-centered, women empowerment work of Las Krudas, which includes a direct critique of men's treatment of women, as "feminist," while Magia's socioeconomic and gendered analysis of women's prostitution is not considered to be explicitly feminist but another kind of discourse. This kind of discourse that is "less harsh" is a version of the socialist revolutionary view of women's inequality that frames women's problems as rooted in material inequality.

Hernández Baguer also identifies two other groups of women that represent still more variations of hip hop feminism. The first group of popular women artists in the movement were members of the group Instincto. She describes the group as very "light." It is important here to note here, however, that time plays an important role in Hernández Baguer's comments. She is speaking as the vice-president of the Agency of Rap, an institution that did not exist and was not in the realm of possibility at the point when Instincto began to perform. At the time of their emergence, they were a very powerful reference point for many future MCs, as they were the first women to rap onstage with men and establish themselves as serious artists within the movement. Their music and image focused primarily on being sexy and cool and having a good time with their boyfriends. Therefore they were considered to be "light" for a movement that later defined itself as socially critical, politically conscious, and underground. Still, Instincto was one of the groups that established the basis for Cuban hip hop to evolve into a recognizable artistic genre and laid the foundation for the feminist debates that would later emerge. Pacini Hernández and Garafalo (1999) discuss the importance of Instincto's sense of rhyme and assertiveness as products of their own experiences. They note that Instincto's professionalism and stage presence were a result of intense work with one of Cuba's preeminent artistic directors, Silvia Acea, who also worked with groups such as S'ntesis, one of Cuba's well-known fusion groups (Moore 2006; Pacini Hernández and Garafalo 1999, 33). Instincto was one of the first all-women groups to claim a public space for women onstage.

Hernández Baguer also mentions another woman, Maygori MC, who represents a fourth type of feminist discourse—that of women from "the hood," "women from El Ghetto" (Maygori MC, personal communication, 2008; Michael Oremas, personal communication, 2008). The representative figure here is a woman who can "hang with the boys," "who rolls with the best of them," and "isn't afraid to be themselves [sic] and refuses to just follow any guy around" (Maygori MC, personal communication, 2008). Artists that fit into this category include Maygori MC, NoNo12, Odalys Cuesta Rosseau (Wanda of Las Krudas), and Cristiane.[10] NoNo, who is both a graffiti artist and an MC, said the following when I asked her what I should know about the Cuban Underground Hip Hop Movement:

NoNo: Bueno que la cultura que es hip hop no se revoluciona como en otros países que es más lo comercial, no. Aquí está un poco más el underground. No es un hip hop para comercial y si lo vas a comercializar estás comercializando underground, porque sus letras van a ser underground. Nunca vas a oír una letra, que si el culo, que si la teta, que si la muchachita, no, eso no, eso no va a suceder y si va a ver videos, las vas a ver más muchachitas, pero no van a estar que sin con el culo fuera, no. Sí van a estar ahí, pero nuestra letra no dice nada de eso, es puro underground, es lo social, lo vivido. Eso es nuestra cultura hip hop y nuestras canciones en cuanto al hombre como a la mujer. Bueno si nos has escuchado sabes que las mujeres no estamos flojas. No es ni, ni, ni, no, estamos ahí en el underground, en lo que no se puede publicar, porque en muchas canciones a nosotros nos han censurado.

Tanya: ¿De verdad?

NoNo: Sín muchas, de las mujeres y de los hombres.

Tanya: ¿Cómo qué? Explícame.

NoNo: Bueno, como yo misma tengo una canción que se llama Alta Demanda como el mismo nombre de mi grupo, pero es cantándole al hombre y una parte de la letra dice, yo no soy un búcaro, cabrón.

Tanya: ¿Búcaro cabrón?

NoNo: Un búcaro es un objeto que se pone en la mesa, un florero, me entiende, eso es un búcaro. Y entonces mi coro el estribillo de la canción dice: Quién te dijo que no puedo ser graffiti, quién te dijo que puedo ser DJ, quién te dijo que no puedo ser MC, quién te dijo que no puedo ser B-girl, Yo no soy un búcaro cabrón, entiende.

Tanya: ¿Y por qué no lo puedes poner?

NoNo: Porque simplemente digo, cabrón. Es una estupidez muy grande, porque a parte que estoy diciendo una realidad, no estoy diciendo malas palabras.

Tanya: Como media hijo de puta.

NoNo: También, eso es una cosa que es en un momento. Hay muchas canciones que no son de hip hop y dicen demasiadas cosas obscenas.

Tanya: ¿Cómo el reggaetón?

NoNo: De madre, es candela y sin embargo la ponen en la radio, me entiende. Y no solamente el reggaetón, mira hay muchas canciones de trova que lo que dicen es horrores, y como es una cosa muy melódica y muy floja ya, pero simplemente en hip hop ya, porque es hip hop. Porque yo creo que mi tema no dice nada. Sí digo muchas palabras fuertes, no fuertes, la realidad de un hombre que maltrata a una mujer. Y yo estoy señalando esto, es una cosa que es realidad, porque la gente no la pueden saber. ¿Qué voy a cantar en mi canción, que linda es la flor y que linda es la pared que yo pinté? No, tengo que cantar la realidad porque es mi hip hop y es mi música.

> NoNo: Well, hip hop culture doesn't revolutionize the same way as hip hop in other countries, which is more commercial. Here it's a little more underground. You're never going to hear some lyrics about an ass, or a tit, or the chickenheads/hoochies with their ass out, nope.[11] Yeah they're going to be there, but our lyrics don't talk anything about this, it's pure underground, it's that which is social, what's lived. This is our culture, hip hop and our songs are about men as much as women. Well, if you have listened to us you know that the women are not whack. Nope, none of this, no, we're there in the underground, on that which can't be published, because in a lot of our songs, they have censored us.
>
> Tanya: For real?
>
> NoNo: Yeah, a lot of us, women and men.
>
> Tanya: How? Explain.
>
> NoNo: OK, like I myself have a song that's called "The Highest Demand," the same name as my group, but it's being sung to a man, and a part of the lyric says, "I am not your ornament [*búcaro cabrón*], dumbass."
>
> Tanya: What is *búcaro cabrón*?
>
> NoNo: An ornament is an object that you put on the table, in a vase, understand me? It's an ornament. And so my chorus, the refrain of the song says: "Who told you that I can't do graffiti, who told you that I can't be a DJ, who

told you that I can't be an MC, who told you that I can't be a B-girl. I am not an ornament, dumbass, understand?"

Tanya: So why can't you play it?

NoNo: Only because I said dumbass. It's a big stupid thing, because part of what I am saying is a reality, I'm not saying bad words.

Tanya: Like you son-of-a-bitch.

NoNo: Also, it's a thing that's in the moment. There are a lot of songs that aren't hip hop that say a bunch of obscene things.

Tanya: Like reggaetón?

NoNo: My God, it's out of control and nonetheless they put it on the radio, understand me. And not only reggaetón, look, there are a lot of Trova songs where the things that they say are horrible, and because it's something with a melody and it's whack right, but only because it's hip hop, it's because it's hip hop. Because I believe that my songs don't say anything [bad]. If I say a lot of strong words, it's not strong . . . the reality of a man that mistreats a woman? I am signaling this, it is something that's reality, because people might not know about it. Am I going to sing in my songs about how beautiful a flower is and how beautiful that painted wall is? No, I'm going to sing about reality because it's my hip hop and it's my music.

NoNo12 discusses how hip hop serves as an important means for expressing the realities that she faces as a woman, including domestic violence. She talks about the abuse and sexism that women face in a way that is honest, blunt, and reflective of her own anger and frustration. She does not attempt to talk about life in a way that is expected of "ladies," while men are able to display a range of human experiences in their music. NoNo12 also declares her identity as an specifically underground MC: "You're not going to find any hoochies here." She means that her music is about consciousness-raising, respecting yourself, and not relying on being a sexual object of men in order to be a part of the movement. Music by underground women MCs ruptures existing silences concerning domestic violence and challenges hegemonic discourses surrounding femininity: these women are not weak. In fact, the interior sections of NoNo's apartment building leading to her apartment are covered with her graffiti (fig. 3.15). When I walked into her house, she asked her boyfriend to restrain her pit bull, which had a tendency to bite. She then told the boyfriend to leave so that she could complete her interview. After he was gone, she laughed and made a comment about how you have to be straight-up with guys: this particular guy was crowding her space, and she was thinking that maybe it was time to tell him to move on. We both chuckled and began the interview.

Regardless of which particular subgenre they are part of, the women in the Cuban Underground Hip Hop Movement are very politicized. These women did not become that way by attending a university or reading a book. Through their engagement in Cuba's cultural sphere (specifically CUHHM) they began to interact with like-minded people and actively seek additional information that was useful to them in terms of being able to historicize, frame, and express their thoughts and ideas. NoNo12 argues that the women in the Cuban Underground Hip Hop Movement are strong, critical women who are going to be blunt about their experiences and unafraid to talk about them in their music. She rhetorically asks: "Am I going to sing in my songs about how beautiful a flower is and how beautiful that painted wall is? No, I'm going to sing about reality because it's my hip hop and it's my music." NoNo challenges the expectations surrounding what is an appropriate song for a woman MC to sing. She rejects the imposition of hegemonic discourses concerning femininity that would limit the topics that she is able to discuss. In the quotation above NoNo also discusses one of her songs that was censored but that she still performs and distributes via the unedited version on her CD. In the song she says to a guy: "I'm not your ornament, you dumbass." Then in the chorus she demands: "Who told you that I can't do graffiti? Who told you that I can't be a DJ? Who told you I can't be an MC? Who told you I can't be a B-girl? I'm not a ornament, you dumbass." NoNo is saying that she is not an accessory for a man. She is not just some pretty object that he can pin onto his jacket and do with her as he pleases.

Despite this confident language, women MCs nonetheless have to negotiate contradictions between their lived experiences and their efforts to establish an identity as artivists and to create a space for strong women artists. To get at this issue, I sought out some of the women MCs who had left the movement because of family or relationship obligations. Internalized expectations concerning a woman's place in society, the persistence and cultural entrenchment of systemic sexism and domestic violence, a forty-year state silence on gender, and an economic downturn have compounded a difficult situation for women in Cuba—particularly those seeking to keep a sense of independence while maintaining a family and an intimate relationship with a man. When women are caught in a domestic violence situation in Cuba, there is no special hotline to call for help and no shelters for women and their children who are victims of domestic violence. Women have had to figure out how to navigate their reality on their own, in a country that proclaims that gender equality has been achieved but also has a massive housing shortage. It is not only revolutionary discourse that defines the category of women as citizens around their naturalized role as mothers, caregivers, and dependents of men. An economic reality also reinforces this dependence.

In the case of the CUHHM, the ideology of women's "biological" obligations as mothers and caregivers in both families and intimate partnerships with men manifests itself in the absence or disappearance of women with children or a new male partner from the music scene. During this period, the overwhelming majority of women hip hop artists still understand their gender as rooted in "biology" or "nature," which centers on motherhood and conjugal unions with men. The demands of motherhood are often invoked to explain why some women never enter the movement in the first place and, even more interestingly, to explain why some women artists "mysteriously" disappear once they do have children. An awkward silence surrounds the departure of these women. Hernández Baguer noted two women MCs, Mariana and Cristiane, both of whom seemed to have left the CUHHM scene entirely. I heard from some artists that in Mariana's case this was due to her boyfriend, who would not allow her to continue to perform; others reported that Mariana also now had a baby in addition to the boyfriend.

But perhaps no artist more clearly illustrates the contradictions between the efforts of women MCs to carve a space for themselves within the world of hip hop and their actual lived realities than Cristiane MC.[12] Hernández Baguer mentioned Cristiane several times in her interview, noting that she had a tremendous amount of talent but that her performances were erratic because she did not have the opportunity to improve her abilities. Hernández Baguer specifically identified Cristiane's having two children as seriously limiting her ability to participate in the movement. This was a recurrent explanation that I heard about many of the women who entered into the movement but then suddenly stopped performing and in many cases disappeared from the scene all together. One of the few exceptions to this pattern was DJ Leydis, a single mother who brings her daughter, Erykah, to hip hop shows and events, including those in which DJ Leydis is performing (fig. 6.3). While some feel that Leydis is being an unfit mother by refusing to stay home to raise her daughter, many men and women respect and admire Leydis's decision.

Cristiane's situation was often whispered about, especially when discussion turned to her husband, who was described as "strange" by male and female members of the movement. Cristiane was the only woman artist who had left the CUHHM after having children that I was fortunate enough to interview. Combined with some of the responses from other women MCs, Cristiane provides tremendous insight into the ways in which hegemonic discourses concern-

Figure 6.3. Erykah. (Courtesy of Leydis Freire)

ing femininity are so internalized and subtly reinforced by the state-imposed silence on women's continued oppression after the "revolution within the Revolution." During my interview with Cristiane, her husband refused to leave the room and continuously interrupted our discussion to offer his views on the questions asked and on Cristiane's responses. He frequently requested a snack or told Cristiane that it was time for her to feed the children or change their diapers. He did all this while sitting in a chair playing video games and watching movies with a neighbor. The experience of interviewing Cristiane was one of the most blatant reminders of the limitations and contradictions of a revolutionary discourse that proclaims women to be equal but also prescribes lived realities that disempower them.

Cristiane began her artistic career in a group with two men. Before long she grew tired of the group and started a group with another woman MC. But shortly after that she decided to perform by herself for the first time at the 2001 Hip Hop Festival. In Havana in 2006 she described how things started:

Cristiane: Bueno, empecé a rapear porque fui yendo a las peñas y me fue gustando. Y a medida que me iba gustando y oyendo a los raperos como cantaban, las letras, lo que hacían. Yo anteriormente escribía mucho, era compositora, me gustaba mucho escribir en mi casa. Me entre tenía haciendo eso. Hasta que ya un día decidí que eso mismo que yo escribía lo podía llevar al rap y empecé a rapear. Empecé a todo lo que escribía ponerle background, hasta que empecé.

Tanya: ¿Cuáles serían los raperos o las raperas que te inspiraron para . . . ?

Cristiane: Pues fíjate no, que me influyeron en mi letra en el sentido de que me ayudaron a cantar, nadie, ninguna. Yo fui por mis propios medios. Y la música desde que salió a las personas le gustaron todo lo que hacía.

Cristiane: Well, I began to rap because I was going to the MC battles and I enjoyed them. And since I was enjoying them and hearing the how the rappers sang, the lyrics, the things that they did. I had been writing a lot, I was a composer, I liked to write in my house. I began having done this. Until one day I decided that I could rap what I wrote and I began to rap. I began to do all that I had written, I put the background in, that's how I started.

Tanya: Who were some of the rappers that inspired you?

Cristiane: Well, look, it wasn't them that influenced my lyrics in the sense that they helped me to sing . . . no one, not one. I went by my own means. And when the music came out people liked all that I was doing.

Cristiane worked tirelessly and independently to become one of the most popular women MCs in the movement. She was an extremely self-driven independent artist. She began her career by herself, established herself, produced her own music, and chose which songs she would sing and perform and when. In her music she focused on themes such as Yoruba/Afro-Cuban religion and social, political, and economic issues. She embraced her African heritage and identified as Black, even though she is often viewed by others as mulata and could have chosen to distance herself from blackness. Describing this early period, Cristiane spoke clearly and forcefully, proud of what she had accomplished as an artist. Her pride is not misplaced. Cuban Agency of Rap officials, musicologists, and hip hop artists all mentioned Cristiane as being among the best women MCs.

So why was her name now so often only whispered and surrounded by an awkward silence within the movement? Those commenting on her absence often said that it had something to do with having two children, but no one said anything further. Some influential MCs and state officials within the movement told me that they had reached out to her to invite her to return, but with no success. The silence surrounding Cristiane was impressive, for she was certainly not the only woman to have a child or children within the Cuban hip hop scene. And given the communitarian nature of the scene and some of the childcare resources available to women, Cristiane could easily have had a babysitter or requested someone in the movement to help care for her children while she performed. As noted above, DJ Leydis took advantage of these resources with her daughter Erykah—but notably, although Erykah's father was also an MC, DJ Leydis was a single parent. In Cristiane's case, she is married to another MC, which in many ways can be an asset in the underground hip hop movement. For Cristiane, however, the results have been mixed at best, though she herself is quick to argue that neither being a woman nor being a mother has impeded her professionally in any way. As she put it in our interview in Havana in 2006:

> Igual también significa lo mismo porque las mujeres, le don que nos dio la naturaleza fue ser mujer y es lo que nos tocó ser. Y entonces lo que nos dio la naturaleza es que como mujer podemos tener hijos, podemos tener un hombre o una mujer. Y lo que nos dio también la naturaleza como mujer y como madre es ser lo que queremos ser como ser humano. Yo soy mujer, soy madre, y como ser humano tengo mis puntos, y tengo, cómo se puede decir, tengo mis logros. Yo quiero ser alguien, no me impide nada, mis hijos no me impiden nada, ser madre no me impide nada. . . . Ser mujer tampoco me impide nada. Y como ser humano no me impido a nada, yo mismo no me impido a nada.

> Because for women, the gift that nature gave us was to be a woman and that's what we have been called to be. And so what nature gave us is that as a woman we can have children, we can have a man or a woman. And what nature gave us also as a woman and a mother is to be what we want to be as a human being. I am a woman, I'm a mother, and as a human being I have my points, and I have, how can you say it, I have my achievements. I want to be somebody, it does not prevent anything, my kids do not prevent me from doing anything, being a mother does not stop me from doing anything. . . . Being a woman never impeded me. And just as being human has not impeded me, I have not impeded myself.

In our interview Cristiane stated that she has never had a problem as a woman. She said that the reason why she didn't perform is because other women artists stopped contacting her after she had children. I have to wonder, however, if the situation is one in which her husband has deliberately overburdened her with "female" responsibilities. Interestingly, she seemed not to question the expectations of her as a woman, so she may not realize how she is being kept from the hip hop community.

As I arrived at Cristiane's apartment in Havana for our interview, I heard a woman yell from the kitchen, "Tanya, I'll be there in a minute."

When I walked into the kitchen, she said: "Hi Tanya, nice to meet you. I'm making you some lunch." We kissed. She introduced me to her neighbor and her husband.

"Sit down and chat," her husband said. "She'll take care of everything." In that moment I wondered why her husband had not offered to finish cooking and to set everything up. I compared this scenario with that of Magia, who had the privacy that she needed to take care of her work as an artist. For our interview Magia and I left the house, walked the streets, and sat out on the rooftop of the apartment that she shared with Alexey. Meanwhile Alexey cleaned the house, made dinner and tea, and stayed out of sight and, most importantly, out of earshot. Similarly, in the case of DJ Leydis, a male neighbor helped take care of her daughter during most of her interview. This was not the situation when I interviewed Cristiane.

When I asked Cristiane about the accepted wisdom in the CUHHM that she had disappeared from the scene, she insisted that she was still very much involved, only working now from her home:

Cristiane: Realmente muchas personas han querido llegar y no los han dejado. Dicen que no estoy trabajando, que hace rato no me ven. Hace rato no me ven porque realmente estoy trabajando, pero en mi casa. Estoy haciendo mi disco, mi disco no lo puedo hacer en la calle ni en un concierto. El disco lo tengo que preparar en mi casa o donde exista la posibilidad de prepararlo. Aparte de que tengo mis hijos también, aunque para mí mis hijos nunca han sido, ni fueron, ni serán obstáculo en mi trabajo. Porque hasta con ellos trabajé hasta los ocho meses de embarazo y después que parí estuve el mes de recién paría yendo a festivales.

Tanya: Es interesante porque estuve aquí otros años y he preguntado dónde están las mujeres raperas, a parte de Las Krudas, Magia, NoNo, Leydis y Margorie. Y siempre me han dicho: Ah, sí hay algunas que tienen hijos y no pueden trabajar y no sé donde están.

Cristiane: No, porque no saben realmente de uno, que yo no trabajo porque no me han llamado para actividades. Mis hijos me ocupan mucho espacio, de veinticuatro horas que tiene el día, me ocupan las veintitrés con cincuenta y ocho segundos, es decir, tengo dos segundos nada más para hacer lo demás mío [*flustered*]. Pero en estos dos segundos me convierto y hago realmente todo lo que voy a hacer. Pero si en un momento determinado me llamaran para cualquier actividad, yo en este caso iría. En mí nunca ha existido el no para ir a trabajar, ni representar al rap cubano, ni representar al rap femenino, ni representarme yo. Yo trabajo, lo que pasa es que no me llaman. . . . Yo no tengo porque promoverme yo sola, porque si entonces yo me promuevo yo sola, entonces tengo que estar tres años o cuatro años metida en mi casa y buscando otros medios. . . .

Porque yo me voy con mis hijos, cojo todo lo que pueda coger, arranco con mis hijos y me voy para los conciertos. Que muchos de ellos están conscientes que yo he ido con mis hijos a trabajar, porque se los he tenido que dejar casualmente al público para poder subirme a una tarima. Y después he bajado y he tenido que irme porque no he podido estar en el concierto completo porque tengo mis hijos que son pequeños, que tengo que llegar a la casa, que le toca la leche y entonces trato. . . .

Tanya:　¿Pero, has estado?

Cristiane:　Sí, he estado. Hace alrededor de un año y medio que yo no voy a trabajar, pero bueno porque estoy haciendo mi disco, mi video que me lo está haciendo mi esposo. Pero, sí, sí yo me mantengo. Fíjate que me mantengo que llegaste hasta donde yo estoy.

> Cristiane:　Really a lot of people have wanted to come here and they won't let them. They say that I'm not working, that it's been a while since they've seen me. That it's been a while since they've seen me because really I am working, but in my house. I'm doing my record, and my record can't be made in the street or in a concert. I have to prepare the record in my house or where the possibility of preparing it exists. Apart from this I have my children as well, although my children have never been, never were, and never will be an obstacle in my work. Because with them, I worked until I was eight months pregnant and after that I stopped, it was last month that I stopped going to festivals.
>
> Tanya:　It's interesting because I have been here other years, and asked where are the other women MCs besides Las Krudas, Magia, NoNo, Leydis, and Margorie. And they always say to me: there are some more but they all have children.
>
> Cristiane:　No, because they don't really know that one, that I am not working because they have not called me for activities. My children occupy a lot of space, of twenty-four hours that I have in a day, they occupy twenty-three hours and fifty-eight seconds, that to say, I have two seconds [*flustered*], nothing more to do things for myself. But in these two seconds I use them and I do what I am going to do. But if there is a determined moment in which they call me for whatever activity, in that case I would go. In me there has never existed a tendency not to work, not to represent Cuban rap, not to represent feminine rap, and not to represent myself. I work and what happens is that they do not call me. And I don't have opportunities because I have to promote myself by myself, then if I have to promote myself I have to be three or four years stuck in my house looking for other ways. . . .
>
> Because I go with my children, I take advantage of whatever I can take advantage of, I get my children together and I go to concerts. A lot of them know I go with my children to work, because I've sometimes have had to leave them in the audience so that I can go up on the stage. And afterward

> I go down and I have had to go because I could not be in the whole concert because I have my kids and they are little, and I have to go home, and heat the milk and so I try. . . .
>
> Tanya: But have you been there?
>
> Cristiane: Yes, I've been. It's been about a year and a half that I have not worked, but because I'm doing my record, my video that my husband is doing. But yes, yes, I'm maintaining. Look, I'm maintaining because you've arrived where I am.

In this dialogue Cristiane says that being a mother has never prevented her from participating in the movement; but only minutes later she comments that taking care of her kids takes up all her time and that she barely has two seconds left to focus on her work. Still, whatever time she does have she uses to further her career. Throughout the interview she talks about how her husband is helping her to produce and distribute her music. She says that people don't invite her to do shows. But later, when I commented that some artists say that they have called her and I suggested that she call them, she explained that she lost her phonebook when her young son ate all of the numbers.

I couldn't help but notice a marked change in Cristiane's discourse as we shifted from how she started to her work now. Cristiane went through two hip hop groups before finally deciding that it was better for her to work alone. She chose to leave the first group of two men because they were not as strong as she would have liked. Then she used to work independently before she was married: she wrote, self-promoted, and actively sought out opportunities to work. But now she waits for her husband to produce and release her music and videos and waits for people to contact her for events. She says that she takes her kids to hip hop events, gets up onstage, and then leaves, so it only seems as if she is not there. But in the next breath she says that it has been a month since she has been to any events. She later amends this to a year and a half and notes that she has been at home for three or four years working on her album when she could. The contrast with her earlier work could not be more striking, and I couldn't help thinking about all the contacts, resources, and concerts that she used to disseminate her music originally—all things that she now says she can't depend on to produce her music. Even as we talked, she sometimes commented on the songs that were being played in the background. But if she wanted to talk about a song she asked her husband for permission to play it for me.

Again, it is important to note that the interview was conducted in Cristiane's home, in the intimidating presence of her husband, who would not leave the room. Cristiane's spouse repeatedly intimidated her during the interview. He did so by recording it—a constant reminder in Cuba that he always had evidence that he could use to argue that she was saying something counter-revolutionary, which could result in numerous problems with the state and local community officials. He also repeatedly interrupted the interview in order to control her answers to questions. At various moments Cristiane became obviously flustered and complained of confusion and a headache, while nervously looking at her husband. She left the interview several times in order to make dinner for her husband and to attend to her two babies. It is also important to note here that I was not able to do a lyrical analysis of Cristiane's music. I asked her if I could buy a CD or a few songs.[13] She got excited and said: "Yes!" But when she asked her husband to burn a CD for me, he responded: "No, I need to finish mixing a few songs. I can play a song for you, but we are not selling Cristiane's music yet. When I think it's ready, I'll release the CD."

While I was in the apartment I realized that Cristiane's husband and his neighbor were not watching a regular TV. They were watching movies on their 27-inch LCD monitor and using really expensive computer hardware to play DVDs. It was then that I noticed the soundboard and all of the studio equipment he had. They had high-tech sound equipment that easily cost $3,000 U.S. Cristiane's husband explained to me that he was producing her music, that no one else had access to her music, not even Cristiane. He told me that he was in charge of her development and promotion and would release and promote her music when *he* felt that she was ready. He had big plans for her, he said. While he talked about his plans, I heard Cristiane rush to attend to her newborn and then rush back to the kitchen to finish frying the chicken and to check on the rice and beans.

What I did hear of the music was shocking in terms of the poor sound quality: I could barely hear Cristiane's voice. I thought of Randy Acosta, who made music and videos on a one-gigabyte computer, in his one-room house, shared with about six other family members. Randy managed to accomplish what at the very least sounded like studio-quality lo-fi sound production to my untrained ears. But when I listened to what Cristiane's husband played me, I could not make out her voice behind the static and background noise, which seemed all the more strange given his large trove of high-tech production equipment.

Cristiane and other women artists, to a varying extent, have internalized a notion of revolutionary femininity in which motherhood is understood as a natural duty and priority for all women. The result, in the case of Cristiane, is a role contradiction in which women eventually acquiesce, through familial and social pressure, to the expectations placed upon them to stay in the home. Cristiane began her career as an MC by attending women-centered hip hop events.

Though it could be argued that she could have found the support and resources necessary to be both a mother and an MC within the movement, the gender relations that structure her home life provide a vivid reminder of the contradictions still faced by women in Cuba more generally.

Conclusion

Sianne Ngai (2007) ends her book with an "Afterword: On Disgust." She argues that the postmodern turn has also influenced notions of democracy, in which the idea of tolerance, associated with the multiplicity of views within a society, is implicitly conflated with equality, democracy, and freedom. The limit of this perspective is that tolerance can function as forms of indifference. The concept of desire has also been implicated in how multiplicity within a democracy has come to be understood as equality, as good, and as something desirable. Yet forms of socioeconomic inequality persist in democracies, including Cuba, which presents itself as a socialist democracy. Ngai (2007) writes:

> It is rather that with its tropes of semantic multiplicity, slippage, and flow, with its general logic of inclusivity and strong centripetal pull, the academically routinized concept of "desire" is simply more concordant, ideologically as well as aesthetically, with the aesthetic, cultural, and political pluralisms that have come to define the postmodern than an emotional idiom defined by its vehement exclusion of the intolerable. If, in the context of a hegemonic pluralism that willfully misidentifies multiplicity with commensurability, the risk of "desire" is that of devolving into a "convenient receptacle" or "friendly abyss" for any form of "literary heterogeneity" or perceived transgression of the symbolic status quo, disgust's vulnerability as a poetics would seem to derive in part from pluralism's ability to manipulate the rhetoric of consensus and inclusivity in order to reduce oppositional and exclusionary formations to "monolithic totalitarianism[s]." (344–345)

What Ngai argues here is that the way in which desire has come to be understood aesthetically converges with a larger political discourse where that which is desirable is associated with aesthetic, cultural, and political pluralisms. The limit of desire, however, is that the boundaries of what is desirable are not clearly defined and can result in the friendly inclusion of heterogeneity and even "perceived transgressions" within democracies. Disgust is useful in policing the boundaries of that which is desirable, that which is acceptable in capitalist democracies. In order to seem to be inclusive, the idea of desire is manipulated discursively to reject that which is oppositional to pluralism and even socially exclusionary as being totalitarian (oppressive). Through an analysis of disgust we are able to see how desire is policed: we can see the limits of desire as well as the limits of democratic pluralism. Ngai (2007) writes:

> For disgust is never ambivalent about its object.... Whereas the obscuring of the subjective-objective boundary becomes internal to the nature of feelings like animatedness and paranoia, disgust strengthens and polices this boundary. Even if disgust is boiled down to its kernel of repulsion, re-pulsion itself tends to be a fairly definite response, whereas the parameters of attraction are notoriously difficult to determine and fix.... [William Ian] Miller notes, "the avowal of disgust expects concurrence" ... whereas we tend not to ask for supplementary ratification of our desired object's desirability, or demand that others share our affective relation to it or our valuation of it, once that object has actually been established. Hence, while disgust explicitly blocks the path of sympathy ... there is a sense in which it seeks to include or draw others into its exclusion of its object, enabling a strange kind of sociability.... Disgust's "expectation of concurrence" also distinguishes it from a particular kind of contempt character-ized predominantly by indifference. (335)

Feelings of disgust are social and political. Such feelings force people collec-tively to take a stand against something in a context where freedom, equality, and plurality are hailed as social realities. These discourses are also used in Cuba to represent the nation as being a socialist democracy vis-à-vis ensuring eco-nomic equality as a means of eliminating discrimination and ensuring demo-cratic plurality. In the case of Las Krudas, or lesbians in general, the disgust ex-perienced reflects the symbolic challenge, and by extension the political threat, posed by lesbian visibility, which is a direct challenge to Cuban machismo (heteropatriarchy). Cuba's heteropatriarchal welfare state claims to empower women via economic equality. While feminists sometimes see some improve-ment in economic measures in addition to the public policies that offer women control over their reproductive health, the ability of women to be able to access the privileges associated with socialist citizenship is severely curtailed by race, by sexuality, and, after the Special Period, by economic class. The effect of Cuba's stalled Revolution (from the mid-1960s until the late 1990s, when the economic crisis ushered in a new wave of profound social change) is that Cuban citizens have been limited in their ability to challenge the ways in which the symbolic is also the underpinning of social inequality. After 1959 the rest of the region went through fifty years of various phases of feminist, LGBTQ, and antiracist political activism that targeted the reproduction of social inequality in the realm of the symbolic.

In Cuba, however, the Revolution's paused in its progress in challenging the elements of the reproduction of social inequality rooted in the cultural and the symbolic (because of its successes in the struggle for material parity). This effectively undermined the possibility of those material-based policies actually decreasing and even eliminating social inequalities, especially gendered and racialized social inequalities. Additionally, in this context political dissent is understood as counter-revolutionary and as a potential threat to Cuban society. It might possibly destabilize Cuban society to such an extent that it would allow a possible violent invasion by the United States—something that most Cubans would not want even if they are dissatisfied with their current government. The visibility of a lesbian *and* feminist body (again, feminism was tolerated in the CUHHM as long as it did not destabilize heteropatriarchy, which the lesbian body symbolically does) resulted not only in disgust at the lesbian body. It also produced a horror at the possibility that some women genuinely reject heteropatriarchy and by extension what it means to be a Cuban (woman). This symbolically occurs via the rejection of their defined role as a female Revolutionary subject, a (potential) mother who is seen as the foundation of a healthy and stable family. The healthy, stable family is symbolically framed as the foundation of a stable Cuban nation. The family is also threatened by a person whose very being is also not defined in terms of her sexual relationship to men. In rejecting sex with men, the lesbian threatens (or eliminates) the possibility of reproducing a family and therefore destabilizes the foundation of the Cuban nation.

Magia, like many heterosexual women who have struggled with defining their woman-centered identity during this formative period of contemporary Cuban Black feminism, was forced to make a political choice. Magia and other artivists were able to bring attention to the racialized nexus of gender and class inequality through their discussions of motherhood, domestic violence, and the contextualization of the *jinetera* (sex worker) within a larger sociopolitical context. But the emergence of Las Krudas highlighted another aspect of women's inequality: the need for women's erotic autonomy as a central element of Black/Cuban women's liberation. The visibility of a publicly articulated lesbian subjectivity (the visible lesbian) embodies the demand for women's erotic autonomy. M. Jacqui Alexander (1991) calls for Caribbean women's erotic autonomy as a central element of their citizenship. Erotic autonomy disrupts the colonial-based connection of respectability, ownership, and citizenship. In this way erotic autonomy can disrupt racialized heterosexuality as a constitutive element of citizenship such that a citizen's loyalty to the nation is not imbued with the colonial relationship of race, gender, reproduction, heterosexuality, and the erotic. As a feminist emancipatory project, erotic autonomy has transformative possibilities for the nation. It will allow all citizens, especially women, the possibility of being fully included in the nation as autonomous subjects.

To this end there is a need for an autonomous space for women and people assigned female at birth in Cuba, run by women and people assigned female at birth. The Cuban Underground Hip Hop Movement provided an important space for initiating public discussions about the experiences of women, particularly Black women and lesbians. But movement leaders such as Magia, while she was the director of the Cuban Agency of Rap, missed an opportunity to claim, develop, and institutionalize a woman-centered space in which women could organize among themselves. If the Agency of Rap had institutionalized such a space, it would have had an effect in terms of mobilizing women across the Island. This could have included support of the independent Women's Hip Hop Festival organized in Holguín, Cuba, and support of the work of women MCs such as the group Las Positivas, based in Santiago de Cuba. The public sphere is almost completely dominated by men in Cuba. Women are still expected to defer to their interests, to stay at home, and to fulfill their roles as spouse/partner and mother. Precisely for this reason the first and most important step was—and still is—to claim space for women. Women artists such as the artistic collective Omegas KILAY attempted to do this, but movement leaders forbade "excluding" men from any public space. While the collective has had some successes (every member now lives in the diaspora and is making a living as a musician), the potential for Omegas KILAY to have a broader impact on creating space for women was also limited but not eliminated.

Magia has recently begun to identify as a feminist once again. This is partly the result of some recent experiences in Cuba in which her creditability and authority in the movement were directly challenged in an overtly sexist and aggressive way. But it is also because of her ongoing conversations with other women MCs and activists affiliated with the movement, especially the lesbian activist and psychologist Norma Guilliard. Additionally, CUHHM feminists are no longer likely to preface their feminist identity politics with a claim to male solidarity. But now Magia is no longer the head of the Agency of Rap, having been replaced by a male MC who is known for his sexist attitudes. Additionally, frustrated with the limited options available to them as artists who are women, nearly all of the members of Omegas KILAY have left Cuba in order to pursue their careers abroad. As a result of the 2006 mass exodus of members of the first generation of CUHHM artivists, there has been a pause but clearly not an end to the activism within the movement. During my visit to Cuba in 2014, it was clear that women artists have continued the underground hip hop movement through their feminist activism despite the end of the movement among their male counterparts (see chapter 8). Women in the CUHHM made some important gains in establishing a Black feminist discourse within Cuban society, but during the period from 1998 to 2006 questions remained about the limitations of this discourse and what issues it is and is not willing to address, as the next chapter discusses.

7

Kruda Knowledge, Kruda Discourse

Las Krudas CUBENSI, Transnational Black Feminism, and the Queer of Color Critique

To all the women in the world. . . .
To all the women that are fighting like us,
To all the sisters,
especially the most Black,
especially the most poor, especially the most fat. . . .
No one has ever spoken to you like this. . . .
Never here.

    "You Are Beautiful" (2003), Las Krudas

We have to keep working a lot, a lot, a lot and to be stronger every day,
stronger, stronger, stronger, [in order] for our men to listen and for our voices
to rise.

    Olivia Prendes Riverón of Las Krudas CUBENSI, Havana, 2006

In the lives of homosexual Cuban women there remains an anonymity that makes
us feel relegated [to second place] . . . In a female history of relegation to second
place with respect to men, where we are assigned the role of wife, mother, and de-
pendent of the male, [the existence of] women who reject these norms in order to
make their life with another woman "is almost an offense."

    Grupo OREMI 2005

People are very neighborly in Cuba. Neighbors visit each other regularly. In the case of musicians, houses are often crowded for jam sessions, loud singing, and dancing with neighbors and their children. My journal in 2006 describes a visit to the apartment of Las Krudas:

During one of my trips to Cuba in 2004, I was surprised to see a little girl, about three or four years old, entering Las Krudas' apartment. Las Krudas lived in a large and crowded apartment building. Children always skipped past Krudas' apartment when they were outside playing and chatting with neighbors. The little girl, however, would enter the apartment, sit on the bed, play, watch TV for a while and then leave. She always said hello to Las Krudas when passing by their apartment door. We joked that maybe she was a budding lesbian and that she had found her people. During subsequent trips, I would see the girl. Her visits continued for about a year and a half. They stopped sometime in 2005. . . .

During a visit to Cuba later that year, I sat with Krudas in their apartment. The little girl walked by the door but instead of stopping as she used to, she quickly walked or ran by the door like the other kids. "Strange," I thought. A few weeks later, while sitting with Krudas in their apartment, the girl walked by the door, stopped and peered into the doorway, staring at us. She did not come in. Apparently our jokes about the girl's lesbian future were also something that possibly concerned her parents; I realized that the moment I heard a woman yell the little girl's name, and the girl promptly responded "No!" and started to cry. The girl's name was repeated a second time, louder, and more harshly, with a "Get away from there!" The little girl ran away from the door. I heard her getting a spanking, crying, and heard the adult loudly whispering something at her. "¡¿Viste?!" ("You see?!") Odaymara of Las Krudas said while we listened to the girl getting a spanking. It was then that the particular form of social isolation that Las Krudas faced as lesbians became clear.

Over the three years that I visited Las Krudas in Cuba, I never saw their neighbors or their children stop by to play drums or sing in Las Krudas' apartment. If the neighbors spoke to Las Krudas, they stood at least fifteen to twenty feet from the apartment. The little girl was the first and only neighbor that I witnessed actually entering their space.

In many societies the hegemony of masculine discourses in public space reproduces and reinforces patriarchal, sociopolitical, economic, and racial structures in ways that reinforce heteronormativity and make it difficult for non-heteronormative women to access power. Cuba is a socialist country where notions of rebelliousness and resistance are highly symbolic and permeate most social discourses. It is also a country in which the state has claimed among its primary victories the achievement of racial equality, women's equality, and sexual liberation for its citizens. In reality, however, while there have been some gains for heterosexual women and gay men over the last fifty years in Cuba, the situation of lesbians seems to have stagnated and in recent years even deterio- rated (Acosta et al. 2003; Más 2003; Grupo OREMI 2005).

The social existence of lesbians in Cuba is further compounded by the issue of race. In contemporary Cuba cultural norms persist that evaluate women in terms of their physical appearance, specifically how "feminine" they are. Black women face a particularly harsh social environment: they are deemed unfemi- nine or even mannish because blackness is perceived as a marker of aggressive- ness and hyper-masculinity (Candelario 2007; Saunders 2009a, 2009b). As a result of Cuba's tenuous racial history, the possibilities for community support and organizing among Black lesbians in particular are limited. Until about 2012 social spaces for them were often so underground that many Black lesbians were unaware of their existence (Saunders 2009a, 2009b). Though there are now gay clubs and lesbian nights at clubs (always run by men, staffed by male DJs, and featuring music by almost exclusively male artists), the clubs deal in Cuban Convertible Currency.[1] As a result of Cuba's emergent racialized material inequality, they are largely attended by very light-skinned and white Cuban women. This chapter focuses on the activism of Las Krudas from 1995 to 2006, the year that the last members of the group left Cuba for the United States. It also discusses the activism of artivists like Las Krudas CUBENSI by document- ing the profound social effects that the CUHHM has had on national discourse in post–Special Period Cuba. Las Krudas CUBENSI use their art-based activism within the hip hop movement and as independent street theater artists to bring attention to the intersecting ideologies of race, gender, and sexuality.

Las Krudas' discursive intervention has been to argue that race, gender, and sexuality serve as the basis for social oppression, particularly oppression of Black lesbians. The group has described their activism as contributing to "the third revolution within the Revolution":[2] the revolution of Black women and lesbian equality. In their music and hip hop performances, they highlight contradictions within hegemonic discourses and systems of representation, as a means to develop an alternative liberatory discourse that includes the citizen- ship demands of socially marginal groups such as Black women and Black lesbi- ans. Like their peers within the Cuban Underground Hip Hop Movement, Las Krudas have focused on consciousness-raising among fellow citizens as a means to spur grassroots social change.

In this chapter I am interested in analyzing a key aspect of Las Krudas' work: their participation in a form of discursive activism that centers on creating an emancipatory discourse that names and challenges multiple intersecting forms of inequality. Despite their ideological isolation in Cuba, where they had limited access to transnational lesbian and gay, Black feminist, and queer discourses, Las Krudas have been able to articulate a Cuban queer of color critique—a "Kruda" discourse—as a centerpiece of their discursive activism. Their emancipatory discourse is in conversation with arguments made from broader Black feminist and queer of color critical perspectives throughout the Caribbean and the Americas that address the experiences of nonheteronormative subjects. Here I also frame what I see in their work as central elements for a hemispheric (Black) queer of color critique as an epistemological orientation and an emancipatory praxis.

The CUHHM is very popular among socially conscious activists in Cuba and a larger public who value the movement's antiracist and anticolonial critiques. By rupturing the silences concerning heteronormativity and its exclusions within the movement, Las Krudas have also been able to critique many of the silences concerning Black women and lesbians that exist at the national level. They could command the attention of the larger public mainly because they have challenged a key authenticity claim within both the CUHHM itself and Cuban society at large: that it is necessary to censor critiques of discourses concerning racism, sexism, and homophobia in order to ensure social cohesion in a nation under constant threat that claims to have eliminated the material basis for social inequality. Las Krudas argue that they have experienced invisibility in the CUHHM, as in Cuban society, as poor women who are Black lesbians, despite the existence of discourses that advocate for the diverse interests and needs of a population marginalized by race, gender, and material inequality.

Through their framing of racism, sexism, and homophobia as "colonial legacies," a central theme within Cuban underground hip hop, Las Krudas have addressed the ways in which racism has been corporalized and institutionalized at the state level and at the psychic level, at the level of the erotic, while simultaneously interrogating the ways in which culture and material inequality are racialized. Several key theorists, such as Manolo Guzmán (2005), Roderick Ferguson (2004), and José Muñoz (1999), implicitly connect a queer of color critique to a challenge to colonialism and Western modernity. Las Krudas build on this critique by also including sexuality within their rejection of discourses affirming Western European modernity as a cultural and developmental ideal. In this way, Las Krudas have developed an alternative vision of modernity that emerges from the intersection of their multiple subjectivities as Black feminists, Cuban revolutionary subjects, and queers of color—a specifically Kruda queer of color critique.

It is important to note that the sex/gender system in Cuba is different than in the United States and that the type of discrimination that sexual minorities face in Cuba is mediated by gender in different ways. Sara Más (2003) notes that more than half of the people in a study said that they treat homosexuals normally, but almost all of the women reported being disgusted by lesbians. The study indicates that lesbians continue to be the most obscure and marginalized population within the homosexual population. The subject of women's attitudes toward lesbians, in particular, deserves much attention. It is very likely that women are more likely to police gender/sexual boundaries than men, given the narrow framework for performing acceptable femininity in Cuba and the high social cost of performing inadequately.

Smith and Padula (1996) note about seven colloquial terms for lesbians but at least twenty-four terms for gay men. Only three official classifications are used to describe female sexuality: heterosexual, bisexual, and lesbian. The Spanish terms publicly correspond to their English translations. "Bisexual" is a newer term in Cuba, while "lesbian" and "heterosexual" have been used for the most part for women.

Given this context, it is important not to read Las Krudas' particular interventions as simply reflecting second-wave U.S. feminism, even though one member of the group in particular, Odaymara Cuesta Rosseau, is very much invested in being in conversation with Caribbean and Black U.S. feminisms. The key here is the idea of conversation. Las Krudas are not completely isolated actors in a totalitarian state who are appropriating second-wave U.S. discourse. They come from a country whose global ideological weight, in terms of discourses concerning social change and liberation, easily rivals the global reach of U.S. ideologies. Historically, many of the key figures of the U.S. Black political Left have gone to Cuba to learn about and from the discourses of liberation there or have actively engaged in learning about Cuban revolutionary theory. As Cheryl Higashida (2011) writes:

> Understanding the internationalist, anti-colonial antecedents of Black feminism is integral to and transformative of the ongoing efforts within these fields to contest the historical amnesia about U.S. imperialism and racism, and the radical movements that have challenged them. This forgetting perpetuates and is perpetuated by beliefs about American exceptionalism; the notion that U.S. social, political, and economic formations disavow and break with "European" feudalism, class conflict, and imperialism; and the idea that the United States is leading the world to democracy and freedom. Such beliefs isolate the United States from hemispheric and global histories and processes. Nation-based frameworks based on beliefs about U.S. exceptionalism narrow the scope and substance of Black

freedom struggles by disconnecting them from radical and often international, or transnational, movements. (6)

Some elements of Las Krudas' work certainly resonate with second-wave
feminism, given the hemispheric nature of the legacies of colonialism and Black
feminist mobilization against the classism, sexism, and homophobia that are
constitutive of American national identities and nation-states. But it is important to remember that feminists are in conversation with women across geopolitical boundaries, especially at the international grassroots level, beyond the
halls of academia. The exchange of knowledge and ideas concerning feminism
in the Americas was never unidirectional, from the United States to everywhere
else, but was instead a dynamic transnational interchange, albeit one shaped by
asymmetrical structures of power.

Reducing the work of Cuban and global feminists such as Las Krudas to
a reflection of U.S. second-wave feminism is an example of how ideological
production within the United States becomes discursively disconnected from
the rest of the Americas. This exceptionalism assumes that transnational perspectives do not influence feminist thought in the United States. It also limits
our understanding of the local context in which American (regionally speaking) feminists and Black feminists are operating. Instead such points of overlap should be critically engaged as nodes of convergence in regional systems of
power that also have the potential for understanding oppression in the United
States. Transnational feminists, specifically leftist Black feminists and feminists
of color, have certainly recognized that. In this chapter I frame the work of Las
Krudas CUBENSI using Higashida's framing of the work of Black internationalist feminists. Higashida (2011) quotes Chela Sandoval's description of *feministas
de la planeta tierra* (feminists from planet earth): as "those who break apart *national* borders," women who create "revolutionary, mobile, and global coalitions
of citizen-activists" (8; emphasis in the original). This, I argue, describes the core
of Las Krudas' work as Black feminists and queer of color activists.

The first section of this chapter discusses the key components of a queer
of color critique. I then analyze the history of Las Krudas as independent artists, their emergence in the Cuban Underground Hip Hop Movement, and their
place within Black feminist epistemology. I examine how Las Krudas' work centers on consciousness-raising as a means of encouraging Cuban women, particularly Black women and lesbians, to work for their own empowerment by developing a critical consciousness that embraces all forms of diversity. The second
section of the chapter discusses their hybrid "Kruda" identity or queer of color
critique, which is constructed at the intersection of their identities as lesbians,

Black women, and socially conscious revolutionary artists. The third section examines the effects of Las Krudas' activism on the CUHHM and their continued work within Cuba and the Cuban diaspora. In the conclusion I discuss how Krudas CUBENSI's queer of color critique (after approximately 2008) makes an explicitly hemispheric and anticolonial intervention into queer theory, which they and other queer Cuban activists refer to as *queeridad*.

While in Cuba, Las Krudas CUBENSI were highly skeptical of academic production and saw themselves solely as artists. It was in the realm of music, painting, poetry, filmmaking, and public theater that they sought to make their socially critical and theoretical interventions. The group members argue that their Kruda identity first emerged as a Black feminist identity when they started to realize how significant aspects of their experiences were not addressed by antiracist and socialist discourses. Higashida (2011) notes that this was recognized by many U.S. Black international feminists who saw the limits of revolutionary nationalism. Las Krudas sought to make a cultural intervention within Cuba's institutionalized cultural sphere by highlighting the issues that they faced as Black Cuban women and lesbians. Like the Combahee River Collective in the United States, they link their culturally based oppression to the legacies of colonialism, particularly slavery and imperialism. In their music and performance, Las Krudas work tirelessly to challenge the ideological basis of social oppression by creating a critical framework that participants in Cuban hip hop can use to recognize the intersecting nature of social oppression. While the majority of the women within the Cuban Underground Hip Hop Movement critique the treatment of women within their music, only Las Krudas have connected the ways in which heteronormativity—as a racialized system through which culturally based notions of gender conformity and heterosexuality are policed—is constitutive of and reinforces Black women's oppression.

Introducing Las Krudas CUBENSI

Las Krudas are sisters Odaymara Cuesta Rosseau (also sometimes known as Pasita), Odalys Cuesta Rosseau (also known as Wanda), and Olivia Prendes Riverón (also sometimes known as Pelusa), the long-term partner of Odaymara (figs. 7.1 and 7.2). Olivia met Odaymara in the Havana arts scene in the mid-1990s. She was struck by Odaymara's talent as a musician and by her knowledge of Cuban and global popular music. Because of their complementary artistic interests (Olivia has a background in theater and production), Odaymara and Olivia decided to work together within Cuba's politicized cultural sphere.

Odaymara strongly identifies as an artist. She is what some would describe

Figure 7.1.   Las Krudas CUBENSI (Krudxs) in Austin, Texas, 2010.
(Courtesy of Las Krudas CUBENSI)

Figure 7.2.   The members of Las Krudas CUBENSI (Krudxs) (*left to right*): Odalys Cuesta
Rosseau, Odaymara Cuesta Rosseau, Olivia Prendes Riverón. (Courtesy of Sahily Borrero)

as an organic intellectual who is a Black feminist: she expresses her ideological interventions through interviews, lyrics, and performances. Disillusioned by her experiences at the professional arts institutions, Odaymara rejects the idea of the academy, specifically print media, as being the only legitimate resource for intellectual production. She is integral to the group's critical and theoretical interventions into everyday discourses and lived experiences. Odaymara's activism did not begin with Las Krudas: she was interviewed in the 1996 film *Gay Cuba* by Sonia de Vries, in which she talked about her experiences as a lesbian youth in Havana. Odaymara has been very active in the LGBT community in Havana since 1994, when she and several other youths attempted to form Cuba's first LGBT organization and host Cuba's first Gay Pride Parade.[3]

Olivia has a postsecondary degree in theater production. She is primarily responsible for helping the group develop and perfect their stage performances and unique sound. She is also a key contributor to the group's social critiques. While she is skeptical of the ideological monopoly held by the academy, she wants to obtain a postgraduate degree, as she is interested in making an intervention into academic discourses concerning women via publications. Wanda, who is Odaymara's older sister and is known for her knowledge of and investment in African and traditional Afro-Cuban music, joined the group as an auxiliary member in 1998. Wanda is integral in maintaining the African, "natural," or "aboriginal" aspect of Las Krudas. She does this through her deep raspy voice, which she uses to sing traditional African-Cuban songs. She also accomplishes this through her incorporation of West African religious rhythms and symbolism in Las Krudas' music. Wanda is respected among her underground peers as someone who is incredibly strong and independent. She was the first member of Las Krudas to leave for the United States via Russia in 2005.

Tropazancos: The Early Years of Las Krudas CUBENSI

Before joining the Cuban Underground Hip Hop Movement, Olivia and Odaymara entered the performance art scene in 1997 as the founders of the independent art troupe Agrupación de Creación Alternativa CUBENSI, a precursor to their internationally acclaimed street theater group, Tropazancos. Tropazancos has about twelve members, though this number varies depending on the needs and availability of the performers. The group is composed of performance artists who use the opportunity to participate as a way to make extra money as artists and to have professional-level work experience in their portfolios. Las Krudas continued their involvement with the troupe until they immigrated to the United States. The members of Tropazancos have received national and international attention for their work. They were invited to international festivals such as the Festival Cervantino in Mexico in 2005 and 2006 and national festivals such as the 2002 Festival del Caribe in Santiago de Cuba. They have been photographed and featured in journals in Bolivia (2005),[4] in Italy (2002),[5] and in Cuba's influential cultural magazine *Bohemia*,[6] all of which represents recognition of their work as a significant contribution to Cuban culture. Because of this official recognition, Tropazancos has received state permission to perform in areas of Old Havana that are frequented by tourists. Wanda joined Odaymara and Olivia during their Tropazancos years. Olivia writes the following about their group (Prendes Riverón 2006):

> en 1997 fundo la Agrupación de Creación Alternativa CUBENSI, junto a Odaymara Cuesta y otras artistas con intereses comunes: centrar en nuestra obra temas como el orgullo nacional, el cuidado a la naturaleza, el maravilloso deleite en las frutas y vegetales, el espíritu festivo, la educación ambiental, el respeto al amor, a la amistad, a la diversidad. En nuestra trayectoria investigábamos formas de llegar a las comunidades, experimentábamos trabajos eminentemente visuales (concentrándonos en las artes plásticas), componíamos temas musicales, teatralizábamos historias y así buscando, encontramos para completar nuestro arte comunitario: los zancos y el rap. Estos recursos fueron de absoluta popularidad, recorrimos en la Casa de Cultura de Centro habana y con la Asociación Hermanos Saiz muchos barrios y calles de La Habana y así rapeando y zanqueando llegamos en 1998 al IV Festival de Rap de Alamar.

> in 1997 I founded the Group of Alternative Creation CUBENSI, together with Odaymara Cuesta and other artists with common interests, [in order] to center our work on themes of national pride, protecting nature, the marvelous delight of fruits and vegetables, a festive spirit, environmental awareness, respect for love, for friendship, and for diversity. In our trajectory we looked for forms of going out into the communities, we experimented with visual art,[7] doing theater performances of history and also looking for a way to do our community art: stilt walking and rap. The resources were popular resources, ranging from the Casa de Cultura of Central Havana to the Asociación de Hermanos Saíz: [we worked in] a lot of neighborhoods and streets in Havana and so [in] rapping and performing zancos [stilt walking] we ended up at the 1998 Fourth Festival of Rap of Alamar.

Olivia points out the communitarian orientation of their work as artists. This grassroots, social justice orientation is linked to a revolutionary ideology.

Tropazancos follows the tradition of Cuban artists and intellectuals who sought to socialize culture after the revolution (Camnitzer 2003; Chanan 2002; Craven 2006; Navarro 2002; Vitier 2002). This movement seeks to make art and theater available to all people, especially those who cannot afford to attend paid performances in closed theaters.[8] By locating their performances in the streets, as Olivia notes, Las Krudas make an effort to bring culture to Cuban citizens and to integrate art and alternative social perspectives into people's daily lives.[9]

The goal of Tropazancos is to reestablish the carnival aesthetic in Havana. Odaymara and Wanda noted in 2004 that they had heard that Havana used to have carnival festivities during the colonial period that created a similar type of atmosphere. Besides street performances, Tropazancos offers free art classes and workshops providing instruction in stilt walking, theater makeup, music, dance, costume making, acting, fire eating, and percussion. The group has also organized public conferences on percussion rhythms as well as popular and folkloric dance. These workshops offer free fun and entertainment, but they also provide education by encouraging people to use the arts as a means to think critically about their everyday lives. For example, Tropazancos encourages people to embrace diversity, especially in areas such as human expression, animal rights, and environmental rights. In street theater work, Tropazancos focuses on pedagogical activities for children. The plays and performances leave children with messages such as to love the earth, to treat all of fellow human beings with care, and to embrace diversity in all its forms. This focus on embracing diversity and "difference" regardless of race, gender, sexuality, class, gender expression, appearance, and ability is a common theme throughout Las Krudas' work. Tropazancos teaches people to use their own creative energies to express themselves and to interpret their social world.

The only pay that members of Tropazancos receive is in the form of donations from tourists and Cuban citizens who participate in performances or workshops. Unfortunately, foreign tourists who do not understand Cuba's approach to culture often take them for beggars and refuse to give donations. Tourists take pictures and record shows but will not offer money when Tropazancos requests donations. Members of the group evenly split the donations that they do receive from their performances. But in the actual performances it is the white members of the group who consistently receive the overwhelming majority of the donations from tourists. How these artists are treated is linked both to racism on the part of the tourists who arrive in Cuba and to the Western capitalist valuation of art, which assumes that people have to pay beforehand to attend the performance if it is something of value. Because the performances are free and occur in the streets of central Havana, they are often not recognized as valuable cultural work. Additionally, most tourists are not aware of Cuba's history of community art and performance.

In 1998 Odaymara, Olivia, and Wanda emerged as Las Krudas CUBENSI in Cuba's underground hip hop scene at the Fourth Annual Hip Hop Festival, held in Alamar. Known for their work with Tropazancos, they were asked by the festival organizers to perform at the 1998 event. They chose the name Las Krudas, which means "the crude ones" (referring to something natural, uncooked, unprocessed, or raw). Like uncooked vegetables, Las Krudas' lyrics may be difficult for many Cubans to digest; but in the end they are good for your health. The name of the group itself, Las Krudas CUBENSI, can be translated as "the crude ones," the "crude women," and even as "the crude feminine subjects" who are also "Cuban?" "Yes!" (CUBEN-SI). This name reflects a critique of and challenge to the resistance and the disgust evoked by the mere mention of anything "lesbian," which is also viewed as "foreign," and "un-Cuban." They went onstage in Tropazancos costumes that included stilts and colorful makeup. In later work that emphasized the diversity and openness of Cuba's emerging hip hop scene, Las Krudas have been described as "stilt-walking lesbians," who, to the "disgust" of the audience, talked about menstruation in their song "120 Horas" (120 Hours) (Perry 2004; West-Durán 2004). Though their initial performance was not well received, they were encouraged by Pablo Herrera, the most popular hip hop producer in Cuba at the time, to perform again. Thus Las Krudas did their first non-Tropazancos solo performance, as a trio, at the 2000 Havana Hip Hop Festival, marking the beginning of their work as a group of hip hop artists who are openly lesbian feminists.

Las Krudas: Underground Rappers

Las Krudas decided to pursue their activism within the Cuban Underground Hip Hop Movement because it was part of a global phenomenon that lent itself to the creative energies of Cuban youths of African descent. They saw the CUHHM as a global platform where Cuban youth could finally have a voice. Olivia writes:

Al conocer lo que en aquel entonces era un joven movimiento quedamos maravillad@s, Hip Hop en Cuba, una gran masa de artistas y público de mayoría afrodescendiente se manifestaba, una cultura surgida y desarrollada en los Estados Unidos de Norteamérica, se había asentado en la isla y se aclimataba perfectamente, transformándose, convirtiéndose en voz populis de tantos jóvenes revoluciónari@s de nuestra generación, la fusión de elementos heredados, la auténtica fuerza de noveles creador@s era más que un resultado, una alucinación . . . estimuladas por las posibilidades de expresión que ofrecía la ocasión fundamos en 1998 Krudas CUBENSI, con la intención de saciar nuestras propias expectativas de representación y también para incorporar un discurso feminista a la ebullente propuesta de mayoría masculina, lo cual significaba un gran reto reto.

> There we came to know a young movement that came to be marvelous, Cuban hip hop, in which a great mass of artists and an audience that was mostly of African descent appeared, a culture that appeared and developed in the United States, that had settled itself on the Island and acclimated itself perfectly, [while] transforming itself, converting itself into the popular voice of so many revolutionary youth from our generation, [it became] a fusion of inherited elements, [it is] the authentic force of new creators that was more than a result of a hallucination . . . stimulated by the possibilities of expression that this occasion offered, we founded Krudas CUBENSI in 1998, with the intention of offering our own perspectives of representation and also to incorporate a feminist discourse into the prevalent discourses of masculinity, which signified a great challenge. (Prendes Riverón 2006)

Olivia explains that Las Krudas viewed Cuba's hip hop as the voice of Afro-Cuban youth. Las Krudas were inspired by their experience in the hip hop community, which they came to understand as an open community for free expression. Odaymara commented: "You can't imagine what it was like. To go to a concert and see a woman with an Afro, rapping, and who declared herself a feminist out in the open and in public [referring to Magia MC], and who talked about being proud to be a Black woman. That made my head explode to see something like that. It was very revolutionary" (personal communication, 2006).

During the early years of Cuban hip hop (1995–2002), a few women participating in the movement offered a positive, woman-centered, empowering message. As discussed in chapter 6, Magia MC was one of a very small number of women who commanded the stage at that time, openly talked about blackness as beautiful, and told Black women to love themselves, their bodies, and their hair. Realizing how important this message and these images were, Cuban women interested in hip hop were bothered by the lack of women's groups, particularly groups that challenged stereotypes of women. They also realized that the disproportionately small number of women MCs was related to an attitude of machismo that is far from specific to hip hop culture but is a broader aspect of Cuban culture, as discussed earlier. Impressed by the artistic and revolutionary potential of underground hip hop as a critical, anticapitalist culture with a communitarian ideology, Las Krudas decided to begin performing at hip hop shows. They created Las Krudas CUBENSI, the formal name of the group, as a means of offering their feminist perspective on the critical discourses circulating within the hip hop community.

A few groups such as Atómicas and Explosión Femenina as well as a few critically conscious female performers at the time similarly tried to inject a critical feminist perspective and were respected in the underground scene (Prendes Riverón 2006). Las Krudas found inspiration in Magia, who won critical acclaim in Cuba for Obsesión's song "Le llaman puta" (They Call Her a Whore"), about the dire material issues facing poor women who turn to prostitution and other activities in Cuba's underground economy. After Las Krudas' performance in the 2000 festival, where they were better received, they were again approached by the pioneering Cuban hip hop producer Pablo Herrera, who also encouraged them to produce a CD and to pursue work within the nascent movement. It was then that Las Krudas realized that the critical artistic and intellectual arena of hip hop offered a space in which they could make a feminist intervention in hegemonic discourses surrounding women.

Las Krudas' activism has two key goals. The first is to raise awareness of the particular social issues facing Black women, such as issues of self-respect, independence, and beauty. By establishing a feminist presence in the hip hop movement, Las Krudas worked to ensure that the diverse interests of women were addressed. Additionally, they aimed to raise awareness of and increase respect for gender and sexual diversity in the hip hop community. Their identity is not only one of Black female subjectivity but also one of lesbian subjectivity. Olivia spoke about their agenda as artivists in our interview in Havana in 2005:

> Entonces cuando nosotras sentimos que había otras mujeres que tenían un discurso feminista, nosotras sentimos que ya podíamos subir a otro escalón. Y el otro escalón es el escalón de salir del closet totalmente, de abrirnos como raperas lesbianas y continuar subiendo la escalera que nos lleva a la emancipación absoluta de Krudas ... en ese caso también tenemos una contradicción que también nos parece hermosa. Porque la aceptamos, es real y no podemos negarla. .... A nosotras que somos mujeres lesbianas nos gusta hip hop.

> Then when we feel that there are other women who have a feminist discourse, we felt that we could take it up another step. And the other step is

the step of coming out of the closet completely and come out as lesbian rappers and continue going up the ladder until we arrive at the absolute emancipation of Krudas . . . in this sense we also have a contradiction that for us is beautiful. Because they accept us, that is real and we cannot negate that. . . . For us, we are lesbian women who like hip hop.

The contradiction that is "beautiful" is to be out as lesbian feminists who also like hip hop and are working in a music genre associated with machismo and homophobia. The irony is that the public would (and have) come to respect the women that they loathe. As Las Krudas gained acceptance and respect as women artists who revealed much of the complexity of life surrounding women, they gradually began to come out of the closet.

Las Krudas' Black Feminist Discourse

Las Krudas represent themselves as poor, Black, lesbian feminists from a marginalized and isolated but revolutionary nation. It is also a nation in which "resistance" is at the center of nationalist discourse in a context that informs their challenge to capitalist ideological and economic structures. Las Krudas' politics of a linguistic and ideological intervention into hegemonic discourses surrounding, gender, and sexuality problematize and name oppression through the critique of their individual experiences, which they use to highlight common experiences shared by their audience. They then use these shared individual experiences as a way to show how systemic forms of social oppression operate. These individual experiences are not simply personal problems but representative of larger social issues that affect all Cubans. After describing the systemic nature of individual experiences, Las Krudas offer liberatory discourses that help to address these particular forms of social oppression.

Las Krudas argue that they support a basic form of feminism in which women are liberated and feel in control of their lives and respected for the decisions that they make. Odaymara spoke of the limitations of revolutionary discourse to address the particular needs of women in our interview in Havana in 2005:

Entonces, o sea, cuando triunfó la revolución, hubo una primera tarea: ser revolucionaria o revolucionario y las causas de grupos o de comunidades quedaron pospuestas para después. Lo más importante era aunar a todo el pueblo en la lucha contra el imperialismo. . . . Entiendes. Entonces las causas como de razas, de género, de sexo, quedaron relegadas a un plano, no segundo ni tercero, décimo, doce planos por allá atrás que aún hoy estamos sufriendo las consecuencias de eso porque era necesario unificar a todo el pueblo en la lucha contra el imperialismo, el enemigo, los ataques, el terrorismo y todas esas cosas.

> At the triumph of the revolution, there was the primary project: to be a revolutionary [woman or man] . . . the causes of [particular] groups or communities were left until later. The most important thing was to unite all of the people to fight against imperialism. . . . So causes like race, gender, sex, they were left on the shelf, not the second one or the third one, but around the tenth or twelfth shelf so that now we are suffering the consequences of this because it was necessary to unify all of the people against imperialism, the enemy, the attacks, the terrorism, and all of those things.

Odaymara argues that the problem with revolutionary culture is that it assumes that the state's focus on equal education and work has solved all the problems facing women. She argues that women are oppressed in all of the world's cultures and that simply focusing on women as workers is not going to end gender inequality. This limitation of the government discourse has been critiqued by numerous writers on women in Cuba (see Bunck 1994; Fleites-Lear 2003; Leiner 1994; Murray 1979; Smith and Padula 1996). During the early years of the revolution, social critiques of social policy and persistent social inequality were discouraged. Thus many people could not speak out about the social issues that they were facing.

State official discourse argued that it was necessary to police ideology in order to ensure unity on the Island. The state wanted to ensure the homogeneity of political discourse as a means of making sure that Cubans would not embrace a capitalist or other competing discourses. These discourses were seen as creating the possibility of Cuban citizens siding with the ideological interests of the United States and working to overthrow the government. Policing of discourse was not carried out only by the state but also by Cubans policing themselves and their fellow citizens. Anything that fell outside of revolutionary discourse was excluded, even if it was not directly counter-revolutionary. Those who wanted to critique or address social issues beyond the boundaries of revolutionary discourse took the risk that their demands would be considered counter-revolutionary. It was in this context that Las Krudas' feminism developed.

During my discussions with Las Krudas, I asked what feminism means for them. Odaymara's first comment in our interview in Havana in 2006 was: "We are not talking about the feminism of Gloria Steinem!" She went on to say:

> ¿Qué es una feminista para mí? Una mujer que defiende las razones de vivir y la necesidad que tenemos las mujeres de ser felices y respetadas

en una y cada una de nuestras decisiones ante la vida. O sea, te estoy hablando del feminismo básico. No te estoy hablando del feminismo académico de Gloria Steiner [Steinem] ni de ninguna de esas mujeres blancas de por allá. ¿Me entiendes? Te estoy hablando de un feminismo elemental que lo puede tener una mujer iletrada. ¿Me entiendes? Hasta analfabeta pueden entender lo que yo estoy hablando. Pienso que para sentirse una mujer feminista no hay que estar sentada doce horas en una universidad para entenderlo. Ni tener un vocabulario de 2,603 palabras por minuto, sino sentirse mujer y sentir las cosas que nos suceden a nosotras las mujeres y a partir de ahí levantarte y decir sí soy feminista, lo soy. Primitiva, primaria, cruda, aborigen, pero defendiendo siempre a las mías porque pienso que estamos en super, super desventaja. Y yo pienso que para mí esto es feminismo.

> What is feminism for me? It is a woman defending the reasons to live and the necessity that we have to be happy and respected in . . . [every one] of the decisions we make in life. Or better, I'm talking about a basic feminism. I am not talking about the academic feminism of Gloria Steiner [Steinem] or any of those other white women over there. You understand me? I am talking about an elemental feminism that an illiterate woman could have. You understand me? So that an illiterate person can understand what I am saying. I think that to feel yourself to be a feminist woman, you don't have to sit for twelve hours in a university to understand it. Nor do you need to have a vocabulary of 2,603 words per minute, but to feel yourself to be a woman and feel the things that happen to all us women and from that to stand up and say, yes I am a feminist, that I am. Primitive, primary, raw, aboriginal, but always defending my thing because I think that we are at a super, super disadvantage. For me, that is feminism.

Odaymara points to the importance of lived experience in forming feminist subjectivity. For Black Cuban women, identity and experience cannot be found in the canonized feminist texts of (white U.S.) scholars such as Gloria Steinem. Given the multiple forms of oppression that Black Cuban women face, it is important first to have that moment of acknowledgment that, as many Black feminists have commented, multiple "isms" are kicking your "behind" and "making [you] crazy" (Smith 2000, xxxiv). For Las Krudas, a feminist consciousness emerges in the moment when you realize that multiple forms of oppression face Black women *and* that you should be happy, be respected, and respect yourself as a woman.

Cubans are somewhat skeptical about feminism. It arrived in Cuba as a discourse concerned primarily, if not entirely, with the interests of elite white women on the Island. During the early Republic years, white feminists from the United States sometimes intervened in Cuban politics; some U.S. feminists tried to prevent universal suffrage in Cuba, as they felt that Black and mulat@ Cubans were not fit to run their country (Stoner 1991). Many Cuban and U.S. women were unabashedly racist and classist (Stoner 1991). Even within this elite environment, however, some antiracist and anticlassist feminists began joining the socialist movements of the 1920s and 1930s.

Aware of this complicated history of global feminist identity and theory, Las Krudas locate their work within the tradition of Black Cuban women such as Gloria Rolando and Nancy Morejón, who have offered their social critiques through the arts. When Las Krudas invoke the names of feminists, they cite influential figures in Cuban and world history (often Black). They also include the names of the women ancestors of their families. They do this in order to locate their work as part of a broader tradition of everyday women, especially poor and working-class women who have not been written into Cuban history, and also to link their struggle to the global struggles facing women, especially Black women. Las Krudas center their critiques not just on Cuba but on issues facing Black women regionally and globally.

Odaymara and Olivia are exceptionally well read and well versed in global feminist theory. While living on the Island, Odaymara and Olivia actively sought out foreigners as a means of accessing information about the experiences of lesbians (particularly Black and Latina lesbians) living outside of Cuba. Las Krudas developed connections with their foreign peers in order to gain access to books and videos not otherwise available. In a 2006 interview Odaymara explained: "You see, the blockade and the restrictions on information don't stop the exchange." Though Las Krudas had been somewhat disconnected from a larger global community during Cuba's global isolation, they are very much in conversation with global feminisms and have been offering their critiques through their local work as performers.

While the three members of Las Krudas may agree on what it means to be a feminist, each one has a different story of how her particular form of feminism arose. For example, Wanda argued that her feminist consciousness developed differently from that of most self-identified feminists. She insists that her feminism came to the fore in total isolation from global feminist discourses. Her notion of feminism was not developed through reading feminist theory or through discussions of feminism with tourists. The term "feminism" itself meant little to her until she began to think about it. Her feminism, which she considers indigenous Cuban feminism, is very much informed by her experiences as a woman, particularly a Black woman, on the Island. She defines her feminist consciousness as something that developed through her own personal experiences and the teachings of her mother, who raised Odaymara and Wanda to be strong, confident, and conscious Black women. Their mother, Señora Bárbara, rejected social norms that discouraged women generally, and Black women specifically, from embracing their body and hair. She rejected the pressure to encourage her daughters to conform to European male-centered notions of beauty, teaching them instead to remember that they have the right to be happy and loved as they are. In this way Señora Bárbara manifested a feminist consciousness that Las Krudas refer to as a natural or aboriginal consciousness.

Odaymara, in contrast, actively sought information on feminism, Black women, and sexuality. She was acutely aware of the isolation that Cuba faced and the international discussions that were occurring concerning these topics. Odaymara talked about the development of her feminist consciousness in our interview in Havana in 2005:

Odaymara: Algunas poetas de por allí y chicanas eso. Sí, todo está muy bien, en palabras, literatura y eso y para mí yo siento que hay distintas maneras de hacer feminismo, y pienso que nosotras, más que ser feministas en una isla que como dice ella, está como aislada, como que no está conectada con las corrientes feministas del mundo ¿entiendes? Con las redes de feministas del mundo, estamos así, eso mismo ha hecho que nuestro trabajo, nuestro activismo, sea aún más activo en dar un mensaje que en estar escrito en un libro, yo tengo conciencia de que el feminismo surgió en tal año, y que empezó por allá por Francia, más que saber la historia del feminismo, con mí feminismo estoy haciendo activismo y es vivirlo, ¿entiendes? Para mí opinión.

  Pero que siento que estamos ahora aquí y que podemos conectarnos con las redes feministas, porque de hecho hay muchas y es bueno hacer puente entre mujeres e intercambiar, saber . . . y que sepan, que conozcan que estamos y que existimos, esto es feminismo crudo, puro.
Tanya: ¿Y dónde leíste estos libros? ¿En un curso de Women Studies?
Odaymara: En mi juventud. Libros que llegaban a mis manos, . . . personas que traían esos libros. Investigaba, buscaba, quería saber.

Odaymara: Some poets from here [the United States] and Chicanas. Yes, all of it is very good, in words, in literature and this for me. . . . I felt that there are distinct ways of doing feminism, and I think that ours, more than to be feminists on an island, as she [Olivia] said, is like being a little isolated, as if we are not connected to the feminist currents of the world. Understand me? . . . with the networks of feminists in the world, we are in that situation, this is exactly what we have done with our work, our activism, it was to be more active in giving a message than is written in a book. I know that feminism started in a certain year and that it began over there in France, but to know the history of feminism, with my feminism I'm doing activism and it's all of it, understand me? That's my opinion.

It's for this reason that I feel that we are here now and that we can connect ourselves with feminist networks, because there are a lot and it's good to be a bridge between women and to have an exchange, to know . . . and that they know, that they know that we are here and that we exist, this is crude feminism, pure feminism.

Tanya: And where did you read these books? In a Women's Studies course?

Odaymara: In my youth, books that came into in my hands . . . persons that bought books. I researched, I looked, I wanted to know.

Through her engagement with tourists, academics, and activists on the Island, Odaymara was able to engage the international community and finally participate in transnational discourses concerning feminism. She consciously compared the different theories, histories, and experiences that were articulated in transnational discourses concerning race, gender, and sexuality. She was not simply a passive recipient of knowledge but actively engaged in filling in the gaps in feminist scholarship that did not address the situation of women in Cuba. Through her activism as an artist, Odaymara worked to help disseminate feminist theory and to present a discourse of Cuban (particularly Black Cuban) feminism. She did this as a conscious subject who wanted to represent herself and the situation of Cuban women within transnational discussions of feminism. She wanted herself and her nation to be included and to contribute to canonical discussions of feminism. At the same time, she also recognized how canonical, mainstream feminism has not been able to include the histories of women who were not in the class, racial, or geopolitical position to represent themselves. Thus she argues that her feminism is an active feminism.

During a 2006 interview with all the members of Las Krudas in Austin, Texas, I asked if they knew other feminists in Cuba. With the others nodding in agreement, Olivia stated that they did not know of any women who were organized in groups that discussed feminist theory or actively embraced a particular identity. She explained:

Olivia: Empezar como a tener el poder de hacer cosas y lo dejaron en la historia del feminismo, mujeres blancas, y como sólo algunas como las que Odaymara mencionó, pudieron insertarse a esa historia de feminismo.

Odaymara: Pero yo creo que existe, existe una historia del feminismo que no puede contarse, que no puede contarse.

Olivia: En sentido [real], yo creo poco en las historias, porque creo mucho en la historia real de la gente pobre que no puede hacer historia porque no tiene acceso a los medios de hacer historia porque no puede escribir, tiene que trabajar para comer, y yo pienso que muchas de las grandes feministas que hemos tenido en nuestra historia real no han tenido tiempo de estar escribiendo, han tenido que hacer otras cosas, quién sabe, espíritus de mujeres cubanas, como, qué sé yo, nuestras madres, nuestras abuelas, gente que sabe pero que no sabe cómo hacer la historia, como que saben muchas mujeres que desde siempre supieron que tenían que ir a trabajar que era necesario pedir los derechos sobre que las mujeres trabajaran. Esas mujeres trabajan y punto. Necesitaban trabajar, muchas mujeres latinas y negras, trabajaron siempre y eran feministas.

> Olivia: To begin with how to have power and how to do things and they are left in the history of feminism, the white women, and only some, the ones Odaymara mentioned, could insert themselves in this history of feminism.
>
> Odaymara: But I believe that there exists a history of feminism that could not speak for itself.
>
> Olivia: In a real sense, I don't believe much in the histories, because I believe a lot in the real history of poor people who could not make history because they did not have access to the means to make their history because they could not write, they had to work to eat, and I think that many of the great feminists that we have had in our real history did not have the time to be writing, they had to do other things, who knows, [the] spirits of Cuban women. Like, I don't know what, our mothers, our grandmothers, people that know, but do not know how to make history, how many women who have known forever that in order to go to work they needed to demand the right for women to work. These women worked and that's it. They needed to work, many Latina and Black women, they always worked and they were feminists.

Olivia and Odaymara note that there is a feminist history that has not been recorded. They argue that many women were feminists but had to focus on working and surviving. They had no time to document themselves and were not of interest to the privileged women who documented their own histories. Las Krudas see feminism in practice among Cuban women in the high divorce rates and in women's willingness to work for and make decisions for themselves. They know some lesbians who say that they are feminists, but, as Olivia stated, "To be a lesbian and to be a feminist is not the same thing." Many lesbians, like many Cuban women, also have internalized revolutionary notions of femininity that are linked to their disempowerment as women (see chapter 6).

Las Krudas did not want to give the impression that feminist identities did not exist in Cuba, but they noted that no sociological study has been undertaken to assess how many women in Cuba self-identify as feminists. While Las Krudas identify as feminists, they also theorize about pushing the boundaries of feminism by exploring other identities, such as *mujerista* (literally "womanist" but more accurately referring to an identity and perspective akin to Black feminism), a key identity that forms part of their larger Kruda identity. Olivia commented that feminism is simply a counterbalance to patriarchy and that they both maintain and reinforce one another. But a *mujerista* is completely outside of the feminism/patriarchy dichotomy and focuses particularly on all women's experiences, without limiting the analysis to women's experiences of oppression under patriarchy. For Krudas, being a "super-feminist" is not enough. Olivia argues that women have to be stronger and more assertive and to learn everything they can from men, because men dominate knowledge of music production within hip hop, as she emphasized in our interview in Havana in 2006:

Pero a mi ver líricas que adolecían del sentido que para nosotras era necesario en ese momento, que eran demostrar que podían existir y ser colegas, competencia y absoluta mayoría de hip hop masculino, unas mujeres, en este caso fuertes, lesbianas, defendiendo a toda costa a las nuestras. Muchas veces se nos dijo: Krudas, están cayendo en el extremismo. Si tú estás criticando el machismo, porque eres tan feminista. En mis canciones, en mis entrevistas y siempre en mi actitud trato de hacerles entender que por favor nunca será suficiente el feminismos para contrarrestar el gran machismo del mundo. Nunca será suficiente.

Porque es tanto el machismo, mi hija, que ni porque todas las mujeres fuéramos superfeministas podíamos hacer nada, ellos son muy fuertes. Nosotras podemos lograr espacio, y de hecho se han hecho muchas cosas lindas y hemos logrado cosas buenísimas desde que estamos ahí en el movimiento, hemos tratado de unificar a las mujeres y hacer conciertos de mujeres solamente, hay ya proyectos de discos de mujeres, hemos tenido ahora nuestro proyecto Omegas KILAY para conciertos, para espectáculos, para cosas de libros de poesías y cosas, tenemos muchos proyecto, y se han logrado cosas, pero ... cuánto han logrado los hombres en el hip hop de Cuba, en el hip hop del mundo, cuánto, cuánto, cuánto. No tiene comparación, o sea, tenemos que seguir trabajando mucho, mucho, mucho y ser cada día más fuerte, fuerte, fuerte para que nuestro nombre se escuche y nuestras voces se levanten.

> For us it is necessary in this moment that we can show that we could exist and be colleagues, be competent and be the absolute best of male hip hop [as] some women, in this case strong, lesbians, defending everything that is ours. A lot of times they say to us, "Krudas, you are going to the extreme. If you are criticizing machismo [it is because] you are *so* feminist." In my songs, in my interviews, and always in my attitude, I try to make them understand that please, feminism will never be enough to counteract the huge machismo in the world. It will never be enough. . . .
>
> Because there is so much machismo, sweetie, that not even if all women were super-feminists could we do anything, they [machos] are really strong. We can achieve space, and having made [space], they have done many beautiful things and we have achieved some really good things from where we are in the movement, we have tried to unify women and do concerts with women only, there already are CD projects from women, right now we have our project Omegas KILAY for concerts, for events, for [poetry readings] and stuff, we have a lot of projects, and we have achieved things, but . . . how much have men achieved in Cuban hip hop, in world hip hop? How much? How much? You don't have a comparison, or better, we have to keep working a lot, a lot, a lot and to be stronger every day, stronger, stronger, stronger, [in order] for our men to listen and for our voices to rise.

Many women do not have access to the resources necessary to develop a feminist consciousness through printed texts, courses, seminars, and the other means by which canonical feminist theory is disseminated. Even though feminist theory has its origins in feminist praxis and activism, Odaymara has focused primarily on an active form of feminism to help change the situation of women and to raise consciousness. Las Krudas express solidarity with all feminists and all women working for social change. They reject the homogenizing impulses of feminism as well as the homogenizing impulses of hegemonic revolutionary discourse. When I asked Las Krudas in our interview in Austin in 2006 if the women mentioned in their songs identified as feminists, the collective answer was "No." When I asked if they believed that a woman could be a feminist and not know it, their answer was a resounding "Yes." Las Krudas state that feminism is about practice, not simply about theory. It is women making the best decisions for themselves and working to make society better for themselves and for all people.

Odaymara said in our interview in Havana in 2006 that the situations of women in Cuba are linked through local, national, regional, and global forms of gender and sexual oppression:

> Lo nuestro es trabajar en contra de la postura del mundo entero, específicamente la de la cultura cubana, la cultura latina, la cultura caribeña, las cuales son muy ricas en sabor pero al mismo tiempo muy machistas, homofóbicas, lesbofóbicas y misóginas. Nuestro trabajo es el de poner todos estos aspectos negativos y ponerlos sobre la mesa, discutirlos, reconocer que existen y luego decidir qué es lo que vamos hacer para erradicarlos.

> So our thing is working against the posture of the entire world, specifically that of Cuban culture, Latin culture, Caribbean culture, which are very rich, very flavorful but at the same time very *machista*, very lesbophobic, very misogynistic. The problem with revolutionary culture is that they say that women already have a lot of rights, lots of equality. You can go to school at night, and work during the day, and I think the problem of women is more than to work and to study, there are problems that are much more profound. We are pushed to the side in the culture of the world. So our project is to take all of this negative stuff, put it on the table, acknowledge that it exists, and decide what we are going to do to resolve this problem.

Odaymara argues that Cuban women's oppression is related to larger transnational issues, to regional dynamics within Latin and Caribbean cultures, and to local praxis within Cuban culture. At each of these levels, she contends, Black women face sexism and lesbophobia. In this quotation Odaymara is connecting the way in which local, culturally based, systems of thought (which are systems of power) are connected to regional and global ideologies (systems of power). This perspective is central to their critique of race, sexuality, and gender-based inequalities as being linked to colonial legacies and ongoing local and regional forms of coloniality.

The Lyrical Intervention of Las Krudas

One area that Las Krudas target in their discursive activism is the realm of self-esteem and self-consciousness. The following excerpt from their song "Eres

Bella" (You Are Beautiful) on the album *Krudas Cubensi* (2003) is an example of how their poetry and lyrics encourage women (particularly Black women) to embrace themselves and their inner beauty. In the song they talk about all the possibilities available to women in which they no longer settle for being subordinates of men. They ask the women in the audience how long Las Krudas will be the only women performing onstage—a question that highlights the glaring absence of women in public life.

[*Voice of Odaymara AKA Pasa MC*]

Dedicado a todas las mujeres del mundo	This is dedicated to all the women in the world
A todas las mujeres que como nosotras están luchando	To all the women that are fighting like us
A todas las guerreras, campesinas, urbanas	To all the [women] warriors, rural [women], urban [women]
A todas las hermanas	To all the sisters
Especialmente a las más negras	Especially the most Black
Especialmente a las más pobres	Especially the most poor
Especialmente a las más gordas	Especially the most fat
Soy yo Pasa Mc	It is me, MC Pasa
Nunca nadie te hablo así	Never has anyone spoken to you like this
Nunca aquí	Never here
Me fui	I left
. . .	. . .
Artificios, desrices y postizos son	Artificial, without roots and artificial we are
Continuación del cuento colonialista	A continuation of the colonial story
No te cojas pa' eso	Don't you be fooled because of this
Deja esa falsa vista	Drop this false view
Tienes talento y pregunto	You have talent and I ask
¿Hasta cuándo seremos esta poca cantidad en tarima?	For how long will be so few of us on the stage?
Maldita y machista sociedad que contamina	This evil and *machista* society that contaminates
No es racismo	It's not racism
(*Coro*)	(*Chorus*)
Siente, siente	You feel it, you feel it,
Siendo tú	Being you
Eres bella siendo tú,	You are beautiful being you

Ébano en flor,	Ebony in bloom
Negra luz	Black light
Eres bella	You are beautiful
Siendo tú, cuerpo no es única virtud	The body is not your only virtue . . .
. . .	. . .
Necesitamos mujeres en la vida pública, en la filosofía, en la política	We need women in public life, in philosophy, in politics

Las Krudas begin with a Yoruba call to ancestral warrior women and dedicate the song to all women, especially the poorest, Blackest, and fattest ones, whom they consider to be some of the most stigmatized members of Cuban society. Odaymara says, "No one has ever spoken to you like this before," meaning that no one in Cuba has publicly spoken with love and respect to poor, fat, and Black women since the Revolution. She begins the song with a temporal play, a key component of African-based music and culture (Mbembe 2001; Rose 1994): "Never has anyone spoken to you like this"/ "Never here"/ "I left." This temporal and spatial play on people's consciousness definitely captures the listeners' attention, especially when seeing them onstage. Odaymara says that she was never present in front of the audience; but while she was never present, she also has disappeared: she left. This disrupts the linear temporal/spatial logic that listeners may expect when hearing a song. How is it possible that she was never there? The audience hears her performing the song, sees her on the stage. Despite the materiality of her presence via sound and visibility, how is it possible that she has never been present but then left? One possibility is that she's a phantom that is able to move through time and space as it pleases, only to choose to make itself visible at various moments. Such a temporal rupture may spur the audience to think about and try to understand what is happening at that moment—how the past and the present can exist and never exist all at once; how something that seems real never was real; how something that was never real can also disappear. At this point Odaymara tells the audience what the performers are doing: they are going to talk about a "colonial story."

As a disarming mechanism, temporal play allows Odaymara and Wanda, the main voices in this song, to draw from the past (from residual values and meanings) and to draw from the future, where they envision liberation. Odaymara stated in a 2005 interview in Havana that she tries to draw on ideas that people may have heard at one point but have since forgotten. By evoking these residual discourses and popular discourses, Las Krudas attempt to develop an emergent discourse that helps people to understand their present predicament. The goal of their music and lyrics is to anchor listeners in an understanding of how the factors of race, gender, class, and sexuality affect the present moment. The song reveals the historical basis of a shared truth and shared material inequality: racism, sexism, and heteronomativity are oppressive ideologies rooted in the colonial history of the Americas. Las Krudas want the audience to be able to see that the realities of today are linked to a history of colonial oppression and anti-neo-colonial struggle. Temporal shifts are used throughout the song. The reference to a "colonial story" is a call to remember the past as it bears directly on the present. Through reflecting on past colonialism and framing the present (the lack of women performing onstage), they ask Black women to remember that they are beautiful, to envision a process of liberation, to work together, and to leave false colonial consciousness behind. Toward the end of the song, Oday-mara shifts to the future, in which women will be truly liberated by learning to value themselves and each other.

By focusing on how women are sexualized and devalued, Las Krudas direct the attention of male listeners to how male perceptions of women are part of women's oppression. They help men *and* women to see how their actions are responsible for women's oppression. At one point, Wanda slips in the line: "It's not racism." This is a claim about the specificity of Black women's oppression: some issues facing Black women are not attributable to racism. Men (including Black men), as well as women themselves, are also responsible for the oppression that women face. Las Krudas address this wider responsibility by asking women not to see themselves as sexual objects or to compete with each other for successes that are based on the superficial criteria surrounding beauty. According to Las Krudas, these criteria do not embrace the complexity and diversity of women: they actually devalue the intelligence and physical diversity of women. Instead Las Krudas ask women to participate in socially significant arenas normally dominated by men, such as politics, academia, or the arts.

Las Krudas use the image of an ebony tree in bloom to describe women. They want women to remember that blackness is beautiful and is also feminine. Black women are often encouraged to straighten their hair in order to appear beautiful or feminine. Black women with well-defined hips and buttocks are assumed to be fat and careless about their appearance. Strangers on the street, usually other women, often feel comfortable in making hair and weight suggestions to women whom they believe can make themselves more attractive. In Cuba women are primarily judged according to their appearance (Más 2003). In my experiences in Cuba, passing as a Cuban woman exposed me to numerous comments that I often found shocking. These comments ranged from women on the bus who whispered that I should straighten my hair to Cuban colleagues who commented that I would be a lot prettier with straight hair and a little less weight. These comments are often tied to the very corporal features to which Black women are often reduced: hair, buttocks, weight, hips, and skin color.

In other songs, such as their most recent popular song, "Gorda" (Fat Woman), Las Krudas reject the Cuban obsession with thin, white, European bodies. In the public sphere Black and fat women often do not often hear that they are beautiful just for being a human being. In fact they usually hear the opposite: that they are less human because they are fat or Black. For many women, to hear their size and their color praised as beautiful is a profound statement, whether in a large concert hall or at home on a recently purchased CD. The continuation of what Las Krudas describe as colonial thinking has inadvertently been allowed through government social policy centered on national health. For example, in an effort to promote a healthy population, the revolutionary government has run numerous public service ads concerning obesity. This is not to say that the rejection of fatness arrived in Cuba with the Revolution, but the public health campaign added "official facts" to people's preexisting biases against fat people. People who are not thin are considered lazy and unhealthy. Most importantly, in a society where women's bodies are assumed to be used for reproduction and male pleasure, a fat woman is assumed to be less feminine: undesirable to men and unable to maintain herself, much less a family.[10]

Another counterhegemonic message can be found in the Las Krudas song "120 Horas" (120 Hours), which focuses on the theme of menses. This song is an attempt to bring another aspect of women's subjectivity (the functioning of their bodies) out from the realm of privacy into public discourse. The very audacity of writing and publicly performing a song about this taboo subject encourages women to reject hegemonic discourses that say women's bodies are disgusting. These songs challenge the way in which the functioning of women's bodies, including sexual pleasure, is rendered disgusting, immoral, unspeakable, and invisible. This is a means of culturally institutionalizing the primacy of the lived experiences (corporal, affective, and even racialized) of those born with penises as "human experience." Anything that deviates from this experience is pathologized. Thus women find their own bodies to be disgusting, dirty, and immoral and feel ashamed about their functioning. When Las Krudas first performed "120 Horas," it angered a lot of people to have a group of women onstage who openly and graphically talked about a woman's bodily functions as normal, sanitary, natural, and even beautiful. Las Krudas talked about the functioning of women's bodies in a way that was not dismissive, demeaning, or sophomoric. They rejected the equation of menses with excrement, a typical method used to affirm the subordination of the female body. By focusing on the intellectual attributes of women and their potential to be independent and comfortable with themselves, they encourage women to leave behind false consciousness and colonial thinking and work together in solidarity to end oppression. As Las Krudas sing in "Eres Bella," a song calling women to action, "intelligence is *your* virtue."

The Incorporation of Las Krudas into the CUHHM

Las Krudas had to work exceptionally hard to overcome many social limitations to become one of Cuba's best known underground hip hop groups. Their presence in the CUHHM community shows that discussions are occurring within Cuban hip hop about how to advocate for the continued liberation of women and how to fight against sexism and homophobia. Some male artists have asked Las Krudas why there are only a few Black lesbians within the hip hop community. Lesbian attendance at hip hop shows is lower than in other musical genres such as Nueva Trova or reggaetón, which have historically drawn a larger lesbian population. This is largely linked to the perception of hip hop as an overwhelmingly Black and therefore masculinist, aggressive genre for Black males and aggressive Black women. This speaks to some of the rigid expectations about femininity as well as racism, which are definitely a part of Cuban lesbian life. Las Krudas argue that life is very difficult for poor Black lesbians in terms of family responsibilities and economic resources, and they work hard to find ways to survive.

Olivia spoke about the social reality of Black lesbians in our interview in Havana in 2006:

> Por ejemplo hay otras mujeres artistas cubanas lesbianas, que tienen una música más suave como trova.... Que para la comunidad lesbiana ese tipo de música es más aceptable, se identifican con ese tipo de música. También es una música que atrae mucho a personas blancas y es un fuerte de la comunidad blanca, lesbiana. Entonces hay muchas mujeres que van a otro tipo de música, no al hip hop. Entonces en el hip hop hay muchos hombres y pocas mujeres. Para ser una mujer lesbiana y estar dentro del hip hop hemos tenido que atravesar años de lucha, respecto y amor. Entonces, preguntarnos siempre: ¿Por que las mujeres lesbianas negras no se acercan a la comunidad del hip hop y no les gusta? Y no tenemos mucha respuestas, pero realmente hay respuestas un poco tristes.... Es que, por ejemplo, a las mujeres negras lesbianas no tienen mucho tiempo para ir al hip hop, tienen mucho trabajo para hacer, para sobrevivir, para buscar dinero. En el hip hop no hay mucho dinero, no hay dinero y las mujeres negras lesbianas no tienen dinero, no tienen maneras de ... [*pauses*] Para

muchas mujeres negras cubanas lesbianas es difícil su vida, muy difícil. Ellas necesitan trabajar mucho, todo el tiempo. Y ya te digo, es difícil como unificar dichas cosas: mujer, lesbiana, hip hop, negra, es dificilísimo. La mayoría de mujeres lesbianas negras van a otro tipo de reuniones, a otro tipo de lugares donde puedan, no sé, conseguir para sobrevivir.

> For example, there are other women artists who are Cuban lesbians that have softer music like Nueva Trova. For the lesbian community, this kind of music is much more acceptable and they identify with this kind of music. Also it is a type of music that attracts a lot of white people, and it is very strong within the white lesbian community. So there are a lot of women that go to this type of music, not to hip hop. Then in hip hop there are a lot of men and very few women. To be a lesbian woman and be within hip hop, we have had to overcome years of fighting with respect and love. So they always ask us: Why don't Black lesbian women join the hip hop community? They don't like it? And we don't have very many answers, but really we have answers that are a little sadder. . . . It is that Black lesbians don't have a lot of time for hip hop, they have a lot of work they have to do in order to live, to look for money. In hip hop, there is not a lot of money, and Black lesbian women do not have money, they don't have a way to . . . [*pauses*] For many Black lesbian Cuban women, life is very difficult, very difficult. They need to work a lot all the time. And as I said, it is hard to unify these things: woman, lesbian, hip hop, Black . . . it's very difficult. The majority of Black women go to other types of activities, other places where they can, I don't know, find a way to survive.

Outside of hip hop shows and other activities related to their work as artists, women artists rarely visit Las Krudas in their Havana apartment. The women who do stop by just to chat usually either arrive with their boyfriends or husbands or are out as lesbians. Likewise, in public space, the only women who speak to Las Krudas are women with husbands or boyfriends, other lesbians, or women working on artistic products with the group. The isolation that Las Krudas face outside of work is palpable. Nonetheless, the level of respect and solidarity that they have within the hip hop community does not exist on the same scale for the rest of the lesbian community. This may be a result of the high premium placed on performing appropriate femininity. Openly talking about gender transgression via sexual deviancy is frightening for a lot of women, and many women are scared of being implicated in such acts by virtue of their association with "out" lesbians.

When Las Krudas first started to perform as a group, though they wanted to stay true to their message and themselves they realized that they had a lot of educating to do in order to create the foundation needed for their audiences to understand their complex identity as Black lesbians. Some people in Cuban society see a lesbian as repulsive, as a disgusting woman. The silence surrounding women's sexuality—outside of male penetration—is so profound that being "lesbian" is hard for many to imagine. Being lesbians who are publicly out of the closet is in and of itself a major social statement in Cuban society. Through their work within the Cuban Underground Hip Hop Movement, Las Krudas began to realize the profundity of the silence on women's sexuality: women were only able to stake a claim of self-autonomy by stating that their goal was not to alienate men. Heterosexual women had so deeply internalized heteronormativity that the threat of being labeled a lesbian, equated with being a man-hater, was preventing women from even attempting to organize around gender equality.

Olivia spoke about stereotypes of women rappers and their experiences with heterosexual female artists within the hip hop community in our interview in Havana in 2006:

> Mira, ha sido simpático porque en el historia del rap de mujeres en Cuba yo siento que, mira, ser una mujer lesbiana y hacer Hip Hop fue algo muy lindo. Porque en cuanto vi algunas mujeres haciendo rap, me pareció que parecían muy lesbianas y me daba tristeza, cuando sabían que no eran lesbianas porque parecían, porque muchas veces su proyección era muy fuerte, se ponían pantalones, porque hacían gestos muy viriles, muy masculinos y era bonito. Pero luego cuando el acto terminaba ellas eran muy suaves y hablaban muy suaves y, quizás, muchas de ellas no hablaban con nosotras porque sabían que nosotras éramos lesbianas y ellas solamente hablaban con sus maridos o con otras mujeres heterosexuales. Entonces nosotras comenzamos a acercarnos a esas mujeres y a hacer como el intento de ser sus amigas o al menos sus compañeras, y con mucho esfuerzo logramos ser simpáticas para ellas, y hablar con ellas y preguntarles cosas. Luego también con las letras de nuestras canciones ellas comenzaron a sentirse muy incluidas en nuestros mensajes, ellas comenzaron a sentirse como muy respetadas por nuestras letras. Ya entonces las relaciones fueron mejorando entre ellas y nosotras, pero nosotras continuamos adelante.

>> Look, for us it has been very nice because in the history of women's rap in Cuba I think that, look, to be a lesbian woman doing hip hop is something very beautiful. Because we have seen a lot of women doing rap that to me seem very lesbian-like and it made me sad when I found out that

they weren't lesbians because they appeared to be, because a lot of time their project is very strong, they put on pants, because they make very masculine gestures, very masculine and very beautiful. But later when the act ends, they are very soft, and they speak very softly, and maybe a lot of them don't talk to us because they know that we are lesbians and they only talk to their husbands or to other heterosexual women. So we began to surround ourselves with these women with the intent to be their friends and at least their peers, and with a lot of strength, we came to be very nice to them and to talk to them and to ask them questions about things. Later, with the words of our songs, they also began to feel very included in our messages, they began to feel very respected by our words. Then the relationship began to get better between them and us, and we continue forward.

Olivia talks about how she initially thought that there might be more lesbian women within the hip hop movement. But she began to notice the contradictory roles of women performing hip hop: they comported themselves as assertive independent women, but in reality they were still controlled by the men in their lives. As discussed in chapter 6, several women artists do not write their own lyrics: their husbands and boyfriends do. Furthermore, the straight women themselves policed sex-gender boundaries by refusing to talk to Las Krudas—some out of fear of being considered man-haters, others because they simply found them disgusting and unfeminine because of the topics that they addressed in their music. After their performances, other women would not speak to Las Krudas or only did so when their husbands or boyfriends were nearby.

As Olivia notes, once Las Krudas became aware of these dynamics within the movement, they realized that they had to change their activist strategy. They decided to design their songs and general activism according to both the specific needs of women within the CUHHM and the broader goals of the movement itself. First, Las Krudas worked hard to show that they were in solidarity with other female artists. They focused on performing songs that addressed experiences that they shared with other Black women. They worked hard to create a sense of community with fellow women artists by starting women's hip hop collectives such as Omegas KILAY. They tried to engender solidarity among female artists by creating women-only spaces away from the watchful eye of male peers.

After Las Krudas spurred discussions of women's issues and worked to increase women's participation in hip hop shows through the creation of all-female collectives such as Omegas KILAY, which toured the United States in

2007, they also began organizing workshops on gender at Havana's hip hop symposia. The workshop centered on educating the general public about gender inequality: how it is manifested in language and leads to other social issues such as domestic violence and homophobia. The symposia also focused on why feminism is a useful political identity and why men should also identify as feminists or at least support feminism. The symposium offered a space to debate and discuss what constitutes women's liberation and to deconstruct gender and sexuality. In this way Las Krudas implemented a strategy of first addressing issues affecting Black women and increasing the representation of solo women artists focused on these issues and independently writing and producing their own songs. Only after these gains were made could Las Krudas also address their identity as lesbians.

Como Existe la Heterosexualidad, Existe la Homosexualidad/ Just As Heterosexuality Exists, Homosexuality Exists

Once Las Krudas felt that they had successfully contributed to Cuban hip hop feminists' work in these areas, they decided to come completely out of the closet as lesbians. Odaymara explained their perspective on sexuality in our interview in Havana in 2006:

> Ser lesbiana es un camino. Ser bisexual es un camino. Ser transgender es un camino. Cada persona tiene su camino y entre más diverso ser mundo, más rico, más rico y más variada ser la funda mundial. Entonces no podemos meternos en el drama que todo el mundo tiene que ser esta talla . . . ooooo!! Tú te imaginas que fue el mundo igual? *¡Cono!* riqueza variedad diversidad porque han diferentes criterios y diferentes maneras de vivir la vida entonces, la . . . como explicarte . . . la . . . la transcendencia de la especie humana es más variedada porque su orígenes es de diferentes componentes que se mesclaron y entonces al final es una persona que es mas en talla porque tiene un open mind, un miente abierta hacia todos que venga porque está bien.

> > To be lesbian is a path. To be bisexual is a path. To be transgender is a path. Every person has a path and within the most diversity is the world, the richest . . . variety covers the surface of the world. So we cannot focus ourselves on the drama that all the world has to be this [one] thing . . . oooh!! Can you imagine if the world were equal. *Damn!* The varied richness, the [varied] diversity because there are different criteria and different ways of living life, then . . . the . . . how do I explain this to you

... the transcendence of the human species is more varied because of the
different origins of the different components that have mixed, and so at
the end a person who is more on point has an open mind toward all that
comes because it's [all] OK.

Las Krudas argue for the embracing of difference. Odaymara envisions a
future in which people can simply *be* without any requirements on what that
being entails. For Las Krudas, and for the many artists working within the alternative music scene, that would mean true freedom, true diversity, real humanity.

Given the difficult conditions facing lesbians, such as isolation, social sanctions, and the possibility that speaking about their particular experiences may
be seen as a severe social transgression (Grupo OREMI 2005), I asked Odaymara about their experiences discussing these issues publicly in our interview
in Havana in 2006. She explained why Las Krudas focus on sexuality within
their music:

Chica, mira nos sentimos tan cómodas, tan relajadas, tan en casa, que decimos mira esta tema también. ¿Por qué no? si es parte de mí. Yo soy también esta parte y no puedo dejarla allá y defender las mujeres y no defen-
derme a mí como lesbiana que lo soy y que lo sufro, no solamente en el
mundo del hip hop, sino en la comunidad cubana en su totalidad. ¿Me
entiendes? Y entonces, pues, nada. Decidimos incorporarlo en nuestros
temas también. Hablar de nuestra sexualidad, de que tú puedes elegir
libremente con quien quieres estar, con quien quieres irte a la cama y que
para nada significa una falta. Todo lo contrario. Demostrándole al mundo,
estamos hace casi diez años juntas, de que es posible de que dos mujeres
se amen y demostrándole a todas las personas, no del hip hop, ¡sino de
Cuba entera de que mira que me vas a decir tú con tu falsa moral heterosexual! Yo estoy aquí hace nueve años juntas, amándonos y qué me vas a
decir, intachable. ¡Qué quieres! ¡qué pasa! Y entonces yo pienso que igual
la comunidad ha dicho ese es un ejemplo. ¿Me entiendes?

Girl, look, we feel very comfortable, very relaxed, so very much at home
that we decided to look at this theme also. Why not, if it's a part of me? I
am also this part and I cannot leave it and defend women and not defend
myself as a lesbian, that which I have suffered, not only in the world of hip
hop, but in all of the Cuban community. You understand me? And then,
well, that's it. We decided to incorporate our themes as well. To speak of
our sexuality, saying that you can liberally choose to be with whoever you
want to be with, whoever you want to go to bed with, that it doesn't rep-

resent a fault. It's the opposite. [We are] demonstrating to the world that we have been together for almost ten years and that it's possible that two women love each other and show it to everyone, not just in hip hop, but to all of Cuba that sees with your false heterosexual morals! We've been here for almost ten years, together, loving each other and inseparable, what do you want?! What's up?! So I think, as the community has said, this is an example. You understand me?

Despite the male-dominated and *machista* cultural sphere in which Las Krudas work, they feel very relaxed discussing the difficulties they face as Black women, particularly their experiences as Black lesbians. This relates in part to the recognition of the cultural sphere in Cuba as a space of debate and political deliberation (at least at the level of civil society) but also to the space that Las Krudas have carved out for women and especially lesbians within the hip hop community. Many people never thought about the existence of lesbians, and very few had come into contact with open lesbians. Las Krudas' very presence as out lesbians in the hip hop scene dispelled many of the Cuban cultural myths about lesbians. For example, through her long-term relationship with Olivia and their contributions to Cuban society, Odaymara hopes to challenge established notions of morality that depict lesbians as morally deviant or generally morally suspicious (even if they are well liked and respected), and socially unproductive. By being "out" within the underground hip hop movement as Black lesbian feminists, as "Krudas," the group has developed a unique discourse that calls for greater awareness and acceptance of human diversity.

Their song "Candela" (Fire) is from their first album, *Cubensi* (2003):

[Voice of Olivia, with Wanda and Odaymara sounding in agreement]

Y aquí también me quemas una realidad muy dura,	And here it also burns me, a very hard reality
injusta y constantemente somos ignoradas,	injustice and constantly we are ignored
maltratadas, descriminadas	poorly treated, discriminated against
casi nunca bien representadas	almost never well represented
caballero esa expresión no me incluye	gentlemen, this expression does not include me
el hombre esa expresión no me incluye	man [as a universal term], this expression does not include me
los humanos esa expresión no me incluye	human beings, this expression does not include me

somos hembras todo eso influye en lo que voy a explicarte aquí adelante	we are women and all of this influences that which I am going to explain to you in a moment
. . .	. . .
continuamos que en la resistencia	we continue the resistance
defendiendo derechos	defending rights
educando a la audiencia	educating the audience
escucha, audiencia	listen, audience!
existe la diversidad	diversity exists
como existe la delgades	as the thin exists,
existe la oversidad	ovalness exists
como existe lo claro	as the light exists,
existe la oscuridad	the darkness exists
como existe lo masculino	as the masculine exists
exista la feminidad	the feminine exists
como existe lo heterosexua	as heterosexuality exists,
existe la homosexualidad	homosexuality exists
todas y todos tenemos derecho a la libertad	and all women and all men, we have the right to liberty

At the beginning of this song, Olivia shouts: "Audience, listen!" After assertively commanding the audience's attention, Las Krudas then directly plant a seed for people to reflect on: embracing human diversity also means embracing sexual diversity. They talk about their feelings of being poorly treated and ignored because they are women (implicitly meaning lesbians). But their references to darkness and light may also be a reference to the issue of race, of which all or most of their audiences are aware. Their reference to being skinny and fat applies to the judgment of bodies, another judgment of which most audiences are aware. However, by stating these realities first, and couching them in terms of persisting inequality, Las Krudas create the space necessary to assert a reality that is often invisible to most Cubans: homosexuality, and in particular female homosexuality, exists. Their intervention in this song is a direct statement: just "as heterosexuality exists, homosexuality exists." Again Las Krudas draw from past and present discourses to elevate the consciousness of the audience members in an effort to help them consider future discourses, to consider discursive change.

The song "Amikemiñongo" on their album *Candela* is an example of this. Las Krudas directly engage the intersections of race, gender, sexuality, and their relationship to Cuba's colonial legacies:

[*Wanda Kruda primary voice*]

Cojoba, taina, siboney	Cojoba, taina, siboney
. . .	. . .
¿Qué más tú quieres de mi,	What do you want from me
si todo yo te lo he dado?	if I have given you all of it?
. . .	. . .
De África de adueñaron	They took control of Africa
y me trajeron aquí	and brought me here
. . .	. . .
que violento	what violence
Hasta cuando permitir	When will I be permitted
que me lo cuenten	to tell it
500 años	500 years
Basta	Enough
. . .	. . .
Que te creías pequeña	What do you think that
que el mundo	the world is small enough
De estar organizado seria	to be organized like
como tu cuarto	your room
. . .	. . .
Bruja, tuerca,	Witch, dyke
Yo mujer, yo	I am woman, I [am]
Libertad por siempre	Freedom forever

In the beginning of this song Las Krudas call out the names of all the native Caribbean nations that suffered near or total genocide during the initial colonization of the Americas. They ask those representing the colonial legacies of genocide: "What else do you want, when I have given all?" The central theme of the song is "enough with the colonialism, it is time for those who have suffered for five hundred years to be free." They focus on the social organizing agenda of colonialism; in essence, they focus on modernity. They ask: "Do you think that the world is small enough to be organized like your room?" Las Krudas challenge that which represents colonialism.

But what are the legacies of colonialism? They include the capitalist state and its colonial ideologies (racism, sexism, homophobia, classism) that attempt to organize subjects, including "nature," in an effort to prepare them for capital's productive interests. Those who pursue a capitalist agenda may do so through the continuation of colonial violence (imprisonment, legislation) or through ideological structures (social norms, notions of morality). Ideological structures are not just embedded in social institutions such as the state and the family, however; every individual also perpetuates colonial thinking through internalized prejudices. In their music Las Krudas are able to link sexual oppression to other oppressions. In this song they directly focus on women, calling for them to fight and to liberate themselves. They also slip in the word *tuerca*, which is slang for "dyke." By naming exploitation and discrimination together, Las Krudas connect them to colonial violence and thus link race, gender, and sexuality to colonization. Through making these connections of racism, sexism, classism, exploitation, and homophobia, Las Krudas attempt to help the audience to see that liberation is for everyone who has suffered as a result of the organizing impulses of modernity.

Olivia commented on how their message about lesbian visibility has been accepted by the hip hop community in our interview in Havana in 2006:

> Bueno, realmente nosotras hemos sido muy dulces. A pesar de que somos Krudas y que siempre hemos tenido una proyección fuertísima, no hemos sido todo lo fuerte que podíamos haber sido, porque sabemos que nuestro auditorio es muy machista y que nosotras debíamos ir como periódicamente dando una información que es hoy día para mucha de nuestra audiencia, mucho de nuestro público, mucha de nuestra gente, una información muy fuerte, que es que somos mujeres, músicas, raperas, mc, protagonistas de un acto artístico único, defendemos a las mujeres, todas, heterosexuales, bisexuales, amas de casa, trabajadoras, artistas, a todos, pero, además, somos lesbianas, que practicamos sexo entre nosotras y creemos en la independencia casi absoluta de la mujer.
>
> Entonces ese mensaje es muy fuerte para todas las comunidades del mundo. Entonces, yo pienso que hemos tenido como mucha fuerza para continuar. Hubo días que el público nos recibió en silencio, otro día nos aplaudieron un poquito más, otro día comenzaron a identificarse mucho con lo que hacemos y aplaudirnos mucho. Otro día nos aplauden mucho, mucho, mucho y nos gritan: Bravo, bravo, bravo. Y no sé, cada día ha ido creciendo el respeto hacia nosotras, porque nos lo hemos ganado, porque nuestro trabajo ha sido serio durante todos estos años, porque realmente nosotras también respetamos mucho a nuestra comunidad y todo lo que decimos, lo decimos con mucho amor y mucho respeto. Y yo pienso que ese ha sido el secreto, nos quieren porque nosotras también queremos.

> OK, really things have gone very well for us. To carry the weight that we are Krudas, and we always have had a strong projection, we have not

been the strongest that we could have been, because our audience is very *machista* and we ought to go with periodically giving information that today is a lot for our audience, it's a lot for our public, for many of our people, [it is] strong information that we are women, musicians, rappers, MCs, protagonists of the only artistic act that defends women, [that defends] all, heterosexuals, bisexuals, unemployed, workers, artists, all, but also we are lesbians . . . and we believe in the absolute independence of women.

So this message is very strong for all of the world's communities. So I think that we have had a lot of strength to continue. There have been days where the public receives us in silence, other days when they applaud us a little more, other days when they begin to identify a lot with what we have done and applaud us a lot. The other day they applauded us a lot, a lot, a lot, and they yelled at us: Bravo, bravo, bravo. And I don't know, every day the respect for us has been growing, because we have won it, because our work has been serious during these years, because really we respect our community very much and all that we say, we say with a lot of love and a lot of respect. And I think that this has been the secret, they love us because we also love them.

Olivia attributes the success of Las Krudas to their hard work as artists, their attempts to develop a more inclusive message, and their efforts to reach out to other female MCs. By this point in 2006 Las Krudas were beginning to reach a larger public and receiving more respect in general, including from some of the macho artists they were challenging with their music. Olivia says that initially they were very strong in their stage presentation. When they realized that people were not open to their message and were actively resistant, they took some time to figure out what their goals were as artivists. It was then that they understood that the general population had not been exposed to a lot of ideas and realities that Las Krudas had had their whole lives to process and understand. Thus they decided that it was a good idea to change their stage presentation slightly and to refocus the process on slowly raising the public's consciousness about Las Krudas' realities as poor Black lesbians. Even though their audience may not always understand them, Las Krudas consistently pointed out in their interviews that they love their people, their communities, their country. As Olivia states in this quotation, it is because they decided to approach their work from a level of love and respect, instead of direct provocation, that they began to receive love and respect in return. This, she says, is part of the reason why they have been so successful as artists.

Kruda Discourse and the Queer of Color Critique

Despite being ideologically isolated in Cuba, with limited access to transnational lesbian and gay, Black feminist, and queer discourses, Las Krudas have been able to articulate a queer of color critique as a centerpiece of their discursive activism. Las Krudas' queer of color or Kruda critique emerged along a trajectory similar to that of the queer of color critiques emerging from North America and the Caribbean. Las Krudas initially emerged as *mujeristas*, in terms of having an identity and perspective akin to Black feminism. In their *mujerista* discourse, Las Krudas speak to the limitations of canonical feminist and socialist theories in addressing the needs of poor Black women. *Mujerista* describes their particular feminist identity, which is constructed at the intersection of their identities as Black feminists and socially conscious revolutionary artists. Las Krudas themselves coined the term in order to name a discourse of Black women's liberation that reflects their experiences as Black women in Cuba. When they realized that the way that Black feminist epistemologies were articulated within the CUHHM did not address key aspects of their oppression as nonheteronormative subjects, however, they developed their specific Kruda discourse. They have sought to make both an intervention in Black feminist politics and an explicit intervention in discourses concerning gayness in Cuba. The emergence of the Cuban Underground Hip Hop Movement in Cuba offered Las Krudas an opportunity to disseminate this discourse to a large national and international public.

For this reason I describe Las Krudas' "Kruda" discourse as a critical intervention into Western notions of non-normativity and nonheteronormativity (what has been referred to as queerness in various countries outside of Cuba). It is also for this reason that contemporary work on Las Krudas has to take the context in which they emerged and their ideological interventions within the CUHHM into consideration when analyzing their contemporary queer identity politics. But in an effort at transnational solidarity and communication they attempt to translate their politics and perspectives by using the language available in whatever local context they are in and then articulating their theoretical interventions into local and transnational discourses concerning oppression. They actively theorize new terms to describe dynamics at play that have yet to be named. This is a hallmark of activists in the 1990s CUHHM generation: their activism centered on largely naming systemic forms of inequality that are difficult to name or have not been named.

In this section of the chapter on their work in Cuba, I focus on Las Krudas' usage of the terms "Kruda discourse," "Kruda knowledge," and "Kruda thought" and place them in conversation with the queer of color critique that was also emerging at the same time in the United States. The overlap of Kruda CUBENSI's Kruda discourse with the queer of color critique in terms of content is important, because it highlights the hemispheric basis of many of the systems of power that racialized subjects face in the Americas as well as being formative in the development and articulation of national racialized subjectivities.

Las Krudas CUBENSI's Kruda discourse, Black feminist discourse, and the queer of color critique are also an anticolonial discourses that challenge the hegemony of Western European notions of modernity.[11] They accomplish this, first, by focusing on the transnational nature of racialized oppression and revealing how a racialized organization of erotic desire is central to the ideologies of race, gender, sexuality, and national identity—in this case what it means to be Cuban or Caribbean. Through their framing of racism, sexism, and homophobia as colonial legacies, Las Krudas address the way in which racism has been internalized at the psychic level, at the level of the erotic, while they simultaneously interrogate the ways in which culture and material inequality are racialized. Their work reflects the way in which the Western cultural logic of race is also a transnational, regionally based ideology.

Second, Las Krudas' key contribution to black feminist and queer of color critiques is the clear articulation of how the origins of these dynamics are linked to Western colonial history and the transatlantic slave trade. By relating their analysis of social inequality to colonial legacies, the work of Las Krudas is certainly in conversation with Black feminist and queer of color critiques in that it is a challenge to hegemonic ideologies that characterize the emergence of national identities and the idea of each nation as exceptional. Kruda discourse, coming from a Cuban national context and a Caribbean context, challenges the idea that each form of inequality is disconnected and nationally specific and therefore not connected to global Western European capitalism, and in this case the legacies of colonialism in the Americas as larger transnational systems of power with interconnected regional and localized effects. Their discourse makes a clear statement that the dissociation of inequality from contemporary global capitalism is flawed. The inequalities embedded in Cuban culture and society are linked to those faced by Afro-descendant and indigenous populations regionally and globally and should be thought of as interconnected.

While Las Krudas talk about queerness in their post-2006 period, it is important to note that they briefly used the term *queeridad* in their solidarity work with younger generations of Black Cuban queer activists such as Logbona Olukonee but still refer to their "Kruda consciousness" or "Kruda knowledge" in their songs. Although they may engage various discourses within the various transnational contexts in which they move, their identities and discourse cannot be reduced to any local discourse. In the end Las Krudas have their own theories of power and liberation. Like those of many intellectuals using what we call art as a medium to articulate their theoretical orientation, their ideas and ideological contributions should be respected as intellectual interventions into transnational and regional discourses concerning power and social change.

Reactions to Las Krudas' Work

Besides producing and performing their music, much of Las Krudas' activism has centered on the development and empowerment of female hip hop artists. Part of their strategy was first to present their experiences as Black women to the hip hop community. The issue of race is an experience with which most of the hip hop community identifies. This community also recognizes the lack of perspective on women's experiences within the music scene as an overwhelmingly male-dominated sphere. Even though the community tends to be very *machista*, as a majority of hip hop concertgoers are men, the artists themselves recognize the value of women's intervention.

Male hip hop artists, such as Randy Acosta of Los Paisanos, Yompi and Michael of Junior Clan, DJ D'Boys, and Alexey of Obsesión, often cite Las Krudas when talking about solidarity among Cubans who are fighting oppression. They are considered artists with tremendous insight into the experiences of oppressed people, particularly Black women and lesbians, whose experiences are often not included in solidarity work. As a result of their community work and their ability to use hip hop as a consciousness-raising mechanism, Las Krudas are viewed as pillars of Havana's contemporary underground hip hop scene. While they have great support and respect within the hip hop community, the topics of their songs are considered socially and by extension politically radical. Yompi of the Junior Clan in our interview in Havana in 2006 said:

OK, Las Krudas are, within the hip hop community, something that is very important, primarily within the feminine branch . . . because this is the area in which they have advanced the most. It is with a force for women, so that they fight not just because they think that their life is a house, or having kids, but that they can have much more apart from being mothers. They can have much more than that. They can also be free in their thinking, so that man is not exploiting them and they say that they [women] have to do this and they [women] have to do this. They [women] can be capable of doing whatever men do equally. They can go, in any determined moment, if they have to and defend themselves for whatever reason because they are capable. You know what I mean? They don't have to be discriminated against, in any way, that they are never again objects of the home. This is the part that Las Krudas defend, the value of women in the entire world.

Yompi echoes a sentiment felt by many male and female hip hop artists, producers, and fans: Las Krudas have been integral in pressing the issue of women's oppression and in offering insight into how women have the power to liberate themselves. Their male counterparts are definitely listening and thinking about what Las Krudas are saying. The song "Usted" (You) on Las Krudas' CD *Candela* is an example of the collaborative work that they have produced with their male peers and features the all-male trio the Junior Clan:

Recuerden que nosotros	Remember that we are doing
hacemos algo por la patria	something for the country
Seguidores del Che somos	Followers of el Che we are
Si usted quiere darse	If you want to censor
censura a lo que hacemos	yourself from what we are doing
Que está bueno	Then that's fine
Esto es piano pa' usted	This is the piano for you
. . .	. . .
Krudas, Júnior Clan	Krudas, Junior Clan
echando un están	making a stand
. . .	. . .
luchar con equivalencia aquí	to fight with equivalence here
Vegetal conciencia	Vegetated recalcitrant
recalcitrantes	consciousness

In this excerpt Mamen "El Invisible" is the voice speaking. He notes that he is creating revolution, spurring social change with his songs. He asks the listener to remember the path of Las Krudas and Junior Clan: that they are contributing something to their country through their positive message. They follow in the footsteps of resistance leaders such as Che, who believed that all work, including artistic work, should be for the betterment of society. El Invisible tells members of the audience, especially those who have vegetated, recalcitrant minds, that they can stop listening if they want (they can censor themselves). He shows that he is strong and so secure in his identity and ideas that he does not care if recalcitrants who are not interested in changing their mind-sets ignore the message of Junior Clan and Las Krudas. El Invisible can only present a positive message; he cannot force his audience to listen and change. He offers to give them the piano (to play the exit music), for them to leave/stop listening and continue in their ignorance. This comment is a challenge to listeners. Hip hop draws people who view themselves as enlightened because they are seeking to elevate their consciousness through music. El Invisible is challenging the authenticity of the listeners as people who say that they are underground but are recalcitrant: they are *machista* and refuse to listen to a positive message about women's liberation.

El Invisible goes on to say that this song, a collaborative work between Las Krudas and Junior Clan, redefines what they called intersexual spiritual communion. Men and women can have a solidarity-based connection. Their spiritual connection can be one of mutual collegial respect; men and women do not need to connect only through sexual intercourse. This directly challenges Cuban heteronormativity and machismo by suggesting that women can be socially respected without being objects of male sexual desire. El Invisible says that it is possible for men and women to fight equally together. He is also directly challenging men within the hip hop movement who dislike the work of Las Krudas because it directly challenges their assumptions concerning women's relationship to men. They are also disturbed that Las Krudas are serious in their critiques of machismo. As lesbians, Las Krudas are off-limits to men: they are sexually unavailable to men and demand respect. Male MCs collaboration with Las Krudas is symbolic of the acceptance of Las Krudas as established MCs with an underground message that challenges the public (including their peer artists) and spurs positive conscious change. The collaboration of male artists such as the Junior Clan indicates that male artists not only support the message of Las Krudas but also support women.

In another collaborative work called "Mujeres y madres" (Women and Mothers, also on *Candela*), performed by Las Krudas and the all-male duo Anónimo Consejo, the men also directly challenge machismo:

[*Voice of Olivia*]	
Lucha, luchando	Fighting, fighting
contra el machismo del mundo	against the machismo of the world
. . .	. . .
Siempre, siempre	Always, always
. . .	. . .
[*Voice of Sekou*]	[*Voice of Sekou*]
Minuto a minuto golpeada	Minute by minute beaten
por el bruto machista	by a macho brute
absoluto hombre dimunuto	absolutely a small man

Mujer no significa	Woman does not mean
objeto, sexo, abuso	object, sex, abuse
Prostituto vienes de su fruto	Prostitution comes from her fruit
Escupo destupo oídos brutos	I spit, I unclog brute ears
Respecto absoluto a usted	I absolutely respect you
Señora madre creadora	Mrs. creative mother
Autoestima adora	Adores self-esteem
Siempre luchadora	Always the fighter
Mirando cada hora	Looking at every hour
Negra, tu voz enseña	Black woman, your voice teaches
Negra, princesa, dueña	Black woman, princess, owner
Negra belleza esa	That beautiful Black woman
Negra mujer que sueña	The Black woman that dreams
Negra purez eterna	Black woman eternal purity
Negra mi madre	Black woman my mother
Bella, bella	Beautiful, beautiful
. . .	. . .
¡Mujer, con tu autoestima	Woman, with your self-esteem
siempre vencerás!	you will always win!
¡Mujer, con tu autoestima	Woman, with your self-esteem
siempre vencerás!	you will always win!

At the beginning of this song Sekou of Anónimo Consejo addresses something that many men have had to witness: the abuse of their mothers or other women who are dear to them. Together with Las Krudas, Anónimo Consejo relays the message that Black women with self-esteem are beautiful, while men who abuse women are disrespectful machos. There is nothing manly about beating down a woman's self-esteem. But Sekou also points out that a woman with self-esteem will always win, she will always be happy, because she will not be afraid to take care of herself. Many women feel that they have to have male partners in order to feel beautiful and feel worthwhile. In the song Las Krudas warn women against men who are controlling. They ask women to establish their independence as a way to avoid potentially abusive men. The men's solidarity with this message is an attempt to show all women within the hip hop community that they have support there: macho men will not be tolerated by anyone, including other men.

Of course Las Krudas does not represent the voices of all lesbians in Cuba, although it is generally recognized within the CUHHM that they have their finger on the pulse of the issues affecting many Black women and lesbians. During my time in Cuba, I interviewed lesbians who were part of Cuba's underground lesbian party scene. These women were wealthy enough to afford frequently going to underground lesbian parties and hosting them themselves. When I asked them their thoughts about Las Krudas, many referred to their "low cultural status" as being offputting. They disagreed with Las Krudas' message of embracing fatness, discussing menstruation, and discussing homosexuality. These lesbians, who saw themselves as of a higher cultural and by extension social status than Las Krudas, often viewed them as reactionary and crass. Part of this resistance centers on Las Krudas' open discussion of their sexuality and identifying as fat, Black, poor women. For many Cubans, this is another sign of Las Krudas' lower-class tendencies: they are not trying to lose weight and they openly identify as feminists who are just as strong as men.

Though there may be some resistance to Las Krudas' discourses and messages even from other Cuban women and lesbians, some of these contrary impulses can be attributed to deeply entrenched homophobia, machismo, racism, and sexism in Cuban culture. Two salient discourses can be used to ameliorate the contradiction between the existence of pervasive social discrimination and a revolutionary national discourse that argues that all forms of social marginality have been or are about to be eliminated. One discourse is the revolutionary discourse of social inclusion through ideological unity and an identity politics in which individual identifications, which are understood to represent personal interests, are sacrificed to one singular identification. At the national level, this singular identification is "Cuban." As discussed in the introduction, post-1959 state discourse at the national level has suggested the following idea: there are no men or women, Blacks or whites, rich or poor in Cuba, there are only Cubans. Anyone who tries to claim a specific identity is seen as supporting the demise of Cuba, by creating the conditions for a civil war by pitting different groups against each other. State discourse portrays the country as being at war, dating back to the U.S. Bay of Pigs invasion, and vulnerable to disintegration, which would allow the United States to invade and return Cuba to its pre-1959 neo-colonial status. Underground artists deploy this logic in their fight against racism. Antiracist critique is privileged above all, and a rhetoric of unity and one identification is used to silence the concerns of women and sexual minorities. Specifically, women and male artists alike commonly consider any discussion of gender inequality, feminist identity, or sexual identity politics to be a sign of man-hating or a belligerent division between the sexes. Similarly, as discussed in the introduction, any discussion of racial inequality at the national level is seen as a belligerent division of the races.

The second discourse that artists employ to dismiss the contradiction between active discrimination and marginalization within the movement is the association of queer critiques with bourgeois class interests. This is also a common national discourse, which serves the same purpose of eliminating a contradiction within the Cuban nation. This discourse underlies much of the framing of homosexuality within the Cuban Underground Hip Hop Movement. Such discursive moves set the stage for determining which battles are worthy of being fought. Because the movement is dominated by male subjects whose primary grievance is racial discrimination, race is framed as the source of social inequality, while homophobia and sexism are not. For example, two male artists within the movement said the following about the work of Las Krudas in our interview in Havana in 2005:

Artist 1: Esos son pasiones, esas cosas son pasiones. Yo no tengo porqué mezclar mi vida sexual, mi orientación sexual con mi música. Me entiendes. La mía no, no me importa te digo. Mi poesía es modestia, barrió. Eso es chisme, eso es de cada uno como es. Quien quiera tener una jeva que la tenga y el que quiera tener un tipo que lo tenga. A mí eso no me importa. Ahora que no me ponga el pie arriba a mí, porque ahí sí le tiro. Pero si tú quieres estar aquí con su tipo es su problema. No me gustan que maltraten una mujer delante de mí, tampoco me gusta que maltraten un hombre, me entiendes.

Artist 2: Los Cubanos son machistas, pero también hay una pila de maricones, pero bueno, lo que creo es que están orientados hacia otro tipo de, de . . . se reservan para otras manifestaciones artísticas, no para el hip hop.

> Artist 1: These are passions, these things are passions. I don't have to mix my sexual life, my sexual orientation with my music. You understand. Mine, no, I tell you I don't import it. My poetry is modest, from the streets. That's *chisme* [simple talk or gossip], that's what every bit of it is. Whoever wants a girlfriend, she should have her, and whoever wants some guy, he should have him. But if you want to be here with your guy, that's your problem. I don't like to mistreat a woman in front of me, and I don't like that they mistreat men, you understand.

> Artist 2: Cubans are *machista*, but also there are a bunch of faggots, but whatever, I think that it is more oriented toward another type of . . . they reserve that for other artistic manifestation, not for hip hop.

While many male hip hop artists support the music of Las Krudas and value their insights, not all of them feel that this work is appropriate. These artists take issue with Las Krudas' discussion of homosexuality but rarely publicly challenge them, given the high level of respect that they enjoy within the hip hop community. These men believe that discussion of homosexuality does not have a place within hip hop. They argue that these discussions belong at gallery openings, ballets, and theater performances. In essence these particular artists still associate homosexuality with a type of white bourgeois culture that is disconnected from the culture of average Cuban citizens or Black artistic expressions. Luckily, while some do not value Las Krudas' work and see it as a form of *chisme* (gossip), many more value the revolutionary implications of their activism.

Despite the controversy surrounding Las Krudas' work, the number of women and men attending their shows since 2003 has markedly increased.[12] Las Krudas have been able to cultivate the respect of male peers and have established their own diverse following. They are on the informal list of the CUHHM's best performers; they are must-haves at hip hop festivals and frequently headline underground hip hop shows, including those being organized internationally. In addition, their work is produced by renowned Cuban producers such as Pablo Herrera, who encouraged them to join the movement in 1998.

While in Cuba, Las Krudas have collaborated on CDs with groups such as the Junior Clan and Anónimo Consejo and are acknowledged in the work of popular artists such as Obsesión, Randy Acosta of Los Paisanos, and Papo Record. Even after moving to the United States in 2006 in order to seek opportunities to engage the global feminist and hip hop communities, they have been included in Cuban hip hop concerts, often as headliners (such as the 2013 Outer Spaces Tour with Invincible and Climbing Poetree). They are constantly touring in Central America, South America, and North America. During their first Mexican tour, they were shocked to see bootleg copies of their CDs sold with other Cuban hip hop artists' CDs on the streets. Like that of other Cuban MCs such as Randy Acosta and Anónimo Consejo, their reputation as one of Cuban hip hop's most established underground hip hop groups has continued in the Cuban diaspora. Their web presence shows that they frequently tour and work within Cuba's hip hop diaspora.[13] They also receive messages of love and support from their male and female counterparts who live in and outside of Cuba, many of whom are themselves also among Cuba's most famous underground hip hop artists.

Though some women may be wary of Las Krudas' sexuality and feminist ideology, none of the female hip hop artists that I interviewed said anything against any of their social demands. Even those women who do not want to be allied with Las Krudas' particular agenda manage to find subtle ways of distancing themselves and are careful not to disrespect their discourse and poetry.

Las Krudas have been able to foster a remarkable amount of solidarity among women within the hip hop community, even among those who do not self-identify as feminist.

Las Krudas' Return to Cuba in 2010

A lot has changed since that moment that I discussed at the beginning of this chapter, when I sat in Las Krudas' apartment and the little girl passed by the door. I completed the fieldwork for this project in 2006, the same year that Las Krudas moved to the United States. I was able to return to Cuba nearly five years later, in 2010, when Las Krudas also returned for their first hip hop symposium in five years. In my field notes (2010) I reflected on the effects that Las Krudas have had on the movement:

> I was shocked at the audiovisual images that were part of the stage props. There were images of the bathroom sign for women with an equality sign to the male bathroom sign and a white male bathroom sign being equal to a Black male bathroom sign. However, I notice with the male being equaled to a woman sign, though it is a black backdrop, it seems that it is the white male being equal to a white female . . . which is interesting to see in a space that presents itself as a pro-Black anti-racist movement. Additionally, the woman has straight hair, there is no Afro or any of the images that would encourage the embracing of a Black femininity, even though the head of the Agency of Rap is a woman who advocated for such. Signs that included disability. There were images that stated "Stop Homophobia." The signs argued for inclusion and diversity of all kinds. The MC took to the stage. He was a Black Cuban, male, very tall, physically fit with broad shoulders and a bald head. People were waiting for Danay to come onto the stage. She is another one of the new rising stars to come out of the Cuban Underground Hip Hop Movement. The MC started making jokes about women MCs and women artists. He made fun of Danay and argued that women should not hate men so much (a reference to Las Krudas). After stating a range of disparaging things against women for a few minutes, ranging from women should not be on the stage to simply joking about women performers, there was silence.
>
> People were nervous, they stirred in their seats, surprised that the MC had the nerve to say such things on the stage. Very few showed support, virtually no one cheered. Odaymara and Olivia stood up and shouted, "Fuck you," and with their middle fingers in the air began walking down

the aisle to the stage. Initially people turned to see where the noise was coming from. As Las Krudas got closer to the stage—with a large group of women following them—people started to cheer loudly. So loudly that the MC could not talk over the audience. The reaction was amazing. The *machista* elements in the audience who support those comments could not control the discourse coming from the stage—or frame who was to be respected and disrespected and who was to be included and excluded from the stage. The crowd shouted "Krudas! Krudas!" The next day he was no longer the MC. I think even Magia MC, the director of the Agency of Rap, was shocked and disappointed at how someone could think that he could reclaim the stage as a legitimate platform for machista and sexist discourse.

When I was in Cuba in 2010, I asked several young women attending the Cuban Hip Hop Symposium who came of age after Las Krudas left Cuba in 2006 if they had heard of the group or met them. The young women commented that while they had never had the opportunity to meet Las Krudas, they had heard about them while living in distant cities such as Camaguey and Santiago de Cuba. They had learned about Las Krudas' activism and Las Krudas had achieved legendary status for them. During the 2010 symposium, nearly every hip hop group that took the stage, and every woman MC who took the stage, acknowledged Las Krudas' presence, offered their respects, and thanked them for the work that they did in the CUHHM.

In a 2013 interview in Havana with Jorge Enrique, previously the director of the young Cuban artists association called La Asociación Hermanos Saíz and now the editor in chief of the Cuban hip hop magazine *Movimiento*, he talked about the process of incorporation that followed the emergence of the CUHHM. In his discussion about the process of appropriation, he mentioned CENESEX, the national institution whose research is centered on sexology in Cuba. CENESEX became the face of Cuba's new sexual revolution in the early to mid-2000s:

Jorge: Por tanto, el poder absorbió esos dos grandes temas. Las raperas y raperos empezaron a involucrar a la sociedad cubana, empezaron a empujar estos dos grandes temas para arriba, para arriba. Otra cosa, el CENESEX tiene que darle las gracias al movimiento de rap en Cuba, como muchas otras instituciones que ahora dicen que ... [*pauses*] Te pongo el ejemplo del CENESEX, porque las primeras personas que asumieron su homosexualidad en un escenario público fueron las raperas, no fue absolutamente más nadie, aún cuando figuras emblemáticas de la cultura cubana como la difunta Sara González, era abiertamente lesbiana.... Repito: aquí, excepto las mujeres raperas lesbianas, nadie antes de ellas, había tocado ese tema. Lo puedo asegurar.

Tanya: ¿En la historia de Cuba?

Jorge: Si, de Cuba. . . . A ver, a ver, a ver. . . . La historia de Cuba. . . . Bueno, estaba Sara González, Tanya, Albita Rodríguez. Te puedo mencionar un millón de artistas lesbianas, pero los que sabíamos que eran lesbianas, era porque de algún modo estábamos en ese círculo . . . pero públicamente; como discusión social, nunca. De hecho, en Cuba las expresiones gay siempre fueron más visibles en lo masculino. . . . Yo me he puesto a pensar: ¿Jorge, machismo también dentro de lo gay? ¡Esto está jodido!, pero es real, porque de algún modo era más natural ver a un hombre gay, la gente decía: eh, mira a la loca esa, pero cuando se trataba de una lesbiana, ya el asunto era más chocante.

> Jorge: Therefore the power absorbed those two big issues. The women rappers and male rappers began to engage the Cuban society, began to push these two big issues up and up. Otherwise, CENESEX must thank the rap movement in Cuba, like many other institutions that now say . . . I give the example of CENESEX, because the first people who came out on a public stage about their homosexuality were the women rappers, absolutely no one else, even when they were emblematic figures of Cuban culture, like the late Sara González, who was openly lesbian. . . . I repeat here, except for the lesbian female rappers, nobody before them had touched the subject. I can assure you.
>
> Tanya: The history of Cuba?
>
> Jorge: Yes, of Cuba let's see, let's see, let's see. . . . The history of Cuba. . . . Well, there were Sara González, Tanya, Albite Rodríguez. Here I can mention a million lesbian artists, but those that we knew we were lesbians, it was because somehow we were in that circle . . . but publicly, as in a social discussion, never. In fact, in Cuba gay expressions were always visible in terms of the male. . . . I began to think, Jorge, is there machismo within the gay community, that's fucked up! But it's real, because in a way it was more natural to see a gay man, people would say: hey, look at that [effeminate gay male], but when you talk about a lesbian, that is something that has more resistance.

In another interview Jorge argued that it was the women MCs who brought the issue of gender inequality (economic and cultural) and homosexuality back into the public sphere and did it with an attention to racial inequality. The Cuban women MCs took an intersectional approach to understanding their own inequality and as a result touched upon several issues that affected nearly everyone in Cuban society. The first thing that the state did was to appropriate these discourses, which resonated with the larger Cuban public, as a way to address the issues raised by CUHHM MCs and then to control them. Jorge argued that a lot of the work of CENESEX, in the area of sexual equality, involved the appropriation of the discourse and activism of feminist MCs, specifically the discourses of Krudas CUBENSI. In chapter 2 and elsewhere in this book I have referred to the lesbian social group OREMI. This is an example of CENESEX's attempt at discursive co-optation: the creation of OREMI was an effort for the state to show (and therefore argue) that it was addressing the needs of Cuban lesbians. CENESEX reached out to Las Krudas and other lesbian activists to start a lesbian social group, only to shut it down and then co-opt it several months later. In commenting on the historical significance of Las Krudas CUBENSI's work in Cuba, Jorge argues that while Cuban history offers examples of many well-known lesbian artists and intellectuals, none of them were out in public. The way that people knew that they were out was because they encountered these artists when socializing among friends or in specific social scenes. Las Krudas CUBENSI were the first women to do so in Cuban history.

One of the reasons why Las Krudas have been able to continue to gain and maintain respect within the movement is because they have stayed true to their underground Kruda discourse. When Las Krudas moved to the United States, they moved to the Rhizome Collective, an anarchist collective, in Austin, Texas. They lived there for three years before the collective was closed by the city for housing violation codes in 2009. Las Krudas also continue to work as socially conscious artivists abroad and often return to Cuba to organize workshops for women artists. These workshops have centered on helping women learn how to market themselves and how to become comfortable with their creative energies as women within a *machista* society. Las Krudas continue to collaborate with other artists and community activists in order to help women to learn how to take more control of their careers as artists but also to increase visibility of Cuba's lesbian, bisexual, and transgender population. They also still produce songs and collaborate with women MCs from abroad, in the diaspora. They have now established themselves as transnational artivists working for social change, with a particular focus on people of color, queers, women, immigrants, lesbians, Latinas and Black Latinas, trans-identified folks, Caribbean feminists, and a whole host of identities that they share as artivists experiencing multiple intersections of social life as they move throughout the Americas.

This chapter has focused specifically on Las Krudas CUBENSI's work in Cuba because their critical interventions and artivism are an important part of

Cuban history and need to be critically engaged and documented. They are the first publically open lesbian group to exist in the history of Cuba. The group's recent shift from the name Las Krudas CUBENSI, to Krudxs CUBENSI reflects changes in their gender identities (they have dropped the feminine article *Las* and replaced *a* with *x*), ushering in an new period of artivist intervention in the United States, Cuba, and globally. Krudxs also now employ Spanish terms that they have developed such as *elles* as a third gender term, as part of their rethinking of gender from the experience of Caribbean *queeridad*. Again, their rethinking of gender identity politics cannot be reduced to having engaged with queer activists in the United States, as they spend much time traveling in the Americas. Krudxs are also coming from a Cuban context where *transvestis* and *bugarrones* are already a part of the cultural landscape. Their theorization of gender identity is a result of multiple experiences in multiple contexts within the Americas.

This is a key point in understanding Krudxs CUBENSI's work. They are revolutionary artists formed by their social context: Black and antiracist lesbians coming of age in a Cuban revolutionary and underground hip hop context. Krudxs, like their peers from the 1990s generation of Cuban Underground Hip Hop artivists, are consciously making an ideological intervention into local (wherever they are) and global discourses concerning social inequality. For those who will continue engaging the work of Krudxs CUBENSI, it is important to remember to resist the urge to reduce their activism, their queer identity politics, and whatever identity politics they decide to engage in their future activism to a mimicking or acceptance of any ideological framework, including hegemonic notions of queerness and now *latinidad* in the United States, for example.

Krudxs are also aware of how their identities shift and their bodies are read in various geopolitical and cultural contexts: Olivia's identity moves between being an antiracist ally who is socially classified as white in Cuba and being an antiracist Latina (now a person of color) in the United States. Odaymara's identity has shifted from being a Black Cuban woman in Cuba to navigating the political boundaries that separate blackness and *latinidad* in the United States. Both live a Latin@ immigrant existence when they are in the United States *and* in Brazil, Colombia (with DJ Leydis), Guatemala, Mexico and beyond (fig. 7.3). As they both move through social contexts they experience new ways of being, they experience new identities and work to bring those multiple and varying identities into conversation with each other to fight social oppression, wherever they are. Their goal is to eliminate boundaries and engage whatever ideas or terms are useful in their work to articulate, critique, define, and break

Figure 7.3.   Las Krudas CUBENSI (Krudxs) at the Afrolatinidades Festival in Brasilia, Brazil, July 2013. (Photo by Tanya L. Saunders)

systems of power, in the multiple contexts they inhabit. Krudxs CUBENSI use language, and language play, as part of a politic of establishing conversations, activist, and solidarity networks across geopolitical borders with the aim of exposing interconnected systems of power, which are not always bounded by geopolitical borders.

8

Conclusion

In this conclusion I engage with the notion that the Cuban Underground Hip Hop Movement "ended" as such, in order to highlight what the movement was, what it accomplished, and what its legacies are today. Attempts to assess the success of the CUHHM based simply on whether or not it exists today in the same form as it did between 1995 and 2006 misread and seriously underestimate both what Special Period Cuban youths were able to accomplish and the struggles and forms of state opposition that they faced. Geoffrey Baker (2011), for example, relates the "fall" of the CUHHM to the "rise" of reggaetón—an analysis that dismisses the idea that the Cuban state would have a vested interest in curtailing any kind of organized social movement and ignores the state's history of attempting to control autonomous social movements through institutionalization and nationalization, both forms of cooptation. In order to understand what the CUHHM was, it helps to differentiate between the arts-based social movement (CUHHM) that has been the focus of this book and the more general music genre of Cuban underground hip hop. It is also important to specify the period analyzed in this book, from 1998 to 2006.

I started going to Cuba in 1998, the year that the group Amenaza disbanded. Up to that point, some would argue that Cuban underground hip hop was still "just" an art and music scene, not yet a movement per se. A number of groups were prominent at this point and could have claimed leadership of the scene. Things began to shift gradually, however, as large numbers of foreigners began entering Cuba during the 1990s, drawn by the arts and music being developed there. LGBT activists, pan-Africanists, environmental activists, and other creative people started arriving in Cuba from the United States and Canada, many of whom were themselves immigrants to those countries from Puerto Rico, Jamaica, and several places in the Americas. According to Herrera, this creative influx had an impact on how the first generation of CUHHM artists engaged with activism.

Record companies were also coming to Cuba looking for new talent, and Amenaza was one of the groups discovered in this way. This discovery and the marriage of one of the members to a foreigner resulted in the disbanding of the group (later formed again, with new members, as the Orishas in France). At approximately this time the CUHHM became conscious of itself as a movement. The disbanding of Amenaza, a group poised to become one of the first international acts to establish Cuban underground hip hop, in 1998 and the arrival of activists from the Malcolm X Grassroots project in the same year marked an important turning point. It could be argued that the rise of Los Aldeanos and the exodus of a significant number of the first CUHHM generation mark the movement's substantial transformation.

The group Los Aldeanos is an example of both the rise of a new generation within Cuba and the nationalization of Cuban hip hop. Los Aldeanos emerged as a force during the 2006 exodus of artists from Cuba and did not follow the traditional activist route of rising through the ranks of the CUHHM. From 1998 to 2006 the CUHHM was, as Herrera (personal communication, 2013) describes it, "a movement without a head. Leadership was collective and leadership was shared because there was no other choice." There were a number of amazing hip hop groups and arts collectives, so no single group or figure represented the face of the movement or could be considered a superstar. All of the groups were exceptionally talented by this point, and the limited number of resources on the Island to support Cuban underground hip hop as a genre compelled people to work together.

The other important thing to emphasize about the CUHHM versus the Cuban underground hip hop scene as it exists today (whether it's called a movement or not) is that the CUHHM discussed in this book was centered around hip hop, to be sure, but was also a more general arts-based social movement. The artivists were invested in their art, entertaining and educating for the purposes of effecting social change and disseminating their work to a broad, even global audience. The CUHHM was very much in conversation with Nueva Trova and other parts of Cuba's alternative music scene, as well as with the various art scenes that existed in Cuba. The artists within the art world in which the CUHHM is rooted also incorporated an activist ethos as a central outlook and practice (hence the term "artivists"), making the CUHHM an arts-based social movement and not simply an arts and music scene. The movement developed an agenda for social change that encompassed everything from making anti-racist and antiheteronormative aesthetic interventions to mobilizing community projects and consciousness-raising programs designed to empower people to work for their own social change.

When scholars and others conflate the two, reducing the social movement element of the CUHHM to the arts scene out of which the movement grew, they miss another major contradiction within the history of socialization (and politicization) of Cuban culture. Part of the state's argument for the socialization of Cuban culture was to support and encourage cultural production as part of a larger process of decolonization. By shielding Cuban cultural producers from the global capitalist market and subsidizing their cultural production, they would not have to compete with giant corporations and institutions such as Warner Brothers, EMI, Hollywood, and Penguin. Additionally, empowering Cuban cultural producers and cultural workers would help to limit the ideological hegemony of U.S. cultural institutions and allow the creation of cultural work that reflected Cuban culture, worldviews, and experiences. It was assumed that the centralization of state resources and the creation of cultural institutions would help to achieve the goal of making Cuban culture both accessible and globally marketable.

With the creation of institutions such as the Instituto Cubano del Arte e Industria Cinematográficos (ICAIC) and the Casa de las Américas, Cuba established itself as a global center of cultural production and facilitated Cuban cultural producers' access to local and global cultural markets. This endeavor was largely successful for decades: institutionalization, at least in theory, guaranteed support and protection for Cuban artists and intellectuals. This is also the reason why the question of whether or not Cuban underground hip hop was authentically *Cuban* was so important, because artists working in a genre that became recognized as authentically Cuban could demand access to various material resources and forms of state support. Cuban underground hip hop and Cuban rock won an important political battle in 1999 when both genres were recognized as Cuban music genres by Abel Prieto, then the minister of culture.

Nonetheless, a contradiction emerged: along with state recognition came the risk of state cooptation, containment, and new forms of exclusion. With the creation of the Cuban Agency of Rap in 2002, for example, Cuban underground hip hop attained a new level of institutionalization that paradoxically enabled the state to justify the *artistic* exclusion of certain CUHHM artists by pointing to the dictates of the market and the artists' ability (or lack thereof) to sell out shows. While the state may have supported Cuban underground hip hop as a genre, it did not support the Cuban Underground Hip Hop Movement and sought in many ways to defuse its grassroots activism.

Indeed, as more recent events have continued to demonstrate, the involvement of the state remains a dubious benefit at times. The 2013 Puño Arriba awards are an excellent example of how the state used passive techniques of power to ensure that the remaining CUHHM artivists living in Cuba and newer generations of Cuban youths are not able to reproduce the same broad-based social movement that existed prior to 2006.

In 2013 I arrived in Cuba to attend the Puño Arriba hip hop awards. The event had been advertised nationally and internationally for several months and was to be held at the Trompo Loco circus tent, a venue that can hold two thousand people. But on December 12, just a few days before the event, the state decided to move it to the Avenida film theater, a smaller event space that holds only about two hundred people and is known for its faulty technical equipment.[1] Two of the concert organizers—Soandry, from the CUHMM group Hermanos de Causa, and Michel Matos, of the independent music project Matraka— organized a protest with about eighty participants in front of the Cuban Music Institute (Instituto Cubano de la Música: ICM) on December 10 (Fernández 2013). The artists were protesting not only the new location proposed for the event but also the confusion that was sure to result after months of marketing efforts by the artists and organizers.

Writing in the *Havana Times* on December 12, 2013, Alfredo Fernández reported that the officials at the ICM requested a meeting but said that they would speak only with protesters who were associated with the Cuban Agency of Rap; "those present replied in the negative, saying 'either you speak to everyone, or you speak to no one.'"[2] Several hours later the ICM apologized and reversed its decision, telling the organizers that the awards show could go on as planned. Fernández (2013) writes that the protesters stood for hours in front of the ICM building saying, "'Either you give us authorization or you throw us in jail—there's no other option.'"

Much like the meetings that resulted when the state canceled the 2004 International Hip Hop Festival (see chapter 3), the Puño Arriba protest reveals only one of many moments of frustration that artists and artivists experience in their relations with the state. When I arrived in Havana, I went directly to Trompo Loco, not having heard about the protests yet. I immediately noticed that a lot of people were there, but the venue was not filled to capacity. Thus, although the organizers were able to continue with the event, it is probable that the state's actions had had some effect. Days after the event, I continued to hear people saying that they had heard it was canceled or that they were not sure where it was. The circumstances surrounding this event highlight the passive aggressive tactics used by the state to sabotage (for lack of a better word) politicized movements and individual actors within Cuba's public sphere, particularly within the politicized cultural sphere. First, the state undermines the ability of people to find an event by changing location, providing misinformation, or placing it in a difficult location. The state also makes it hard for the event to happen by using tactics such as canceling an event (let's say due to weather) and then never rescheduling it or providing a venue where the technological equipment is so poor that it breaks or creates some other difficulty. Over the years, I attended multiple CUHHM events at which people who were accustomed to the technological difficulties would stay four or even five hours for an event that should have taken only two or three hours but ran long because of frequent pauses to fix or simply find equipment.

It remains unclear whether we should speak of the end of the CUHHM or its transformation. In the dissertation on which this book is based (Saunders 2008), I noted that every Cuban generation after 1959 has included a mass exodus of frustrated young (usually 30-something) artists, who leave a power vacuum that is then filled by the next generation of artists. Though the first few generations of artists were targeted for harassment and imprisonment by the state, later generations faced more frustration associated with constant impediments to their ability to produce and freely disseminate their work, including their ability to travel abroad and to live their lives as globally engaged artists and intellectuals. After a significant number leave the Island, a vacuum is created until members of a new generation come of age and become critically engaged citizens. I expected the same dynamic to happen for the CUHHM in 2006, and there is some evidence that it did.

After the 2006 exodus, energetic Cuban youths of the new wave are now undertaking activism that reflects, as expected, the realities particular to their generation. For example, while the continued existence of the CUHHM remains in question, my fieldwork in Cuba leaves little or no doubt that Cuban underground hip hop feminism has continued and even flourished since 2006 (a relatively new development that is just now becoming formally captured by media outlets such as the blog http://negracubanateniaqueser.com/). The invisibility of the evolution of Cuban underground hip hop feminism vis-à-vis the assumption that organized hip hop activism has ended in Cuba reveals the continued male-centric focus of most discussions of the CUHHM, particularly those announcing its total demise. The following sections discuss the 2006 exodus of CUHHM artivists from Cuba in terms of not only the impact that the exodus had but also why artivists left in the first place and why it is so important to differentiate this exodus from earlier movements of people away from the Island. I focus on what happened to the CUHHM after so many artivists left, noting in particular the emergence of Los Aldeanos—the first artists since 1998, I argue, who successfully engaged Cuban underground hip hop solely as a music genre, not as a movement. Drawing on my follow-up fieldwork in Cuba in 2010 and the winter of 2013–2014, I discuss the longer legacies of the CUHHM in terms of the discourses regarding race, class, gender, and sexuality, focusing in particular on the continuation and evolution of Cuban underground hip hop feminism.

The Transformation of the Movement

During a conversation with CUHHM producer Pablo Herrera in 2011, he reacted to a video of a concert with Los Aldeanos, in which the group dissed the Ministry of Culture and attacked the minister of culture, Abel Prieto. During that conversation, Herrera lamented what had happened to the Cuban Underground Hip Hop Movement. He also discussed the guilt that he sometimes feels for having left Cuba. He was part of the generation that began to leave the Island around 2005, culminating in the largest number of CUHHM artivists leaving in 2006. The last of the key leaders of the CUHHM started living abroad in 2012, when groups like Anónimo Consejo and members of Hermanos de Causa changed their primary countries of residence to the United States, Spain, and Venezuela. I very deliberately state that these artists have taken up primary residency outside of Cuba rather than simply saying that they left. For many of these artists, their primary intention was being able to travel and becoming truly global citizens and were frustrated by state attempts at manipulation and control of artistic production. This is an important marker of a generational difference: younger generations of Cubans are not leaving for explicitly political reasons or, more specifically, due to antistate ideologies. Rather, they are choosing to have a different relationship to their country. It is thus frustrating to hear people outside of Cuba use Cold War discourse such as "defection" to refer to the various visa statuses that the artists may use to take up residency somewhere else.

Cuba is a marked country, and its citizens live a precarious global citizenship existence. They have do not have the same range of choices in terms of visa options as North Americans or Europeans do. They negotiate as they must in order to live the life that they want. Reducing the investments of the artists in the diaspora to their limited visa options does not reflect new Cuban realties. Younger generations of Cubans are choosing to live abroad to achieve a better quality of life. Although they are often critical of the contradictory actions of the state, the last thing that they would support is Cuba becoming another neo-colony of the United States. Cuban artivists' continued presence on the Island and their continued work there even after moving indicate their investment in working in Cuba even as they now live as globally engaged cultural producers.

Reflecting on his experiences and the development of the CUHHM while he was still in Cuba, Herrera wished that he had been mature enough to understand what they were doing at such a young age. He acknowledged that the movement (and he used the word itself, because we talked about these issues in English) had a lot of power and potential because it was organized by Black youths. It was only after the artists decided to reside primarily outside of Cuba and had time to reflect that they really began to understand the significance of what they had created in Cuba. Artivists such as Pablo Herrera (now living in Edinburgh), Ariel Fernández (now living in New York City), Alexis "DJ D'Boys" Rodríguez (now living in Toronto, Ontario), Las Krudas/Krudxs CUBENSI (now living in Austin, Texas), DJ Leydis (now living in Oakland, California), and Randy Acosta (now living in Spain) are experiencing a reflective moment as they think back on the movement and its past *and* present possibilities (figs. 8.1, 8.2, 8.3, and 8.4). Becoming members of the Cuban diaspora (a process that Celiany Rivera captures so well in her 2012 documentary *Queen of Myself: Las Krudas d'Cuba*) has required these artivists to renegotiate their relationships with the movement that they helped to build.

Ariel Fernández spoke about the possibilities of being involved in the movement from the diaspora in 2008 at the El Proyecto conference, where he saw some of his fellow CUHHM artivists for the first time in about four years:

> We cannot be a movement in the diaspora, we can't really be connected, we never were connected in Cuba, so at some point the hip hop movement in Cuba was marketed like a movement, I mean if people looked Cuban and wait, you know what I mean, and people were assuming that we were doing in Cuba was going to be the answer to the world, people were going to go to Cuba and say, "Oh, hip hop in Cuba is unique, because they don't have record companies." You know what I mean, Cuban hip hop is unique because they don't get permission, and at some point they don't really want it to be based on your lyrics getting approved to perform in the festival, it was seen as a movement, *Washington Post, New York Times*, they were treating us like we were a movement but more like people never understood what was really happening to us, the contradiction that we were having, you know what I mean, people were thinking like we were the Che Guevaras and Fidel Castros of the global hip hop, and it wasn't that, this is the truth, it was young Black people that were going to do something possible with their lives to make a change, we

Figure 8.1. Miki Flow (from Explosión Suprema) performing in New York City, 2011. (Photo by Tanya L. Saunders)

Figure 8.2. Alexis "DJ D'Boys" Rodríguez performing in Toronto, Ontario, 2011. (Courtesy of Alexis DJ D'Boys)

Figure 8.3. Advertisement of DJ Leydis's weekly *Jet Set* in Oakland, California. (Courtesy of Leydis Freire)

Figure 8.4. Advertisement for Randy Acosta in Spain, 2011. (Courtesy of Randy Acosta)

were poor, we didn't have anything but at the end of the day we got a place to sleep every day and we got food every day, what we were doing? Why we are here now? It's all connected, mostly not to be able to do what we wanted to do in Cuba, it's not like you left Cuba because you couldn't do business in Cuba, we left because we couldn't do what we wanted to do in Cuba, we couldn't say what the country should be, I mean the people that educated us, and the people that showed us how to be the way we are, so at some point the revolution educated us, to be revolutionary and critical, I did the classes, I got my tie, so *escenario* [scenester], critic, *pensador* [thinker] . . . *¿me entiendes?*

I didn't even know where we were going before and that's what . . . we didn't know, like the fact that my friends, they started doing it, you know what I mean. . . .

In a political context, before me being in the hip hop, I wasn't aware of the situation that was happening in Cuba, that's the game, I spent fourteen years of my life in the hip hop culture and hip hop, it's not my thing anymore, I mean, hip hop was something that made the way for where I wanted to go, I wanted to be part of the movement that fights against oppression, I want to do a day-by-day activism, I did it for fourteen years . . . and somebody needs to do that, I think you are an artist and you are focused in your art . . . and that was the thing, we were able to deliver reality and see people, we have a high-level education, and for people that went to Cuba, we never had a deep education on your cultural background, and I was always impressed with the capacity, of what could be said in a four- or five-minute song, that it speaks to you, you can be easy and talk political speech, you know what I mean?

Here Fernández is processing as he speaks. He notes that the Black youths of the 1990s did not realize what they were doing. They were just doing it. Fernández also mentions that they were raised in a revolutionary context, to be critical. He comments that he did everything he needed to do to be a revolutionary citizen in Cuba. He went to the classes for Communist youth and got the tie that symbolizes that someone has come of age and can be recognized as a revolutionary youth. As in my conversations with other producers and organizers such as Pablo Herrera and DJ D'Boys, however, Fernández sometimes struggles with calling the CUHHM a movement per se. At the same time, he notes that people outside of Cuba presented it as this revolutionary movement, as a movement for change. He rejects the depiction of the CUHHM as some sort of iconic movement for a global audience and argues that they were simply

Black youths who were addressing the contradictions and the oppressions that they faced. Interestingly, he mentions that housing and food were taken care of through state policies, so they were able to have the time and energy to invest in the movement, even though they were still materially poor and did not have access to the technology that hip hop demands. Fernández gave fourteen years of his life to the CUHHM because he believed in its capacity for change. This is all reflective of the idealism of Cuba's critical artists and intellectuals who, like Fernández, were focused on art as a way to present reality, to work for change. Herrera, Fernández, and DJ D'Boys all expressed a frustrated idealism in their interviews, which seems to be a hallmark experience of being one of the Cuban Revolution's primary contradictions: the critical artivist.

The exodus of the CUHHM's first generation reflects a general pattern among Cuba's socially critical artists, intellectuals, and artivists. They emerge into Cuba's cultural sphere idealistic, frustrated, and eager to work for change. After about ten years of slow progress, however, after the constant "no" from the Cuban state in the form of the various obstacles that the state places in front of these artivists, many of them get so frustrated that they leave, usually around the age of thirty. Ultimately, these folks are artists who want to see the world and live their life to the fullest, which means realizing their potential and intense calling as an artivist. The overwhelming majority of CUHHM artists living abroad are involved in artistic production and also stick to their underground roots. Nonetheless, the Cuban state seems to be aware of this pattern and simply waits for frustrated artivists to get tired and leave. David of Grupo OMNI expressed this frustration in Havana in 2010:

Tanya: Oye, ¿por qué . . . por qué lo quitaron el rock y después hip hop?
David: Lo quitan porque lo quitan, porque quieren tener el dominio y el dominio, en verdad, del espacio donde nace, de la gente que lo organiza y tú sabes que este gobierno quiere tener todo organizado y todo controlado.

> Tanya: Hey, why? . . . why did they take away rock and then hip hop?
> David: They take it away because they take it away, because they want to have control and dominion, in truth, of the place where it began, of the people that organized it, and you know that this government wants to have everything organized and everything controlled.

David is talking about the government's move to incorporate and censor the critical performance arts scene, in which Grupo OMNI in particular has been at various moments a target of state censorship since about 2006.

A lot has changed since I completed the research for this project in 2006, with follow-up trips to Cuba in 2010 and again in 2013–2014. At the state level, notable changes have included increased liberalization of the economy and the right to travel, but at the same time, at various moments since about 2010, there has also been an increase in state intimidation and repression of those who are openly critical of the state, including Cuba's artivists. In 2013 this seemed to have decreased somewhat with the easing of travel restrictions between the United States and Cuba. We can only hope that the state does not undertake a policy of eating its own as it did in the 1970s. But given the direction of United States/Cuba relations, Cuba/Brazil economic ties, and Cuba/China ties, and as Cuba increases its economic (in)dependence and regional integration, it becomes more difficult to argue that a U.S. invasion could happen at any moment and thus to find support for increased restrictions at 1965–1970s levels.

Herrera worries that many left at a time when people needed them, when younger generations needed guidance. His concerns are certainly valid. In 2010 older activists and some young activists within the younger generations referred to members of the millennial generation in Cuba as "the lost generation," which had heard much about how hip hop was once a movement but often felt that this was a myth, given their own experiences of coming of age after 2006.

Many of the CUHHM artivists who left have started returning to Cuba to mentor and support these younger generations left behind. Upon their return, however, they often have to deal with being framed as "non-Cuban." As such, the work of the artivists is usually dismissed as being "foreign" while they are on the Island; once they leave, they are seen as literally being foreign. Needless to say, this is a very complicated dynamic, from which the state benefits discursively. Any division that can be fomented among like-minded artivists helps the state to reject critiques and to dismiss as illegitimate and irrelevant the work of Cuban artivists who choose the diaspora. Meanwhile, on the Island, Black artists complain that the movement is being co-opted by people interested in material success without doing anything to help people at the community level. For a short time (from about 2006 to 2011), some worried that the movement was being slowly co-opted by the state through a mulat@cracy, whereby the persistent racism in Cuba was no longer discussed and focus shifted instead to a general malaise as a means of selling records. This was a common critique of Los Aldeanos, who were not invested in doing the type of community-based work that CUHHM artivists did during the peak movement years (see fig. 8.5).

Los Aldeanos were in a position to become the leaders of the Cuban underground hip hop scene. Importantly, they did not go through the activist ranks and were not associated with the underground hip hop art world and thus marked a generational shift within Cuban underground hip hop. They are an exceptionally talented group that came onto the scene with a new discourse, built on the older generations' discourses. They made their own music, they produced themselves, and they openly stated a sentiment that many young Cubans felt: "Fuck the government." For many artists, their emergence marks the nationalization of Cuban underground hip hop: Los Aldeanos' members are white or fall within the realm of nonblackness in Cuba. The fact that they could openly denounce the government is linked to their racial and class privilege.

Many politicized Black Cubans who were part of the CUHHM shared an understanding that directly challenging the Cuban state could be dangerous. This silence has been in place since the 1920s, linked to the Black political mobilizations of 1912 that resulted in the race-based massacre of Cubans in the western provinces of the Island (Helg 1995; Herrera, personal communication, 2013; Rolando 2014). Black Cubans came up with a way to communicate with the government and to make their needs known without openly confronting or challenging it. One artist described it to me: "Do you like Mike Epps? There was this one routine that he did that talked about the difference between Black kids and white kids. That if Black kids got into trouble, they would not dare to talk back to their parents. But in the case of white kids, white kids could be building a bomb in their room, and if their mother walked in and asked what they were doing, the kids would say, 'Fuck you, Mom!'"

The ability of Los Aldeanos to get away with critiques and not be constantly harassed on the level of Black artists (who are sometimes stopped, questioned, and detained in the venue of their own show for being "suspicious") was seen as a result of their sharing racial privilege with those of the Cuban state, which gave them the power to speak openly and bluntly. When I asked Herrera his thoughts on this topic, he commented that he personally thinks that it is important to remember that the older generation of Cuban underground hip hop artists were heavily influenced by Nueva Trova. They were influenced by the idea of working for a revolution within the Revolution and inspired by the brilliance and challenge of using poetry to write songs that had double meanings. Even through poetry and these kinds of songs, they could say something that was really powerful and subversive, without using vulgarity.

Los Aldeanos marked a discursive generational shift and for many the final step in nationalization of Cuban underground hip hop. When a "white" group performed hip hop this meant that it was available to whites and maybe eventually nearly to whites only (see chapter 4 on the relationship between whiteness and mulat@ness).

In short, a form of Cuban underground hip hop emerged that was no longer connected to the CUHHM, revealing the power vacuum that Pablo Herrera refers to, left by the artivists who began leaving the Island. Key to this power vacuum is the break in the knowledge transfer from members of the older hip hop generation, who were unable to pass on what they had learned as organizers and what they had learned in terms of understanding the potential of the movement. Older generations of artists and intellectuals started journals such as *Encuentro* and other forums after leaving the Island but continued to engage in public life in Cuba and in the diaspora. Members of the old-school generation of the CUHHM have also developed ways of continuing to support the movement at home: by returning to participate in concerts and organizing symposia where they can pass on the knowledge and experiences that they have developed as artivists, while raising awareness and support of the CUHHM abroad.

What makes this generation different from other generations is that it was the first generation of artivists to leave Cuba not in direct reaction to the state but as a means of securing opportunities for development as artivists and finding ways to support artists at home. This is one thing that has become clear to younger generations of CUHHM artivists, who are now emerging to redefine CUHHM leadership and the movement itself. If the CUHHM is to continue as a movement (if it still needs to be a movement, as Cuba is a very different place than it was in 1995), what comes next is up to the younger generations.

What is clear, however, is that the changes in U.S. policy toward Cuba first under Bill Clinton (whose encouragement of people-to-people exchanges was seen as being integral to the emergence of the CUHHM) and then under Barack Obama have allowed a different type of collaboration between artivists in the diaspora and those on the Island. The members of the new Cuban diaspora are not nearly as reactionary as older generations of Cuban immigrants. Instead of following the precedent set by older generations of Cuban Miami exiles and immigrants, these artivists are working for change via the institutions available in Cuba's public sphere and nascent civil society. It is also clear, however, that the artists who stayed face a new era of struggle. At least for the moment, older artivists are choosing to stay and participate in a new generational shift in Cuban pressures for social change. The movement is now at a stage where it has to make sense of the relationship between the CUHHM diaspora, those from the old-school generation still living on the Island, and the younger generations and how to form newer networks for political mobilization and change.

The CUHHM had the ear of the Cuban state, which was trying to figure out whether or not an organized Black movement was forming that might challenge state policy. The breaking point came with the creation of the Cuban Agency of Rap in 2003. Actors within the CUHHM leadership pushed for state incorporation via the creation of an Agency of Rap, while others rejected any form of state cooptation. Those who rejected incorporation took one key stance: once you begin to depend on an institution for resources, you lose any form of independence and become vulnerable to cooptation. Those who pushed for incorporation had faith that the Cuban state was going to allow the Cuban Agency of Rap to be a representative institution, operating in the interests of the CUHHM. As a result the first director of the Cuban Agency of Rap was Susana García Amorós, a Latin American literature expert who specialized in Afro-Cuban literature.

Amorós had no background in music and knew nothing about hip hop but was an accomplished Black woman who lived in Alamar. For those familiar with Cuban history, this is reminiscent of the appointment of Armando Hart Dávalos (a lawyer and technocrat) as the first minister of culture. Reflecting on this moment, artists now in the diaspora recognize that they did not really realize *who* was placed in this position. Some now think that Amorós was appointed as director because some people in the state's cultural institutions had a desire to see her fail, as they knew she would find resistance. Additionally, artists did not think to ask a Black literary scholar who had been the vice-president of the Cuban Institute of the Book what she could offer them in terms of mentorship—they rejected her for not being a hip hop artist.

In 2006, in response to pressures for change, Magia López (Magia MC of Obsesión) was appointed to be the second director the Cuban Agency of Rap. She was pressured to leave her position in 2011. Some artists felt that she was chosen because she was the most likely to adhere to the state policy of stifling representation and dissent through the politics of omission and, looking back, felt that she did exactly that. Women artists also shared this critique of Magia. While she was the director of the Agency of Rap, only one woman was represented by the agency. Since her departure, there are now at least six. Las Positivas, for example, is a nationally known and well-respected CUHHM group composed of women MCs based in Santiago de Cuba. They have also emerged as part of what is now called the old-school generation of CUHHM artists. For years they asked Magia to let them be a part of the agency, as a popular professional CUHHM artivist group, but they were repeatedly denied. Finally the members moved from Santiago to Havana; only after Magia left did they became one of the groups represented by the agency.

For these artists, both directors had done exactly what they had feared would happen—the directors found excuses to explain why important events such as the International Hip Hop Symposium could not be held, found excuses to explain why so few artists were releasing CDs, and failed to address why the releases were happening so slowly (approximately one CD release every two to three years). In short, the artists became frustrated with the constant "no" of the agency, which artists described as the "no" of socialism. While one of the major and widely acknowledged legacies of the CUHHM has been the discursive intervention in the question of race and the place of Black Cubans in the new Cuba, a central intervention in what that would look like came from women artivists.

New Caribbean Feminism: The (Re)Emergence of Cuban Black Feminism in Post–Special Period Cuba

During a December 2013 trip to Havana, I went out to a club with Las Positivas, La Fina, La Javá, and Odaymara Cuesta of Las Krudas CUBENSI. I was really happy to see how well received they were by people in the club. The hosts of the night, recognizing that there were nationally known Cuban MCs at the party, asked the MCs to free-style on the microphone (figs. 8.6 and 8.7). To my dismay, while La Javá was MCing, two men pushed through the crowd. One man (fig. 8.6), to the shock of everyone present, tried to grab the mic from La Javá's hand. The men were pushed away by fans who were present, and the MCs closed the circle to make sure they could not return. I followed the men outside to hear what was happening.

Outside of the DJ booth, one of the men yelled: "It's not fair. The women get to speak, and the men have the right to respond." What is interesting is that the MCs were not making any particular references to men, they were having fun battling each other (fig. 8.7). But the very fact that women were speaking over the mic bothered this particular group of three men, who felt that women did not have the right to claim the space to speak without men intervening. After a back and forth between the men and the MCs, I talked to one of the men and asked him what happened. To the amusement of those standing nearby, he started to whine and nearly cry about how it was not fair that they did not have a chance to challenge the women speaking. He went on to say that the organizers would not let him and his friends get on the mic, because they were not famous and these MCs were. He could not understand why the women, and not the men, would be given the right to use the mic just because they were well known and respected.

Such customary forms of aggression that Cuban women face are a direct challenge to women who dare to claim their right to speak. This continues to be reflected in how women artists, specifically Black and mulata artists, are treated in Cuba. It is still understood that a woman who is invited to perform at a hip

Figure 8.5. Lourdes "La Cimarona" Suárez giving a community leader copies of books as part of a grassroots community initiative in the arts. (Courtesy of the community group Somos Más)

Figure 8.6. Unknown person attempting to take the microphone from the hands of the MC Javá. (Photo by Tanya L. Saunders)

Figure 8.7. MC Battle, Havana, 2013 (*left to right*): MC La Fina, Orielis Mayet and Yaneidys Tamayo of the hip hop group Las Positivas, MC La Javá, [unknown spectator waiting for his turn to MC], Pasa MC (Odaymara Cuesta Rosseau) of the hip hop group Las Krudas CUBENSI (Krudxs). (Photo by Tanya L. Saunders)

Figure 8.8. DJ Leydis performing in Oakland, California, 2012. (Courtesy of DJ Leydis)

Figure 8.9. New Generation Cuban MCs: La Real (*left*) and La Reyna (*right*).
(Photo by Tanya L. Saunders)

hop artistic event and promised a certain amount of time is lucky to get half the
time at best when she gets onstage. This is not unique to Cuba, of course; I have
seen this happen at hip hop shows in the United States, Cuba, Brazil, Puerto
Rico, Canada, and many other countries.

Men within hip hop globally collude to exclude the women who are present,
yet no one can figure out the reason for the "absence" of women within hip hop.
In reality, however, the question should be about women's (in)visibility, because
they are certainly present (figs. 8.8 and 8.9). In recent years in Cuba, I have seen
women attempt to organize events at nightclubs and other state-run venues,
only to be told that the venue would charge a cover fee but that the women
artists would not be paid for their performances. In Cuba this is not only particular to hip hop scenes but is reflective of the struggle for Cuban women to
have autonomous space that is respected in the same ways that male-only autonomous space is respected. Thus the women hip hop artists of Cuba have had
to become more united and organized in their efforts to accomplish their work.
The socially conscious Black feminist movement spurred by the Cuban Underground Hip Hop Movement has continued within and outside of it and has resulted in an quasi-autonomous feminist movement. The interesting thing about

the contemporary feminist movement is that few (if any) white, openly feminist women are actively producing blogs and texts about Cuban feminism. Instead it has primarily been Afro-descendant women who have been on the forefront of the emerging feminist movements in Cuba: see, for example, the work of Sandra 'Abd Allah Álvarez Ramírez.[3]

The online and offline publications of Afro-Cubanas like 'Abd Allah Álvarez Ramírez are additional manifestations of the emergence of mobilized Cuban Black feminism. As in the case of Black feminisms throughout the region (whether it be the Combahee River Collective or the work of Brazilian Black feminists at Geledés: the Black Women's Institute), it is clear that Cuban Black feminism and what queer activist Logbona Olukonee calls "Afro-Caribbean feminism" and *queeridad* have benefited from the door that Instincto, Magia MC, Las Krudas CUBENSI, and the many other feminist MCs kicked open. The Black feminist movement and the Black queer movement in Cuba are one of the many legacies of the CUHHM. Independent artist collectives have continued in other areas, such as the spaces created by Grupo OMNI and Grupo Uno in Alamar and Puño Arriba based out of El Vedado. The legacy of the CUHHM has also had a significant impact in supporting scholars who are working to put the question of race on the national agenda, including in Cuban academic research.

Cuban scholar Yesenia Fernandes Selier, for example, is credited with being the first person to initiate empirical work on the question of racial identity in the post-1949 period. She did this as an undergraduate in the Department of Psychology at the University of Havana in the late 1990s and continued her research with the Juan Marinello Center in the early 2000s. Selier undertook this work because of the discourses and identity politics of the CUHHM.[4] In sum, this was a broad-based movement. The goal of this text has been to engage the activism of these artivists and to situate this movement within its national and regional context.

Concluding Remarks

This book is a case study of a movement for social change. It examines a movement centered on a challenge to the social inequalities embedded in Cuban society that are linked to its continued coloniality. This is a particularly important context in which to undertake such an analysis, as the 1959 Cuban Revolution initially gave primacy to the importance of grassroots cultural change. The contradiction is that through both political repression and the imposition of a Eurocentric aesthetic ideal the state further reentrenched the seeds of some elements of the social inequality that it sought to eliminate.

The stance of the contemporary state is not a result of being socialist but a result of the continuation of centuries-old forms of social oppression: specifically, negating the cultural and ideological significance of African cultural legacies and their implications for an independent and decolonized Cuban nation. The state, though anticolonial, actually continued a longer historical colonial process within the realm of Cuban culture. By embracing a Black subjectivity as a positive political identity, CUHHM artivists were able to address the ways in which racism affects nearly every aspect of social life, including consciousness, affect, and the taken-for-granted notions of "nation" and who is considered a good, trustworthy, productive, healthy, and law-abiding citizen.

The centrality of race, specifically blackness as the fulcrum of social inequality in the countries associated with the Caribbean, and the Americas more broadly, is reflected in Cuba's three-tier racial structure. This functions as a way to allow white supremacy and Eurocentrism to exist as viable ideological structures in Cuba, a majority Afro-descendant and former colonial society that has yet to complete its process of decolonization, much like all countries in the Americas. The CUHHM, though not always necessarily conscious of itself as a social movement, is what Agustín Lao-Montes describes as a decolonial move, spurred by a group of youths who realized that something needed to change and, as the movement evolved, that change was clearly linked to colonial legacies manifested via persistent racism. Las Krudas CUBENSI played a particular role in broadening the anticolonial discourse of the CUHHM to include consideration of how coloniality via heteronormativity (itself a racialized sex/gender system) affects all Cubans, especially Black Cubans.

The important thing that this movement did was to create a space of discussion and debate about these issues. It helped people to mobilize and develop an alternative ideological framework through which to seek social change—all in a country that is classified as totalitarian. The social sciences need to show greater recognition of the way in which art can be consciously taken up and used as a propeller of social change in this region. The social significance of art is also understood in a fundamentally different way than in Western European liberal capitalist democracies, where the importance of art is primarily based on the market and the arts' role as "catharsis." This analysis is particularly important in a region where the struggles for equality are centered not only on economic and environmental justice but also on challenges to cultural hegemony and consciousness as central to the reproduction of society and as a site for liberation. Attention to their worldview and its relationship to these political actors' investments is necessary too.

Though the Americas are of the West, they are not Western European; and even though the United States seeks to define itself as a European nation, it is not. In essence, the next stage of decolonization in the Americas will focus on large-scale social change centered on culture, worldview, ways of being, ways of knowing—in short, the decolonization of episteme. It will be/is a struggle over cultural hegemony, over which identity politics will take on new levels of significance, and over the role of transnational movements in challenging Eurocentric epistemology in multiple national contexts in the Americas. Therefore I would like to return now to the way in which I have situated Cuban hip hop within the African diaspora and how I conceptualize that term.

In this book I have employed the formulation of Agustín Lao-Montes, who argues against the reduction of the African diaspora (specifically Blacks in the West) to a group of people who share the legacies of the terror of enslavement and social subordination. Lao-Montes (2007) argues that the African diaspora also signifies a cosmopolitan project. He makes a connection between the interests and worldviews of the African diaspora in the Americas and competing visions of Western modernity, in which the Haitian Revolution holds an important symbolic place in Western history. As a result of the success of the Haitian Revolution, in addition to all of the insurrections, revolts, and maroon societies that occurred during that tumultuous historical period, Black and African agency and self-determination scared the elites of the American colonies. It was clear that Africans and their nonwhite descendants had their own ideas about what types of societies would emerge upon liberation.

Thus it is important to take a hemispheric approach to understanding the origins of blackness in the West and analyzing what it means globally. The severing of blackness from American regional context(s) flattens and distorts a multiplicity of Black experiences and the various ways in which blacknesses inform and structure each other. Blackness did not arrive in the Americas with European ideas of "nation," "nation-state," "citizenship," and "humanity." Within the Americas, blackness emerged as these ideas were also in formation. Additionally, Africans and their descendants were heavily involved in how these idea(l)s were contested and how they would evolve.

For people from the Americas, the question of blackness emerged as a result of the history of colonization. This history was not only about racializing a subject but also about delegitimizing African cultural logics and ignoring the syncretism of African cultures in the Americas: cultural forms which also serve as the basis of Western modernity and subjectivity. Blackness challenges the ways in which Africans and their descendants have been written out of the formation of the West. Hence many have argued that in the Americas blackness became a point around which members of the African diaspora could come together, regardless of geopolitical boundaries and spoken/linguistic differences, to define themselves as cosmopolitan subjects and as a diverse group that had a formative role in defining Western modernity. When we think about the impact of hip hop on CUHHM artivists and the impact of hip hop on the consciousness of American youth (regionally speaking), we are reminded that the question of racial identification with Blackness, nonBlackness, or whiteness was about maintaining an emergent Eurocentric capitalist structure. The threat of Blackness in the Americas is about the social and economic threat to European hegemony in the West. It is also about the possibilities—dare I say probabilities—of what would happen if the African diaspora in the Americas, like the CUHHM artivists, continued to demand recognition of anothern vision of Western modernity and credit for their formative role in the emergence of Western nations, such as Cuba. This would have global implications for the Eurocentric version of Western modernity.

Notes

Chapter 1

1. This excerpt has been slightly edited.

2. In this book I refer to members of the CUHHM as artists and "artivists." Importantly, this does not include all Cuban hip hop artists. Only those who identify themselves as part of the CUHHM specifically define themselves as activist-artists working for social change within the cultural sphere. M. K. Asante Jr. (2008) describes the artivist as the artist + activist: someone who is aware of having an obligation both to reflect reality and to provide a vision of change. He writes: "The artivist uses her artistic talents to fight and struggle against injustice and oppression—any *medium* necessary. The artivist merges the voice, the body, and the imagination. The artivist knows that to make an *observation* is to have an *obligation*" (Asante 2008, 203; emphasis in the original).

3. Throughout this text "Island" is capitalized when referring to Cuba.

4. Scholars such as Sujatha Fernandes and Geoff Baker presented their work at the conference. Geoff Baker references this in his book *Buena Vista in the Club* (2011).

5. Rensoli is using the general term "centric" to refer to the Eurocentrism and universalism of Western European cultures.

6. In the United States there is a movement to use "@" in place of "o" in Spanish words that end in the masculine form, where it is meant to reflect everyone, including male and female and other genders. "@" looks like the masculine and feminine endings together. Also, in Portuguese-speaking and Spanish-speaking countries in recent years the use of "x" instead of "o" is appearing in order to represent a diversity of genders, beyond the male and female binary. This has particularly taken off in Cuba in the last few year, as a result of the CUHHM group Las Krudas CUBENSI. Las Krudas have been playing with language a lot over the last three to four years, in an effort to develop language in Spanish that reflects gender and sexual diversity. They encountered this usage when they were in a feminist event in Guatemala in about 2007. Olivia Prendes Riverón felt that it was a great alternative to "@" and decided to use it.

7. In this text I use the term "Black U.S." instead of "U.S. Black" to challenge the idea that blackness has been bounded, in the Americas in particular, by some sort of national specificity based on by geographical boundaries as opposed to a relational subject position influenced by national discourses but not only bounded by and determined by them.

8. Here I am referring to Audre Lorde's definition of the erotic as "an assertion of the lifeforce of women; of that creative energy empowered, the knowledge and use of which we are now reclaiming in our language, our history, our dancing, our loving, our work and our lives" (Lorde 2007, 55). While her definition is primarily focused on women, I am generalizing this to people who are now reclaiming their erotic power as part of a larger decolonizing strategy. For this book I want to leave the notion of affect, pleasure, and desire open-ended; I am interested in the idea of people being able to connect openly with whatever the erotic means for them, something that will vary according to context. Thinking about this in a Cuban context is central to the arguments of the CUHHM group Las Krudas CUBENSI (see chapter 7).

9. In Latin America and much of the Caribbean, the intermediary racial category of mulat@ defines large parts of the Afro-descendant population as neither Black nor white (see chapter 2). The category is often noted in efforts to validate the ideology of race-lessness or racial intermixture: that racism does not exist in Cuba. Here I am as careful as I can be in my discussions of Black, mulat@, and white, in an effort to challenge the hegemony of the U.S. racial system, which is certainly used to dismiss racial inequality in Latin America and the Spanish-speaking Caribbean. These categories *do* exist in Latin American and Caribbean nations and mark important ontological boundaries in American societies (which are racialized/racially stratified societies), especially those with large Afro-descendant populations.

10. I use "heteronormativity" instead of "homosexuality" because the various intersections of gender, race, sexuality, and their normative performances have differing logics of organization and representation across Western contexts. Heteronormativity is a better term to convey these differences in meanings, while acknowledging the existence of a (regionally based) gender/sex system at play. This system shares points of convergence and divergence in various national and local contexts (see chapter 4).

11. Drawing from the work of Anibal Quijano (2000b), I use "modernity" to refer to a cultural, economic, and corporally based project in which regional European capitalists sought to organize non-European populations and resources for their own productive interests. Because many of these non-European populations possessed their own cultural logics (such as differing notions of time, ideas about ownership, and systems of value) the colonial project involved the imposition of one cultural logic over another as a means of controlling material resources, including labor, while creating markets. Non-European countries in the Americas were integral to the formation of "Western modernity," but their place within that history and even their designation as modern or Western remains contested, given the racialization of their Afro-descendant, indigenous, and mulat@/mestiz@ populations and their position in the racialized global economic order.

12. Here I am also referring to the United States. For a significant portion of its early history, the initial thirteen colonies had such a large enslaved population that the African and African-descendant population neared a majority at various points. This would change after the Haitian Revolution, however, when planters began to rethink developing colonial economies based on the Haitian model of a large enslaved population and a numerically smaller free population.

13. The debate in this case focuses on the methods used for animal sacrifice and whether such methods constitute cruel and inhumane treatment of animals. The absence of any comparative perspective that also examines the treatment of animals in modern industrial agriculture reveals the racial and cultural biases of the debate.

14. In earlier state usage, "LGBTT" rather than "LGBT" was sometimes used to refer to "transgender" and *transvesti*. This has now been placed under the umbrella of transgender, which in Cuba incorporates identities that are not included in English, such as *transvestis*, who are gay men who publicly dress as women in their everyday lives. This is different from transvestites, who are overwhelmingly heterosexual men who dress as women.

15. Kwame Dixon and John Burdick (2012) define blackness and more specifically hemispheric blackness as follows: "Blackness is, variously, a form of consciousness among Black people, a deliberate project to produce such consciousness, and ideas about Blacks held by non-Blacks. . . . Throughout the hemisphere, consciousness and projects of Blackness cluster around the ideas of common descent from Africa, a common history of enslavement and emancipation, and common experiences of social oppression . . . while ideas non-Blacks have about Black people center on racist stereotypes that articulate white fears of loss of dominance . . . the contents of each of the categories—'Africa,' slavery, emancipation, oppression, fear, and dominance—and how these concepts cluster together vary from place to place and context to context" (2).

16. Louis Althusser conceptualized the term "interpellate." Here I am recognizing that interpellated subjects can also feel coerced into accepting the social identity applied to them and understand that they are expected to perform that role, consciously or unconsciously. Individuals can be very much aware of this dynamic: regardless of their reluctance they will be read and treated according to their social classification.

17. In Canada, for example, I think of the invisibility of First Nations peoples and Canadians whose ancestors were runaway U.S. slaves and the silences on the forced integration/destruction of Africville as examples.

18. Frank Guridy (2010) addresses how exchanges between African Americans and Black Cubans have been integral in the development of the political strategies used by both to challenge enslavement and anti-Black racism. He goes a step further and discusses Black Cubans who attended historically Black colleges in the United States. Guridy engages the significance of Marcus Garvey, a Jamaican (not a Black U.S. American) who started the contemporary Back to Africa Movement, and Cuba's key role in the UNIA-ACL (Universal Negro Improvement Association and African Communities League) movements. Guridy situates the Black identity politics of Cubans and U.S. Americans within a regional context.

19. I specifically refer to post–Special Period Cuba here because it is the economic crisis and its process of reintegration into the global capitalist system that has been the propeller of recent historical changes in Cuba. I am wary of the term "postsocialist" to refer to contemporary Cuba because it has resonances in which Cuba is reduced to being a part of the Soviet bloc, which it was not. And it also reduces what became known as Cuban socialism to Soviet socialism. In my opinion what became known as Cuban socialism and the ideals of that socialist project are more embedded in ideological currents that exist in the Americas, represented by Cuba's national heroes, José Martí and Antonio Mace.

20. The Zulu Nation is a hip hop activist collective. See http://www.zulunation.com. For CUFA, see http://www.cufausa.blogspot.com.br/.

21. Bakari Kitwana (2002) writes the following about the hip hop generation: "we are the first generation to come of age in an America that has ended legal racial segregation. We are the first generation of African Americans to enjoy the fruits of the civil rights and Black power movements. . . . At the same time, we've witnessed the steady erosion of the euphoria of racial integration and in some cases civil rights gains themselves. . . . Although we lack a broad national movement, we are not without smaller-scale activist movements . . . young activists are more likely to focus on a particular issue. . . . For us, these are the many heads to the same monster" (147–149).

22. By "Atlantic" I mean the part of the world, bounded by the Atlantic, whose populations and cultures were formed by the transatlantic slave trade and Western European colonialism.

Chapter 2

1. This fear would later be tempered by a competing narrative of Black and white solidarity around Cuban independence and revolution.

2. As with blackness, it is important to remember that whiteness should not be taken for granted as being stable across national boundaries and geographic locations. While my discussion of whiteness locates it within the specific history of the Americas, a number of scholars have discussed its construction and evolution over time in more general terms and in other contexts: see, for example, Stoler 2010 and McClintock 1995.

3. These fears were not unfounded, as slave revolts were common throughout the colonial period. See Barcia 2012.

4. For a well-researched and very enriching analysis of the political context of the 1912 massacre and its effects in Cuba, see Gloria Rolando's documentary *1912: Breaking The Silence* (2010, 2011, 2012).

5. Robin D. Moore adds an additional layer to this moment in Cuban history. In *Nationalizing Blackness* (1997), he argues that much of Cuba's white elite began to take an interest in "Cuban" music when it became popular in Europe in the 1930s and 1940s. The interest in non-European cultures later intensified when Europeans themselves were going through an identity crisis. They had considered themselves to be civilized, but

the Nazis' actions in World War II showed that Europeans were no different from those that Europeans labeled "warlike savages." Therefore, within artistic spheres, Europeans began to embrace that which was "primitive" and gave a second look at the cultural production from regions considered to be "non-European." Cuba was one of those non-European countries whose music became popular. The Cuban elite studying in Europe during this time started to embrace what they considered to be the "primitive" aspects of their culture.

6. Marisela Fleites-Lear (2003) defines machismo as "the idea that men are superior to women and should dominate them socially, economically, physically, and sexually" (214).

7. Here I am referring to Gayle Rubin's (1975) definition of a sex/gender system.

8. The term "bisexual" is also a fairly recent classification. In 2005, Celiany Rivera-Velázquez and I had a meeting with CENESEX officials and discussed some of the history and confusion regarding the category of bisexuality. In the eyes of many, bisexuality for women simply did not exist and was not comprehensible, because bisexual women still sexually desired men. Bisexuality posed a serious identity crisis for women, much more serious than a lesbian identification, because of the confusion surrounding their sexual desire. The term "bisexual" did not exist for men either, but the word *bugarrones* describes men who are the active partner in sex with men. The partner who is penetrated is considered to be "gay." No similar term exists for women.

9. Carrie Hamilton and Elizabel Dore (2012) note a gender difference even in the way that the UMAP policies were carried out against homosexuals. They argue that lesbians were not targeted in terms of homosexual deviancy because women's sexuality was largely invisible. But the state's homophobia played out in boarding schools and other state-controlled areas understood as "feminine" spaces outside the purview of the larger public sphere. In these spaces girls and young women were disciplined for gender deviancy and same-sex desire. Being dismissed from a boarding school or other state institution was a form of social stigmatization that could result in profound social exclusion.

10. State-run clubs, operated by men, offer nightlife. Underground lesbian parties, which were mostly run by women (regardless of sexuality) and were a communal effort among neighbors, who would divide the profits from the party, have largely ended. The works of women artists were frequently played at these parties, which rarely happen now. In the state-run clubs all of the music that is played is by men. Sometimes over the course of a night the music of a woman artist is played or her video is shown—always a foreign woman artist, never a Cuban. Usually all of the bouncers, DJs, and bartenders are men. Women entering these events are frequently lectured by male bouncers and managers about how to conduct themselves in a public space, without any other provocation other than knowing that the women attending the events are gay. The commercialization of lesbian events has also restricted the amount of space available to Black and mulata women: entry into these parties costs $5 Cuban Convertible Pesos (CUC). The average salary of a Black Cuban professional is about $18 CUC per month.

11. Mark Sawyer (2005) focuses on changes in racial identities and racial politics during the Special Period.

12. Hugh Thomas (1971) argues that there was a power struggle between these two perspectives within the revolutionary government during its early years. As a compromise, it was decided that Castro would articulate state-level consensus. Thus, while Castro himself may have enjoyed abstract art, it is unclear whether or not all of his policy announcements are reflective of his personal perspective or the evolution of those perspectives over time.

13. Heberto Padilla was a writer and poet who initially embraced the Cuban Revolution. As the revolutionary process progressed, however, he became critical of the path it was taking. In 1968 he published a book of poetry, *Outside of the Game*, in which he criticized the state's increasing censorship of artistic production. His work garnered public attention when he was awarded a prize at the 1968 National Poetry contest. As the power struggle between the state and artists and intellectuals continued to intensify, the government targeted Padilla in 1971 with one month of imprisonment and interrogation and a forced public confession that he and other writers harbored counter-revolutionary sentiments. Padilla's treatment led to the end of much of the international support for the Cuban Revolution.

14. The Casa de Cultura of Alamar, for example, hosted the first Cuban Hip Hop festival in 1995.

15. One of the goals of the Agency of Rap as an institution within the Ministry of Culture is to bring independent artists into the organization. This is an effort to establish more control over the competing discourses offered by the underground hip hop movement.

16. See http://webcache.googleusercontent.com/search?q=cache:NQHhC4wGH3wJ:www.min.cult.cu/loader.php%3Fsec%3Dprogramas%26cont%3Dprogramanacional+&cd=2&hl=en&ct=clnk&gl=us.

17. Ministry of Culture, available at http://www.min.cult.cu/loader.php?Sec=programas&cont=programanacional. It appears that this link no longer works, unfortunately, and at the time of writing the Ministry of Culture's website was down.

18. Unlike Jacques Attali (1985), who argues that commercialized music manufactures (or at least attempts to manufacture) identities, Joaquín Borges-Triana (2009) contends that music represents preexisting identification. This approach to understanding the relationship between music and identification, in addition to the work on Black music cultures by scholars such as Neal (2003), Gilroy (1993b), Rose (1994), and Weheliye (2005), has more explanatory power, at least for music cultures in the Americas. The artist manifests a feeling of identification already present among the people who will become the artist's public. Efforts by the music industry to manufacture identities via music simply do not work in terms of supporting music that has staying power.

19. Unpublished Grupo OMNI promotional materials.

Chapter 3

1. I would encourage people interested in this topic to check out the debates that oc-curred in Cuba's national media and Cuban academic journals, including *Revista Temas*, and the Cuban Underground Hip Hop journal *Movimiento*. An anthology concerning Cuban underground hip hop is going to be published in Cuba by the Instituto de la Mú-sica Cubana, which was organized by Cuban musicologist Dr. Grizel Hernández Baguer.

2. The more consumer-oriented hip hop was not easily accessible to Cuba until about 2000, when state liberalization that increased the size of the tourism sector allowed for a massive influx of numerous types of musics and consumer-oriented ideologies.

3. Available at http://www.zulunation.com.

4. Hip hop moves beyond the Americas, of course, but the focus of this book is how hip hop, as an American phenomenon (regionally speaking), functions as a challenge to coloniality in the Americas.

5. I want to note here that U.S. Americans also includes Puerto Ricans, who are U.S. citizens due to the neo-colonial relationship of the United States to Puerto Rico, as well as immigrants from much of the Caribbean.

6. https://mxgm.org/about/why-we-say-new-afrikan/.

7. Ibid.

8. http://mxgm.org/blackaugust/black-august-hip-hop-project/.

9. For more information about Steve Marcus and his work, see http://www.smarcus .com/.

Chapter 4

1. Copies of Soandry's lyrics can be found at http://www.cubaencuentro.com /revista/revista-encuentro/archivo/53-54-verano-otono-2009/poesia-rap-250584.

2. In a new song entitled "Hoy" on their 2014 CD *Poderosxs*, Krudxs CUBENSI di-rectly engage race. Odaymara focuses on the African diasporic experience with race, while Olivia directly addresses the coloniality of whiteness. Things change quickly both in Cuba and in the diaspora, so I have limited the amount of updated information added to this text and will address newer developments elsewhere.

3. This term, developed by the Cuban anthropologist Fernando Ortiz (1995), refers to the process of cultural production in which he challenges notions of "acculturation" and "assimilation" to argue that all cultures that are introduced to a society contribute to its overall culture. As such, no "stronger" culture absorbs a "weaker" culture: they all func-tion together to create cultural change and the emergence of different cultures. Jossianna Arroyo (2003) and Walter D. Mignolo (2000) are suspicious of this term: although Ortiz attempts to give some power and importance to cultures defined as "inferior," national culture is still defined by those classified as white.

4. This phrase is borrowed from Scott Nakagawa of the Race Files blog, available at http://www.changelabinfo.com.

5. The original names of Alejandra and Marta have been changed for anonymity.

6. *Achabon cruzado* is the color of the brown wrapper of a popular Cuban candy.

Chapter 5

1. For example, Cuban blogger and activist Yoni Sánchez discusses the critical/artivist intervention of Cuban artivists on her blog Generation Y, available at http://www.desdecuba.com/generationy, especially as they relate to the direct engagement of social issues such as violence against women. Sánchez writes the following on her blog: "On finishing at the University I realized two things: first, that the world of the intellectual and high culture is repugnant to me and, most painfully, that I no longer wanted to be a philologist." What is interesting is that this is one of the central critiques of how censorship and repression works in Cuba, through the imposition of a Eurocentric aesthetic while at the same time classifying indigenous Cuban political and cultural thought that does not support hegemonic state discourse as being "foreign" or threatening. This is one reason why Rensoli's comment at the beginning of the introduction is so significant: he "others" the Eurocentrism that is imposed on Cuban society. Other artivists such as David of Grupo OMNI signed a petition to free writers who have been detained by the state (petition available at http://www.porotracuba.org/?p=604). There certainly seems to be another increase in repressive tactics used by the state, designed to target all of Cuba's activists who challenge it (see chapter 8).

2. This aspect of Cuban culture has changed significantly in recent years.

3. An analysis of the history of the ACR from 2002 until the present would merit its own long chapter. While the subject is interesting, engaging this continuous history is outside of the focus of this book.

4. Available at http://www.walterlippmann.com/abelprieto-11-7-2004.html.

Chapter 6

1. Sara Más (2003) writes that more than half of the people in a 2002 nationwide study said they treat homosexuals normally. But almost all women (it is not clear whether the sample only included people who self-identified as heterosexual) were disgusted by lesbians. The study indicates that lesbians in particular continue to be most marginalized within the homosexual population. Women's attitudes toward lesbians are an area that deserves much attention.

2. Using Kitwana's (2002) definition of the hip hop generation as the post–civil rights generation, the women of the hip hop generation would be approximately forty-five and younger.

3. I talk about the formation and the significance of the Cuban Agency of Rap in chapter 3.

4. All quotations from Magia in this chapter are from my interview with her in Havana in 2006 unless otherwise noted.

5. Siguaraya is a sacred tree in Afro-Cuban religious practices.

6. La Madriguera is an aficionado arts space primarily used by the Asociación Hermanos Saíz in Havana, Cuba.

7. This issue is now being openly discussed in Cuba. See http://www.cubanet.org /otros/expertos-de-naciones-unidas-preocupados-por-la-situacion-de-violencia-contra- la-mujer-en-la-isla/.

8. The influence of Las Krudas CUBENSI is the focus of the following chapter; this chapter focuses on how other women, particularly Magia, related to Las Krudas and their specific critique of heteronormativity in the hip hop community.

9. Women were asked what they *thought* about lesbians, so we do not know whether they are basing their answers on their reaction to encountering lesbian or gender- nonconforming women or if their responses are entirely based on their imagination.

10. I talk about Odalys Cuesta Rosseau of Las Krudas (known as Wanda) in more detail in the following chapter.

11. "Chickenheads/hoochies" is my slang-to-slang translation of the word *muchachi- tas*, which literally translates to something like tiny little girls.

12. For the privacy of this particular artist, I have changed her name.

13. During this period, purchasing music was a key way to show artists that you sup- ported their music in Cuba. Interestingly, when I went back in 2010, it was clear that this custom had stopped. Artists were giving CDs away. They were surprised when I offered them money for their music. For example, one newer artist was about to refuse my offer of 10 Cuban Convertible Pesos, when another artist whom I had known for just over seven years said: "Asere, that's how it used to be. Tanya's from the old school. She sup- ports artists' work." After a few seconds it seemed as if he understood the exchange dif- ferently. Instead of seeing it as a handout or as me interpreting him as asking for money, the young artist now understood that the aim of the transaction was supporting artistic production. He accepted the money and nodded.

Chapter 7

1. I discuss Cuban Convertible Currency (CUC) in chapter 2. Cuba has a dual econ- omy that is in the process of ending. The convertible currency started in the 1990s as a way to stabilize the economy. 1 CUC = $1 U.S., while Cubans who worked for the state (most Cubans) received pay in Cuban pesos. So a doctor who made 460 Cuban pesos per month made about $18 per month. This has become a problem in a country that now is using CUC for its official currency, while phasing out the Cuban convertible peso.

2. This quotation refers to Fidel Castro's 1966 speech, in which he stated that the women's movement represented a revolution within the Revolution (Bunck 1994, 87).

3. The "T" of "LGBT" is more often used in Cuba to refer to *transvestis* (gay men who dress and sometimes live as women).

4. "Tropazancos: La calle como escenario en Cuba," in *La Razó*, La Paz, Bolivia, Decem- ber 18, 2005: http://www.la-razon.com/versiones/20051218_005394/nota_277_230748.htm.

5. They were mentioned in the Italian travel magazine *I Viaggi di Republica*, February 7, 2002, 14.

6. *Bohemia*, May 2002, 14.

7. For example, performance art and film.

8. In 2001, for instance, Las Krudas began working with performance artist Beth Ferguson of Austin, Texas. Ferguson has worked with the Canadian (Toronto) troupe the Bread and Puppet Theater. See the website at http://www.breadandpuppet.org/.

9. See Celiany Rivera-Velázquez, *Reina de mi Misma, Queen of Myself: Las Krudas d' Cuba*.

10. The *Sociology of Sport Journal* published a special issue in 2008 (25, no. 1) entitled "The Social Construction of Fat." The text challenges the various ways in which the sociocultural meaning of fat as negative, immoral, unhealthy, and unwholesome is justified and reproduced.

11. What I am referring to here is that it is quite common for LGBT populations in the Americas to be drawn to Afro-descendant spiritual traditions such as Cándomble, Ifá, Santería, and indigenous practices.

12. I have noticed from videos of Las Krudas' performances that the number of women in the audience has increased. Additionally, the number of parents (women and men) who attend events with their children and speak to Las Krudas after the shows has grown. The discussion of gender at the first Hip Hop Symposium, which Las Krudas and several other women organized, drew a room packed with both women and men, while others stood outside of the room in order to hear the discussion.

13. www.krudascubensi.com.

Chapter 8

1 .See http://fusion.net/culture/story/obama-castro-shaken-hands-island-cubas-hip-hop-307131.

2. http://www.havanatimes.org/?p=100552.

3. See her blog at http://negracubanateniaqueser.com/.

4. Her work can be found at http://www.yeseniaselier.net/.

Bibliography

Acosta, D., S. Más, D. Edith, and M. Ramírez Corría. 2003. "¿Qué pensamos sobre homosexualidad? Un acercamiento a la visión de la población cubana." Paper presented at the 16th World Congress of Sexology/XVI Congreso Mundial de Sexología, March 2003, Havana, Cuba.

Alexander, M. J. 1991. "Redrafting Morality: The Postcolonial State and the Sexual Offences Bill of Trinidad and Tobago." In *Third World Women and the Politics of Feminism*, ed. C. T. Mohanty, 133–152. Bloomington: Indiana University Press.

Alexander, M. J., and C. T. Mohanty. 1997. *Feminist Genealogies, Colonial Legacies, Democratic Futures*. New York: Routledge.

Alim, H. S. 2006. *Roc the Mic Right: The Language of Hip Hop Culture*. New York: Routledge.

Allen, J. S. 2011. *¡Venceremos?: The Erotics of Black Self-Making in Cuba*. Durham, NC: Duke University Press.

Almendros, N., and O. Jiménez-Leal. 1984. *Mauvaise conduite*. Film, 110 min. Les Films du Losange et Antenne 2: France.

Alvarez, S. E., E. Dagnino, and A. Escobar. 1998. *Cultures of Politics, Politics of Cultures: Re-visioning Latin American Social Movements*. Boulder, CO: Westview Press.

Arguelles, L., and B. R. Rich. 1984. "Homosexuality, Homophobia, and Revolution: Notes toward an Understanding of the Cuban Lesbian and Gay Male Experience, Part 1." *SIGNS: Journal of Women in Culture and Society* 9, no. 4: 683–699.

Armony, A. C. 2005. "Theoretical and Comparative Reflections on the Study of Civil Society in Cuba." In *Changes in Cuban Society since the Nineties*, ed. J. S. Tulchin, L. Bobea, M. P. Espina Prieto, and R. Hernández, 19–34. Washington, DC: Woodrow Wilson International Center for Scholars.

Armstead, R. 2007. "'Growing the Size of the Black Woman': Feminist Activism in Havana Hip Hop." *NWSA Journal* 19, no. 1: 106–117.

Arroyo, J. 2003. *Travestismos culturales: Literatura y etnografía en Cuba y Brasil*. Pittsburgh, PA: Editorial Iberoamericana.

Asante, M. K., Jr. 2008. *It's Bigger Than Hip Hop: The Rise of the Post-Hip-Hop Generation*. New York: St. Martin's Press.

Attali, J. 1985. *Noise: The Political Economy of Music*. Minneapolis: University of Minnesota Press.

Avritzer, L. 2002. *Democracy and the Public Space in Latin America*. Princeton: Princeton University Press.

Baker, G. 2005. "Hip-hop, revolución! Nationalizing Rap in Cuba." *Ethnomusicology* 49: 399.

———. 2006. "La Habana Que No Conoces: Cuban Rap and the Social Construction of Urban Space." *Ethnomusicology Forum* 15, no. 2: 215–246.

———. 2011. *Buena Vista in the Club: Rap, Reggaetón, and Revolution in Havana*. Durham, NC: Duke University Press.

Barcia, M. 2012. *The Great African Slave Revolt of 1825: Cuba and the Fight for Freedom in Matanzas*. Baton Rouge: LSU Press. Available at: http://muse.jhu.edu/books /9780807143339.

Barnet, M. 1968. *Biografía de un cimarrón*. Barcelona: Ediciones Ariel.

Becker, H. S. 2008. *Art Worlds*. Berkeley: University of California Press.

Bejel, E. 2001. *Gay Cuban Nation*. Chicago: University Of Chicago Press.

Black Public Sphere Collective, ed. 1995. *The Black Public Sphere: A Public Culture Book*. Chicago: University of Chicago Press.

Borges-Triana, J. 2001. "Música cubana alternativa: Del margen al epicentro." Available at http://www.iaspmal.net/wp-content/uploads/2012/01/JoaquinBorgesTriana1.pdf.

———. [1970] 2009. *Concierto cubano*. Barcelona: Linkgua.

Bourdieu, P. 1984. *Distinction: A Social Critique of the Judgement of Taste*. Cambridge, MA: Harvard University Press.

Brock, L., and D. Castañeda Fuertes, eds. 1998. *Between Race and Empire: African-Americans and Cubans before the Cuban Revolution*. Philadelphia: Temple University Press.

Bronfman, A. 2005. "Measures of Equality: Social Science, Citizenship, and Race in Cuba, 1902–1940." *JLCA Journal of Latin American Anthropology* 10, no. 2: 469–471.

Brown, W. 1992. "Finding the Man in the State." *Feminist Studies* 18, no. 1: 7–34.

Bunck, J. M. 1994. *Fidel Castro and the Quest for a Revolutionary Culture in Cuba*. University Park: Pennsylvania State University Press.

Camnitzer, L. 2003. *New Art of Cuba*. Rev. ed. Austin: University of Texas Press.

———. 2007. *Conceptualism in Latin American Art: Didactics of Liberation*. Austin: University of Texas Press.

———. 2009. *On Art, Artists, Latin America, and Other Utopias*. Austin: University of Texas Press.

Candelario, G. E. B. 2007. *Black behind the Ears: Dominican Racial Identity from Museums to Beauty Shops*. Durham, NC: Duke University Press.

Casas-Cortés, M. I., M. Osterweill, and D. E. Powell. 2008. "Blurring Boundaries: Recognizing Knowledge-Practices in the Study of Social Movements." *Anthropological Quarterly* 81, no. 1: 17–58.

Castellanos, J. C., and I. Castellanos. 1988. *Cultura Afrocubana: El negro en Cuba, 1492–1844*. Miami: Ediciones Universal.

Castro, F. [1961] 2011. *Palabras a los intelectuales*. Mexico City: Ocean Sur.

Castro-Gómez, S. 2008. "(Post)Coloniality for Dummies: Latin American Perspectives on Modernity, Coloniality, and the Geopolitics of Knowledge." In *Coloniality at Large: Latin America and the Postcolonial Debate*, ed. M. Morana, E. Dussel, and C. A. Jáuregui, 259–285. Durham, NC: Duke University Press.

Chanan, M. 1986. *The Cuban Image: Cinema and Cultural Politics in Cuba*. London: BFI Publishing.

———. 2001. "Cuba and Civil Society, or Why Cuban Intellectuals Are Talking about Gramsci." *Nepantla: Views from the South* 2, no. 2: 387–406.

———. 2002. "We Are Losing All Our Values: An Interview with Tomás Gutiérrez Alea." *boundary 2* 29, no. 3: 47–53.

———. 2004. *Cuban Cinema*. Minneapolis: University of Minnesota Press.

Chang, J., and D. J. K. Herc. 2005. *Can't Stop, Won't Stop: A History of the Hip-Hop Generation*. New York: St. Martin's Press.

Clay, A. 2008. "Like an Old Soul Record: Black Feminism, Queer Sexuality, and the Hip-Hop Generation." *Meridians: Feminism, Race, Transnationalism* 8, no. 1: 53–73.

———. 2012. *The Hip-Hop Generation Fights Back: Youth, Activism, and Post–Civil Rights Politics*. New York: New York University Press.

Clealand, D. P. 2013. "When Ideology Clashes with Reality: Racial Discrimination and Black Identity in Contemporary Cuba." *Ethnic and Racial Studies* 36, no. 10: 1619–1636.

Cohen, C. J. 2005. "Punks, Bulldaggers, and Welfare Queens: The Radical Potential of Queer Politics?" In *Black Queer Studies: A Critical Anthology*, ed. E. P. Johnson and M. G. Henderson, 21–51. Durham, NC: Duke University Press.

Combahee River Collective. 2000. "A Black Feminist Statement." In *Home Girls: A Black Feminist Anthology*, ed. B. Smith, 264–274. Camden, NJ: Rutgers University Press.

Condry, I. 2006. *Hip-Hop Japan: Rap and the Paths of Cultural Globalization*. Durham, NC: Duke University Press.

Craven, D. 2006. *Art and Revolution in Latin America, 1910–1990*. New Haven, CT: Yale University Press.

Davis, A. Y. 1998. *Blues Legacies and Black Feminism: Gertrude "Ma" Rainey, Bessie Smith, and Billie Holiday*. New York: Pantheon Books.

de la Fuente, A. 2001. *A Nation for All: Race, Inequality, and Politics in Twentieth-Century Cuba*. Chapel Hill: University of North Carolina Press.

D'Emilio, J. 1983. "Capitalism and Gay Identity." In *Powers of Desire: The Politics of Sexuality*, ed. A. Snitow, C. Stansell, and S. Thompson, 100–113. New York: Monthly Review Press.

Dennis, C. 2012. *Afro-Colombian Hip-Hop: Globalization, Transcultural Music, and Ethnic Identities*. Lanham, MD: Lexington Books.

Díaz, V., and L. Díaz. 2006. *Cuban Hip Hop: Desde el principio*. Film, 75 min. Riverside, CA, Independent.

Dilla Alfonso, H. 2005. "Larval Actors, Uncertain Scenarios, and Cryptic Scripts: Where Is Cuban Society Headed?" In *Changes in Cuban Society since the Nineties*, ed. J. S. Tulchin, L. Bobea, M. P. Espina Prieto, and R. Hernández, 35–50. Washington D.C.: Woodrow Wilson International Center for Scholars.

Diouf, M., and I. K. Nwankwo. 2010. *Rhythms of the Afro-Atlantic World: Rituals and Remembrances.* Ann Arbor: University of Michigan Press.

Dixon, K., and J. Burdick. 2012. *Comparative Perspectives on Afro-Latin America.* Gainesville: University Press of Florida.

Dubois, L. 2004. *A Colony of Citizens: Revolution and Slave Emancipation in the French Caribbean, 1787–1804.* Chapel Hill: University of North Carolina Press.

Durham, A. 2007. "Using [Living Hip Hop] Feminism: Redefining an Answer (to) Rap." In *Home Girls, Make Some Noise!: Hip Hop Feminism Anthology*, ed. G. D. Pough, E. Richardson, A. Durham, and R. Raimist, 304–312. Mira Loma, CA: Parker Publishing.

Durham, A., B. C. Cooper, and S. M. Morris. 2013. "The Stage Hip-Hop Feminism Built: A New Directions Essay." *SIGNS* 38, no. 3 (Spring): 721–737.

Erni, J. N. 1998. "Queer Figurations in the Media: Critical Reflections on the Michael Jackson Sex Scandal." *Critical Studies in Mass Communication* 15, no. 2: 158–180.

Ferguson, R. A. 2004. *Aberrations in Black: Toward a Queer of Color Critique.* Minneapolis: University of Minnesota Press.

Fernandes, S. 2003. "Fear of a Black Nation: Local Rappers, Transnational Crossings, and State Power in Contemporary Cuba." *Anthropological Quarterly* 76, no. 4: 575–608.

———. 2006. *Cuba Represent!: Cuban Arts, State Power, and the Making of New Revolutionary Cultures.* Durham, NC: Duke University Press.

Fernández, A. 2013. "Cuban Rappers Stage Successful Protest." December 12. Havana Times.org. Available at http://www.havanatimes.org/?p=100552.

Fernández, N. T. 2010. *Revolutionizing Romance: Interracial Couples in Contemporary Cuba.* New Brunswick, NJ: Rutgers University Press.

Fernández Robaina, T. 1990. *El negro en Cuba, 1902–1958: Apuntes para la historia de la lucha contra la discriminación racial.* Havana: Editorial de Ciencias Sociales.

———. 1994. *Hablen paleros y santeros.* Havana: Editorial de Ciencias Sociales.

———. 1998a. *Historias de mujeres públicas.* Havana: Editorial Letras Cubanas.

———. 1998b. "Marcus Garvey in Cuba: Urrutia, Cubans, and Black Nationalism." In *Between Race and Empire: African-Americans and Cubans before the Cuban Revolution*, ed. L. Brock and D. Castañeda Fuertes, 120–128. Philadelphia: Temple University Press.

———. 2003. "El proyecto revolucionario y los homosexuales." Unpublished manuscript.

———. 2005. "Género y orientación sexual en la santería." *La Gaceta de Cuba* 1: 36–40.

Ferrer, A. 1999. *Insurgent Cuba: Race, Nation, and Revolution, 1868–1898.* Chapel Hill: University of North Carolina Press.

First Cuban Hip Hop Symposium 2005. Declaration presented on November 27, 2005, at the House of Culture, Plaza of the Revolution, Havana, Cuba.

Fleites-Lear, M. 2003. "Women, Family and the Cuban Revolution." In *Cuban Commu-*

nism, ed. I. L. Horowitz and J. Suchlicki, 276–302. 11th ed. New Brunswick, NJ: Transaction Publishers.

Flores, J. 2000. *From Bomba to Hip-Hop: Puerto Rican Culture and Latino Identity*. New York: Columbia University Press.

Forman, M., and M. A. Neal. 2004. *That's the Joint!: The Hip-Hop Studies Reader*. New York: Routledge.

Gaunt, K. D. 2006. *The Games Black Girls Play: Learning the Ropes from Double-Dutch to Hip-Hop*. New York: New York University Press.

George, N. 1998. *Hip Hop America*. New York: Viking.

Gilroy, P. 1993a. *The Black Atlantic: Modernity and Double Consciousness*. Cambridge, MA: Harvard University Press.

———. 1993b. *Small Acts: Thoughts on the Politics of Black Cultures*. New York: Serpent's Tail.

González Chacón, C. 2011. "Pelos." In *Afrocubanas: Historia, pensamiento y prácticas culturales*, ed. D. Rubiera Castillo and I. M. M. Terry, 170–186. Havana: Ciencias Sociales.

Grupo OREMI 2005. Project proposal. Havana, Cuba. Unpublished.

Guevara, C. [1965] 1989. *Socialism and Man in Cuba*. New York: Pathfinder Press.

Gupta-Carlson, H. 2010. "Planet B-Girl: Community Building and Feminism in Hip-Hop." *New Political Science* 32, no. 4: 515–529.

Guridy, F. A. 2010. *Forging Diaspora: Afro-Cubans and African Americans in a World of Empire and Jim Crow*. Chapel Hill: University of North Carolina Press.

Guzmán, M. 2005. *Gay Hegemony/Latino Homosexualities*. New York: Routledge.

Hall, S. 2008. "What Is This 'Black' in Black Popular Culture?" In *Popular Culture: A Reader*, ed. R. Guins and O. Zaragoza Cruz, 285–293. Los Angeles: Sage.

Hamilton, C., and E. Dore. 2012. *Sexual Revolutions in Cuba: Passion, Politics, and Memory*. Chapel Hill: University of North Carolina Press.

Helg, A. 1995. *Our Rightful Share: The Afro-Cuban Struggle for Equality, 1886–1912*. Chapel Hill: University of North Carolina Press.

Higashida, C. 2011. *Black Internationalist Feminism: Women Writers of the Black Left, 1945–1995*. Chicago: University of Illinois Press.

Higginbotham, E. B. 1992. "African American Women's History and the Metalanguage of Race." *SIGNS* 17, no. 2: 251–274.

Hill Collins, P. 2000. *Black Feminist Thought: Knowledge, Consciousness, and the Politics of Empowerment*. New York: Routledge.

hooks, b. 2000. *Feminist Theory: From Margin to Center*. Cambridge, MA: South End Press.

Howe, L. S. 1995. *Afro-Cuban Cultural Politics and Aesthetics in the Works of Miguel Barnet and Nancy Morejón*. Madison: University of Wisconsin-Madison.

———. 2004. *Transgression and Conformity: Cuban Writers and Artists after the Revolution*. Madison: University of Wisconsin Press.

Jameson, F. 1984. "Postmodernism, or the Cultural Logic of Late Capitalism." *New Left Review* 146: 59–92.

Jasper, J. M. 1997. *The Art of Moral Protest: Culture, Biography, and Creativity in Social Movements*. Chicago: University of Chicago Press.

Joffe, M. 2005. "Working Paper #3: Reshaping the Revolution through Rhyme: A Literary Analysis of Cuban Hip-Hop in the 'Special Period.'" Working Papers, Duke University Literature Program: www.duke.edu/web/las/Council/wpapers/working papersJoffe.pdf.

Johnson, E. P. 2003. *Appropriating Blackness: Performance and the Politics of Authenticity*. Durham, NC: Duke University Press.

Keyes, C. L. 2011. "Empowering Self, Making Choices, Creating Spaces: Black Female Identity via Rap Music Performance." In *That's The Joint!: The Hip-Hop Studies Reader*, ed. M. Forman and M. A. Neal, 399–412. New York: Routledge.

Kitwana, B. 2002. *The Hip Hop Generation: Young Blacks and the Crisis in African American Culture*. New York: Basic Books.

Knight, F. W. 1970. *Slave Society in Cuba during the Nineteenth Century*. Madison: University of Wisconsin Press.

Kofsky, F. 1975. *Black Nationalism and the Revolution in Music*. Atlanta: Pathfinder.

Kutzinski, V. M. 1993. *Sugar's Secrets: Race and the Erotics of Cuban Nationalism*. Charlottesville: University Press of Virginia.

La Fountain-Stokes, L. 2002. "De un pájaro las dos alas: Travel Notes of a Queer Puerto Rican in Havana." *GLQ: A Journal of Lesbian and Gay Studies* 8, nos. 1–2: 7–33.

Lane, J. 1998. "Blackface Nationalism, Cuba 1840–1868." *Theatre Journal* 50, no. 1: 21–38.

Lane, N. 2011. "Black Women Queering the Mic: Missy Elliott Disturbing the Boundaries of Racialized Sexuality and Gender." *Journal of Homosexuality* 58, nos. 6–7: 775–792.

Lao-Montes, A. 2007. "Decolonial Moves: Trans-Locating African Diaspora Spaces." *Cultural Studies* 21, nos. 2–3 (March/May): 309–338.

Leiner, M. 1994. *Sexual Politics in Cuba: Machismo, Homosexuality, and AIDS*. Boulder, CO: Westview Press.

Lipsitz, G. 2007. *Footsteps in the Dark: The Hidden Histories of Popular Music*. Minneapolis: University of Minnesota Press.

Lorde, A. 2007. *Sister Outsider: Essays and Speeches*. Rev. ed. Berkeley, CA: Crossing Press.

Lumsden, I. 1996. *Machos, Maricones, and Gays: Cuba and Homosexuality*. Philadelphia: Temple University Press.

Manduley López, H. 2001. *El rock en Cuba*. Havana: Atril.

Marable, M., and V. Agard-Jones. 2008. *Transnational Blackness: Navigating the Global Color Line*. New York: Palgrave Macmillan.

Marcuse, H. 1978. *The Aesthetic Dimension: Toward a Critique of Marxist Aesthetics*. Boston: Beacon Press.

Martí, J. 1999. *José Martí Reader: Writings on the Americas*. New York: Ocean Press.

Martín-Sevillano, A. B. 2008. *Sociedad civil y arte en Cuba: Cuento y artes plásticas en el cambio de siglo, 1980–2000*. Madrid: Editorial Verbum.

Más, S. 2003. *Lesbianas, las más rechazadas*. Havana: Servicio de Noticias de la Mujer.

Mbembe, J. A. 2001. *On the Postcolony*. Berkeley: University of California Press.

McClintock, A. 1995. *Imperial Leather: Race, Gender, and Sexuality in the Colonial Contest*. New York: Routledge.

Mignolo, W. D. 2000. *Local Histories/Global Designs: Coloniality, Subaltern Knowledges, and Border Thinking*. Princeton, NJ: Princeton University Press.

———. 2006. "Citizenship Knowledge and the Limits of Humanity." *American Literary History* 18, no. 2: 312–331.

Miller, I. 2009. *Voice of the Leopard: African Secret Societies and Cuba*. Jackson: University Press of Mississippi.

Ministerio de Justicia. 1975. *Código de familia*. Havana: Editorial Orbe.

———. 1977. *La mujer en Cuba socialista*. Havana: Empresa Editorial Orbe.

Moore, R. D. 1997. *Nationalizing Blackness: Afrocubanismo and Artistic Revolution in Havana, 1920–1940*. Pittsburgh: University of Pittsburgh Press.

———. 2006. *Music and Revolution*. Berkeley: University of California Press.

Morgan, J. 2011. "Hip-Hop Feminist." In *That's The Joint!: The Hip-Hop Studies Reader*, edited by M. Forman and M. A. Neal, 277–282. New York: Routledge.

Morgan, M., and D. Bennett. 2011. "Hip-Hop and Its Global Imprint." *Daedalus* 140, no. 2: 176–196.

Moten, F. 2003. *In the Break: The Aesthetics of the Black Radical Tradition*. Minneapolis: University of Minnesota Press.

Muñoz, J. E. 1999. *Disidentifications: Queers of Color and the Performance of Politics*. Minneapolis: University of Minnesota Press.

Murray, N. 1979. "Socialism and Feminism: Women and the Cuban Revolution, Part I." *Feminist Review* 2: 57–73.

Nakagawa, S. 2012. "Blackness Is the Fulcrum." From the "Race Files: A Project of CHANGE-LAB" website: http://www.racefiles.com/2012/05/04/blackness-is-the-fulcrum/.

Navarro, D. 2002. "In Medias Res Públicas: On Intellectuals and Social Criticism in the Cuban Public Sphere." *boundary 2* 29, no. 3: 187–203.

Neal, M. A. 1999. *What the Music Said: Black Popular Music and Black Public Culture*. New York: Routledge.

———. 2003. *Songs in the Key of Black Life: A Rhythm and Blues Nation*. New York: Routledge.

Negrón-Muntaner, F. 2004. *Boricua Pop: Puerto Ricans and the Latinization of American Culture*. New York: Routledge. Available at http://public.eblib.com/EBLPublic /PublicView.do?ptiID=865685.

Ngai, S. 2007. *Ugly Feelings*. Cambridge, MA: Harvard University Press.

Nwankwo, I. K. 2005. *Black Cosmopolitanism: Racial Consciousness and Transnational Identity in the Nineteenth-Century Americas*. Philadelphia: University of Pennsylvania Press.

Ortiz, F. 1995. *Cuban Counterpoint, Tobacco and Sugar*. Durham, NC: Duke University Press.

Osumare, H. 2007. *The Africanist Aesthetic in Global Hip-Hop: Power Moves*. New York: Palgrave Macmillan.

Pacini Hernández, D., and R. Garafalo. 1999. "Hip Hop in Havana: Rap, Race and National Identity in Contemporary Cuba." *Journal of Popular Music Studies* 11–12, no. 1: 18–47.

Pardue, D. 2008. *Ideologies of Marginality in Brazilian Hip Hop.* New York: Palgrave Macmillan.

Perry, I. 2004. *Prophets of the Hood: Politics and Poetics in Hip Hop.* Durham, NC: Duke University Press.

Perry, M. D. 2004. "Los Raperos: Rap, Race, and Social Transformation in Contemporary Cuba." PhD dissertation, Anthropology, University of Texas–Austin.

———. 2008. "Global Black Self-Fashionings: Hip Hop as Diasporic Space." *Identities: Global Studies in Culture and Power* 15, no. 6: 635–664.

Pough, G. D. 2007. "An Introduction of Sorts for Hip-Hop Feminism." In *Home Girls, Make Some Noise!: Hip Hop Feminism Anthology,* ed. G. D. Pough, E. Richardson, A. Durham, and R. Raimist, iv–ix. Mira Loma, CA: Parker Publishing.

———. 2011. "Seeds and Legacies: Tapping the Potential in Hip-Hop." In *That's the Joint!: The Hip-Hop Studies Reader,* ed. M. Forman and M. A. Neal, 238–289. New York: Routledge.

Pough, G. D., E. Richardson, A. Durham, and R. Raimist, eds. 2007. *Home Girls, Make Some Noise!: Hip Hop Feminism Anthology.* Mira Loma, CA: Parker Publishing.

Prendes Riverón, Olivia. 2006. "Representando grandeza de mujer cubana: Maternizando lo patriarcado: Féminas y Hip Hop." Online at www.myspace.com/3krudas.

Quijano, A. 2000a. "Coloniality of Power and Eurocentrism in Latin America." *International Sociology* 15, no. 2 (June): 215–232.

———. 2000b. "Coloniality of Power, Eurocentrism, and Latin America." *Nepantla: Views from South* 1, no. 3: 533–580.

Richardson, E. B. 2006. *Hiphop Literacies.* New York: Routledge.

Rivera, R. Z. 2003. *New York Ricans from the Hip Hop Zone.* New York: Palgrave Macmillan.

Rivera-Velázquez, C. 2008. "Brincando bordes, cuestionando el poder: Cuban Las Krudas' Migration Experience and Their Rearticulation of Sacred Kinships and Hip Hop Feminism." *Letras Femeninas* 24, no. 1: 97–123.

———. 2012. *Queen of Myself: Las Krudas d'Cuba.* Film. Tortuga Productions in association with Las Krudas CUBENSI.

Robinson, C. J. 2000. *Black Marxism: The Making of the Black Radical Tradition.* Chapel Hill: University of North Carolina Press.

Rolando, G. 2010. *1912: Breaking the Silence, Chapter 1/1912, Voces para un silencio, capítulo 1.* Film, 46 min. Available at http://www.afrocubaweb.com/gloriarolando/breakingthesilence.htm.

———. 2011. *1912: Breaking the Silence, Chapter 2/1912, Voces para un silencio, capítulo 2.* Film, 58 min. Available at http://www.afrocubaweb.com/gloriarolando/breakingthesilence.htm.

———. 2012. *1912: Breaking the Silence, Chapter 3/1912, Voces para un silencio, capí-*

tulo 3. Film, 58 min. Available at http://www.afrocubaweb.com/gloriarolando /breakingthesilence.htm.

———. 2014. *Reembarque/Reshipment*. Film, 59 min. Available at http://www.afrocuba web.com/gloriarolando/reembarque.html.

Rose, T. 1994. *Black Noise: Rap Music and Black Culture in Contemporary America*. Middletown, CT: Wesleyan University Press.

Roth-Gordon, J. 2012. "Linguistic Techniques of the Self: The Intertextual Language of Racial Empowerment in Politically Conscious Brazilian Hip Hop." *Language and Communication* 32, no. 1: 36–47.

Rubin, Gayle. "The Traffic in Women: Notes on the 'Political Economy' of Sex." In *Toward an Anthropology of Women*, edited by R. R. Reiter, 141–210. New York: Monthly Review Press, 1975.

Saunders, T. L. 2008. "The Cuban Remix: Rethinking Culture and Political Participation in Contemporary Cuba." PhD dissertation, University of Michigan.

———. 2009a. "Grupo OREMI: Black Lesbians and the Struggle for Safe Social Space in Havana." *Souls: A Critical Journal of Black Politics, Culture and Society* 11, no. 2: 167–185.

———. 2009b. "La Lucha Mujerista: Krudas CUBENSI and Black Feminist Sexual Politics in Cuba." *Caribbean Review of Gender Studies*. Available at https://sta.uwi.edu /crgs/november2009/journals/CRGS%20Las%20Krudas.pdf.

———. 2011. "Black Lesbians and Racial Identity in Contemporary Cuba." *Black Women, Gender and Families* 4, no. 1 (Spring): 9–36.

———. 2012. "Black Thoughts, Black Activism: Cuban Underground Hip-hop and Afro-Latino Countercultures of Modernity." *Latin American Perspectives* 39, no. 2: 42–60.

Sawyer, M. Q. 2005. *Racial Politics in Post-Revolutionary Cuba*. New York: Cambridge University Press.

Schloss, J. B. 2009. *Foundation: B-Boys, B-Girls and Hip-Hop Culture in New York*. New York: Oxford University Press.

Scott, R. J. 1985. *Slave Emancipation in Cuba: The Transition to Free Labor, 1860–1899*. Princeton, NJ: Princeton University Press.

Selier, Y. F. 2005. "Movimiento de Rap Cubano: Nuevas identidades sociales a través de la cultura Hip Hop." Online at http://bibliotecavirtual.clacso.org.ar/ar/libros /becas/2005/demojov/selier.pdf.

———. 2010. "The Crossroads of Cuban Rap." Online at http://www.angelfire.com /planet/islas/English/v5n14-pdf/49.pdf.

Selier, Y. F., and P. Hernández. 2009. "Black Cubans: A Social Identity." Online at http:// www.angelfire.com/planet/islas/English/v4n12-pdf/32-39.pdf.

Smith, B., ed. 1983. *Home Girls: A Black Feminist Anthology*. New Brunswick, NJ: Rutgers University Press.

Smith, L. M., and A. Padula. 1996. *Sex and Revolution: Women in Socialist Cuba*. New York: Oxford University Press.

Snorton, C. R. 2013. "As Queer as Hip Hop." *Palimpsest: A Journal on Women, Gender, and the Black International* 2, no. 2: vi–x.

Somerville, S. B. 2000. *Queering the Color Line: Race and the Invention of Homosexuality in American Culture*. Durham, NC: Duke University Press.

Somoroff, M. 2006. Review of *Phonographies: Grooves in Sonic Afro-Modernity*, by Alexander G. Weheliye (2005). Available at http://newblackman.blogspot.com/2006/02/book-review-phonographies-grooves-in.html.

Stoler, A. L. 2010. *Carnal Knowledge and Imperial Power: Race and the Intimate in Colonial Rule*. Berkeley: University of California Press.

Stoner, K. L. 1991. *From the House to the Streets: The Cuban Woman's Movement for Legal Reform, 1898–1940*. Durham, NC: Duke University Press.

Sweig, J. E. 2002. *Inside the Cuban Revolution: Fidel Castro and the Urban Underground*. Cambridge, MA: Harvard University Press.

Thomas, H. 1971. *Cuba: The Pursuit of Freedom*. New York: Harper and Row.

Thompson, R. F. 1983. *Flash of the Spirit: African and Afro-American Art and Philosophy*. New York: Random House.

Vidal-Ortiz, S. 2005. "Sexuality and Gender in Santería: Lesbian, Gay, Bisexual, and Transgender Identities at the Crossroads of Santería Religious Practices and Beliefs." In *Gay Religion: Continuity and Innovation in Spiritual Practice*, ed. S. Thumma and E. R. Gray, 115–138. Lanham, MD: AltaMira Press.

Vitier, C. 2002. "Resistance and Freedom." *boundary 2* 29, no. 3: 247–252.

Walker, S. S. 2001. *African Roots/American Cultures: Africa in the Creation of the Americas*. Lanham, MD: Rowman and Littlefield.

Weheliye, A. G. 2005. *Phonographies: Grooves in Sonic Afro-Modernity*. Durham, NC: Duke University Press.

West-Durán, A. 2004. "Rap's Diasporic Dialogues: Cuba's Redefinition of Blackness." *Journal of Popular Music Studies* 16, no. 1: 4–39.

Williams, R. 1977. *Marxism and Literature*. London: Oxford University Press.

Young, C. A. 2006. *Soul Power: Culture, Radicalism, and the Making of a U.S. Third World Left*. Durham, NC: Duke University Press.

Yúdice, G. 2003. *The Expediency of Culture: Uses of Culture in the Global Era*. Durham, NC: Duke University Press.

Zurbano Torres, R. 1994. *Poética de los noventa: ¿Ganancias de la expresión?* Havana: Ediciones Universales.

———. 1996. *Los estados nacientes (Literatura cubana y postmodernidad)*. Havana: Ediciones Universales.

Index

Page numbers in italic indicate illustrations.